POPE FRANCIS
and the
SEARCH FOR GOD
IN *AMÉRICA*

BIBLIOGRAPHY

*Ian Wright t*he Autobiography, Constable 2016
*Playing at Home, John Aizle*wood, Orion 1998
*Stan the Man, S*tan Ternent, John Blake 2004
Swanny, Confessions of a Lower League Legend. Peter Swan. John Blake 2008
The Burnley Express
The Lancashire Telegraph

Also available at all good book stores

9781785316548

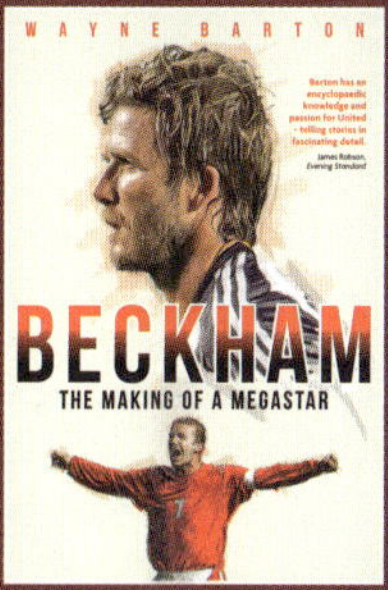

9781785316760

9781785314995

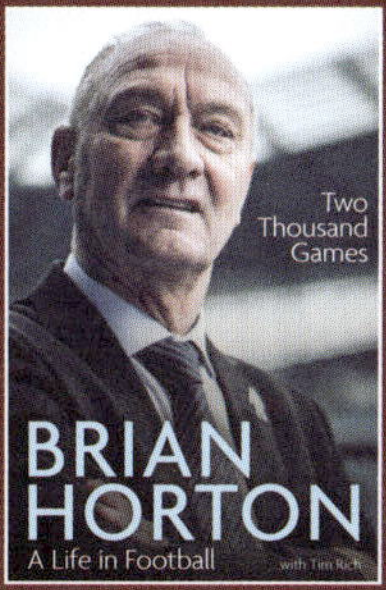

9781785316685

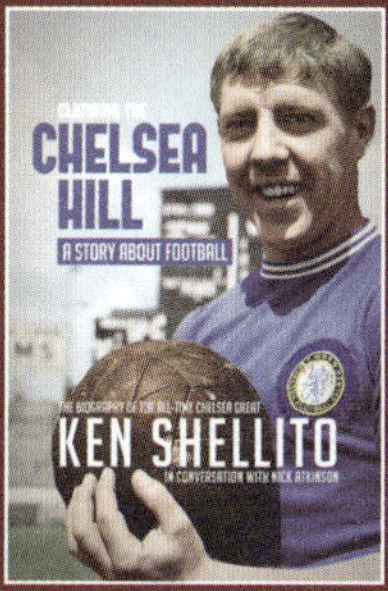

9781785316807

9781785315008

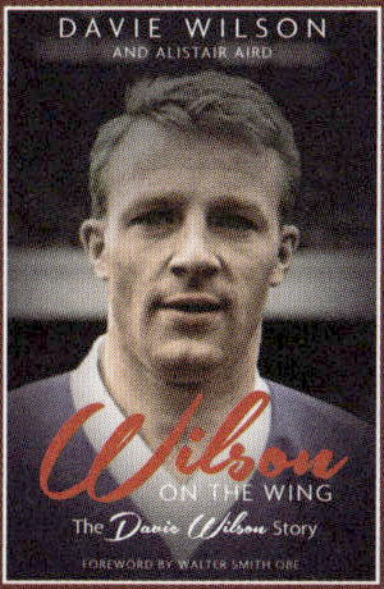

9781785316333

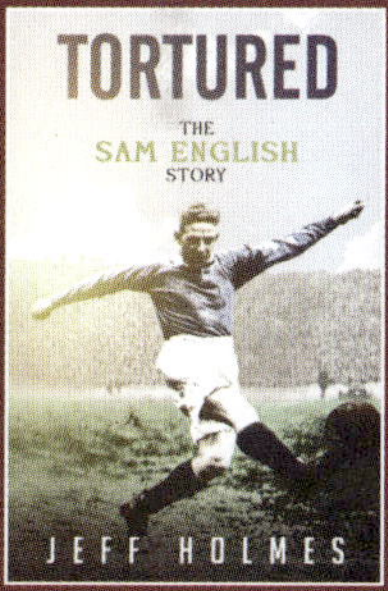

9781785317255

9781785315510

POPE FRANCIS *and the* SEARCH FOR GOD IN *AMÉRICA*

The Significance of His Early Visits to the Americas

Edited by Maria Clara Bingemer and Peter J. Casarella

Foreword by Archbishop Christophe Pierre

The Catholic University of America Press

Washington, D.C.

The paper used in this publication meets the minimum requirements of American National Standards for Information Science--Permanence of Paper for Printed Library Materials, ANSI Z39.48–1984.
∞

Library of Congress Cataloging-in-Publication Data

Names: Bingemer, Maria Clara Lucchetti, editor. | Casarella, Peter J., editor. | Pierre, Christoph, 1946- other.
Title: Pope Francis and the search for God in América : the significance of his early visits to the Americas / edited by Maria Clara Bingemee and Peter J. Casarella ; foreword Archbishop Christoph Pierre.
Description: Washington, DC : The Catholic University of America, [2021] | Includes bibliographical references and index.
Identifiers: LCCN 2021035688 (print) | LCCN 2021035689 (ebook) | ISBN 9780813233789 (paperback) | ISBN 9780813233796 (ebook)
Subjects: LCSH: Francis, Pope, 1936---Travel--Latin America. | Papal visits--Latin America.
Classification: LCC BX1378.7 .P65475 2021 (print) | LCC BX1378.7 (ebook) | DDC 282.092--dc23
LC record available at https://lccn.loc.gov/2021035688
LC ebook record available at https://lccn.loc.gov/2021035689

Table of Contents

Foreword

NEARLY FIVE YEARS AGO, the Holy Father appointed me as apostolic nuncio to the United States, having served previously as his representative to Mexico. With this unique perspective, I am happy to present this collection of essays edited by Dr. Maria Clara Bingemer and Dr. Peter Casarella: *Pope Francis and the Search for God in* América*: The Significance of His Early Visits to the Americas.*

It is important to be aware that Pope Francis's apostolic exhortation *Evangelii Gaudium* is strongly connected to the final document of the Fifth General Conference of the Bishops of Latin America and the Caribbean that took place in Aparecida in 2007, in which the then archbishop of Buenos Aires played an important role.

There is also a need to become more familiar with the sources of the thinking of Pope Francis and the various authors who have contributed to his intellectual and pastoral formation. I want to mention in particular the profound study done by Massimo Borghesi entitled *The Mind of Pope Francis: Jorge Mario Bergoglio's Intellectual Journey.*

Borghesi's work explores how the Holy Father's pastoral activity and his words and gestures have been influenced by the theologians and philosophers whom he has studied and appropriated over the years, including Europeans like Fessard, Guardini, Balthasar, De Lubac, and Giussani, as well as Latin Americans like Methol Ferré, Tello, and Scannone. The pope's ability to synthesize many great thinkers allows him not only to touch the reality of people's concrete situations and circumstances, but also provides him with an instrument of dialogue with contemporary culture.

I heard Dr. Peter Casarella for the first time during an international symposium held in October 2018 at the Sacred Heart Seminary in Hales Corners, Wisconsin that explored Pope Francis's thought and brought it to the American public. The symposium's contributions have been published under the title *Discovering Pope Francis: The Roots of Jorge Mario Bergoglio's Thinking*, and Dr. Casarella's contribution is titled "Pope Francis, the Theology of the People and the Church in the United States."

The present collection serves to bridge the gap between the church in the United States and North America and that of South America so that we can use the term *Ecclesia in America* with authenticity and integrity.

At the beginning of my mission to the United States, preparations had begun for the V National Encuentro. The success of the Encuentro was more necessary than ever because of the burgeoning presence of Hispanics and Latinos in the US church. This presence and the gifts of these persons have the potential to be a source of renewal and a force for evangelization in the United States, but the appropriation of these gifts will be dependent upon the building of an authentic culture of encounter. It was for this reason that the Holy Father sent a message to the American bishops that included these words:

> Our great challenge is to create a culture of encounter that encourages individuals and groups to share the richness of our traditions and experiences, to break down walls and to build bridges. The church in America, as elsewhere, is called to "go out" from its comfort zone and to be a leaven of communion—communion among ourselves, with our fellow Christians, and with all who seek a future of hope. We need to become ever more fully a community of missionary disciples, filled with love of the Lord Jesus and enthusiasm for the spread of the Gospel. (Video message to the General Assembly of the USCCB, November 14–17, 2016)

I believe that this collection of essays seeks to create this culture of encounter. The Holy Father is constantly speaking about encounter, dialogue, and more recently, fraternity. There must be a concerted effort by theologians from both the North and South to have a mutual understanding of one another and of the cultural influences that have shaped Catholicism in the region so that the church can mount an effective effort of evangelization on the American continent(s).

The development of Catholicism in North America, and specifically in the United States, involved by and large the arrival of waves of immigrants from Europe who brought with them their own clergy. The result was a European form of Catholicism that subsequently grew up in a democratic, American context and that had to encounter Protestantism.

A particular form of Catholicism emerged from this encounter, one that is different from Catholicism in Central and South America.

This volume then is timely inasmuch as it affords an opportunity for an intellectual encounter that can lead not only to a mutual understanding but also to a creative synthesis of ideas, which will hopefully bear much fruit for the church in America, as it carries out the mission of evangelization.

I conclude with the words of Pope Francis from *Evangelii Gaudium*:

> An evangelizing community is always concerned with fruit, because the Lord wants her to be fruitful. It cares for the grain and does not grow impatient with the weeds. The sower, when he sees weeds sprouting among the grain does not grumble or overreact. He or she finds a way to let the word take flesh in a particular situation and bear fruits of new life, however imperfect or incomplete these may appear. (*EG*, 24)

Archbishop Christophe Pierre
Apostolic Nuncio
Oct. 17, 2020

CHAPTER 1

Introduction

POPE FRANCIS IN AMÉRICA

A South-North Encounter

Peter J. Casarella

WHEN THE POPE TRAVELS to a foreign country to visit its people in his role as the successor to St. Peter, the Vatican Press Office issues a statement regarding the pontiff's *viaggio apostolico*, his "apostolic journey." The term seems better fitted to an heir of St. Paul than St. Peter, since the former is the true paradigm of "the one sent" (the word "apostle" means "one who is sent") to carry the message of Jesus Christ to faraway lands.[1] In any case, the journey is not a business trip or diplomatic mission. It is different in kind from that of a CEO or secretary of state. The voyage itself speaks of the church as a reality that has a center and a periphery. In the case of the current pontiff's trips to Latin America, the pope "from the ends of the earth" is traveling back home to the ends of the earth.[2] This book examines the travels of the pope back to his native continent and its neighbor to the north not just as an accomplishment in diplomacy, but as a sign of how the church under Pope Francis needs

1 The legacies of Peter and Paul are linked beyond the historical period in which they lived, and their bond of discipleship adds life to the contemporary church. Pope Paul VI spoke eloquently about the joint martyrdom of Peter and Paul, the two princes of the church, in Rome. Some have argued that the establishment of the see of Rome may be linked to their burial in that city. See William R. Farmer and Roch Kereszty, O.Cist., *Peter and Paul in the Church of Rome: The Ecumenical Potential of a Forgotten Perspective* (New York: Paulist Press, 1990).

2 In his first appearance in St. Peter's Square, Pope Francis stated that his brother bishops had chosen a new occupant of the see of St. Peter "from the ends of the earth."

to be reexamined in terms of the relationship of center and periphery, in terms of its center being in the periphery and vice versa. This book is about the church no longer being conceived as a sphere but rather a polyhedron.[3] In this polyhedron, the inequalities in the relationship between center and periphery are acknowledged because uniformity across the outer surface is no longer the tacit ideal. The unity of the church is established by Christ and can never be exchanged for an indifferent pluralism, but for Pope Francis the unity of the church exists and is nourished by productive differences. These differences include but are not limited to the relationships that exist between the local churches and the see of Rome. The polyhedral church offers a new definition of catholicity, one that is truly catholic in its universality and solidly Catholic by virtue of its diverse manifestations of faith.

The specific task given to the contributors of this book was to write about the apostolic journeys of the Argentine pope to the Americas in the year 2015. At that point, he had already made one visit to the Americas. Jorge Mario Bergoglio was elected pope in April of 2013 and went to Rio de Janeiro for the World Youth Day in June. By going to Rio, he was fulfilling a promise that Pope Benedict had made, but he also set a fresh new tone of openness to dialogue in a hub of global Catholicism. On the beach of Copacabana, he said Mass for more than three million young people (almost equivalent to the population of Uruguay). Later in a meeting with Brazil's leaders he insisted on "dialogue, dialogue, dialogue."[4] Because there was a torrential downpour at Copacabana, the last-minute change of venue to the beach created security issues; in the end, the residents of Rio de Janeiro offered hospitality to the innumerable foreign pilgrims because neither the state nor the church was prepared for the huge number of people.

Between 2013 and 2015 there were important apostolic journeys to Jerusalem and other sites of global conflict.[5] The first American

3 Francis, Apostolic Exhortation *Evangelii Gaudium* (November 24, 2013), 236. All documents published by the Vatican, including this one and many others cited below, including papal addresses, may be found at the vatican.va website.

4 "When leaders in various fields ask me for advice, my response is always the same: dialogue, dialogue, dialogue." Francis, *Meeting with Brazil's Leaders of Society*, Rio de Janeiro, July 27, 2013.

5 These included Israel, Jordan, and Palestine (May 24–26, 2014), South Korea (August 14–18, 2014), Albania (September 21, 2014), France (November 25, 2014), Turkey (November 28–30, 2014), Sri Lanka and the Philippines (January 13–19, 2015), and Bosnia and Herzegovina (June 6, 2015).

pope did not want to give the impression that he was only or in the first instance a pope of the Americas. As the bishop of Rome and occupant of the office of Peter, he was in the first instance a messenger of global peace.[6] The witness of Pope Francis to the Americas cannot be separated from his role as the first pope to incarnate global Catholicism. Saint John Paul II broke the centuries-old mold of there being an Italian pope, but Cardinal Bergoglio was the very first holder of the Petrine office to come to it bearing wisdom from the Global South. Pope Francis seems to be conscious of the fact that he carries the responsibility of his office for all of those Catholic peoples at the ends of the earth who have been ignored by the church in the past.

The trip to Rio may have been Pope Francis's much-celebrated debut as bishop of Rome in Latin America, but it took place as the fulfillment of a promise made by his predecessor. The apostolic voyages of 2015, by contrast, were undertaken out of his own initiative and on his own terms. In that year, Pope Francis made two relevant journeys from Rome: one to Bolivia, Paraguay, and Ecuador and another to Cuba and the United States. The individual chapters of this book examine the talks and events that took place in each of these nations. He did not travel to all regions of the Americas, but the breadth of these trips taken together offers us a window into the pope's initial vision of this intercontinental church.

For now it suffices to note that he began his journey to the Americas in Bolivia, one of the poorest countries, with one of the highest indigenous populations, located on these two continents. It is noteworthy that he did not make his debut in his native land of Argentina, a land which today is not as heavily populated with indigenous peoples as are the countries in the central region of the Andes. In fact, on July 9, 2015 in Santa Cruz de la Sierra, Bolivia, the Holy Father participated in the Second World Meeting of Popular Movements, having already participated in the first meeting in Rome itself. This initiative was undertaken by Pope Francis

6 The pope's visit to the Holy Land included praying at the Western Wall, a visit to the Dome of the Rock and the tomb of the father of modern Zionism, an acknowledgement of the tragedy of the Shoah at the Yad Vashem Holocaust Memorial, and an invitation to the presidents of Israel and the Palestinian people to visit the Vatican. They both accepted.

so that he could address the economy of exclusion and inequality.[7] Since Bolivia, the group has had a third meeting in Rome and a regional meeting in Modesto, California. In Bolivia, he said,

The Bible tells us that God hears the cry of his people, and I wish to join my voice to yours in calling for the three "L's" for all our brothers and sisters: land, lodging and labor. I said it and I repeat it: these are sacred rights. It is important, it is well worth fighting for them. May the cry of the excluded be heard in Latin America and throughout the world.[8]

The sacred right to "land, labor, and lodging" has become a refrain of this pope. But he is not content with the repetition of slogans; he is more interested in an analysis of global systems. In fact, he accuses the global system that imposes a mentality of profit at any price of being the "invisible thread" running through every form of exclusion, thereby linking the problem of social exclusion to the destruction of nature. In general the pope is trying to implement the method of "see, judge, act" enshrined by John XXIII in *Mater et Magistra* (236) in order to spur greater participation of the peoples of the world in political, economic, social, and cultural systems. He is defiant about the need to act defiantly. We cannot sit on the sidelines of history and watch the forces of consumerism destroy the human community and the environment. The global engagement with the *movimientos populares* (popular movements) in Bolivia thus set the stage for the pope's entrance into the church of the Americas.

The trips to *América* in 2015 do not stand alone. In 2016 he traveled to Mexico and made a historic visit, the first one by any pope, to the US-Mexico border, praying before a cross on the border between Ciudad Juárez and El Paso in an event billed as "Two Nations, One Faith." About 28,000 people in El Paso's Sun Bowl erupted in cheers when Pope Francis talked to them during his televised Mass from Juárez, where another two hundred thousand-plus people attended.[9] If it had not been so hot, there might have been even more. The

7 On the economy of exclusion and inequality, see Francis, *Evangelii Gaudium*, 53–54.

8 Francis, *Participation at the Second World Meeting of Popular Movements: Address of the Holy Father*, July 9, 2015, introductory remarks.

9 Cf. Vic Kolenc, "Sun Bowl's 28,000 Part of Papal Binational Mass," *El Paso Times* online, February 17, 2016, http://www.elpasotimes.com/story/news/local/juarez/pope/2016/02/17/pope-francis-juarez-mexico-elpaso-sun-bowl-catholics/80393464/.

pope in his homily from Mexico thanked his brothers and sisters in El Paso. There are reports that this was the largest "binational" Mass ever celebrated. The event included blessings for the people of Ciudad Juárez, the people of El Paso, and the refugees and others present at a border levee near the Juárez Mass site. The Eucharist thus embraced not only two countries, but also the pilgrims en route from one to the other.

Then, in September of 2017, he went to Colombia to lend a hand to the bishops and pastors in the implementation of the new peace accords intended to end years of conflict between rebels and the government. When the Colombian peace process started, it was difficult to see the scope of its importance, but Pope Francis's support for and encouragement of this process sheds light on his ongoing commitment to *América*. In 2018 he visited Chile, where he faced criticism over the church's sexual abuse scandals, as well as Peru. In 2019 he returned to the Americas for World Youth Day in Panama. Even though the pope always travels on an Argentine passport, he has still not fixed a date to return to his native country.

Affirming and Moving Beyond *Ecclesia in America*

Pope Francis's apostolic journey in 2015 came sixteen years after a similar trip made by John Paul II. The Polish pope issued his apostolic exhortation *Ecclesia in America* on January 22, 1999 in Mexico City, notably at the Shrine of Our Lady of Guadalupe. In it he called upon Catholics in North America and Latin America to consider the church to be part of one *América*.

I asked that the Special Assembly of the Synod of Bishops reflect on America as a single entity, by reason of all that is common to the peoples of the continent, including their shared Christian identity and their genuine attempt to strengthen the bonds of solidarity and communion between the different forms of the continent's rich cultural heritage. The decision to speak of "America" in the singular was an attempt to express not only the unity which in some way already exists, but also to point

---

An image of this event is contained at the beginning (p. 181) of Julia Young's contribution to this volume titled "A Century of Mercy: The Catholic Church and Immigration along the U.S.-Mexico Border."

to that closer bond which the peoples of the continent seek and which the Church wishes to foster as part of her own mission, as she works to promote the communion of all in the Lord.[10]

John Paul II was an ardent defender of the intercultural Christian presence in this one *América*. His call for a new evangelization was unveiled at the fourth general conference of CELAM in Santo Domingo. But the plea that he made almost twenty years ago seems to have fallen on deaf ears. Although one can find a few ongoing academic and ecclesial collaborations that exist either as a result of *Ecclesia in America* or in accord with its basic spirit, very few people in either North or South America adopted this way of thinking about the church. Most Catholics are still myopic and do not think about their ecclesial bonds beyond their own culture and nation, focusing either on their own diocese or the see of Rome. They do not think, for example, about what Miami and Rio de Janeiro have to do with one another.

The election of an Argentine pope was, however, a game-changer. Although Pope Francis never emphasized *Ecclesia in America* in his apostolic voyages of 2015, his journeys to Latin America and the United States during these voyages recall and reconfigure the Polish pope's vision. Our first pope from the Americas strengthened the existing bonds that were in place from the time of Aparecida Conference in 2007 (at which he served as the chair of the drafting committee for the final document) and opened up new paths for dialogue. Speaking of Latin America, Pope John Paul II coined the phrase "a continent of hope," but Pope Francis put flesh and bones on that vision, especially by entering into the United States from the south. In fact, Francis's first wish was to come into the United States by crossing the Mexican border.[11] In *Ecclesia in America*, Pope John Paul II said that trinitarian communion has as its fruit social solidarity.[12] Pope Francis introduced

10 John Paul II, Postsynodal Apostolic Exhortation *Ecclesia in America* (January 22, 1999), 5.

11 Francis, interview with Mexican reporter Valentina Alazraki, *Catholic News Agency* online, March 13, 2015, https://www.catholicnewsagency.com/news/pope-francis-says-he-wanted-to-enter-us-from-mexican-border-44087.

12 John Paul II, *Ecclesia in America*, 52: "Solidarity is thus the fruit of the communion which is grounded in the mystery of the triune God, and in the Son of God who took flesh and died for all. It is expressed in Christian love which seeks the good of others, especially of those most in need." See also Peter J. Casarella, "Solidarity as the Fruit of Communion: Ecclesia in America, 'Post-Liberation Theology,' and the Earth," *Communio: International Catholic Review* 27 (Spring 2000): 98–123.

solidarity into the journey by bringing the fruits of his trip to Cuba, including his earlier behind-the-scenes efforts to help with the thaw in US-Cuban relations, to the White House.

We conceived of this book as a South-North dialogue that would be born from a place in the center of the Americas; namely, Havana. The pope traveling from south to north thus has special significance for us. As editors we are particularly drawn to these words uttered by Pope Francis as he spoke on the South Lawn of the White House in his greeting to President Barack Obama: "I am deeply grateful for your welcome in the name of all Americans. As the son of an immigrant family, I am happy to be a guest in this country, which was largely built by such families. I look forward to these days of encounter and dialogue, in which I hope to listen to, and share, many of the hopes and dreams of the American people."[13]

It is no accident that this son of immigrants introduced himself to the president of the United States and to the entire nation by expressing his solidarity with the sons and daughters of immigrants that came there. The pope introduced himself to the president and the people of the US in order to make a point about identity. If the essence of being from the US is linked to immigration, then a very different sense of nationhood and peoplehood emerges than the usual one.

Like the pope, the editors of this volume, I myself and Maria Clara Bingemer, are not only committed to the South-North encounter but, as it happens, are also both the direct descendants of Italian immigrants to *América*. The contributions in this volume are meant to foster a new vision of the church in *América*, but they also strike a chord deep in our hearts as immigrants to the two neighboring continents that make up *América*.

Mario Bergoglio, the pope's father, left the Piedmont region of Italy in 1929 because he feared being persecuted by the fascist Mussolini. His son's Italian roots help to explain his fascination with Peronism—which in its

---

13 Francis, *Address of the Holy Father at the Welcoming Ceremony*, South Lawn of the White House, Washington, D.C. (September 23, 2015), introductory remarks. For the full text of this ceremony, see the White House Office of the Press Secretary website, "Remarks by President Obama and His Holiness Pope Francis at Arrival Ceremony," https://obamawhitehouse.archives.gov/the-press-office/2015/09/23/remarks-president-obama-and-his-holiness-pope-francis-arrival-ceremony.

early Catholic manifestations appealed to such immigrant families—as well as his solidarity with immigrants throughout the Americas.

We have similar stories. My coeditor Maria Clara Bingemer's paternal grandfather, Marco Lucchetti, was born in a little village in Lombardy. When he was a young adult, he traveled to Barcelona to find work; finding jobs in the north of Italy, close to the powerful and wealthy city of Milan, was not easy at that time. In Barcelona he met a beautiful and strong Catalonian woman named Josefa, whom everyone called Pepita. She agreed to marry him under one condition: that they would always speak Catalan at home. They were married and immediately after that migrated to Brazil. At that time, Spanish and Italian immigration to the south of *América* was an important phenomenon. The couple settled in Rio de Janeiro, and Marco started working in a hat factory.

My paternal grandfather came from Campania in the South. The name of my grandfather's town was Bisaccia; the language of that town of about one thousand people is still today known as Bisacessi or Bisaccian. Employment there was scarce, and the US offered opportunity to Italian manual laborers that was simply not available in the south of Italy. Michele Angelo Casarella came through Ellis Island in 1910 and went to Connecticut because his brother had already gone there. Although he wanted to build houses, he eventually found work as a nonunionized factory worker making spoons with the International Silver Company. He married Maria, a girl from Avellino who had also settled in the area around Meriden in Connecticut. Casarella's father, Mario Casarella, was the fifth of five brothers in the home of "Mike" and Maria Casarella.

These are three early twentieth-century stories of emigration from Italy to Buenos Aires, Rio de Janeiro, and Ellis Island. In this book we do not just speak from one point in the North and another in the South. We inhabit a polyhedral matrix of immigration stories and opportunities for dialogue.[14] North America and Latin America have intertwined destinies. Both continents depend on an ongoing flow of new blood and new cultural identities, contrary to what certain doomsayers may predict. Dialogue is always about entering into relationships

14 On dialogue as polyhedral, see Francis, *Evangelii Gaudium*, 236, and Juan Carlos Scannone, "Pope Francis and the Theology of the People," *Theological Studies* 77, no. 1 (March 2016): 118–35.

that undergo a process of transformation through the dialogue, and often the parties to the dialogue partners begin it in an unequal relationship. There are many different ways of grasping the relationship between the center and the periphery. All of these considerations were in play when Pope Francis introduced himself on the South Lawn. He was setting a tone for and painting a picture of how dialogue could unfold between an Argentine pope and a people that he had never met before on their own turf. What makes the polyhedron into a living web of belief is catholicity.

The pope's distinctive style and rhetoric was in evidence during these trips. His style of speaking is very different from that of his Polish predecessor because it was forged alongside the so-called Argentine *teología del pueblo*, the "theology of the people." Let us consider for a moment the Argentine roots of this rhetoric. The word "people" is perhaps the most well-known word in the lexicon of Pope Francis. In Spanish, the word can refer generically to any social unit with a common history, identity, or sense of belonging, specifically a social unit on the lower rungs of the socioeconomic ladder or in a small town. These three separate senses of the word are all folded into the one word "people" in Spanish. English speakers often miss the multivalency of the word, especially if they think that it means the same thing as the phrase "We the people" in the social imaginary of the US's founding.

Emilce Cuda from Buenos Aires notes that one cannot assimilate the pope's use of the antithesis between people and antipeople (*pueblo y antipueblo*) into the Marxist dialectic of a struggle between the proletariat and the owners of the means of production.[15] Cuda maintains that the Latin American political ethics favored by Bergoglio "de-structures" the values of the aggressor not for the sake of a class struggle, but in search of a new synthesis and a new semantics.[16] His use of this ethical framework is not just a preference for an irenic resolution and the avoidance of physical and moral violence, although the language of peace is central to his new vocabulary. By means of an analysis of

15 Emilce Cuda, *Para leer a Francisco: Teología, ética, y política* (Buenos Aires: Manantial, 2016), 174–83. Cuda has the deepest grasp of the complexity and fruitfulness of political theory of anyone in Argentine Catholicism today. In this article, she develops the way in which the cultural hermeneutics of Juan Carlos Scannone dovetails with the pope's theology of the people.

16 Cuda, *Para leer a Francisco*, 177.

Juan Carlos Scannone, Cuda highlights that a hermeneutics of culture based upon the priority of otherness and difference can contribute to the fostering of a “pluriform harmony” that respects religious liberty and simultaneously unmasks the ideological armaments of social oppression. Culture is not extracted from socioeconomic structures or processes as a neutral field of play in politics, but it is also not reduced to the determinism of either the Marxist dialectic or the radical empiricism of some social scientists. Culture is born of an encounter of diverse peoples, and its fruitful existence is inexorably tied to an avoidance of false, hegemonic totalities.

Pope Francis's address to the US Congress was historic. The fact that no previous pope had ever been invited to address this body is just one dimension of its uniqueness. Authentic appreciation and applause emanated from both sides of the aisle, but the most remarkable fact about the address was its prophetic content. At the heart of the speech was an echo of the words of Dr. Martin Luther King: “I have a dream.” For those around the globe inspired by King and committed to his legacy of civil and human rights, these words have a specific and enduring meaning. But going even further, the Argentine pope interwove King's vision and the visions of Abraham Lincoln, Dorothy Day, and Thomas Merton. Lincoln is an icon of the abolition of slavery and a “guardian of liberty” (the pope's phrase) for both political conservatives and liberals like Barack Obama. He symbolizes a North American dream of freedom in which solidarity and subsidiarity remain in balance. Day represents the Catholic personalism that is close to the pope's own heart, but in a North American key: “Her social activism, her passion for justice and for the cause of the oppressed, were inspired by the Gospel, her faith, and the example of the saints.”[17] Out of his monastic solitude, Merton taught US citizens “a capacity for dialogue and openness to God” that serves as a much-needed antidote to the secular clarion calls for world peace. The dream that Pope Francis set before both the Democrats and the Republicans in the Congress was woven out of the fabric of this nation and its people. King's civic virtue was fused with Day's liturgical piety and radical acts of hospitality, Lincoln's republicanism, and Merton's contemplative insights into world order. The first pope ever to appear in Congress, on

17 Francis, *Visit to the Joint Session of the United States Congress: Address of the Holy Father*, Washington, D.C. (September 24, 2015).

his first trip to the US, was unexpectedly a bard who fashioned a hope for the nation taken from the diverse aspirations of the people itself.

The dream of a better future was also invoked in Cuba. There too, the very notion of a dream for society was based in reality and more on the social dimension of an authentically Christian hope than on pious utopianism. In his meeting with Cuban youth at the Centro Cultural Padre Félix Varela, the pope cited the words of the Guatemalan Nobel laureate Miguel Ángel Asturias (without explicitly mentioning his name) from his 1946 novel *El Señor Presidente*, in which Asturias spoke about a "glass eye" and another "eye of flesh": "Those who see with their glass eye see because they dream. Those who see with their eye of flesh see because they are looking at the reality in front of them!"[18] He alluded to the fact that the youth must dream with two eyes and that those who are not able to dream become entrapped in their selfhood. Using an Argentine expression, he warned them, "Don't get wrinkled up!"[19] The Catholic youth were urged to dream and to share their dreams even if they did not conform to the expectations of their disgruntled peers or of the socialist government. They must keep abreast of the reality in front of them, especially if they hope to change that reality and work for a more just regime and society. The hope for a different future depends on the youth not being enervated and losing their desire to dream.

It is noteworthy that both sets of dreams, one for the US and one for Cuba, are taken from the soil of the people and serve the deepest needs of the people. The contemplative stance of Merton is not directly relevant to Cubans, and the poetry of Asturias would not make much sense to pragmatically oriented Catholic youth in the US. In both cases the great lover of the Argentine epic poem *El Gaucho Martín Fierro* entered into the naked public square not just to console or edify.[20] His goal was and is to forge a new discourse for political inclusion and participation that is grounded in the Christian doctrine of hope. Pope Francis is particularly interested in questions of social memory and time. Past, present, and future need to be brought together into a new synthesis. Political ideologies by themselves cannot create a hope

18 Miguel Ángel Asturias, *El Señor Presidente* (New York: Atheneum, 1964), 24.

19 "No te arrugues!" This might also be translated as "don't get bent out of shape."

20 Cf. Thomas R. Rourke, *The Roots of Pope Francis's Social and Political Thought: From Argentina to the Vatican* (London: Rowman and Littlefield, 2016), 146–47. The pope referenced this work in his address to the United Nations on September 15, 2015.

for this synthesis. Poetry, dreams, and national aspirations are the stuff out of which this synthesis can be created, and new directions for political work can be discovered.

The Field Hospital: Reforming the Church in the Americas

The language that Pope Francis speaks when describing the church is forceful and sometimes shocking: "A field hospital after the battle," "A poor Church for the poor," "Shepherds with the smell of the sheep," "Jesus was a refugee," and "The church in America... is called to go out from its comfort zone and be a leaven of communion."[21] In *Evangelii Gaudium*, the pope not only calls for a new missionary discipleship, but also rebukes an economy of exclusion, the idolatry of money, selfishness and spiritual sloth, sterile pessimism, spiritual worldliness, strife and division within the church, and, above all, ecclesial self-referentiality. These are not mere slogans. They are rooted in a program for the universal church that was articulated in the Constitution *Lumen Gentium* of the Second Vatican Council when it addressed the church as a People of God. The essays in this volume thus also address the idea of the church as the people of God, an idea that Pope Francis prioritizes and the basis of reform of the church that he espouses.

In his trips to the Americas he not only spoke to but also listened—to the bishops, the laity, the holy and faithful people of God, the religious, the popular movements, political leaders, and prisoners and victims of sexual abuse. His idea of a listening church as set forth in *Evangelii Gaudium* is taken from Paul VI's *Evangelii Nuntiandi*, but is also leavened

21 John L. Allen, "Challenges to Vision of a 'Poor Church for the Poor,'" *National Catholic Reporter* online, March 19, 2013, https://www.ncronline.org/blogs/ncr-today/challenges-vision-poor-church-poor; Carol Glitz, "Pope Francis: Priests Should be 'Shepherds Living With the Smell of the Sheep,'" *The Catholic Telegraph* online, March 28, 2013, https://www.thecatholictelegraph.com/pope-francis-priests-should-be-shepherds-living-with-the-smell-of-the-sheep/13439; Dennis Coday, "Pope's Quotes: The Field Hospital Church," *National Catholic Reporter* online, October 26, 2013, https://www.ncronline.org/blogs/francis-chronicles/pope-s-quotes-field-hospital-church; Yasmine Hafiz, "Pope Francis: 'Jesus Was A Refugee,'" *Huffington Post*, June 23, 2014, https://www.huffingtonpost.com/2014/06/23/pope-francis-jesus-refugee_n_5508721.html; *Message of His Holiness Pope Francis for the V Encuentro*, United States Conference of Catholic Bishops website, November 15, 2016, http://www.usccb.org/about/leadership/usccb-general-assembly/2016-november-meeting/message-of-his-holiness-pope-francis-for-the-v-encuentro.cfm.

with distinctively Bergoglian insights.[22] It is here that Pope Francis says that the preacher must *poner un oído en el pueblo* ("keep his ear to the people") in order to discover what the faithful need to hear. Following Montini's pastoral insight, this listening is not restricted to the spiritual realm. His discussion of hopes and dreams described above now meets its application in the realm of a theology of the Word and the reception of the Word in the life of the community. The preacher must enter into the entire web of life of the community to understand not only their mode of prayer but their loves, aspirations, social engagements, and reasons for despair. Through this process of discernment in the light of the Word of God, the pastorally attuned preacher will facilitate God's calling upon his people by means of the proclaimed Word.

Because he speaks about hopes and dreams, one could draw the false impression that Pope Francis is interested in a utopian church, one that always looks optimistically into an unknown future. In fact, he is neither an optimist nor a pessimist, but he is firmly convinced of the need to acknowledge tragedy and grief. Francis maintains that the church weeps because God himself weeps. At Ground Zero in New York City, the pope laid a white rose at the edge of one of the two massive waterfall pools ringed by the engraved names of those who died. He spoke of the meaning of flowing water at this memorial, painting a vivid image of the waterfalls in each of the two pools representing tears of grief, and stating that the pools are receptacles for both past and present tears.

Here grief is palpable. The water we see flowing towards that empty pit reminds us of all those lives which fell prey to those who think that destruction, tearing down, is the only way to settle conflicts. It is the silent cry of those who were victims of a mindset which knows only violence, hatred and revenge. A mindset which can only cause pain, suffering, destruction and tears. The flowing water is also a symbol of our tears. Tears at so much devastation and ruin, past and present. This is a place where we shed tears, we weep out of a sense of helplessness in the face of injustice, murder, and the failure to settle conflicts through dialogue. Here we mourn the wrongful and senseless loss of

22 Francis, *Evangelii Gaudium*, 154, citing Paul VI, Apostolic Exhortation *Evangelii Nuntiandi* (December 8, 1975), 53 and 33, as well as John Paul II's Postsynodal Apostolic Exhortation *Pastores Dabo Vobis* (March 15, 1992), 10.

innocent lives because of the inability to find solutions which respect the common good. This flowing water reminds us of yesterday's tears, but also of all the tears still being shed today.[23]

Tears recur often in the speeches and pastoral practice taught by Pope Francis. One could even speak of his penchant for theological lachrymosity. "God weeps," said Pope Francis on September 27, 2015, in an unscheduled introduction to his address to the US bishops in Philadelphia, which took place just after he had prayed with victims of clerical sexual abuse. The divine weeping is for the victims of this abuse.

What are tears and what do they signify in the worldview of Pope Francis? Tears are a biological function as well as a sign of deep emotion. They flow together with the other waters of the world. At Ground Zero, he reminded us of what his mentor Lucio Gera taught about the embeddedness of tears in the order of creation.[24] Gera did not think that the shedding of tears before the senselessness of violence was futile or of merely therapeutic value. Matthew 5:4, after all, tells us that "blessed are they who mourn, for they will be comforted." For the Argentine school, tears are not an opiate given to the people in order to still their sense of justice; on the contrary, the shedding of tears are the physical manifestation of a cry for new structures that stand in solidarity with God's tears. Luis Herrera writes in his contribution to this volume that the pope's theology of tears redresses the deliberate suppression of subversive memories by political authorities intent upon burying them: "The public recovery of memory is opposed to official policies of silencing, bringing to light what was veiled, bringing to light the truth."[25] The well of tears collected by the church, from the church, and for the church is like the well of eternal life at which Jesus meets the Samaritan woman. Tears are the first sign that reconciliation with God and neighbor may be possible.

---

23 Vatican Radio website, "Pope Francis' Address at Ground Zero Memorial in New York," September 24, 2015, http://en.radiovaticana.va/news/2015/09/25/pope_francis%E2%80%99_address_at_ground_zero_memorial_in_new_york/1174651.

24 *Escritos Teologico-Pastorales de Lucio Gera*, vol. 1 of *Del preconcilio a la conferencia de Puebla (1956–1981)*, ed. Virginia Raquel Azcuy, C. M. Galli, and Manuel Gonzalez (Buenos Aires: Agape, 2006), 113–19 (containing a written text by Gera from 1957).

25 Luis Herrera Rodríguez, SJ, "Whisper to Those in Despair: 'The Best Wine is Yet to Come': Memory, Hope, and Resistance," p. 120.

A final clue to the reform impulse in Pope Francis's theology of the people is the theme of the Samaritan church. It is a leitmotif that predates Francis; Paul VI said in an address of December 7, 1965 at the last general session of the council that "the old story of the Samaritan has been the model of the spirituality of the council."[26] As a cardinal in Argentina, the parable became for Bergoglio the authentic basis for constructing a model of Argentine nationhood.[27] On the eve of Mother Teresa's canonization, Pope Francis spoke with the Workers of Mercy, telling them that "the world needs solidarity and a Samaritan Church." In his General Audience of April 27, 2016, his words were even more forceful: "What does it mean to ignore the suffering of human beings? It means to ignore God! If I do not draw close to that man, that woman, that child, that elderly man or elderly woman who are suffering, I do not draw close to God."[28] In this way, the Samaritan church brings the people to God.

There can be no question of reducing the reality of the church to a communal will to becoming a do-gooder. The church, according to Pope Francis, is an irruption of unbounded maternal love in the world, never a compassionate nongovernmental organization. The image of the Samaritan as forged by Paul VI at the close of the council and reiterated by Pope Francis is that of a church generally disposed to be at the service of the most needy. The Samaritan church of Bergoglio recalls Emmanuel Levinas's statement in *Otherwise than Being* that in the face of the Other I am ready to give, despite myself, the bread torn from my very mouth.[29] In both the Argentine Catholic theologian and the French Jewish philosopher we see that the existential encounter with God and the Samaritan encounter with the stranger are distinct but *not separable* religious acts.

Cultura de Encuentro: On the Origins of this Project in Havana

All of the papers collected in this volume were hatched at a meeting that took place in the Centro Cultural Padre Félix Varela and the Casa

---

26 Paul VI, *Address During the Last General Meeting of the Second Vatican Council*, December 7, 1965.

27 Rourke, *Roots Francis's Political Thought*, 152–53.

28 Francis, *General Audience*, April 27, 2016.

29 Emmanuel Levinas, *Otherwise than Being: Or Beyond Essence* (Dordrecht: Springer, 1991), 56.

Sacerdotal of Havana in October 2016.[30] In a very real sense, these efforts are the fruit of the *cultura de encuentro* (culture of encounter) shared by the participants and extended by our hosts in Cuba.[31] Hospitality was extended and received at this midpoint of the Americas and crucible of a new *América*. Havana, after all, is only a short distance from Hispaniola, the island where Christopher Columbus made the first permanent European settlement in the New World.[32] It is also the site where diplomatic relations between the US and the island recently resulted in a new opening, in no small part due to the intervention of Pope Francis. In short, we met at the crucible of the Americas in order to discuss their future.

The meeting in Havana centered on the visits of Pope Francis to the Americas in 2015 and 2016. The first of the papal trips discussed was his visit to Bolivia, Ecuador, and Paraguay in July 2015, in which Francis focused on the dignity of workers and of the poor and marginalized.[33] The second of these visits was to Cuba and the US in September 2015, which focused on the relations between the two countries and on the 2015 World Meeting of Families.[34] Finally, the group discussed Francis's trip to Cuba and Mexico in February 2016, which had a special focus on the US-Mexican border and the meeting of the pope with the Russian Orthodox patriarch Kirill.[35] Pope Francis has, since, visited the

30 Neither Julia Young nor Sixto García were able to be physically present for the meeting, but their papers were shared and discussed. Luis Fraga attended the meeting and submitted his coauthored paper afterwards.

31 A note of gratitude is due to Fr. Yosvany Carvajal Sureda and Gustavo Andujar of the Centro Cultural Félix Varela and Fr. José Miguel Gonzalez Martin of the Casa Sacerdotal. During this meeting we had the unique opportunity to celebrate the seventy-fifth birthday of Cardinal Jaime Ortega with His Eminence and with the current archbishop of Havana.

32 Today this island is shared by the Dominican Republic and Haiti.

33 The itinerary of this trip may be found at *Apostolic Journey of His Holiness Pope Francis to Ecuador, Bolivia and Paraguay* on the Vatican website.

34 Jonathan Watts and Stephanie Kirchgaessner, "Pope Calls on Cuba and US to Set Global 'Example of Reconciliation,'" *The Guardian* online, September 19, 2015, https://www.theguardian.com/world/2015/sep/19/pope-francis-cuba-us-reconciliation-havana.

35 Francis X. Rocca and James Marson, "Pope Francis Plans Historic Meeting With Russian Orthodox Leader in Cuba," *The Wall Street Journal* online, February 5, 2016, https://www.wsj.com/articles/pope-to-meet-russian-orthodox-leader-in-cuba-1454673252; Juan Paullier, "Los 5 momentos más importantes de la visita del papa Francisco a México" [The five most important moments of the visit of Pope Francis to México], *BBC Mundo* website, February 18, 2016, https://www.bbc.com/mundo/noticias/2016/02/160217_mexico_papa_francisco_analisis_visita_claves_jp.

Americas three times in the 2017 to 2019 period in trips that, although important, will not be reflected upon on in this volume. The first of these visits was to Colombia in September 2017, which centered on peacebuilding. A moment of particular significance on this visit was the prayer in front of the black Christ of Bojayá, a moving act in honor of the victims of the 2002 Bojayá massacre and all the victims of the Colombian conflict, an act that also pointed to the compassionate and healing love of Christ in the midst of suffering.[36] In 2018, the pope visited Chile and Peru, a visit that included several encounters with indigenous communities of the region.[37] Finally, the last of Francis's visits to the Americas was to Panama in January 2019, where he exhorted the youth to say yes to God at the World Youth Day 2019.[38]

The scholars from North and South were accompanied by seventeen undergraduates from the University of Notre Dame, whose presence added to the conference welcome vigor and youthful insights. This group consisted of students enrolled in a seminar led by me and Robert Pelton, a missionary priest of the Congregation of the Holy Cross and the founder in 1985 of the Latin American North American Church Concerns Project at Notre Dame. Although he is not represented in this volume, Fr. Bob's input was vital and needs some elaboration. He was the inspiration for the idea of meeting in Cuba and also inspired several of the undergraduates to pursue research projects on Cuban Catholicism. In fact, his signature essay from 2005, "Learning from the Cuban House Churches," offers an excellent model for the South-North encounter envisioned for this volume.[39] The *casas de oración*, he writes, are places of prayer, social service agencies, and oases of subtle but palpable resistance against an oppressive regime that holds an ambivalent attitude toward Catholicism. In his words,

36 Francis, *Prayer to the Black Christ of Bojayá*, Las Malocas Park (Villavicencio), Colombia September 8, 2017.

37 Inés San Martín, "Both in Chile and Peru, Politics of all Sorts May Vex Pope's Trip," *Crux*, January 13, 2018, https://cruxnow.com/pope-in-chile-and-peru/2018/01/chile-peru-politics-sorts-may-vex-popes-trip/.

38 Vatican News website, "Pope Francis' Speech at WYD 2019 Opening Ceremony: Full Text," January 25, 2019, https://www.vaticannews.va/en/pope/news/2019-01/pope-francis-panama-wyd-2019-opening-ceremony-full-text.html

39 Robert Pelton, CSC, "Learning from the Cuban House Churches," in *Small Christian Communities Today: Capturing the New Moment*, ed. Joseph G. Healey and Jeanne Hinton (Maryknoll, N.Y.: Orbis, 2005), 22–27.

"the unmistakable parallels between the house churches of contemporary Cuba and the house churches of the first century provide clear evidence that the blueprints for the church that can meet the challenges of the third millennium may well be found in the renewal of the first-millennium roots."[40] His essay offers an excellent example of how the principle of "mission *in reverse*," that is, from South to North, undergirds the entire effort of this project.

The two essays that follow this introduction offer a panorama of the volume as a whole. The opening address of the conference was delivered in the auditorium of the historic Centro Varela (in front of which the pope had addressed Cuban youth) and serves as the point of entry to this volume. Austen Ivereigh, author of the most authoritative biography of Jorge Mario Bergoglio yet to appear, develops the notion of *la patria Grande* that underlies much of the pope's thinking about politics and society. In other words, he dreams of a reunification of Latin America, and this dream has now been translated into other goals for the universal church. Ivereigh's rich insight into Argentine and Latin American history sets the stage for grasping the world from which the pope came and to which he returned in 2015.

The next two essays address theological, historical, and pastoral engagements that cut across several of the pope's visits. Sixto García, a Cuban-American theologian and retired professor of theology from St. Vincent de Paul Major Seminary in Boynton Beach, Florida, writes about the Christology of the Aparecida document. The document precedes both the pontificate and the apostolic voyages, but the encounter with the person of Christ as it emerged in a conference in which Cardinal Bergoglio played a key role in the drafting of the final document is a clue to the pontificate. García sets the stage for thinking about the deeply Christocentric orientation of Pope Francis and its resonances with the theodicy of Latino/a theologians in the US.

Ana María Bidegain, a historian of Uruguayan origins who now teaches at Florida International University, looks at the prehistory of Pope Francis's ecclesial engagement with poverty. She provides ample documentation of the origins of being "a poor church for the poor" in the early Catholic Action groups of Catholic youth in Latin America in the 1950s and even before that in the early church and

40 Pelton, "House Churches," 27.

Middle Ages. Any simple narrative whereby Francis is simply imitating certain recent strands of the theology of liberation and ignoring the earlier tradition of the church will need to be rewritten in the light of her lucid analysis.

The next five essays are dedicated to the visits themselves. Paulo Fernando Carneiro de Andrade is an expert on liberation theology from the Pontifical Catholic University of Rio de Janeiro. He focuses on the pope's addresses as they relate to popular movements and reinforces the embrace of a preferential option for the poor articulated by Bidegain. By unveiling the Latin American roots of the engagement with popular movements, he is able to show that the pope's July 9, 2015 address in Bolivia does not stand alone. In fact, the pope's concern for the popular movements is in essence an attempt to forge a new discourse about the subjectivity and agency of the poor in history.

Luis Herrera Rodríguez, SJ, teaches theology in Belo Horizonte, Brazil and wrote a dissertation on the relevance of North American theologian David Tracy for reflecting on the hermeneutical issues involved in the indigenous theology of the peoples in the Peruvian Andes. He focuses here on the trip to Bolivia, Paraguay, and Ecuador. He uncovers discourses of memorializing, resistance, hope, and change in the pope's discourses. He is able to show, through his hermeneutical dissections and reconfigurations, that the poor and other vulnerable people who have been left without hope are actually granted strategies of resistance to structural injustices and conditions of despair.

Roberto Tomichá is director of the Institute for Mission Studies in Cochabamba, Bolivia, and a priest from the Chiquito people in Bolivia. His contribution surveys the talks given on the South American trip from the perspective of the new discourse of theology that is being written by the indigenous people in Latin America. After centuries of being silenced, the peoples who first received the Christian message are now being given a voice in theology. Tomichá's fascinating engagement with Pope Francis is thus groundbreaking in terms of its depth of intercultural thought and reflection.

William Portier, a historian of the Catholic Church in the US from the University of Dayton, surveys the impact of the Latin American theology of the people on the pope's visit to the US. He analyzes the innovative use of language as well as the "encyclical of gestures" that were communicated to the US public.[41] He concludes that the first American pope is an urban gaucho whose novel Catholic discourse about the US church accords in some fashion with the working-class struggle that reverberates in Bruce Springsteen's "Land of Hope and Dreams."

Julia Young is a historian at The Catholic University of America who specializes in the history of Mexican migration to the US. She begins with the defense of the migrant and refugee contained in the speeches of Pope Francis. She draws out the implications of Francis's rich theology of memory as it applies to the historical presence and current situatedness of migrant Mexicans. Specifically, she turns to the century-long story of post-1920 immigration. She elicits parallels between the current predicament along the border and the concerns raised by the National Catholic Welfare Conference in the 1920s and 1930s. She is thus able to show that the current engagement of the church with the question of migration is not new. Furthermore, the pope's recent call to build bridges and not walls can be buttressed and clarified by historical analysis in order to show that Spanish-speaking Catholics in the US are not only not a recent phenomenon but a people that has struggled valiantly and eloquently for a long time to establish their voice and role in this land.

Luis Fraga of the University of Notre Dame and Kiku Huckle of Pace University are political scientists who specialize in the analysis of the politics and political discourse in the US as it relates to Latinos and Latinas. They studied the English and Spanish texts of the pope's visit to the US and the various reactions that these addresses received in the country. By pinpointing language as a field for spiritual enrichment, they are able to demonstrate that the pope was received as a "Latino pope" and as a pope who stands in solidarity with Latino immigrants. Furthermore, they speculate that the overcoming of the language barrier in Pope Francis's words and actions, rather than being a mere crutch, creates a cultural bridge between the pope and Latinos that will help to foster genuine diversity in both church and society in the US.

The pentultimate essay is a trenchant analysis of Pope Francis's critique of clericalism by Allan Figueroa Deck, SJ. Deck teaches at Loyola Marymount University and formerly served as the founding director of the Secretariat on Cultural Diversity in the Church of the United

41 I borrow the phrase "encyclical of gestures" from Carlos María Galli.

States Conference of Catholic Bishops. He not only recites the many instances in which Pope Francis voices his conviction that clericalism is an aberration in light of the conciliar vision of the church as a people of God, but he interrogates the reality of clericalism in the Latin American church and beyond as a neuralgic point. He concludes with a call for a church that is completely shorn of narcissism and self-referentiality and is authentically Samaritan.

Maria Clara Lucchetti Bingemer is a theologian from the Pontifical Catholic University of Rio de Janeiro who completed her doctorate at the Gregorian University in Rome on the trinitarian spirituality of St. Ignatius of Loyola. She offers an overview of the spirituality of the South-North encounter. She looks concretely at the trip to both Cuba and the US through the lens of St. Ignatius's valorization of the lives of saints in the *Spiritual Exercises*. The dynamic she describes is reinforced not only by the pope's deep immersion in Ignatian spiritual theology but also by his frequent invocation of the importance of testimony to communicate the Christian message. People do not listen attentively when you offer only words. They are more likely to react positively when the words and the living witness form a coherent whole. By focusing on this, Bingemer is able to plumb new depths in the pope's American discourses and find a new path to transcontinental dialogue and the building of a revitalized *Ecclesia in America* in the process.

We have given this book the title "Pope Francis and the Search for God in *América*." As editors, we have been enriched by brilliant contributors from both North and South, all of whom reflect in their essays the exciting possibility of mutual exchange, listening to one another, and mutual learning between North and South. In Cuba we exchanged more than information and viewpoints—we celebrated our being together with delicious meals, the holy Eucharist, and late-night rum tastings. Sociality and transcendence were interlaced. In fact, we entered together into a mystery that encompasses *la mística* (the mystical dimension) of what it means to be from *América*. The search for God on our continents is not like the solving of a crossword puzzle. It is a struggle filled with tears, but will nonetheless never become old and used up. No one will ever write a complete travelogue of the spiritual quest of these two massive habitations of faith, learning, resistance, and inquiry. We learned repeatedly from our reflections and time spent together that each of our searches was enriched by the perspective of the other. As a group, we spanned the two continents, and, just as importantly, our encounter was enriched by the presence of diverse undergraduates, in acknowledgement of the generational geography of the Americas. We entered more deeply into the unfathomable mystery of God by virtue of being awakened to God's multiple faces and voices. We offer this volume to the members of the church in *América*, South and North, old and young, with the hope that it will spur even more thought, reflection, prayer, and service. Above all, we hope that it engenders the genuine *cultura de encuentro* that we, by virtue of the generosity of our Cuban hosts, were able to experience in Havana.

CHAPTER 2

THE POPE AND THE PATRIA GRANDE

How Francis Promotes Latin America's Continental Destiny

Austen Ivereigh

IN RESEARCHING MY BIOGRAPHY of Pope Francis, titled *The Great Reformer*, I was struck by the strength of his passion for Latin American continental unity. Above all, in the years between the Fifth General Conference of the Latin American episcopate in May 2007 in Aparecida, Brazil, and his election as the 266th successor of St. Peter in March 2013, Cardinal Jorge Mario Bergoglio appeared convinced that Latin America's hour was at hand in both the church and the wider world. The coming-of-age of the "continent of hope" would have a dual dimension: progress toward a long dreamed-for continental unification would go hand in hand with an active role for the continent modeling a politics and economy of Christian humanism. This consciousness of *La Patria Grande* following Aparecida coincided with commemorations of the bicentenary of independence of the Latin American nations, which in turn provoked soul-searching about what had happened to the dreams of José de San Martín and Simón Bolívar of a *confederación de pueblos libres* (a confederation of free peoples).[1]

The term "Patria Grande" dates from the early twentieth century, when the dreams of the Spanish-American liberators, comprehensively

1 This article is an updated and amended version of a keynote address given in October 2016 at the Centro Félix Varela in Havana, Cuba, at the start of a three-day colloquium examining the significance of Pope Francis's visits to the Americas. On Cardinal Bergoglio and the Patria Grande, see Austen Ivereigh, *The Great Reformer: Francis and the Making of a Radical Pope* (New York: Henry Holt, 2014), esp. chaps. 4, 5, and 7. References to this book herein are to the revised and updated Picador paperback edition of July 2015. On Pope Francis and the Patria Grande, see Austen Ivereigh, *Wounded Shepherd: Pope Francis and His Struggle to Convert the Catholic Church* (New York: Henry Holt, 2019), chap. 8.

dashed in the upheaval and balkanization of Latin America in the decades following emancipation, were revived by the "Generation of 900" intellectuals. They referred to the vision variously as *Magna Patria* or *Gran Patria*. But what stuck was the term coined by the Argentine nationalist visionary Manuel Ugarte in his 1922 tract, *La Patria Grande*.

When *The Great Reformer* appeared in November 2014, Pope Francis had made only one visit to Latin America, for World Youth Day in Rio, a few months after his election. He made no mention of the Patria Grande there, nor did he in the first two years of his pontificate, apart from surprising the then Argentine president, Cristina Kirchner, by using the term in a meeting with her in March 2013.[2] But then came the epic visits to the Americas: in June 2015 to Ecuador, Bolivia, and Paraguay, and in September of that year to Cuba and the United States; in February 2016 to Mexico; in September 2017 to Colombia; and in January 2018 to Chile and Peru. His frequent invocation of the Patria Grande on these trips, as well as his passionate, almost mystical view of the *pueblo* and the *patria*, took commentators by surprise.

In July 2016 Francis marked the anniversary of the Congress of Tucumán—which two hundred years earlier had declared the independence of what was then called the United Provinces of South America—with a bold letter to the president of the Argentine bishops' conference in which he referred to two hundred years "of the journey of a *patria* that, in its desire and yearning for fraternity, projects itself beyond its country's borders: toward the Patria Grande of which San Martín and Bolívar dreamed"; that is, toward "a family of broad horizons and fraternal loyalty."[3]

It had taken two or three years to emerge, but Francis had discerned that this Latin America-specific agenda did not contradict his priorities as universal pastor, and in fact was part of his call. Just as

2 President Kirchner noted after the meeting that in speaking of regional unity the pope had used the term "Patria Grande," which had moved her. "He told me he used the term because it was the term used by San Martín and Bolívar." *La Política Online*, Edición Argentina, March 19, 2013, https://www.lapoliticaonline.com/nota/nota-89383/

3 *Letter of His Holiness Pope Francis for the Bicentennial of Independence of the Argentine Republic*, July 8, 2016. This English-language translation of the pope's letter uses "Great Homeland" for Patria Grande, but there is no real equivalent in English; see below, page XX. All documents published by the Vatican, including this one and many others cited below, including papal addresses, may be found at the vatican.va website.

Saint John Paul II saw his election to the see of Peter as a providential means of liberating Eastern Europe from the Soviet yoke, Francis has sought to promote the unfinished emancipation of Latin America, "always threatened by diverse kinds of colonialism."[4] If the Polish pope sought to open up Eastern Europe to a postcommunist future based on its own Christian-humanist traditions, the Argentine pope seeks to wean Latin America from its attachment to stale dichotomies and false polarizations borrowed from imported ideologies that do not reflect its realities, while nudging the continent to embrace a future rooted in its unique culture and history. In this sense, the Florida Straits and the Mexican-American border are to this pontificate what the Berlin Wall was to John Paul II's.

His is not a defensive, or insular, nationalism; Francis believes passionately in a Latin America open to, and engaged with, the world. Part of his geopolitical strategy as pope has been to unblock its channels to the wider world—above all by restoring the ties between the US and Cuba—and to consistently remind the Americas that their cultures are intrinsically proimmigrant.

At the same time, he is convinced that the logic of globalization means opening the door to continent-states, and that it is Latin America's calling to develop a pancontinental integration faithful to its culture. In other words, it must strengthen its identity, developing a society and politics faithful to a unique identity formed in the crucible of the encounter between the ancestral peoples of Latin America and conquest and evangelization. Key to this development is a strengthening of the continent's internal bonds, which has long been a policy of the Latin American church, ever since the very first continent-wide CELAM (the Latin American Episcopal Council) assembly in the 1950s.

This chapter proceeds in two main parts. In the first I explain the origin of Francis's nationalist vision in the writings of the group of thinkers known as the La Plata school, introducing its key figures and major concepts—above all, its revisionist view of Latin American history in the writings of Alberto Methol Ferré.[5] In the second I show how,

4 Francis, "Presentación," in Guzmán Carriquiry, *Memoria, coraje y esperanza: A la luz del Bicentenario de la Independencia de América Latina* (Granada: Editorial Nuevo Inicio, 2017), ix.

5 Warmest thanks to two Uruguayan sages for help with understanding Methol Ferré's thought and for furnishing important materials: Prof. Guzmán Carriquiry, formerly

on his visits to Latin America and in his bicentenary message to the Argentine bishops in July 2016, he has reflected that message under six major headings: evangelization through culture, pastoral/missionary conversion of the church, the culture of encounter and solidarity, the renewal of politics, true globalization, and the Patria Grande.

I have used the term Patria Grande rather than the official Vatican translation of "Greater Country" or "Greater Fatherland"—the renditions vary—because the connotation of patria in Spanish is very different: "fatherland" has associations with fascism, and Latin American patriots often refer to the *Madre Patria*, the "motherland," which connotes a nurturing entity. I have also kept pueblo in Spanish, a term that, for Francis and the La Plata school, has a powerful, even mystical connotation as a subject of history and a carrier of the seeds of the Gospel, none of which is quite captured in the English word "people."

The Roots of the Vision

Pope Francis has always been open about his debt to his Uruguayan friend and mentor, Alberto Methol Ferré (1929–2009).[6] Methol Ferré was a historian, theologian, and philosopher, a Latin American pan-nationalist and admirer of Juan Domingo Perón who was influenced above all else by the Second Vatican Council, which he saw as giving birth to a new era for the church in Latin America. An eclectic autodidact and brilliant synthesizer, he was an intellectual rather than an academic—he once described himself as "a feral Thomist, without academy or seminary"—who left behind a large catalogue of

---

secretary of the Pontifical Commission for Latin America in Rome and now Uruguayan ambassador to the Holy See, and Prof. José Ramiro Podetti, curator of the Methol Ferré collection at the University of Montevideo.

6 See Alver Metalli, "Introduction," in Alberto Methol Ferré and Alver Metalli, *El Papa y El Filósofo* (Buenos Aires: Biblios, 2013), 19–34; José Ramiro Podetti, "Confluencias entre Francisco y Alberto Methol Ferré: Iglesia, evangelización y mundo contemporáneo" (paper given in the Semana Teológica del Uruguay, Fac. Teología, Inst. Mariano Soler, Montevideo, September 22, 2014); Bárbara Díaz, "Alberto Methol Ferré: Una influencia fundamental en el pensamiento del papa Francisco," *Cuadernos del CLAEH*, second series, 34, no. 101 (2015): 63–85. The best overview of Methol's thought is Javier Restán Martínez, *Alberto Methol Ferré: Su pensamiento en* Nexo (Buenos Aires: Dunken, 2010).

essays and some books and talks, as well as three journals he edited and dominated: *Nexo* (1955–58), *Víspera* (1967–75) and again *Nexo* (1983–89).[7]

Their friendship was rooted in a shared popular nationalism, the conviction that it was time for Latin America to play a larger role in the Catholic Church, a belief that theology and pastoral practice should be geared to inculturation, and a shared skepticism about the dangers of the ideologies of left and right. Bergoglio imbibed from Methol Ferré the conviction that globalization was opening the doors to deeper continental integration, which needed to recognize the role of faith in popular culture if it was not to become yet another "imperial" project. The subject of Methol Ferré's metaphysics, Bergoglio wrote, "is the real being as such—determined and limited—who opens the door to the concrete universal" as opposed to the "imported ideologies that create abstract universals."[8]

From the mid-1970s, Methol Ferré worked for the pancontinental episcopal council CELAM in various capacities: as head of the laity department, as an influential member of its pastoral theology think tank, and as secretary to Antonio Quarracino, then bishop of Avellaneda, after the Argentine bishop became CELAM's general secretary in 1979. Methol's genius was to connect, on the one hand, the new Latin American theologies of liberation sparked by the great CELAM general conference in Medellín, Colombia of 1968 with, on the other hand, the national-popular traditions of Latin American emancipation, thus enabling an engaged Catholic populism rooted in the culture and traditions of the pueblo. Together with the Argentine theologian Fr. Lucio Gera, who was one of the main drafters of Pope Paul VI's *Evangelii Nuntiandi* (1975), Methol Ferré had a major influence on the document that came out of the Third General Conference of CELAM held in Puebla, Mexico in 1979.

---

7 Among his most important books are: *La Crisis de Uruguay y el Imperio Británico* (Buenos Aires: A. Peña Lillo, 1959); *Puebla: Proceso y Tensiones* (Buenos Aires: Documenta, 1978), *De Río a Puebla: Etapas Históricas de la Iglesia en América Latina (1945–1980)* (Bogotá: CELAM, 1980), and a book-length interview with Alver Metalli, *La América Latina del Siglo XXI* (Mexico City: Instituto Mexicano de Doctrina Social Cristiana, 2006), reissued as *El Papa y El Filósofo* (cited in the previous note).

8 Thomas R. Rourke, *The Roots of Pope Francis's Social and Political Thought: From Argentina to the Vatican* (London: Rowman and Littlefield, 2016), 85–87.

Gera was a pioneer of the branch of Latin American theology known as the theology of the people (hereafter TP), which was shaped by the Argentine church's response to Vatican II and Medellín between 1966 and 1973, the year Bergoglio became the Jesuit provincial. TP has its origins in the Episcopal Pastoral Commission (COEPAL) presided over by three of the most dynamic bishops of the time, all of whom had taken part in Medellín: Enrique Angelelli of La Rioja, Vicente Zazpe of Santa Fe—both of whom were close to Bergoglio—and Manuel Morengo of Azul. They appointed a group of theologians whose leading lights were Gera—who had studied under Joseph Ratzinger in Bonn—as well as Rafael Tello and Justino O'Farrell. Others in the so-called La Plata school of Latin American theology included the Jesuit Juan Carlos Scannone, the Chilean Schönstatt priest, Joaquín Allende, and one of Methol Ferré's disciples, the Uruguayan Guzmán Carriquiry. After the CELAM assembly at Puebla, Mexico in 1979, these are among the names that appear regularly in Methol Ferré's journal *Nexo*.[9]

The distinctiveness of TP is its critique of Marxism and other Enlightenment ideologies as alien to both Christianity and the Latin American cultural tradition. Gera looked instead to the tradition of the "simple faithful" who had incarnated the Gospel in culture over time. Although TP shares with liberation theology (hereafter TL) an association between salvation and emancipation, it looks first of all to the rationality and interests of the pueblo as the agent of that emancipation.

If TL was "a critical reflection on historical praxis," in Gustavo Gutiérrez's phrase, TP asked whose historical praxis was involved—that of the Latin American peoples or of the group of intellectuals committed to TL. TP critiqued TL's dependence on Marxist social science, not just because its categories were outside the historical experience of Latin America, but because it looked to class rather than culture. By uncritically adopting Enlightenment rationalist perspectives, TP thinkers

9 The best study of TP is Juan Carlos Scannone, SJ, *La Teología del pueblo: Raíces teológicas del Papa Francisco* (Maliaño, Cantabria: Sal Terrae, 2017). See also Sebastián Politi, *Teología del pueblo: Una propuesta Argentina a la teologia Latinoamérica* (Buenos Aires: Docencia, 2015), 184–92; Rafael Luciani, *El Papa Francisco y la teología del pueblo* (Madrid: PPC, 2016); Emilce Cuda, *Para leer a Francisco: Teología, ética y política* (Buenos Aires: Manantial, 2016); and Rourke, *Roots of Francis's Political Thought.* See Restán, *Alberto Methol Ferré,* 268–76, for a list of contributors to *Nexo.*

argued, TL could become another form of imperialism, a project in the name of the people, but not with them.

TP also rejected what it saw as TL's attachment to dependency theory, which tended to reduce history to a narrative of oppression and exploitation. For the COEPAL theologians, *el pueblo* meant the distinctive hybrid culture of Latin America, born of the twin experiences of racial and cultural *mestizaje*—the blending of White, Black, and Indian peoples—on the one hand, and the evangelization of America on the other. Through baptism, the ancient Indian peoples and the mestizos became a new people (*pueblo nuevo*) with an awareness of their common dignity, who participated equally in pursuing the common good. Of course, this historical project of emancipation has never been fully realized and in fact has been continually frustrated, but there were moments and experiences in the early colonial period—the Jesuit missions of Paraguay and the "village hospitals" of Mexico to name two—that had conferred on the Latin American consciousness the notes of popular sovereignty and self-determination that fitted naturally with a federal, democratic, participatory politics.

For the TP theologians, the pueblo and its religiosity constitute a dynamic historical subject, counterposed, in their reading, to the *imperio*—the enlightened elites linked to the major economic interests tied to the foreign great powers (Great Britain, the US, etc.). The interests of the *imperio* were defended in the nineteenth century by the liberal state, which restricted suffrage to the literate and propertied on the grounds that only "rational" people should be able to vote. Thus, for the La Plata school, Argentine history is a constant back-and-forth story of the pueblo's emancipatory struggles—mobilized by the *caudillos* in the independence era, but then excluded from participation in government until the expansion of suffrage in 1912 and the Radical administrations from 1916 to 1928 dominated by Hipólito Yrigoyen. Expelled by the army in 1928, the pueblo burst forth again in October 1945 to demand Perón's release, but was excluded again from the army when it unseated Perón in 1955.[10]

10 Politi, *Teología del Pueblo*, 226–47. Methol Ferré, "Marco histórico de la religiosidad popular," in *Iglesia y Religiosidad Popular en América Latina* (Bogotá: CELAM, 1977), 45–75.

Methol Ferré's early journal *Víspera* (1967–75) featured theologians from both the national-popular and liberationist currents, but the two groups fell out over the Cuban revolution and the guerrilla strategies it inspired, which Methol Ferré described as both the death of politics and the politics of death.[11] They also split over the papal magisterium. Whereas the liberationists followed the European Marxist paradigm of a "people's church" versus a "hierarchical church" and wanted to see (following Hans Küng) a greatly diminished Vatican, the TP thinkers believed that a strong center (Rome) was necessary to hold in check the strength and wealth of particular churches. Hence the nationalists were quick to defend *Humanae Vitae*, for example, as a bulwark of poor countries against the Malthusianism of the North.[12]

In the run-up to Puebla, the liberationists were furious with the nationalists for shifting the attention in the preparatory document away from sociology and onto history and culture. They painted the La Plata school as conservatives who were rolling back the legacy of Medellín, a narrative that has lasted to this day. And yet it would be the La Plata school that became the dominant theology of CELAM, first at Puebla, and later at Aparecida, and it is now, through Francis's *Evangelii Gaudium*, the most important theological current of the universal church.[13]

In the wake of Puebla, the La Plata school thinkers would form the backbone of the second *Nexo*, which Methol Ferré created to promote and spread Puebla's insights and vision. (Six members of the CELAM pastoral-theological group were on the magazine's staff.) *Nexo* was concerned with helping the Latin American church reconnect with popular religiosity and the national-popular tradition of social and political emancipation. CELAM itself has consistently promoted both

---

11 Methol Ferré, "La revolución verde oliva, Debray y la OLAS," *Víspera* 1, no. 3 (October 1967): 17–45, at http://www.metholferre.com/obras/articulos/capitulos.php?id=1

12 This remains Francis's reading of the encyclical. "The great controversy at the time was over the [contraceptive] pill, but what people didn't realize was the prophetic force of the encyclical, which foresaw the neo-Malthusianism which was then just getting underway across the world. Paul VI sounded the alarm over that wave of neo-Malthusianism. We see it in the way people are selected according to their utility or productivity: the throwaway culture." See Austen Ivereigh, "An Interview with Pope Francis," *Commonweal* online, April 8, 2020, https://www.commonwealmagazine.org/time-great-uncertainty.

13 Restán, *Alberto Methol Ferré*, 14; Ivereigh, *The Great Reformer*, 184–86.

episcopal collegiality and Latin American integration as twin aspects of a single historical movement.[14]

The "Catholic Resurgence"

In his prologue to a book by Guzmán Carriquiry on Latin America's bicentenary, Cardinal Bergoglio praised Methol Ferré for rescuing history from the distortions of the dominant hermeneutics, both liberal and Marxist, of the intellectual elites of the 1950s, who, like the liberals of the nineteenth century, ignored the colonial period, dismissing it as backward, premodern, and superstitious. For Methol Ferré, the three centuries that followed the conquest and evangelization of Latin America were the incubator of the pueblo nuevo. This was missed by the sociology of the 1960s and 1970s in its ignorance of the vital formative role of the church in the experience of ordinary people, whose popular religiosity was the principal carrier of both Gospel and culture.[15]

The distinctive culture and vision of the early colonial period would become for Bergoglio a standpoint from which to critique alien ideologies. "Our people has a soul," he often said as a Jesuit, "and because we can speak of the soul of a people, we can speak of a hermeneutic, a way of seeing reality, an awareness." Repeating that quote as cardinal in 1988 in an essay on Cuba in the year of John Paul II's visit to the island, he described how both Marxism and neoliberalism were alien to Cuba's "soul."[16]

In putting Catholicism back at center stage and telling the story of Latin America from the point of view of the lived experiences of ordinary people, Methol Ferré divided the story of Latin America into three periods. The first, the colonial, was the period in which a unique and distinctive Latin American culture was formed. From the meeting

14 See CELAM, *Promoviendo la colegialidad episcopal y la integración latinoamericana* (Bogotá: CELAM 2016).

15 Jorge Mario Bergoglio, prologue to 2011 edition of Carriquiry, *Memoria, Coraje y Esperanza*, reproduced in the 2017 edition cited in note 4. This was essentially the argument of Methol Ferré in "Marco histórico de la religiosidad popular."

16 Ivereigh, *The Great Reformer*, 237, 250. An early use of the phrase "our people has a soul" can be found in the 1974 article "Una institución que vive su carisma," in Jorge Mario Bergoglio, *Meditaciones Para Religiosos*, rev. ed. (Buenos Aires: Diego Torres, 1982; repr., Bilbao: Mensajero, 2014), 47.

of three races—Indian, Black, and White—there emerged over time an essentially mestizo and baroque cultural substrate symbolized by the dark-skinned, Indian, and compassionate features of Our Lady of Guadalupe. Latin America's distinctively symbiotic civilization emerged within a growing respect for the native peoples, evident in the missionaries' careful cataloguing and recording of the cultures they encountered and sought to understand, above all during the reign of Philip II, following the Council of Trent. This respect for the dignity of the people came initially from the cry of the church against the mistreatment of natives articulated by the Dominican friars Antonio de Montesinos in Santo Domingo and Bartolomé de las Casas in Chiapas, and later from the missions that sought to protect and nurture the indigenous civilizations, pioneered by Vasco de Quiroga in Michoacán, Toribio de Mogrovejo in Lima, Junípero de la Serra in what would become the southwestern US, and—most famously of all—the Society of Jesus in Paraguay. Jesuit settlements, missions, and reductions were the incubators of a unique, baroque humanism and of a distinctive Latin American culture.

Evangelization of the native peoples of America led to a normative "popular Catholicism" lived by the poor. Where the missionary church was close to the poor, standing with the native peoples against exploitation and fostering their cultures, colonial Latin America was linked by shared humanist ideals. These ideals were reflected in a network of colleges present in a chain of cities that form the backbone of Latin America today: all the capitals except Montevideo and Brasilia, Methol Ferré points out, were founded within just forty years between 1520 and 1560.[17]

The second, national period—dating from the mid-eighteenth century to the mid-twentieth—saw the dismantling of this heritage under the enlightened despotism of the Bourbons (who famously expelled the Jesuits and suppressed the reductions), causing a cleavage between elites and people from which Latin America has never fully healed. The Bourbons' attempt to incorporate Latin America into the economies of Spain and Portugal provoked independence movements and the wars of secession, which were followed by many decades of recession and

---

17 Alberto Methol Ferré, *Perón y la Alianza Argentino-Brasileña* (Córdoba, Argentina.: Ediciones Del Corredor Austral, 2000), 9.

political chaos. Without an internal center to hold them together, the metropolitan centers were sundered from one other. As they recovered, their economies were shaped more by their relationships with foreign powers than by each other's, and the nascent nation-states entered into an at-times bloody rivalry.

The liberal states that emerged from independence were ideologically very similar to the Bourbon states: in religious terms, they were hostile to popular religiosity and naturally inclined to assert state control over the church. In former colonies where the church had considerable autonomy and managed vast landholdings that protected native civilizations, national states were formed by taking over and privatizing church lands, creating powerful new landowner and merchant elites who dominated their politics. The landowner-merchant elites were dazzled by France and England as cultural and economic models of progress, and tended to despise what they saw as the archaic, religious, mixed-race world of the interior.

In Methol Ferré's reading, the experience of the eighteenth and nineteenth centuries involved three breakdowns: first, a rupture between elite and pueblo, which also implicated the role of the church; second, the weakening of the institutions of civil society that bound people together, leading to gross inequalities and the impoverishment of the poor; and third, the fragmentation of Latin America into isolated, often feuding, nation-states, which in the nineteenth and early twentieth centuries went to war with each other (including a war between Paraguay and the "triple alliance" of Argentina, Brazil and Uruguay; the War of the Pacific between Chile and Bolivia; and the Chaco War between Bolivia and Paraguay). All three of these breakdowns held back Latin America's development, leaving it vulnerable to foreign domination and interference.

For most of the nineteenth century and into the early decades of the twentieth, the church was institutionally feeble, overtaken by the emergent technocratic, pragmatic, deist culture of the new elites, while clericalism harmed the church's relationship with ordinary people. Yet at the lower levels of society, popular religiosity—scorned by urban elites—thrived in the absence of a strong institutional church presence: the pueblo preserved culture and faith in the face of the foreign ideas of the elites. In many of Bergoglio's writings there are frequent references to the way in which humble people safeguarded in their hearts the ancestral faith of great teachers.[18]

The third period delineated by Methol Ferré was triggered by the Second Vatican Council and its reception by the Medellín conference. By allowing the church to engage with modernity and in rejecting integrism, the Latin American church could once again become an interpreter of reality and a driver of culture, resuming its colonial role as missionary, pastor, and protector of its people, and reconnecting with the pueblo via popular religiosity.

Yet the church remained trapped in the intellectual climate of Latin America in the 1950s and 1960s, a climate that was dominated by sociological frames of modernization emanating from the US, which were underpinned by dualistic paradigms—modernity versus tradition, secular versus sacred, industrial versus agrarian—and a view of history that regarded the second of each of these pairings as condemned to defeat by the first. With the failure of US-promoted developmentalist theories to deliver broad and widespread economic growth, the modernization thesis gave way to Marxist dependency theory, but underpinned by the same technocratic presupposition of the church as a static, antimodern institution irrelevant to the twentieth-century world.

Catholic sociologists were swept up into the Marxist paradigm. In the view of the La Plata school, the liberation theologies of Gustavo Gutiérrez and Camilo Torres suffered from this paradigm's blindness in failing to grasp the significance of culture and history, seeking to shape reality according to ideology and despising popular religiosity. In Methol Ferré's reading, the continued dominance of sociologies of modernization, which all assumed the waning of religion (in spite of all the evidence to the contrary in the Latin American popular classes), was the main reason for the mass exodus of priests and religious in the late 1960s and early 1970s. Methol Ferré's critique of Gutiérrez was that in his theology, the poor were an abstraction, divorced from history, culture, and the experience of God captured in popular religiosity.[19]

The page began to turn with the bishops' synod in Rome in 1974 and Paul VI's apostolic exhortation in response to it a year later. *Evangelii*

18 E.g., "La Memoria," in Bergoglio, *Meditaciones Para Religiosos*, 196–200.

19 Pedro Morandé, "En simposio de Humanitas sobre el bien común global," *Humanitas* 20, no. 79 (2015): 594–600.

Nuntiandi, which Francis has often referred to as the greatest pastoral document ever written by a pope, was in part drafted by Fr. Gera, Methol Ferré, and other TP stalwarts. Their speeches and essays prepared the way for the CELAM assembly at Puebla in 1979, which essentially described Latin America's reception of the exhortation: the final Puebla document quoted *EN* ninety-seven times. Puebla allowed for the missionary dynamic of the church to be restored by reconnecting it with popular religiosity and with the history and culture of Latin America; Puebla, much more than Medellín, was the moment when the Latin American church made the Second Vatican Council its own, just as the Council of Lima in the sixteenth century marked Latin America's reception of the Council of Trent.

At a conference organized by Bergoglio in 1985 on the topic of "the Evangelization of Culture and the Inculturation of the Gospel," he spoke of both faith and culture as the places where divine wisdom is manifested. The Gospel revealed God's saving plan through Jesus Christ, while "the different cultures, fruit of the wisdom of the peoples" reflected "the creative and perfecting Wisdom of God."[20]

Guzmán Carriquiry would later recall how the 1974 synod marked the end of the "iconoclastic" phase of the postconciliar period, which had coincided with a disillusionment in Latin America concerning both the US developmentalist strategy as well as with a Cuba-style socialist revolution.[21] The search for new, homegrown models created space for the emergence of the national-popular Catholicism of the La Plata school, and at the same time, for the recovery of the dream of continental reunification, which the nationalists of the first decades of the twentieth century—thinkers like Manuel Ugarte and Enrique Rodó, and later leaders like Haya de la Torre and Juan Domingo Perón—had sought to revive.

Noting how the experience of the US and postwar Europe showed that the future lay in "continent-states," Methol Ferré argued that the Patria Grande could be reborn from Perón's frustrated "ABC" idea of a tariff-free zone between Argentina, Brazil, and Chile, as outlined in a speech the Argentine leader gave in November 1953.[22] In the

20 Ivereigh, *The Great Reformer*, 186.

21 Guzmán Carriquiry, *En Camino hacia la V Conferencia de la Iglesia Latinoamericana* (Buenos Aires: Claretiana, 2006), 39.

22 Methol Ferré, *Perón y la Alianza*, 25-27.

same essay, Methol Ferré gave strong support to the formation of Mercosur following the Asunción Treaty of 1991, seeing it as similar to the Franco-German Coal and Steel Agreement that paved the way to the European Union. The Argentine-Brazilian agreement was key, for it allowed the vision of the Patria Grande to move beyond the confines of the Spanish-American nations. (Because Brazil was not an independent republic until 1898, San Martín and Bolívar had not included the former Portuguese colony in their vision of a confederation.) For Methol Ferré, the inclusion of Brazil in the Patria Grande meant symbolically recovering that glorious sixty years (1580–1640) in which the whole Iberian Peninsula (and therefore all of the American colonies) were united under one king, Philip II.

In the Methol Ferré-Bergoglio reading, the "Catholic resurgence"—or, as it would later be called, the "new evangelization"—was therefore about healing the ruptures of the second period: reevangelizing the elite by means of the popular religiosity of the pueblo, reinvigorating civil society by means of mechanisms of communion and participation, and returning the continent to the path of integration and unity.

"The multiple Hispanic American states were the response to the crisis of the Spanish empire," wrote Methol, adding: "Today, these multiple states are the problem we must overcome."[23] He described continental integration as "the condition of liberation and development of our peoples," the fruit of the *resurgimiento católico* achieving what he called "an authentic global historical protagonism."[24] The "first thing is the inconclusive nation of Latin America," he wrote in *Nexo*. "We are Latin American nationalists."[25]

Latin America as the "Source Church"

In a 2017 interview to mark the tenth anniversary of Aparecida, Francis noted that there had been great progress in the people's sense of belonging to the continent and that the church in Latin America was

23 Methol Ferré, *Peron y la Alianza*, 10.

24 Alberto Methol Ferré, "El resurgimiento católico latinoamericano," in *Religión y cultura: Perspectivas de la evangelización de la cultura desde Puebla* (Bogotá: CELAM, 1980), 123–24.

25 Alberto Methol Ferré, "Terceros incluidos y excluidos," *Nexo* 1, no. 2 (March 1984): 6–45, http://www.metholferre.com/obras/articulos.php#obr_3

far better equipped to judge the present using its own lenses, rather than ill-fitting foreign ones. But he lamented the waning of the vision of the Patria Grande, which he described as the "true project of Latin America." It was held back, he told Hernán Reyes, by corruption and drug trafficking, as well as the continent's subservience to the "international monetary system." As for the church, Catholicism in Latin America was "still very much halfway there" in terms of its "pastoral conversion," the main obstacle to which was clericalism. The call to lay discipleship, he added, "still has to be discovered and given its proper weight."[26]

It was clear that Francis saw these two incomplete Latin American journeys—the church's pastoral conversion mapped out at Aparecida, and the continent's historical journey to unity and self-realization dreamed of by the liberators—as intertwined. This interconnection was perceived not just by Bergoglio, Methol Ferré, and the La Plata school, but had been a long-standing commitment of the Latin American bishops in CELAM, who at previous CELAM general conferences (Puebla in 1979 and Santo Domingo in 1992) had spoken of *la gran patria latinoamericana* and pledged themselves to "our founding fathers' ideal of the Patria Grande."[27] At Aparecida the bishops renewed this pledge, noting that the Gospel was a key element in synthesizing the peoples of the continent. "In the new cultural situation we affirm that the project of the Kingdom is present and is possible," the bishops declared, "and hence we aspire to a united, reconciled, and integrated Latin America and Caribbean."[28] Developing this idea, the bishops later described the church in Latin America and the Caribbean in terms of "a sacrament of communion of its peoples," linking the church's capacity to embody the unity and fraternity of that communion to the continent's own capacity for realizing the vision of the Patria Grande.[29] As pope,

26 Francis, *Latinoamérica: Conversaciones con Hernán Reyes Alcaide* (Buenos Aires: Planeta, 2017), chap. 1.

27 CELAM, "Puebla: III Conferencia General del Episcopado Latinoamericano, 1979" in *Las Cinco Conferencias Generales del Episcopado Latinoamericano* (Bogotá: Ediciones Paulinas, 2014), para. 428; CELAM, "Santo Domingo: IV Conferencia General del Episcopado Latinoamericano," in *Las Cinco Conferencias Generales del Episcopado Latinoamericano*, mensaje 45.

28 Jorge Mario Bergoglio, ed., *Concluding Document, Aparecida, May 13–31, 2007* (Washington D.C.: United States Conference of Catholic Bishops, 2008), 520 (hereafter "Aparecida Concluding Document").

29 Bergoglio, 524–25.

Francis put it simply: "We yearn for the Patria Grande, yes, but it will only be great—as we read in the Aparecida document no. 527—when it is great for everyone, with greater justice and equity."[30]

For Bergoglio, continental unity is the fruit of the Gospel—of communion, fraternity, and justice—just as Latin America's continued division and subjugation reflect the dominance of a neo-gnostic *pensamiento único* (uniform thinking) arising from an imperialist conception of globalization that has flattened all culture and difference. Just as the Church's cultural generativity and capacity to unite arose from inculturation, which was in turn a fruit of the Incarnation, so the materialist, gnostic ideology of globalization has driven out differences and made unity impossible.

His objection is not to globalization per se—the deepening of ties between peoples as economies become more integrated—but to the imposition of ideological uniformity flowing from a materialist anthropology. He is haunted by Robert Hugh Benson's dystopian 1907 novel, *Lord of the World*, which foresees a united globe in which philanthropy has replaced morality and a single identity is forged in a kind of postmodern totalitarianism. True globalization, Francis told journalists on the flight back from Manila in January 2015, is like a polyhedron rather than a sphere, such that "every people, every part, preserves its own identity without being ideologically colonized."[31] Latin America, he told civic leaders from the continent in Rome in March 2018, "was born *mestizo*, will remain *mestizo*, will only grow *mestizo*, and this will be her destiny." Latin America, he added, was "a Patria Grande in the process of becoming."[32]

For Methol Ferré and Bergoglio, the Patria Grande project relates to the defense of Latin American culture, history, and tradition in the face of this "ideological colonization." Octavio Paz—an important writer for the thinkers of the La Plata school—observed shortly before his death that despite its proximity to and economic integration with the US economy, Mexico had preserved its culture to an extraordinary degree because of the strength of its family, traditional religion, and

30 Francis, "Presentación," in Carriquiry, *Memoria, coraje y esperanza*, x.

31 *In-Flight Press Conference of His Holiness Pope Francis from the Philippines to Rome*, January 19, 2015.

32 *Address of His Holiness Francis to a Group from the Pontifical Commission for Latin America*, March 4, 2019.

popular devotions. "I believe the Virgin of Guadalupe has been much more anti-imperialist than all the speeches of the country's politicians," Paz said, adding, "The traditional forms of life have preserved, to some extent, the very being of Latin America."[33]

In 2005, in a prologue to another Carriquiry book, *Una apuesta por América Latina*, Bergoglio spoke of the need to "recover the paths of integration toward the configuration of the South American Union and the Latin American Patria Grande." Alone and separated, he said, "we count for little and we're going nowhere." Continued fragmentation would condemn Latin America to being "peripheral, impoverished, and dependent on the great world powers." Reiterating almost exactly the view of Methol Ferré that in the future the world would be made up of continent-states, Bergoglio added that "whoever does not form part of a continent-state will end up, in a global world, at the edge of history, where it is only possible to express yourself in terms of lamentation, fury, or silence."[34]

This journey toward Latin American unity and the Patria Grande would mean confronting major challenges: the creation of new models of sustainable economic development to defeat some of the sharpest social inequalities on the planet, as well as a reform of politics and the state to ensure that they serve the common good. Yet none of this could happen without "a vast task of education, mobilization, and participation" of peoples—an "organized community" drawing on "a Catholic and Latin American self-consciousness."[35] In his hour-long speech to the popular movements in Santa Cruz, Bolivia, in July 2015, he spelled out the threat from what he called the "new colonialism" of political ideology and economic hegemony, behind whose "different faces" was "the anonymous influence of mammon: corporations, loan agencies, certain 'free-trade' treaties, and the imposition of 'austerity' measures which always tighten the belt of the workers and the poor."

33 Octavio Paz interview with *El Mercurio*, quoted in Guzmán Carriquiry, *El bicentenario de la independencia de los países latinoamericanos* (Madrid: Encuentro, 2011), 1376.

34 Bergoglio, "Prologo," in *Una Apuesta por América Latina*, by Guzmán Carriquiry (Buenos Aires: Sudamericana, 2005), 2–4. Methol Ferré's vision of continent-states replacing the old colonial powers is outlined in his *Los Estados Continentales y el Mercosur* (Montevideo: HUM, 2013).

35 Bergoglio, "Prologo," in Carriquiry, *Una Apuesta*, 2–4.

He said that Latin America could not allow "certain interests—interests that are global but not universal—to take over, to dominate states and international organizations, and to continue destroying creation."[36]

Equipping the Latin American church for the historic task of reevangelization engaged Bergoglio and his theological collaborators in the run-up to the May 2007 CELAM assembly in Aparecida, Brazil, whose concluding document they drafted.[37] For Bergoglio, Methol Ferré, and Carriquiry, the greatest obstacle to the reevangelization was the church itself. A static, bureaucratic, ritualistic, formalistic Catholicism would be incapable—as the fate of Europe, in their view, has proved—of regenerating culture and resisting ideological colonization. Hence the importance at Aparecida of two key ideas: missionary discipleship and pastoral conversion, which would form the basis of Pope Francis's 2013 exhortation *Evangelii Gaudium,* and which pays tribute—even in its name—to Paul VI's exhortation *Evangelii Nuntiandi*, the document that paved the way to Puebla.

A month after the 2005 conclave that elected Pope Benedict XVI, Bergoglio gave a speech in Lima, Peru, to commemorate the fiftieth anniversary of the founding of CELAM, in which he said that it was time for a continent which included half of the world's Catholics "to lend a service to the universal Church" and to share the gifts that the Holy Spirit had showered on its people. "This is the prophetic dimension which Latin America must assume in this Fifth Conference," he told them.[38] At the synod on the new evangelization in Rome in 2012, it was clear that, to use a phrase of Cardinal Walter Kasper's later adopted by Fr. Carlos Galli, the wind was now "blowing from the south."[39] Later, as pope, Francis described Latin America as "the continent of hope" that could demonstrate "new models of development that include Christian

36 Francis, *Address at the Second World Meeting of Popular Movements: Address of the Holy Father*, Santa Cruz, Bolivia, July 9, 2015, at 3.2, 3.3. Discussed in Ivereigh, *Wounded Shepherd*, 228.

37 Discussed in Ivereigh, *The Great Reformer*, 294–301.

38 Jorge Mario Bergoglio, "Prologo," in Guzmán Carriquiry, *En Camino hacia la V Conferencia de la Iglesia Latinoamericana* (Buenos Aires: Claretiana, 2006), 6.

39 Carlos Galli, "El Viento Del Sur de Aparecida a Río: El proyecto misionero latinoamericano en la teología y el estilo pastoral de Francisco," *Seminarios sobre los ministerios de la Iglesia* (España) 60, no. 211 (2014): 9–48.

tradition and civic progress, justice and equity with reconciliation, scientific and technical development with wisdom."[40]

Aparecida drew heavily on the La Plata school and on the ideas that had continued to develop in Buenos Aires in the 1990s and 2000s. Methol Ferré was too ill to attend the assembly, but Carriquiry was a major influence in its preparation. TP had shaped Bergoglio's (and now Francis's) two key collaborators, Fr. Galli and Fr. (later Archbishop) Víctor Manuel Fernández, who were part of the drafting commission at the assembly headed by the Argentine cardinal. In 2006 Galli and Fernández coauthored a book spelling out the concept of missionary discipleship, a key idea at Aparecida.[41]

Aparecida, as Pope Francis would recall at a Mass in the shrine in August 2013, "was born of the interplay between the labours of the Bishops and the simple faith of the pilgrims, under Mary's maternal protection."[42] The assembly agreed on a continent-wide ecclesial approach and pastoral praxis, committing the church to a "continental mission" springing from a renewal of mission and discipleship, and also pledged the church to the integration of Latin America and the Caribbean as a cultural and pastoral priority.[43] At its heart was "an attitude of permanent pastoral conversion," a renewal of habits and structures that would bring the church closer to the people and their concrete needs—and a spirituality of communion that would expand participation and form laypeople as missionary disciples.[44] Aparecida calls for the church to be permanently moving out from itself, "*una Iglesia en salida*," focused on the peripheries and on the poor and marginalized, with a proclamation focused on God's mercy.[45]

Before he died in 2009, Methol Ferré was convinced that the Latin American church was now set to become the dynamic "source" for

---

40 On the emergence of Latin America as the new "source" for the universal church, see Ivereigh, *The Great Reformer*, chap. 7.

41 Victor Fernández and Carlos Galli, *Discípulos Misioneros* (Buenos Aires: Agape, 2006).

42 *Holy Mass in the Basilica of the Shrine of Our Lady of Conception of Aparecida, Homily of His Holiness Pope Francis*, July 24, 2013.

43 Bergoglio, *Aparecida Concluding Document*, 127–28, 520–28. See also Carlos Galli, "El aporte de la fe cristiana a la formación de la comunidad iberoamericana de naciones," in *El mundo iberoamericano antes y después de las independencias*, ed. M. A. Peña González (Salamanca: Publicaciones de la Universidad Pontificia, 2011), 449–79.

44 Bergoglio, *Aparecida Concluding Document*, 366.

45 Bergoglio, 517–19.

the universal church, as Spain and Italy had been at the time of the Council of Trent and Germany and France had been at the Second Vatican Council. Galli has written that the election of Pope Francis, an icon of the Latin American church because of his pastoral closeness, directness, warmth, and joy, represents a new Pentecost, and that the church of Latin America is no longer embarked solely on a "continental mission," but a "universal mission" signified by the translation of the key precepts of Aparecida into *Evangelii Gaudium*.[46] For Carriquiry, "his pontificate creates the possibility of a Latin American Catholic resurgence, and, linked to that, of a path to Latin America's unity and fraternity in the building of conditions of greater justice and growth in humanity."[47]

Building *La Patria Grande*

At the time of the Argentine bicentenary celebrations in 2010–11 Bergoglio wrote richly and deeply on the process of "becoming a people," distinguishing between a country (a geographical space), a nation (its institutional scaffolding) and the patria, which he described as what is received from our parents and what we hand onto our children: the identity of belonging, the mythical sense of a "foundational being" (*ser fundante*), which people take responsibility for preserving while also developing. "A country can be mutilated, a nation can change, but la patria either keeps its foundational being or dies," he noted in 2011.[48] In the same way, while "citizen" is a logical category, "people" is a mythical one. "One lives in society, but one belongs to a people," as he wrote in a long lecture on the topic the year before.[49]

46 Carlos Galli, "Lectura teológica, espiritual y pastoral de la exhortación *Evangelii Gaudium* de Francisco," in de Mier, *Instauremos el Reino del Padre*, 13–48.

47 Guzmán Carriquiry, "Desde Aparecida a la *Evangelii Gaudium*," in *Instauremos el Reino del Padre*, 49.

48 Francis, "Presentación," in Carriquiry, *Memoria, coraje y esperanza*, xvi.

49 Bergoglio, "Nosotros como ciudadanos, nosotros como pueblo: Hacia un bicentenario en justicia y solidaridad," in Francis, *En Tus Ojos Está Mi Palabra: Homilías y discursos de Buenos Aires, 1999-2013* (Madrid: Claretiana, 2018), 969. For a discussion of Francis's understanding of this distinction, see Austen Ivereigh, "We Belong To A People," in Barbara E. Wall and Massimo Faggioli, eds., *Pope Francis: A Voice for Mercy, Justice, Love and Care for the Earth* (New York: Orbis, 2019), 128–54.

Bergoglio's understanding drew on Lucio Gera's idea of the patria and the pueblo as a phenomenon of solidarity anterior to any political, geographic, or institutional expression, a *ser fundante* to which it needs to remain loyal if it is to be true to itself. The pueblo is an active subject, a historical actor, based on an agreement to live together in justice and solidarity, an agreement that is made real through mechanisms of negotiation and dialogue such as assemblies (which, in the language of the church, are expressions of synodality), from which flow proposals and actions aimed at overcoming everything that undermines the dignity of the people. Hence Francis's encouragement of the popular movements, which he sees as a concrete manifestation of this process of solidarity and participation.[50]

In the section titled "The Common Good and Peace in Society" of his 2013 apostolic exhortation, *Evangelii Gaudium*, Francis speaks of the process of "becoming a people," an ongoing process in which every new generation must take part, noting that it is "a slow and arduous effort calling for a desire for integration and a willingness to achieve this through the growth of a peaceful and multifaceted culture of encounter."[51] He goes on to articulate his four guiding criteria for "the development of life in society and the building of a people where differences are harmonized within a shared pursuit," in terms very similar to those of his 2010 bicentenary essay.[52]

Looking at the messages Francis delivered during his first four trips to Latin America—to Rio de Janeiro for World Youth Day in July 2013; to Ecuador, Bolivia, and Paraguay in July 2015; to Cuba and US in September 2015; and to Mexico in February 2016—as well as his important letter to the Argentine bishops on the bicentenary of Argentine independence in July 2016, we can make out six broad themes closely linked to that vision of "building a people": evangelization through culture, pastoral/missionary conversion, the culture of encounter and solidarity, the renewal of politics, true globalization, and finally, the Patria Grande.

---

50 See Francis, "Prologue," in *La irrupción de los movimientos populares: El "Rerum Novarum" de nuestro tiempo*, ed. Guzmán Carriquiry and Gianni La Bella (Rome: Libreria Editrice Vaticana, 2019), 1–8, and Jorge Maria Bergoglio, "A un ejército invisible: Carta a los movimientos populares, 22 de abril de 2020," in Francis, *La vida después de la pandemia* (Rome: Libreria Editrice Vaticana, 2020), 39–44.

51 Francis, Apostolic Exhortation *Evangelii Gaudium* (November 24, 2013), 220.

52 Francis, 221; Bergoglio, "Nosotros como ciudadanos," 977–80.

Evangelization through Culture

The affirmation of the "seeds of the Gospel" in a nation's past is known as "evangelization through culture," and is the great method and insight of *Evangelii Nuntiandi*. In Ignatian terms, this is comparable to the method of the *Spiritual Exercises*, in which the retreatant discerns the presence of God in his or her past in moments of both suffering and joy. In Philadelphia, Francis noted simply that "the religious dimension is not a subculture; it is part of the culture of every people and every nation."[53]

In each country he visited in the Americas, Francis highlighted how its history showed evidence of God's nearness, usually in the form of the suffering Christ and the consoling Virgin, showing how, in the unique gifts and history of that country it was possible to discern each pueblo's special gift or calling. Speaking to journalists on the flight back to Rome from Ciudad Juárez, he said that Mexico could only be explained by studying Our Lady of Guadalupe.[54] In Brazil, he praised "the dynamic and distinctive character of Brazilian culture, with its extraordinary ability to integrate a variety of elements,"[55] while telling the bishops that the miracle of the black-faced Virgin of Aparecida in colonial Brazil—"divided by the shameful wall of slavery"—showed God's providence in forging that unity.[56]

In Ecuador, he told clergy that an insight received in prayer had shown him that the Andean nation's consecration to the Heart of Mary in colonial times was "a milestone in the history of Ecuador's people," which gave the country "the grace of piety that makes you unique."[57] In Bolivia, he praised the fusion of Spanish with thirty-six native languages, and noted how the Gospel had taken deep root, "contributing to the

53 Francis, *Meeting for Religious Liberty with the Hispanic Community and Other Immigrants: Address of the Holy Father*, Independence Hall, Philadelphia, September 26, 2015.

54 *In-Flight Press Conference of His Holiness Pope Francis from Mexico to Rome*, February 17, 2016.

55 *Meeting with Brazil's Leaders of Society: Address of Pope Francis*, Rio de Janeiro, July 27, 2013, 1.

56 *Meeting with the Bishops of Brazil: Address of Pope Francis*, Rio de Janeiro, July 28, 2013, 1.

57 Francis, *Meeting with Clergy, Religious, and Seminarians: Address of the Holy Father*, Quito, Ecuador, July 8, 2015.

development of the nation and shaping its culture."[58] In Paraguay he praised the perseverance of a suffering people following the devastation of the War of the Triple Alliance, linking it to the closeness of the Virgin of Caacupé.[59] "She has always been part of the history of this country, making it a nation," he later said at the shrine.[60] In Santiago, he said the Cuban patria "was born and grew, warmed by devotion to Our Lady of Charity," who "protects our roots, our identity, so that we may never stray to paths of despair."[61]

He also picked out examples from Latin America's history, highlighting times that the continent's culture and social organization cohered. In Paraguay, for example, he described the reductions as "the most significant experiences of evangelization and social organization in history" where "the Gospel was the soul and the life of communities which did not know hunger, unemployment, illiteracy or oppression," an experience that "shows us that, today too, a more humane society is possible … Where there is love of people and a willingness to serve them, it is possible to create the conditions necessary for everyone to have access to basic goods, so that no one goes without."[62]

Having pointed to the seeds of the Gospel and signs of the divine presence in each nation's past, Pope Francis urged people to recall those roots and be faithful to them. "Never cease to remind your people of how powerful their ancient roots are, roots which have allowed a vibrant Christian synthesis of human, cultural and spiritual unity which was forged here," he told the Mexican bishops.[63] In Ecuador and Bolivia he spoke of his sadness when priests forget the indigenous language they grew up with, or refused to speak it. "Never forget, never deny your roots, don't reject that culture where you learnt from your people just because you now have a more sophisticated, important culture,"

58 Francis, *Welcome Ceremony: Address of the Holy Father*, La Paz, Bolivia, July 8, 2015, 3.

59 Francis, *Meeting with Government Authorities and the Diplomatic Corps: Address of the Holy Father*, Asunción, Paraguay, July 10, 2015.

60 Francis, *Holy Mass: Homily of the Holy Father*, Marian Shrine of Caacupé, Paraguay, July 11, 2015, 3.

61 *Homily of His Holiness at the Minor Basilica of the Shrine Virgen de la Caridad del Cobre in Santiago, Cuba*, September 22, 2015.

62 Francis, *Meeting with Representatives of Civil Society: Address of the Holy Father*, Asunción, Paraguay, July 11, 2015, 3.

63 Francis, *Meeting with the Bishops of Mexico: Address of the Holy Father*, Mexico City, February 13, 2016.

he told the clergy in Bolivia, before going on to speak of "the grace not to lose the memory of the faithful people."[64]

Pastoral/Missionary Conversion

A large number of Francis's messages to the church in each Latin American country were aimed at bolstering the "continental mission" set forth at Aparecida in which evangelization and the building up of unity and fraternity went hand in hand. On his visits he repeatedly stressed the importance of a missionary focus and pastoral conversion and warned against temptations that would distract from that mission, above all clericalism and spiritual worldliness, signs of a church closed in on itself. In Havana he warned religious congregations against storing up money, and in New York, he cautioned against evaluating apostolic works by the standards of efficiency and success.[65] In Mexico he warned the bishops "not to be corrupted by trivial materialism or by the seductive illusion of underhanded agreements; do not place your faith in the 'chariots and horses' of today's pharaohs," and he told them "to overcome the temptation of aloofness … and clericalism, of coldness and indifference, of triumphalism and self-centredness."[66]

At the mass of canonization of Father Junípero Serra in Washington D.C., Francis praised the Franciscan as the embodiment of "a Church that goes forth," a church that "sets out to bring everywhere the reconciling tenderness of God."[67] He told the Mexican bishops that "la Virgen Morenita teaches us that the only power capable of conquering the hearts of men and women is the tenderness of God."[68]

64 Francis, *Meeting with Clergy, Religious, and Seminarians: Address of the Holy Father*, Santa Cruz de la Sierra, Bolivia, July 9, 2015, 2.

65 Francis, *Address to Leadership of the Episcopal Conferences of Latin America*, Rio de Janeiro, July 28, 2013; *Celebration of Vespers with Priests, Men and Women Religious and Seminarians: Homily of His Holiness Pope Francis*, Cathedral, Havana, September 20, 2015; *Vespers with Priests and Religious: Homily of His Holiness Pope Francis*, St. Patrick's Cathedral, New York, September 24, 2015.

66 *Meeting with the Bishops of Mexico.*

67 *Holy Mass and Canonization of Blessed Fr. Junípero Serra: Homily of His Holiness Pope Francis*, National Shrine of the Immaculate Conception, Washington D.C., September 23, 2015.

68 *Meeting with the Bishops of Mexico.*

The Culture of Encounter and Solidarity

One of the main effects of the baptism of Latin America, in the view of the La Plata school, was to integrate the disparate and contradictory elements of society, awakening people to a recognition of a shared humanity and thereby forging a nation. On each visit, Francis used his addresses—especially to civic leaders and the young—to stress the importance of solidarity, encounter, dialogue, and inclusion. Socially and politically, the message was one of social integration—of reaching out to the peripheries to include the elderly, the poor, the indigenous, etc., in order to build up the commonweal. Culturally, it meant listening and dialogue to allow the identity of each person and group to be expressed and integrated into the whole.

He told Bolivian political leaders, including President Evo Morales, that pluralism and integration required "an ever greater appreciation of values by individuals and their growing convergence with regard to common ideals to which all can work together, no one being excluded or overlooked." This was a cultural task that could not be neglected in favor of simply redistributing wealth. "A growth which is merely material will always run the risk of creating new divisions, of the wealth of some being built on the poverty of others," he told them.[69]

In Paraguay, he told civil society representatives that dialogue meant explaining one's identity, not negotiating it. "This means that, for there to be dialogue, that fundamental basis of identity must exist," he said, adding that the "first" identity was to love your nation. Dialogue, he said, "presupposes and demands that we seek a culture of encounter; an encounter which acknowledges that diversity is not only good, it is necessary."[70]

Likewise, at vespers in Havana he warned: "Unity is often confused with uniformity; with actions, feelings and words which are all identical. This is not unity, it is conformity. It kills the life of the Spirit; it kills the charisms which God has bestowed for the good of his people. Unity is threatened whenever we try to turn others into our own image

69 *Welcome Ceremony*, La Paz, Bolivia.

70 *Meeting with Representatives of Civil Society*, Asunción, Paraguay, 2.

and likeness. Unity is a gift, not something to be imposed by force or by decree."[71]

The Renewal of Politics

A clear aim of each visit was the renewal of public and political life toward a politics rooted in concrete realities (rather than abstract ideologies) that serves the needs of the ordinary people (rather than the interests of a few). A key element of that renewal was opening up public life to religion, not just because politics and faith need to be in dialogue, but because it is implicit in a politics that serves the interests of ordinary religious people (in Latin America, secularism is a largely elite phenomenon).

In speaking to Brazil's leaders of a "rehabilitation of politics" that could bring about "greater and more effective participation on the part of the people, eliminating forms of elitism and eradicating poverty" and guarantee "dignity, fraternity and solidarity," he said that politics needed to be open to religion. "It is impossible to imagine a future for society without a significant injection of moral energy into a democratic order that tends to remain imprisoned in pure logic or in a mere balancing of vested interests," he said.[72]

"An ideological approach is useless: it ends up using the poor in the service of other political or personal interests," he told political leaders in Paraguay, adding that "ideologies end badly, and are useless. They relate to people in ways that are either incomplete, unhealthy, or evil."[73] Addressing the popular movements in Santa Cruz, Bolivia, he urged political leaders to "be creative and never stop being rooted in local realities, since the father of lies is able to usurp noble words, to promote intellectual fads and to adopt ideological stances." He urged them instead to "build on solid foundations, on real needs and on the lived experience of your brothers and sisters, of campesinos and natives, of excluded workers and marginalized families."[74]

---

71 *Celebration of Vespers*, Havana.

72 *Meeting with Brazil's Leaders of Society*, 2–3.

73 Francis, *Meeting with Representatives of Civil Society*, Asunción, Paraguay, 3.

74 Francis, *Address at the Second World Meeting of Popular Movements*, 2.

Francis urged Cubans to not be seduced by political rhetoric that uses language of solidarity but is essentially partisan. "There is a way of going about serving which is interested only in helping 'my people, our people,'" he warned at the Mass in Havana's Revolution Square. "This service always leaves 'your people' outside, and gives rise to a process of exclusion." In the presence of Raúl Castro and two other Latin American presidents—of Argentina and Panamá—he added: "Service is never ideological, for we do not serve ideas, we serve people."[75]

True ("Polyhedric") Globalization

Distinguishing between "good" and "bad" globalization was a consistent theme in the pope's messages. He called on Latin America to resist not the growing interdependence of the world through trade and technology, but the "ideological colonization" implicit in new forms of colonialism that brings with it a "neo-gnosticism" that seeks to separate people from their past, their culture, and their religion. That meant affirming Latin America's distinctive culture and traditions and, specifically, shoring up Latin America's religious and family heritage.

During his religious freedom address in Philadelphia, he warned against what he called in *Laudato Si'* the "globalization of the technocratic paradigm," which, he said, "consciously aims at a one-dimensional uniformity and seeks to eliminate all differences and traditions in a superficial quest for unity." Rather than a globalization that "claims to make everyone uniform, to level everyone out" he called for "a globalization that attempts to bring everyone together while respecting the uniqueness and gifts of each person or people," capturing the distinction in the contrast between a sphere in which every point is equidistant from the center and a polyhedron, where "everything is united but each element keeps its own identity."[76]

The social and personal disintegration brought about by the negative elements of globalization can only be countered, he repeatedly noted, by shoring up the family.[77] In Santiago de Cuba, for example,

75 *Homily of His Holiness Pope Francis*, Plaza de la Revolución, Havana, Cuba, September 20, 2015.

76 *Meeting for Religious Liberty*, quoting Encyclical Letter *Laudato Si'* (May 24, 2015), 106.

77 See e.g., *Meeting with the Bishops of Brazil*, 4.

he said that the family "saves us from two present-day phenomena, two things which happen every day: fragmentation, that is, division, and uniformity. In both cases, people turn into isolated individuals, easy to manipulate and to rule. Then in our world we see societies which are divided, broken, separated or rigidly uniform. These are a result of the breakup of family bonds, the loss of those relationships which make us who we are, which teach us to be persons."[78]

In his address to the popular movements in Bolivia, he said it was necessary in humility to recognize humanity's growing interdependence, but he warned against new forms of colonialism that reduce poor countries to "mere providers of raw material and cheap labor, engenders violence, poverty, forced migrations and all the evils which go hand in hand with these, precisely because, by placing the periphery at the service of the center, it denies those countries the right to an integral development." He summed up the message by saying yes to an encounter of peoples and cultures, and no to colonialism.[79]

The Patria Grande

Francis made a few, but potent, indirect and explicit references to the Patria Grande in statements about the growing awareness through Latin American history of the pueblo awakening to its God-given dignity and emancipation.

At the Mass in Quito's appropriately named Bicentennial Park, he recalled how "Latin America's cry for independence ... arose from being conscious of a lack of freedom, of exploitation and despoliation, of being 'subject to the passing whims of the powers that be.'"[80] Later, in Santa Cruz, Bolivia, he noted how "for almost two centuries their history has been dramatic and filled with contradictions, as [Latin Americans] have striven to achieve full independence." Noting the "growth of fraternity between their peoples," he said that the governments of the region "have pooled forces in order to ensure respect for

78 *Holy Mass: Homily of His Holiness Pope Francis*, Santiago de Cuba.

79 *Address at the Second World Meeting of Popular Movements*, 3.2.

80 *Holy Mass for the Evangelization of Peoples: Homily of the Holy Father*, Quito, Ecuador, July 7, 2015, quoting *Evangelii Gaudium*, 213.

the sovereignty of their own countries and the entire region, which our forebears so beautifully called la Patria Grande." Calling on the popular movements to "foster and increase this unity," he again linked a better future for the continent to its integration, arguing that it was "necessary to maintain unity in the face of every effort to divide, if the region is to grow in peace and justice."[81]

Although no text was released of his exchange with the bishops in Bolivia, he later told journalists that during that meeting he touched on Bolivia's appeal to the international court for access to the sea, which it lost in the War of the Pacific. The pope recalled telling the bishops that "brothers have to dialogue, the Latin American peoples have to dialogue in order to create the patria grande, dialogue is necessary," and that it was "not unjust" for Bolivia to long for its access to the sea to be restored. "After a war of that type there are losses, and I believe what's important, above all, is dialogue, healthy negotiation," he told reporters.[82]

Conclusion

Following an initial reluctance to refer as pope to the ideal of Latin American unity, beginning with his second apostolic journey to Latin America in 2015, Francis began to use his pontificate to promote the Patria Grande, a vision of unity, fraternity, and justice that he believed was the true "soul" of Latin America. It was a vision in which the church strengthens dialogue and cooperation, allowing the continent to better resist the disaggregating forces of globalization and the people to act as a historical subject.

The pope's shift in emphasis may have many causes, among them the breakdown of the postwar international order marked by the rise of populist nationalism across the Western world, symbolized by the triumph of Brexit and Donald Trump against all expectations. It is clear from Francis's interviews that he saw parallels with the 1930s and 1940s.[83]

---

81 *Address at the Second World Meeting of Popular Movements*, 3.2

82 *In-Flight Press Conference of His Holiness Pope Francis from Paraguay to Rome*, July 13, 2015.

83 Jonathan Haidt, "When and Why Nationalism Beats Globalism," *The American Interest* 12, no.1 (July 10, 2016). See also Austen Ivereigh, "How Francis Will Respond

Although it would be tempting to place Francis in the "globalist" camp—not least because of his stance over immigration, one of the fault lines of the new polarization—his background suggests, rather, a natural sympathy for the national-popular tradition of Latin American politics, with its rejection of liberal individualism and technocratic, managerial politics. Francis's stinging critique of the European Union for abandoning its founding vision and losing its fertile capacity for integrating and strengthening multiple identities prophetically anticipated the United Kingdom's decision to leave the EU in a popular referendum the following month. Much of his Charlemagne Prize speech, in fact, contained precisely the critique of "ideological colonization" and stale conformity that Francis has put forth in making his case for the Patria Grande. His critique of liberal globalization, in other words, is that in failing to build a people, it has paved the way for a populism that claims to speak for the people yet instrumentalizes it in the service of power.[84]

On October 4, 2020, in the seventh year of his pontificate, Francis published his second social encyclical inspired by Saint Francis of Assisi, on the topic of fraternity. The first chapter of *Fratelli Tutti* gloomily noted how, after decades of steps taken toward integration in Europe and Latin America following World War II, there were now "signs of a certain regression" in the form of "a myopic, extremist, resentful and aggressive nationalism" that is on the rise.[85] But he showed, again, that he was no unthinking globalist: the local has something the global lacks and only the well-rooted can reach out to the other. The local and the global are in polar tension, but they are not antithetical: what is needed is a "healthy relationship between love of one's native land and a sound sense of belonging to our larger human family."[86] There could be few better definitions of the Patria Grande.

---

to the New Anti-Globalism," *Crux*, November 11, 2016, https://cruxnow.com/analysis/2016/11/francis-will-respond-new-anti-globalism/, and Antonio Caño and Pablo Ordaz, "Pope Francis: 'The Danger is That in Times of Crisis we Look for a Savior,'" *El País* online, January 22, 2017, https://english.elpais.com/elpais/2017/01/21/inenglish/1485026427_223988.html.

84 Francis, *Address at the Conferral of the Charlemagne Prize,* May 6, 2016.

85 Francis, Encyclical Letter *Fratelli Tutti: On Fraternity and Social Friendship* (October 4, 2020), 11.

86 Francis, 149.

CHAPTER 3

THE ROLE OF THE POOR AND THE SUFFERING IN THE CHRISTOLOGY AND THEODICY OF POPE FRANCIS

The Theology of the Aparecida Document

Sixto García

"The poor are the Gospel," said Pope Francis.[1] It is commonly held that the Aparecida Document, the final document of the V General Conference of CELAM (the Episcopal Conference of Latin America and the Caribbean),[2] is of decisive importance for understanding Pope Francis's theology, spirituality, and pastoral vision. Cardinal Jorge Mario Bergoglio, now Pope Francis, was its editor in chief. A quick glance at Francis's apostolic exhortation *Evangelii Gaudium*, his encyclical letter *Laudato Si'*, and his postsynodal apostolic exhortation *Amoris Laetitia* reveals texts, intuitions, and theological proposals that can be traced back, sometimes, to the Aparecida Document.

Starting from the commonly held opinion that the Aparecida Document shapes the main lines of Francis's thought in a coherent and rigorous, and at the same time theologically, spiritually, and pastorally *poetic* fashion, this document will be the center and focus of the present analysis. This essay is structured around the themes outlined in its title, albeit in a different order: Christology, then theodicy, then the poor.

1 Francis, *Address to the Latin American Conference of Religious* (CLAR), June 10, 2013.

2 Jorge Mario Bergoglio, ed., *Concluding Document, Aparecida, May 13–31, 2007* (Washington D.C.: United States Conference of Catholic Bishops, 2008). Citations to this document herein are to paragraph numbers.

Christology: A Theology of Encounter

The Aparecida Document speaks of faith as a resounding yes to a personal encounter with Jesus Christ. It is not by accident that the expression "encounter with Jesus Christ" appears forty-nine times in the document. The experience of the encounter with Jesus Christ as a privileged locus of Christian faith and Christology, though easily discernible in the late Patristic Age, particularly in Maximus the Confessor's "Four Centuries on Charity,"[3] finds its contemporary explication in postconciliar theology. Since his Tübingen lectures on the creed in 1967,[4] and especially in his first encyclical *Deus Caritas Est*, Benedict XVI defines Christian faith, and thereby the subject of Christology, in suggestive form: "Being Christian is not the result of an ethical choice or a lofty idea, but the encounter with an event, a person, which gives life a new horizon and a decisive direction."[5] We will examine later the connection between a "Christology of encounter" and the theodicy of Aparecida, a connection originally drawn by Francis. For now, we will confine ourselves to an allusion to Gabriel Marcel's existentialist definition of "person" and "encounter": The "I," argues Marcel, meets the "Thou," and returns to itself forming a "We."[6] Marcel's insight is crucial for the notion of a Christology of encounter, which is the dynamic center of Aparecida.

The theme of an encounter with Jesus Christ is central to the Aparecida Document. The purpose of the V CELAM Conference is defined, in its most seminal form, by this encounter: "What is required is confirming, renewing, and revitalizing the newness of the Gospel rooted in our history, out of a personal and community encounter with Jesus Christ that raises up missionary disciples."[7] The consequences of this

---

3 Maximus the Confessor, "The Four Hundred Chapters on Love," in *Maximus the Confessor: Selected Writings*, trans. and ed. George C. Berthold (New York: Paulist Press, 1985), 33–98.

4 Joseph Ratzinger, *Introducción al Cristianismo*, trans. José L. Domínguez Vilar (Salamanca: Sígueme, 2005), 39–72, 99–115.

5 Benedict XVI, Encyclical Letter *Deus Caritas Est* (December 25, 2005), 1. All documents published by the Vatican, including this one and others cited below, including papal addresses, may be found at the vatican.va website.

6 Gabriel Marcel, *The Mystery of Being*, trans. G. S. Fraser (South Bend, Ind.: St. Augustine's Press, 2001), 33–50, 68–84.

7 Bergoglio, *Concluding Document*, 12, quoting Benedict XVI, *Deus Caritas Est*, 1.

encounter translate into missionary joy: "Being Christian is not a burden, but a gift."[8] Therefore, in what amounts to a programmatic statement, Aparecida proposes that "knowing Jesus is the best gift that any person can receive; that we have encountered Him is the best thing that has happened in our lives, and making him known by our word and deeds is our joy."[9] This clear proposal, devoid of any theological ambiguity, places us before the key Christological section of the document, entitled "The Encounter with Jesus Christ."[10] It is important to note that this section begins with the quotation from *Deus Caritas Est* contained in the previous paragraph, which summarizes Pope Benedict's personalist Christology. The quotation echoes Saint Thomas Aquinas's formula: "*Actus credentis non terminatur ad enuntiabilem, sed ad rem*" (The act of faith does not end in the formula, but in the thing signified).[11] There are similar instances of this insight in Francis's encyclical *Lumen Fidei*: "Faith does not merely gaze at Jesus but sees things as Jesus himself sees them, with his own eye: it is a participation in a new way of seeing."[12] The conception expressed is supported by a text of decisive importance for our pursuit of the Christology and theodicy of Aparecida and Pope Francis: "Christian faith is faith in the Incarnation of the Word and his bodily resurrection; it is faith in a God who is so close to us that he entered our human history."[13] Here we also find Aquinas's beautiful insight: "It is not enough to believe in God if we do not believe in the Incarnation."[14]

In the Aparecida Document, the future pope defines the new evangelization as involving a Christocentric mission. This will allow us to elucidate the intimate connection between the encounter with Jesus Christ and its sacramental expression in the clamor of the poor. This requires, in Walter Kasper's words, a return to a *theological theology*, that is, a theology that begins and ends with God the Father, revealed by

8 Bergoglio, 28.
9 Bergoglio, 29.
10 Bergoglio, 243–75.
11 Thomas Aquinas, *Summa Theologiae,* trans. Fathers of the English Dominican Province (New York: Benziger Bros., 1947), II-II q. 1 a. 2.
12 Francis, Encyclical Letter *Lumen Fidei* (June 29, 2013), 18.
13 Francis, 18.
14 Thomas Aquinas, *Commentary on the Epistle to the Hebrews*, chap. 10, lecture 2, 502, trans. Chrysostom Bauer, O. Praem. (South Bend, Ind.: St. Augustine's Press, 2006), 211.

the paschal event of Jesus Christ, in the power of the Spirit, given to us in a privileged fashion in the life of the poor, the hungry, the despised, the discarded—in sum, the crucified victims of human history.

Aparecida also reminds us that the encounter with Christ, as mediated by the Holy Spirit, happens in the received and lived faith of the church.[15] It is opportune to recall the form and shape of the church proposed by Francis: "I want a Church that is poor and for the poor. They have much to teach us. Not only do they share in the *sensus fidei*, but in their difficulties they know the suffering Christ."[16]

In this regard, Jon Sobrino has recast the ancient saying "*Extra ecclesiam nulla salus*" (There is no salvation outside the church)[17] as "*Extra pauperes nulla salus*" (There is no salvation outside of the poor). He argues that the church does not exist in abstract conceptual formulas, but only in the concrete and suffering reality of the poor. For Sobrino, the poor are not so much a part of the church, they *are* the church. There are obvious links between Sobrino's reformulation and Francis's words, "The poor are the Gospel." Sobrino's proposal rests on the following: if the Gospel's in-breaking into history has taken place in the person of Jesus Christ, on the one hand, and on the other, "the poor are the Gospel," it follows that indeed, "*extra pauperes nulla salus*."[18]

There are conciliar roots for both "the Church that is poor and for the poor" and "*extra ecclesia nulla salus*." Pope John XXIII had already sparked discussion of the topic a week before the inauguration of the council, saying that the church presents herself before the underdeveloped world as she is and as she desires to be: as the church of all, and in particular, of the poor.[19] Cardinal Giacomo Lercaro, an important protagonist in the council's deliberations, lamented at the end of the first session that

15 Bergoglio, *Concluding Document*, 246.

16 Francis, Apostolic Exhortation *Evangelii Gaudium* (November 24, 2013), 198.

17 Heinrich Denzinger and Peter Hünnermann, *El Magisterio de la Iglesia = Enchiridion symbolorum definitionum et declarationum de rebus fidei et morum*, trans. Bernabe Dalmau, OSB, Constantino Ruiz-Garrido, and Eva Martin Mora, 38th ed. (Barcelona: Herder, 2000), 802, 1351.

18 Jon Sobrino, "Extra Pauperes Nulla Salus," in *No Salvation Outside the Poor: Prophetic-Utopian Essays*, translated by Margaret Wilde, Joseph Owens et al. (Maryknoll, N.Y.: Orbis, 2008), 35–76.

19 Gustavo Gutiérrez, "The Meaning and Scope of Medellín," in *The Density of the Present: Selected Writings* (Maryknoll, N.Y.: Orbis, 1999), 67.

> something has been missing in the Council up until now. This is the hour of the poor, of the millions of poor that live all over the world; this is the hour of the mystery of the Church, mother of the poor; it is the hour of the mystery of Christ, especially among the poor . . . [This], in truth, is not only another theme, but, in a certain sense, the only theme of Vatican II.[20]

Aparecida emphasizes the role of the scriptures as a privileged locus for the encounter with Jesus Christ. It recommends rediscovering the ancient practice of *lectio divina*.[21] Benedict XVI, the pope who presided over the conference at Aparecida, would also promote *lectio divina* two years later in his postsynodal apostolic exhortation *Verbum Domini*. The four steps—*lectio*, *meditatio*, *oratio*, and *contemplatio*—take us from the reading of the text to a passionate, vulnerable, and risky encounter with the Living Word Himself.[22]

This passion, vulnerability, and risk is not an unimportant or minor point for Aparecida. The memories of martyrdom and suffering for the sake of the Gospel were very vivid at the time of the conference. Rutilio Grande, SJ, a close friend of Archbishop Oscar Romero, was assassinated by death squads thirty-two days after preaching his last homily at Apopa, in which he said, "I am afraid, my brothers and sisters, that very quickly the Bible and the Gospel will not be allowed to enter through our borders. The bindings of the book will no longer be allowed because all of its pages are subversive! Subversive against sin, naturally!"[23]

Liturgy, particularly the Eucharistic mystery, is identified as a privileged moment of the encounter with Jesus Christ. The Aparecida Document suggests an intimate link between liturgy and the missionary dimension, which, in the context of the theology of Aparecida, is, by definition, a mission to the poor. Aparecida reaches out to the thousands of communities that cannot participate in the Sunday liturgy,

---

20 Gutiérrez, 68–70.

21 Bergoglio, *Concluding Document*, 249.

22 Benedict XVI, Postsynodal Apostolic Exhortation *Verbum Domini* (September 20, 2010), 87.

23 Rutilio Grande, SJ, *Homilies and Writings*, ed. Thomas M. Kelly (Collegeville, Minn.: Liturgical Press, 2015), 119.

inviting them to a Sunday celebration of the Word that makes present the paschal mystery in a community gathering of love. It brings to mind Gerhard Lohfink's meditation on the paschal vigil as the eschatological moment par excellence. Lohfink's intuition allows us to speak about the convergence of all of the pathways of salvation history, on all of which the victims of history suffer and hope.[24]

The most prophetically surprising passage in the Aparecida Document, openly subversive in its boldness, reads, "In the recognition of this presence and nearness [of the poor], and in the defense of the rights of the excluded, the Church's faithfulness to Jesus Christ is at stake."[25] I might add here Archbishop Dom Hélder Câmara's influence on the Latin American church's commitment to the poor. "When I give food to the poor, they call me a saint. When I ask why the poor have no food, they call me a communist," is probably his best-known quote. Dom Hélder's experience reaches back to the Eucharistic Congress at Manaus in 1975, where, as he says, all those present—bishops, priests, religious, laity, and the entire People of God—helped to make the connection between the sacramental Eucharist and the Eucharist of the poor. At the most solemn moment in the congress, an unemployed worker, an abandoned mother, and a prostitute spoke to the assembly.[26] Surely the bishop's account of this congress brings to mind Matthew 21:31.[27]

The text quoted in the preceding paragraph allows us to enter into the manner in which popular piety mediates between Christology and theodicy. The religiosity of the people affords a connection between the encounter with Jesus Christ and the witness of a theological theology.

Pope Francis appropriates the theme of the personal encounter with Jesus Christ in *Evangelii Gaudium*. Francis reads Aparecida's Christology of encounter in the key of mission and contemplation:

---

24 Gerhard Lohfink, *No Irrelevant Jesus: On Jesus and the Church Today*, trans. Linda M. Maloney (Collegeville, Minn.: Liturgical Press, 2014), 154.

25 Bergoglio, *Concluding Document*, 257.

26 Francis McDonagh, *Dom Helder Camara: Essential Writings* (Maryknoll, N.Y.: Orbis, 2009), 157–58.

27 "Amen, I say to you, tax collectors and prostitutes are entering the kingdom of God before you." Unless otherwise noted, this and all other scripture quotations are taken from the New American Bible, Revised Edition (NABRE).

> The primary reason for evangelizing is the love of Jesus which we have received, the experience of salvation which urges us to ever greater love of him. What kind of love would not feel the need to speak of the beloved . . . How good it is to stand before a crucifix, on our knees before the Blessed Sacrament, and simply to be in his presence! . . . We need to recover a contemplative spirit which can help us to realize ever anew that we have been entrusted with a treasure which makes us more human and helps us to lead a new life. There is nothing more precious which we can give to others.[28]

Popular piety, prayer as the clamor of the suffering, contemplation as the mysticism of the crucified of history: these three themes, which we will approach below in detail are present in this chapter of *Evangelii Gaudium*.[29] In popular piety, we find the theme of mystery as the definition of the deepest heart of the Christology of the poor. From the beginning, Aparecida relates popular piety with the experience of the poor. Quoting Paul VI's *Evangelii Nuntiandi*, Aparecida states that popular piety "manifests a thirst for God which only the simple and the poor can know."[30] This affects the deepest layers of the life of the poor: "At different moments of daily struggle, many go back to some small sign of God's love: a crucifix, a rosary, a candle lit to accompany a child in his or her illness, an Our Father murmured amid tears, a tender glance at a beloved image of Mary."[31] Here we see the blossoming of a suffering, genuinely paschal Christology: "Our peoples particularly identify with the suffering Christ; they look at him, they kiss him or touch his wounded feet as though saying: This is he 'who has loved me and given himself up for me' [Gal 2:20]. Many of them, beaten, dispossessed, hold their arms aloft . . . They also find God's affection and love in the face of Mary."[32]

Strictly speaking, popular piety is "a spirituality incarnated in the culture of the lowly."[33] It is not only a concrete form of the Incarnation

28 Francis, *Evangelii Gaudium*, 264.

29 Francis, 264–70, 281–86.

30 Bergoglio, *Concluding Document*, 258, quoting Paul VI, Apostolic Exhortation *Evangelii Nuntiandi* (December 8, 1975), 48.

31 Bergoglio, *Concluding Document*, 261.

32 Bergoglio, 265.

33 Bergoglio, 263.

of the Son of God, but its most preeminent form. The Son becomes incarnate as the sacrament of the preferential option for the poor, the decisive epiphany of the "least of the least" (Mt 25:40).

Christology, as Karl Rahner has reminded us, is the ultimate object of the human being's transcendental drive toward God, of its hunger and yearning for absolute meaning and absolute and decisive personal encounter.[34] This thirst for God defines popular piety and the faith of the poor and simple. Indeed, only the poor and simple can embrace the "foolishness" of the crucified Word.[35] Francis makes his own this "mysticism of the poor" identified at Aparecida: "The bishops refer to it as 'popular spirituality' or 'the people's mysticism' . . . [it is not] devoid of content; rather it discovers and expresses that content more by way of symbols than by discursive reasoning, and in the act of faith greater accent is placed on *credere in Deum* [belief as participation] than on *credere Deum* [belief as propositional assent]."[36]

Theodicy: Theology from the Perspective of the Suffering of the Innocent

The Christology of Pope Francis has been developed from the paschal situation of the poor, and from that perspective we approach, from within the dynamics of popular piety, a defining point of the theodicy of Aparecida and Pope Francis. Pursuing the possibilities of popular piety, Aparecida remarks:

> We highlight pilgrimages, where the People of God can be recognized in their journey. There the believer celebrates the joy of feeling surrounded by myriad brothers and sisters, journeying together toward God who awaits them. Christ himself becomes a pilgrim, and walks arisen among the poor. The decision to set on toward the shrine is already a confession of faith, walking is a true song of hope, and arrival is the encounter of love.[37]

34 Cf. Karl Rahner, *Grundkurs des Glaubens: Einführung in den Begriff des Christentums* (Freiburg: Herder), 206–24.

35 1 Cor 1:18–28.

36 Francis, *Evangelii Gaudium*, 124.

37 Bergoglio, *Concluding Document*, 259.

The encounter with God in Jesus Christ is indeed an encounter of love. But Aquinas reminds us that "*ex amore procedit et gaudium et tristitia*" (both joy and sadness proceed from love).[38] Aparecida echoes Thomas's perspicacity: "Love pauses, contemplates mystery, and enjoys it in silence. It is also moved, pouring out the full load of its pain and dreams. The confident prayer, flowing sincerely, is the best expression of a heart that has relinquished self-sufficiency, recognizing that alone it can do nothing."[39] And, subsuming the category of mystery, the document adds: "In [this lived spiritual experience], the pilgrim undergoes the experience of a mystery that goes beyond them, the transcendence not only of God but also of the Church, which transcends their family and their neighborhood . . . These walls [of shrines] contain many stories that millions could tell of conversion, forgiveness, and gifts received."[40] Love is begotten by the experience of the pilgrim Christ who, risen, walks among the poor. Here we can raise the question: Can we pray to and speak of God from the agonizing suffering of the poor, the oppressed, the despised, and the rejected migrants?

The Son of God's crucified love unveils the mists of the mystery of suffering and identifies it as truly "mystery." Crucified love does not attempt to solve suffering as a problem but rather invites us to embrace it, contemplate it, and participate in it. Can we continue to speak about the God of Jesus Christ in a world where the wealthy societies of Europe and the US compete with each other to erect walls to keep at a distance refugees and migrants clamoring for mercy and where over thirty-five thousand children under the age of eighteen starve to death every day, while sated consumer societies with pretensions of self-sufficiency ignore and despise their plight?

Indeed, we can, if we opt for the preferential option for the poor. Aparecida reiterates the theme of this option: "Our faith proclaims that Jesus Christ is 'the human face of God and the divine face of man.' Hence, 'the preferential option for the poor is implicit in the Christological faith in the God who became poor for us.'"[41] Indeed, "'the suffering faces of

38 Aquinas, *Summa Theologiae*, II-II q. 28 a. 1.
39 Bergoglio, *Concluding Document*, 259.
40 Bergoglio, 260.
41 Bergoglio, *Concluding Document*, 392.

the poor are the suffering faces of Christ' . . . Everything having to do with Christ has to do with the poor, and everything connected with the poor cries out to Jesus Christ."[42] Christology raises the question of theodicy, the challenge of praying to and speaking of God in the suffering of the innocent. Christology already includes and flows into theodicy.

Can we pray after Auschwitz, after El Mozote? Further, can we still pray when we know that thirty-five thousand children died of starvation yesterday and that the same number will die today and tomorrow? Should we hang our heads and concede the truth of Albert Camus's position that life is an absurdity? Should we echo Camus's character in *The Plague,* the tortured Jesuit Paneloux, when he says: "We should accept this dilemma and decide to either hate God or love God. And who would dare hate Him?"[43]

Gustavo Gutiérrez has opted to read the book of Job in the key of the suffering and the oppressed: "How can we speak of God from the side of poverty and suffering? That is the question raised by the book of Job." Indeed, Job is not so much seeking the meaning of suffering, but rather a language to speak of God and speak to God, to complain, to protest. Job is a "believing rebel" who recoils against a suffering that he perceives to be unjustly imposed

Here we have, in my opinion, one of the crucial, albeit implicit, themes of Aparecida. It is the main theme of the book of Job, which can be stated as a question: How do we find a language that speaks about God from the point of view of the suffering of the poor and the oppressed? Gutiérrez argues that the book of Job could only have been written by someone who had suffered God's seeming abandonment in his own flesh: "It is a work written by a faith moist with tears and crimsoned by blood . . . this is someone who has known pain and loneliness."[44] Aparecida echoes this insight.[45] Here we can call to mind Johann Baptist Metz's notion of the "*leiden an Gott*" (suffering on account of God). Only those who have not just studied, but also

42 Bergoglio, 393.

43 Albert Camus, *The Myth of Sisyphus and Other Essays*, trans. Justin O'Brien (New York: Vintage, 1948), 228.

44 Gustavo Gutiérrez, *Hablar de Dios desde el sufrimiento del inocente* (Salamanca: Sígueme, 1986), 53. Cf. Johann Baptist Metz, *Memoria Passionis, Ein provozierendes Gedächtnis in pluralistischer Gesellschaft* (Freiburg: Herder, 2006), 69–78.

45 Bergoglio, *Concluding Document*, 259.

lived, the suffering of the innocent, are qualified to speak of the paschal mystery of Jesus Christ. Alluding to his mentor, Karl Rahner, Metz holds, "Hardly anyone knew better than Karl Rahner that all discourse about God has an authentic linguistic base only insofar as it is rooted in a discourse with God, that is, that the theoretically indispensable linguistic realm for theology is the language of prayer."[46] Prayer offers us a mode of discourse that bears the weight of and expresses the truth of this liminal experience of suffering.

Christology as Theodicy: Mysticism at the Heart of the Option for the Poor

We are called to pray and suffer with the victims of history. Karl Rahner has proposed that "the Christian of the future will be a mystic, that is, someone who has experienced something, or will be nothing."[47] The Aparecida Document sows a mysticism of the poor, made evident in popular piety and in the clamor of those who suffer. The popular mysticism of those who suffer finds an echo in a poetic and theological key in some passages in the document; for example, "Love pauses, contemplates mystery, and enjoys it in silence."[48] Pope Francis adopts this approach in *Evangelii Gaudium*.[49]

Along with Gutiérrez, Metz and Sobrino have inquired into the issue of theology as theodicy. It is not a stretch of logic to propose that theodicy is the future of theology. Wolfhart Pannenberg's insight points in this direction: "Who and what God is, is defined in the Christ event . . . Christ belongs to the definition of God."[50] It follows that if, on the one hand, Christ's paschal event defines who and what God is, and, on the other, theology is coherent and rational discourse about God, then Christology, past and present, must be theodicy. Theodicy attempts to

46 Johann Baptist Metz, *A Passion for God: The Mystical-Political Dimension of Christianity*, trans. Matthew Ashley (New York: Paulist Press, 1998), 115.

47 Karl Rahner, *Theological Investigations*, vol. 7, *Further Theology of the Spiritual Life*, trans. David Bourke (New York: Seabury, 1977), 15.

48 Bergoglio, *Concluding Document*, 259.

49 Francis, *Evangelii Gaudium*, 124. Cf. Aquinas, *Summa Theologiae*, II-II q. 2 a. 2.

50 Wolfhart Pannenberg, *Jesus, God* and *Man*, trans. Lewis L. Wilkins and Duane Priebe (Philadelphia: Westminster, 1968), 130.

argue that it is possible to speak of an omnipotent God whose power is revealed in the powerlessness of love; in particular, crucified love.

This itinerary requires loving and careful listening. Again, consider the words of Metz: "Whoever hears the message of the resurrection of Christ in such way that the cry of the crucified has become inaudible in it, hears not the Gospel but a myth."[51] Aparecida assures us not only that we can pray from within the heart of pain and injustice, but also that within that heart, through radical and subversive forms of popular piety, the poor pray to the God of Jesus Christ every day.

We will proceed toward a conclusion regarding Christocentric theodicy in two parts. First, the theologian living in *koinonia* (communion) with the poor and all of the innocent sufferers should adopt a contemplative attitude, and second, everything is thus resolved in the key of love, and it is love that allows us to proceed into a theological theology. This move presupposes two things: the participation of the theologian in the suffering of the innocent and the recognition of Mary the Mother of God as the cipher or primordial symbol of a Christological theodicy and a theological theology.

In the context of Aparecida, it is clear, as Karl Rahner holds, that the theologian is called to do theology from within the heart of a prayer that flows, like a river from its wellspring, from the anguish, pain, oppression, and humiliation of the poor. The theologian needs to define his or her theology as an always-incomplete attempt to pursue a pilgrimage, always under a cloud of failure, speaking about the God of Jesus Christ from the point of view of innocent suffering—a pilgrimage in which the theologian is called to participate as the most intimate definition of his or her being.

Before the awesomeness of mystery, we can dare to undertake, at least provisionally, a mental genuflection before a crucifix. The crucifix that both Aparecida and Francis so subversively hold before our eyes (perhaps drinking deep from Bonaventure's Christological mysticism) will allow us to enter, and appropriate as our own, the suffering of the victims, thereby establishing the foundations of a theological theology; that is, a theology evincing its legitimacy on the trinitarian and paschal grounds upon which it unfolds.

51 Metz, *A Passion for God*, 55.

The paschal event of Jesus Christ not only defines who and what is God, but also who and what is the human being. We all are *paschal beings*. Again, Rahner has articulated it for the ages: "Christology is self-transcending anthropology. Anthropology is deficient Christology."[52] From this perspective, we can better understand Michael Buckley's and Walter Kasper's lament about the loss of the biblical and kerygmatic freshness of contemporary theology. From different perspectives, both advocate a return to a theological theology. For Kasper, this means recovering the grounding of theology in salvation history.[53] Buckley proposes that

> God has emerged, over and over again in human history, as the direction toward which awe and wonder progresses . . . The Christian God cannot have a more fundamental witness than Jesus Christ, even antecedent to the commitment of faith. Christian theology cannot abstract itself from christology, in order to shift its focus toward philosophy . . . for a Christian, Jesus belongs to the intelligibility of the truth about God. Who God is, and even that God is, has its most primordial evidence in the person and the event that is Jesus Christ.[54]

From the most heartrending cries, the most convulsing expressions of anguish that spring forth from the most forgotten and despised corners of history, there emerges a singular woman: Mary the Mother of Jesus, the living Son of God, fully and radically human, fully and radically God, and therefore a woman who is, in a most radical and decisive way for Christian faith, the Mother of God. Aparecida portrays her as the personal symbol of a Christological theodicy:

> Her figure emerges from the Gospel as a free and strong woman, consciously directed toward the true following of Christ. She has fully experienced the entire pilgrimage of faith as mother of Christ and then of the disciples, and yet

52 Rahner, *Grundkurs des Glaubens*, 206–25.

53 Walter Kasper, *Theology and the Church* (New York: Crossroad, 1972), 73–93.

54 Michael J. Buckley, *At the Origin of Modern Atheism* (New Haven, Conn.: Yale University Press, 1987), 362–63.

> has not been saved from incomprehension and continually having to seek the Father's project. Thus, she came to stand at the foot of the cross in deep communion, so as to then fully enter into the mystery of the covenant.[55]

Indeed, a sober and careful examination of those New Testament texts that allude to Mary forbids any vulgarization or sublimation of Mary's vocation—she has indeed experienced human pain unto its dregs: "From the cross, Jesus Christ entrusts to his disciples, represented by John, the gift of Mary's motherhood *which springs directly from the paschal hour of Jesus*."[56] Aquinas's musings on how suitable it was for the risen body of Christ to bear the scars of the passion come to mind.[57]

Aparecida further remarks: "With her, providentially united to the fullness of time (Cf. Gal 4:4), the hope of the poor and the desire of salvation come to fulfillment."[58] Indeed, "she also indicates what pedagogy should be used so that the poor 'feel at home' in every Christian community."[59] Pope Francis appropriates the Mariology of Aparecida as the privileged key to what amounts, in my judgment, to a Christological theodicy. Indeed, Aparecida proclaims the special place of Mary at the foot of the cross as the wellspring of her privileged pilgrimage among and with the poor. Francis says: "On the cross, when Jesus endured in his own flesh the dramatic encounter of the sin of the world and God's mercy, he could feel at his feet the consoling presence of his mother and his friend."[60] In his own mystical poetry, Francis reflects on how this happens:

> Mary was able to turn a stable into a home for Jesus, with poor swaddling clothes and an abundance of love . . . she is the woman whose heart is pierced by a sword and who understands all our pain. A mother of all, she is a sign of hope for peoples suffering the birth pangs of justice . . . as she

55 Bergoglio, *Concluding Document*, 266.

56 Bergoglio, *Concluding Document*, 267. Emphasis mine.

57 Aquinas, *Summa Theologiae* III, q. 54, a. 4.

58 Bergoglio, *Concluding Document*, 267.

59 Bergoglio, 272.

60 Francis, *Evangelii Gaudium*, 285.

> did with Juan Diego, Mary offers them material comfort and love, and whispers in their ears: 'Let not your heart be troubled . . . Am I not here, who am your mother?'[61]

One of Francis's privileged words, "tenderness," colors and defines the very heart of *Evangelii Gaudium*, as it flows sweetly and compellingly from Aparecida: "There is a Marian style to the Church's work of evangelization. Whenever we look to Mary, we come to believe once again in the revolutionary nature of love and tenderness. In her we see that humility and tenderness are not virtues of the weak but of the strong who need not treat others poorly in order to feel important themselves."[62] Mary is not an alienating figure in the church's new evangelization and commitment to justice and the poor. Rather, in her and through her, there thunder over and over again Francis's words: "The poor are the Gospel."

From this Mariological reflection, we can infer that the commitment to Jesus Christ in the Americas, flowing from the wellspring of Aparecida and deepened by *Evangelii Gaudium*, can only be understood as a Christocentric theodicy. This theodicy is both a thinking about and a speaking of God from the within the suffering of the poor and the victims, in the form of contemplative prayer joined to a mysticism of the poor. Christocentric theodicy is, of its own nature, theological theology; that is, a theology that justifies itself from its very defining principles: salvation history, the church in history, and the scriptures and their interpretation by the faith of the church. As such, this theology reveals the paschal, trinitarian God as the God of Jesus Christ, of the poor, and of all of the crucified in history. In conclusion (and to reaffirm what was said at the outset), the poor are indeed the Gospel.

Appendix: My Pilgrimage to Cuba: November 7–22, 2016

A journey is defined by the commitment and attitude of the sojourner. I opted to go to Cuba last November as a pilgrim, and therefore I

---

61 Francis, *Evangelii Gaudium*, 286.

62 Francis, 288.

choose to call it a pilgrimage, not merely a trip.[63] My awe and wonder at the Aparecida Document, and its appropriation in Francis's *Evangelii Gaudium*, were very much present in my mind and heart as the splendid lights of love and justice that helped me make sense of my pilgrimage.

Since my departure from the island on April 7, 1961, I had been back to Cuba once before, from September 13 to 30, 2003. I had been invited to teach two courses on Christology in the Archdiocese of Camagüey to the priests, deacons, and religious, and to the committed laity, of the local church. After forty-two years, everything seemed like new: somehow the places of my childhood and early youth seemed smaller, shrunken by memory and time. My encounter with the Cuban church revealed a unique situation; that is, the challenging circumstances in which the church attempts to fulfill her mission to witness to and proclaim the Gospel, a situation that I attempted to fathom as I met various people, from lay leaders to parish priests to the archbishop of Camagüey (presently the archbishop of Havana). My visit was a rich encounter with the local faith community, but the purpose of my journey was to teach Christology, and since I spent much of my time in the secluded environment of the Archdiocesan Pastoral Center, I did not get much exposure to the church's everyday ministries of evangelization, nor to the lay Catholics who sustained those ministries, and, in fact, the very survival of the church.

My second time around, last November, was different. I did not go to teach or participate in any official or church activity. I went to Cuba to stay for sixteen days with my brother, Alberto, a Jesuit priest, at the Centro de Espiritualidad Pedro Arrupe. From the moment I decided to go to Cuba, I resolved to walk around and talk to everyday people in the streets. The Jesuit Centro is located near the corner of G and Nineteenth Streets in El Vedado, a convenient location for my seemingly endless walks all over the city. A quick (and neck-risking) ride in a popular taxi, usually a 1949 or '50 Chevrolet or Plymouth

63 Editors' note: Dr. García was not able to join the other contributors for the conference in Cuba because his special residence status as a Cuban-American born on the island in 1961 demanded a visa that could not be procured in time for the trip. The trip described here took place one month after the conference. This *recuerdo* or reminiscence is included here not for sentimental reasons but because social memory and its healing are critical to the vision of Aparecida and of Pope Francis.

(locally called *almendrón*, big almond, for its shape), miraculously kept alive by the ingenuity of Cuban mechanics, took me to Old Havana, "La Habana Vieja," and there I walked many miles along those old, at times cobblestoned streets, talking, asking, and sharing life, heart, and soul with just about everybody.

I spoke to literally dozens of police officers, taxi drivers, construction workers, government officials, and retired men and women idling on the centuries-old corners. I found that, since my earlier sojourn in 2003, Cubans in the streets were more willing to voice their frustrations about the government. These were not ideological complaints ("socialism doesn't work," etc.) but rather a more pragmatic but widespread moaning about the government's failure to deliver on its promises to the people.

But I also devoted considerable time to conversing with people in the church. The local Jesuit community, led by Fr. Benjamín González and my brother Alberto, is radically devoted to its ministry in the local parishes, among the poor and the suffering. I discovered that much had changed since 2003. First of all, in 2003 the Aparecida Document was still four years in the future. I found that the document, mediated by Pope Francis's prophetic ministry, had seeped into the deeper layers of the Cuban church. Lay groups, led by both women and men, have their meeting place at the Centro. I met two female lay leaders, coordinators of a lay prayer and discussion group that convenes at the Centro weekly. One of them actually knew my wife Elena.

I was fascinated by the youth groups that I met. I saw their presence at the Church of San Juan de Letrán, near the Centro, as I attended the Mass for the centennial of the Dominicans in Havana. They wore their T-shirts with the group's name and biblical quotes printed on them. Their faces and conversations revealed a deep, passionate, intelligent faith, and a sense of sure purpose and commitment. The day before my brother and I departed from Cuba (after sixteen years on the island, he has been indefinitely assigned to Belen Jesuit Prep in Miami), yet another youth group arrived at the Centro, wearing their yellow T-shirts. We talked for half an hour, and at the end they invited me to give them a presentation whenever I returned to Cuba—I said I would, and this is a promise that I intend to keep.

The Jesuits at the Centro offered an informal yet joyful and meaningful Eucharistic celebration every day. Parish masses revealed what, to me, is one of the decisive changes, and a harbinger of a truly new church for the future. At one Mass, I sat next to Cubans of African descent, mulattoes, and Caucasians—all races and mixes were there, sharing together, celebrating together. Contrary to some of the nostalgia-driven myths among some Cubans in Miami, this was truly new, wonderfully new, at least to me!

At the parish of the Servants of Mary, there were twelve young women, postulants, doing the readings and guiding the congregation. I could see that, in that brief, rather small sample of sixteen days, women have begun to claim their rightful place as leaders of local churches and small communities.

The spirit, mysticism, and evangelizing soul of Aparecida seemed to be in evidence most everywhere. Most priests, lay leaders, and even youth leaders were familiar with the document and certainly with Francis's deep reflections and pastoral applications flowing from it.

Moreover, the spirituality I breathed whenever I entered spaces of prayer and church communities was decidedly Christocentric. The encounter with Jesus Christ, the guiding theological and spiritual theme of Aparecida, was the main driving motivation behind the commitments of these Cuban church communities.

A commitment to the poor, to the people, which is at the heart of Aparecida's program of evangelization, was also in evidence. The active engagement of those who, in previous times, were not welcome at the more opulent churches, defines the ministry of the local assemblies within the larger Cuban church. Race and even gender seem to have lost most of their power as criteria for selection of ministers and leadership in many local faith communities. At San Juan de Letrán, two Black Cubans, of unmistakable African descent, were the community leaders, and this, as I had the opportunity to find out, was not an isolated case.

I am not attempting to portray an idealized version of the Cuban church. There are issues of leadership among the bishops that beg for a solution. According to reliable sources, many of the seminarians at the new Seminario del Buen Pastor are reverting to clericalist attitudes, fueled by a widespread wave of conservatism and regression. Cuban Catholics are a minority of the general population. Criticism has been leveled at the church's acceptance of popular piety.

I left Cuba, however, with a sense of guarded optimism about the church and the country in general. I am aware that such optimism places me in a very definite minority. Yet, as a Christian who has had the blessing and grace to study and teach theology and scriptures, I hold onto the sense that salvation history has not run its course in Cuba and that seeds (and even some already-sprouting trees) of renewal are signs of an ongoing and future paschal evangelization of the Cuban church that is deeper, more joyful, ever-passionate, ever-vulnerable, always risk-taking. I see that Aparecida's encounter with Jesus Christ is happening, is blossoming within the bowels of the pain, agony, and uncertainty that has been Cuba's lot for so long. Paraphrasing Gerhard Lohfink, the Cuban church is celebrating its paschal vigil, where all the pathways of Cuban history will eventually converge. It is a church unfolding in the spirit of Aparecida, and for the first time in Cuban republican history, it is becoming a true church of the people.

CHAPTER 4

"WE FINALLY HAVE A POPE ON THE SIDE OF THE POOR"

Ana María Bidegain

ONE OF THE KEY CHARACTERISTICS of Francis's pontificate has been the position he has taken on the side of the poor. On his visits to Latin America, he has gone out of his way to meet them, to hug them, and to offer them words of encouragement.[1] In those encounters, he has also recognized that the poor have been the victims of historical injustices, asked for their forgiveness, and affirmed the dignity and value of their cultures and languages. He has asked them not to be disheartened in their daily struggles to secure the basics of life (work, housing, land, etc.) despite the enormous difficulties they face.[2] It is touching to witness the warmth, love, and joy with which Francis is received among communities of persons living in very vulnerable economic, social, and political situations.

"Thank God for our Pope Francis, who comes where the poorest of us are," said Carmen Rodríguez, an eighty-three-year-old Puerto Rican woman, as she welcomed the pope to her New York community.[3] A Paraguayan boy tenderly approached the Holy Father and offered him the only gift he had: a chicken, so that the Pope could cook vori-vori, a typical

1 John Smith, "El Barrio espera con ansias al Papa" [The neighborhood awaits the pope with excitement], *El Diario* online, July 5, 2015, https://eldiariony.com/2015/07/05/el-barrio-espera-con-ansias-al-papa/.

2 Jose Antonio R. Soto, "El gallo que le llevó el niño Ángel al Papa" [The rooster that the boy angel gave the pope], *Periodista Digital*, July 11, 2015, http://www.periodistadigital.com/religion/america/2015/07/11/el-gallo-que-le-llevo-el-nino-angel-al-papa-iglesia-religion-fao-vori-vori-inercia-tierra-economia-politica-corrupcion-pobreza-paro-juvenil-carcel-mujeres-papamovil-aeropuerto.shtml.

3 Smith, "El Barrio espera con ansias al Papa."

Paraguayan dish.[4] At the end of the Mass with the indigenous communities of Chiapas, a native woman gave the pope two bibles, one in Tzotzil and the other in Tzeltal, along with a New Testament in the Tzotzil of Huixtán. The gift of these sacred texts is very significant—these texts were the result of a lengthy effort of translation that was begun a long time ago under the direction of the community's beloved bishop, called by the Tzeltal "*jtatik*" (meaning "father") Samuel Ruiz. This gift also points to the new official status that has been gained by the native languages in liturgical celebrations. For Rosa García, a twenty-five-year-old Tzeltal woman, "the question is not what language we use to pray to God. God always understands us. The difference is that now, in our own language, we will feel God closer to our hearts."[5] At the end of the celebration, against a background of local musical rhythms, one could hear the loud voices of the natives yelling in unison: "We have a Pope on the side of the poor."[6]

Meanwhile in Miami, a group of university students and I were attentively following the historical papal visit and the beautiful celebration in Chiapas, which was broadcast by the Hispanic television networks. One of the American students asked me, "Why would they trust that a pope could be on the side of the poor, since the pope is so powerful and the Catholic Church is so rich?" Another student added, "Where does the strength and conviction of those people who live in poverty that God and the church must be on their side come from?"

The objective of this chapter is to answer the questions posed by those students. We will not focus primarily on Pope Francis himself, but on the historical background behind the movement that, in his warm encounter with the poor, he has been stimulating in communities throughout the Americas. Building a church that is poor and for the poor is part of the core message of the Gospel,[7] and the goal of doing

4 Soto, "El gallo que le llevó el niño Ángel al Papa."

5 Agencia AFP, "Papa Francisco tiende la mano a indigenas y pide person por su exclusion," ABC website, February 15, 2016, http://www.abc.com.py/internacionales/papa-francisco-tiende-la-mano-a-indigenas-y-pide-perdon-por-su-exclusion-1453602.html.

6 Agencia AFP, "Francisco tiende la mano a indigenas y pide perdón por su exclusión," *El Heraldo* online, February 15, 2016, https://www.elheraldo.hn/inicio/930140-465/francisco-tiende-la-mano-a-ind%C3%ADgenas-y-pide-perd%C3%B3n-por-su-exclusi%C3%B3n.

7 The term "church of the poor" does not refer to an entity parallel to or apart from the historical church, but to instances in ecclesial life in which the central impulse of

so has been a strong strand throughout the church's history, a strand that was markedly revitalized in the twentieth century. This goal was present in the documents of the Second Vatican Council and has been enshrined in the contemporary ecclesiastical magisterium and in the social doctrine of the church. In the context of Latin America, it was clearly articulated in the texts that emanated from the Second Episcopal Conference of Latin America held in Medellín, Colombia in 1968. This centuries-old tradition has also nourished the pastoral initiatives and intellectual developments associated with liberation theology.

From where, then, does the openness and joy of the poor originate when they encounter the pope? Their trust in Francis's message and their gladness in his presence is due to their sharing in a collective memory: *the memory of the prophetic history of the church of the poor.*

The Poor in the History of the Church

Even though the poor were the first to receive Jesus's message and the first to build his church in the first few centuries after his death, their ecclesial place was eclipsed when Constantine (r. 306–39) made Christianity the official imperial religion. Linked after this decision to the high-level spheres of political power, the church gradually normalized the cultural and social traits of the imperial elites. It was thus molded by powerful social groups that were incorporated into its ranks—politically, economically, and socially, as well as culturally and intellectually. Nevertheless, the original primacy of humble people, one of the essential aspects of the Gospel message, was never completely forgotten. Early in the history of the church, various communities, leaders, initiatives, and processes emerged that attempted to reach the original Christian ideal and that, for this reason, were in tension with the value system of the imperial world. Every generation has produced followers of Jesus who have been aware of the central place of the poor in the Gospel and in the foundational message of Christianity, followers who have sought ways of living out their fidelity to this outlook in the concrete realm of history. These witnesses

---

the Gospel that situates the poor at the center of the life and mission of Christ, at the center of the Good News of the kingdom of God, is concretized.

constitute an uninterrupted thread, present in every century, although varying in intensity and at times even hidden.

In the following sections, we review some of the significant moments in the life of the church when the evangelical value of the poor gained greater visibility. We will omit an examination of the patristic period, although it is rich in reflections about the theme under consideration. Likewise, we will not be able to explore the origins and development of monasticism, nor will we consider various relevant processes that took place during the Middle Ages, even though the profound transformations that began in the twelfth century continue to impact modernity and were undoubtedly in the mind of Pope Francis when he chose his name.

The Church and the Poor in Early Modernity

In the sixteenth century, we find a new generation of critics that defended sweeping ecclesial reforms—people like Erasmus, Colet, More, Luther, Calvin, and Zwingli. The last three broke with the church and led the Reformation movement, bringing about the birth of national churches that played a fundamental role in the construction of the identities of certain European states. With respect to Calvin, Weber's thesis regarding the affinities between his theology and ethics and the demands of nascent capitalism is well-known. In fact, the poor were not at the center of the reformers' concerns, though they criticized mechanisms that functioned to profit the church, such as the sale of indulgences, the exploitation of the devout, and various forms of corruption. They did not, however, clamor for a church for the poor. On the contrary, when they spoke of the laity they had in mind nobles and the emerging bourgeoisie, not the urban poor or the peasantry.[8]

The elitist attitude of many of the reformers contrasts with that of Thomas Müntzer (1488–1525). Müntzer studied theology and was a companion and follower of Luther, but later distanced himself from him, rejecting the Lutheran alliance with the German nobility, an alliance that resulted in the creation of the German territorial churches in

8 Hermann Tüchle and Cornelis Adrianus Bouman, *Reforma y contrarreforma*, vol. 3 of *Nueva historia de la iglesia*, ed. L.J. Rogier, Roger Aubert, and David Knowles (Madrid: Cristiandad, 1966), 87.

1523.[9] Müntzer led a popular reaction against harsh taxes and levies that increased poverty and misery. The peoples' demands for religious reform intermixed with a reaction against adverse factors of material reality like the emerging money-based economy. Müntzer attacked the arbitrariness of the feudal lords, the most powerful social class of the epoch, who in his judgment illegitimately appropriated natural resources, leaving the majority in misery. Apart from the theological differences between Luther and Müntzer, the principal cause of the divergence between them was the way in which each understood historical reality and the models of Christianity that they proposed following from that understanding. Müntzer opted for a humble and egalitarian Christianity favoring the simple and poor people. He proposed a redistribution of material goods, and in order to achieve this objective he justified the use of violence. Together with other radical elements of society, he brought about a large peasant uprising, sometimes called a "peasant war," in the southern and central parts of Germany.[10]

In 1525, the peasants decided to establish a confederate order—"a Christian community according to the Gospel."[11] They requested support from Luther, Philip Melanchthon, and Huldrych Zwingli in order to resolve problems related to ecclesiastical law, and in order to mediate their conflict with the nobles as put forward in the Twelve Articles—all of which were rather reasonable. Luther had agreed to intercede for them with the nobility. However, when the more radical groups resorted to violence, Luther parted ways with them and publicly declared himself an enemy of the peasant reform. In 1525 he wrote a pamphlet titled *Against the Murderous, Thieving Hordes of Peasants.* He virulently condemned the movement:

> Therefore, let everyone who can, smite, slay and stab, secretly or openly, remembering that nothing can be more poisonous, hurtful or devilish than a rebel. It is just as when one must kill a mad dog; if you do not strike him, he will strike you, and a whole land with you. [...] Stab, smite, slay, whoever you can.

---

9 Under the protection of the nobility, Luther wrote *Temporal Authority: To What Extent It Should Be Obeyed*, in vol. 45, *Luther's Works: The Christian in Society II*, ed. Walter I. Brandt and Walter T. Lehmann (Philadelphia: Fortress Press, 1962), 85–86.

10 Tüchle and Bouman, *Reforma y contrarreforma*, 87.

11 Tüchle and Bouman, 89.

> If you die in doing it, well for you! A more blessed death can never be yours, for you die obeying the divine Word ... and in loving service of your neighbor.[12]

In this and other texts it is clear that Luther was unconditionally on the side of the temporal power. According to Luther, the sovereign exists to protect pious men and impede revolts. The obligation of subjects was to obey, and he even went so far as to claim that they must not defend themselves, a position that put him at odds with the rustic population. Far from discerning the call for social justice and the legitimate evangelical demands that were part of the peasant rebellion, Luther reduced the entire movement to its most violent faction, characterizing it as a diabolical endeavor and Thomas Münzter as an archdevil. He legitimated the subsequent persecution of the peasant reformers, and "is considered the intellectual responsible for the bloody repression" that brought about more than ten thousand deaths, including the execution of Müntzer.[13]

The Lutheran side of the Reformation, which involved an alliance with the nobility, was imposed in the German lands. The work of Luther justified the separation of a segment of Christianity from the Roman church, but gave responsibility for the propagation of the Gospel not to the common people, but to each territory's official and political circles. He thereby maintained in Protestantism the settlement of the system of Christendom and the strong alliance between political and religious power. More nationalist than popular, the Lutheran tradition was not supportive of a poor church, of the poor and for the poor.

Following the critical spirit encouraged by Erasmus of Rotterdam, we find other Christians in the sixteenth century who placed themselves unconditionally on the side of the poor. Erasmus had a large impact in Spain, where he nurtured a rich humanist movement and influenced the ecclesiastical reforms of Cardinal Cisneros.[14] That humanist perspective

12 *Against the Murderous, Thieving Hordes of Peasants*, in *Martin Luther*, ed. E. G. Rupp and Benjamin Drewery, Documents of Modern History (London: Edward Arnold, 1970), 121–26.

13 Tomás Varnagy, "El pensamiento político de Martín Luther" [The political thought of Martin Luther], in *La filosofía política clásica: De la antigüedad al renacimiento*, ed. Consejo Latinoamericano de Ciencias Sociales (Buenos Aires: CLACSO, 1999), 154.

14 Cf. Marcel Battalion, *Erasmo en España* (Madrid: FCE, 1950), 1–71.

had an effect on the missionaries that went to America, such as Fray Antonio Montesino, Fray Bartolomé de las Casas, the bishop Vasco de Quiroga, and the Jesuit missionaries, among many others. The essential thing these men had in common is that they interpreted the Gospel so as to lay bare the inequity of the colonial system. They denounced the total impoverishment of the lives of the New World peoples, which was the result of Iberian conquest and domination. They believed in the moral regeneration of human beings, in their capacity to modify reprehensible conduct. It is because of this that they strove to transform legislation and create new pastoral experiences with the objectives of protecting the indigenous and announcing the Gospel in a genuine, pacific, and fraternal form.

The Dominicans Montesinos, Las Casas, and Vitoria, each from his own social place, were the prophets who began the struggle for indigenous rights. They were conscious of living during a new historical stage characterized by a system that oppressed many human beings who were being integrated into Christianity by force. They asked themselves how to announce the Good News to the indigenous when what they were actually given was slavery, not justice or law. Montesinos denounced the *encomenderos*, accusing them of living in a state of mortal sin because of the exploitation and slavery to which they subjected the indigenous. Las Casas confronted the theory that the indigenous had no rights in Christian societies because they were pagans. Francisco de Vitoria, although he never set foot in America, developed the principle of universal human rights common to all races.[15] These thinkers and pastors put into question the legitimacy and justice of the European conquest and colonization of the rest of the world. Unfortunately, this was a question that, although it made a dent in the consciences of some Catholics, especially Spaniards, did not affect the majority of European Christians and later North Americans, for whom colonization was an obvious right.

Although Las Casas was recognized as the protector of the Indians, he is not an isolated figure in this struggle. Many others, relying on the logic of the Gospel, also rose up against the colonial system in order to benefit oppressed populations. The list of bishops of the Latin American

15 Gustavo Gutiérrez, *In Search of the Poor of Jesus Christ* (Maryknoll, N.Y.: Orbis, 1993), 275–355.

church who did so is fortunately long, and the work of many of these bishops is well-known, thanks to the work of Enrique Dussel.[16] One of these was the bishop of Michoacán, Vasco de Quiroga (d. 1565). His missionary work, inspired by Thomas More's *Utopia*, provided the foundations of the missionary proposals of a number of religious communities, especially the Jesuits, and the building of true Amerindian republics.[17] Entering the continent in order to protect and save the indigenous from Spanish exploitation and Portuguese slavery, the Jesuits built exemplary missions in Orinoco, Brazil and in present-day Bolivia and Paraguay.

Also in the sixteenth century, in Europe, the wars of religion in Germany (1545–55) and in France (1555–98), like all wars, worsened the situation of the most vulnerable populations. In the confrontation between princes, it was the poor who were decimated and who suffered forced displacement toward the urban centers where their poverty became acute, resulting in a huge increase of the numbers of people reduced to begging. The wounded and invalids, mostly poor, were abandoned to their fates. In the rural areas, many peasants were stripped of their lands, contributing to the swelling number of the desperately poor. For the rich, the nobles, the bourgeoisie, and those at the top of the social hierarchy, beggars were like a plague in the social fabric. Instead of doing something about the causes of impoverishment, the elites attempted to eradicate the mass of poor people, imprisoning them and driving them out onto the roads.

Faced with a world that generated such social inequality, many women with a religious vocation searched for ways in which they could consecrate themselves to God and to the service of the poor. Despite the magnitude of the social necessities that they felt called to address, they faced many obstacles thrown up by the ecclesiastical hierarchy. Many of them proposed dedicating themselves to an active religious

---

16 Enrique D. Dussel, *El Episcopado Latinoamericano y la Liberación de los Pobres, 1504–1620* [The Latin American episcopate and the liberation of the poor, 1504–1620] (México, D.F.: Centro de Reflexión Teológica, 1979), http://biblioteca.clacso.edu.ar/clacso/otros/20120131104309/espiscopado.pdf

17 For information about Bishop Vasco de Quiroga's life, see José Aparecido Gomes Moreira, *Conquista y Conciencia Cristiana: El Pensamiento Indigenista y Jurídico Teológico de Don Vasco de Quiroga (+1565)* [Conquest and Christian consciousness: The indigenous theological and legal thought of Don Vasco de Quiroga] (Quito: Abya-Yala, 1990).

life and attending to the needs of the poor, the sick, the elderly, and the children and youth. However, Pope Boniface VIII's (r. 1294–1303) decrees of 1298, apparently required by a previous easing of rules governing female convents, imposed a strict cloistering of women with a religious vocation. There was a strong tension between the desire of consecrated women to live out their understanding of Christianity in a way they saw fit—including engaging in social action for the needy—and the perspective of the masculine hierarchy. The men argued that women needed protection and that they were incapable of managing their lives on their own. Masculine perceptions were expressed in strong masculine control and led to the cloistering of nuns in convents, which were built as impregnable fortresses. Boniface's decree was relativized in practice in a few places and times, and there have always been communities of women who have been able to fulfill their vows without the obligation of monastic cloistering.[18] A little known case that embodied the model of female religious organization in future centuries was that of the Oblates of St. Frances of Rome, who installed themselves in a poor Roman convent in 1433 without vows or cloistering and with the specific mission of practicing charity among the poor.[19] Despite the obstacles they faced, in the early modern period, nuns whose calling was to attend to the necessities of the poor became very numerous.

The Church, the Poor, and the Bourgeois Republican State

After the French Revolution, once the national republican states had been established in the nineteenth century, society began suffering

18 The Council of Trent, in its twenty-fifth session, approved the *De Regularibus et Monialibus*, which treated the requirement of cloistering only in the case of contemplative nuns. In *Acta* 88, it clearly states: "Women who are called Penitents or Converts and who conform to their constitutions are exempted from these prescriptions." See the Latin text at *Actas Apostolicas Sedes*, ann. 43, ser. 2, vol. 18 (January 1951), 38–40, http://www.vatican.va/archive/aas/documents/AAS-43-1951-ocr.pdf. Thus, the existence of tertiary Dominicans and Franciscans and the Sisters of Penance was recognized. Pope Julius II, by means of papal bulls of March 14, 1509, and February 27, 1510, permitted these women to live in common and to make three vows without the obligation of being cloistered. See Berthem-Bontoux, *Sainte Françoise Romaine Et Son Temps (1384–1440)* (Paris: Bloud and Gay, 1931), 25–30. The Vicentines and the Gray Sisters working in the hospitals of France in the fifteenth and sixteenth centuries also had this freedom.

19 Berthem-Bontoux, *Sainte Françoise Romaine*, 35–46.

the negative impacts of the Industrial Revolution. The transformation of economies and the world of labor had a huge impact on families, as the working class increasingly came to include women and children. The liberal state developed new sources of labor and, with them, new forms of exploitation. The social challenges of this context provoked a new wave of works of compassion initiated by Christians, especially beginning around 1830. Religious congregations serving the poorest, especially the female poor, multiplied. Rome quickly approved the work of these women, recognizing the importance of their mission. Religious institutes multiplied all over Europe, but they were also founded in missionary territories. Several male and female congregations decided to accompany the migration process that brought large contingents of landless peasantry, craftsmen, and unemployed urban people to the ports of the Americas—from Boston to Buenos Aires.

By the middle of the nineteenth century, many Catholic parishes had created societies of ladies to attend to diverse social needs. The actions of lay Catholics serving in all kinds of social projects within the parish setting intensified over the course of the century. Conservative aristocratic sectors participated in this process, including well-known figures like Albert de Mun and Patrice de la Tour du Pin, as well as members of the liberal bourgeoisie who were interested in a rapprochement between Catholicism and the ideals of the revolution. Some historians find in these diverse groups the beginnings of the social Catholicism of the nineteenth and twentieth centuries.[20]

Some members of the clergy also responded creatively to social challenges. Antoine Chevrier (1825–79), a diocesan priest, developed a vast social initiative among the poor and founded a house for the formation of nuns present in working-class neighborhoods. He also founded a house that educated priests who were in direct contact with workers so that they could understand their reality. At his death, four priests educated in the juvenile refugee facilities also established by Chevrier created an association of priests, Prado, that aimed at

20 Guillaume de Bertier de Sauvigny and Joseph N. Hajjar, *De La Ilustración a La Restauración*, vol. 4 of *Nueva Historia de la Iglesia*, ed. L.J. Rogier, Roger Aubert, and David Knowles (Madrid: Cristiandad, 1984), 148.

accompanying the impoverished workers in the parishes of the working-class neighborhoods.[21]

After the electoral system had been established and the organization of political parties and workers' associations allowed (the latter of which, in turn, gave rise to unions), the diversity of initiatives among Catholics, especially priests and laity, grew in the face of the extreme poverty that had devastated both rural and urban areas. The high-ranking clergy, however, composed mostly of aristocrats and men of the high bourgeoisie, continued to focus on combatting the rationalism of the Enlightenment and were blind to the great social challenges of the day. They were in general formed without contact with the people and ignorant of the scope of the social processes incubating before their own eyes, but as always, there were exceptions. In 1841, the archbishop of Rouen urged the state to pass a law prohibiting child labor for children under eight years old and to limit working hours, which at the time sometimes reached sixteen hours a day.[22]

Even more radical social proposals were advanced by some Catholics; for example, by Father H. F. Lamennais (1782–1854), who denounced inequality as the source of a new slavery and the negation of the human dignity of the poor. He proposed the creation of workers' associations to defend the rights of workers and called on priests to promote a church for the poor. He invited them to live in material poverty in order to regenerate the church and convert it into a church of justice and of the persecuted, as it had been in earlier times. For the French bishops, profoundly imbued with the Gallican spirit, some of Lamennais's theses (mostly published in the newspaper *L'Avenir*) were very radical because they saw them as promoting the separation of the spiritual from the political and the freedom of the press, of education, and of association. From Rome, they were disavowed in the encyclical *Mirari Vos* (1832). Lamennais continued to denounce capitalism and exhorted the poor and other underprivileged individuals to rebel against their oppressors. His ideas were specifically condemned by the encyclical *Singulari Nos* (1834), which led him to break with the institutional church. Followers

21 Jean Yves Ducourneau, *Jesus, l'Eglise et les pauvres* (Nouan-le Fuzelier: Beatitudes, 2010), 121.

22 Paul Christophe, *Les pauvres et la pauvretê* (Paris: Desclee, 1987), 127; Ducourneau, *Jesus, l'Eglise et les pauvres*, 123.

of Lamennais, especially the Dominican J. B. Lacordaire (1802–61), took up aspects of his reformist views from the perspective of orthodoxy. Lacordaire preached that the cry of poverty was a cry of anguish, and he told the poor that although men did not hear them, God would not forget them. His preaching in the cathedral of Paris put pressure on politicians to legislate in favor of the well-being of workers. He consistently denounced poverty as anti-Christian and against the will of God, and incited his listeners to fight against it.[23]

A young layman, Frederic Ozanam, a professor of history at the Sorbonne who was committed to the charitable works of the Vincentian sisters, openly criticized economic liberalism.[24] He described it as an "ignominious doctrine" that reduced each person's life to the calculus of interest. He announced that "the question that stirs the world today… is the struggle of those who have nothing and those who have much… To restore order through charity is not enough; though it heals wounds, it cannot avoid the blows that produce it."[25] He believed that government should intervene to regulate the labor market through workers' associations and some modicum of state control. Ozanam founded the Society of St. Vincent de Paul, dedicated to social work, which remains active today. He was beatified in 1997.

Between 1860 and 1890, lay groups reacted to the prevailing social situation throughout Catholic Europe, not only concerned with fulfilling the demands of Christian charity, but also with advancing socialism and anarchism among the working classes. These Catholics saw social action from a generally paternalistic perspective as a means to achieve an alliance of the popular masses against the bourgeois and anticlerical oligarchy. Their attitude was, essentially, a reaction to the displacement of old social hierarchies by the power of money. More than just confronting the rising challenges posed by the bourgeois revolutions, they were inspired by nostalgia for patriarchal, corporative societies. These groups maintained contacts with each other and with Rome, the latter of which facilitated the formation of the Catholic Union of Social Studies. Beginning in 1884, this group met in Fribourg with the aim

23 Henri Baptiste Lacordaire, *Lettres a un jeune homme sur la vie chretienne*, rev. ed. (1858; repr., Paris: Cerf, 1988), 25.

24 Marcel Vincent, *Ozanam: Une Jeunesse Romantique, 1813–1833* [Ozanam: A romantic youth, 1813–1833] (Paris: Médiaspaul, 1997), 36.

25 De Bertier de Sauvigny and Hajjar, *De La Ilustración a La Restauración*, 390.

of adapting to the times a version of a corporatist doctrine of society. These socially oriented Catholics prepared the way for Pope Leo XIII's encyclical *Rerum Novarum*.[26]

Rerum Novarum addressed the convergence of challenges that presented themselves to the church from different directions, demanding a pronouncement from Rome. It is bold in language and content and in approaching the realities that emerged out of the Industrial Revolution. It does not advocate for corporatism, but rather favors the formation of professional associations, which in the long run legitimized the formation of labor unions. It was well-received among Catholic groups and is recognized as the beginning of the church's social doctrine, though it did not have much impact on the working class at the time since it had already been organized for half a century by socialist leaders. It was, however, important in the Catholic environment because it called for an end to nostalgically dreaming of an order that no longer existed and for recognition of the dignity of workers. It acknowledged the working class as part of the framework of existing institutions, including trade unions, which the pope explicitly recognized. This implied a subtle call to leave behind corporatist proposals and opened the way to new forms of organizing workers, forms that would soon take shape in Christian democracy. Although it did not directly impact workers who were already radicalized by socialist or anarchist ideals, it greatly impacted many other working people and Catholic societies. For the first time a worldwide moral authority like the papacy had solemnly declared the rights of workers and repudiated the injustices committed against workers by the liberal system. Nevertheless, although many nineteenth-century thinkers and Leo XIII's encyclical at the end of the century had recognized the rights of workers and denounced injustice, neither placed in the hands of the poor the task of social transformation or evangelization—that great shift came in the twentieth century.

The Twentieth-Century Shift Toward the Laity

As we have seen, the influence of the laity in ecclesial organizations increased during the nineteenth century. In the twentieth century, this ongoing process was consolidated in Catholic Action (1922). This

26 De Bertier de Sauvigny and Hajjar, *De La Ilustración a La Restauración*, 152.

organization made it possible for the laity to be part of the hierarchical apostolate. Through Catholic Action, the laity received a mandate that linked them to the pastoral action of the bishops as an integral part of their pastoral work. For Pius XI (r. 1922–1939), the great challenge was to train the laity to perform their own irreplaceable role in the church and in society. Because of Catholic Action, Pius XI no longer saw them as an adjunct to his pastoral work, as did the previous pope. He valued the particular function of the laity in mass organizations, which involved acting in diverse spaces in social and political life to promote the re-Christianization of the norms of private, public, national, and international life. Pius XI gave his full support to Catholic Action, including providing it with a theological and doctrinal basis, and guaranteed its institutional presence throughout the world by means of numerous agreements and concordats. Catholic Action offered diverse proposals and many of the old associations and undertakings were integrated into Catholic Action as auxiliary projects. The heart of the new organization lay in the formation of groups in all the parishes that included men, women, and youth of both sexes. Although it integrated laity from various sectors of society, its pastoral objectives were not centered on the poor. The parish-based Catholic Action organizations were coordinated at the diocesan level and these, in turn, at the national and international level. Each country adapted the model according to its own needs.

Something different occurred in the Belgian movement called the Young Christian Workers (YCW), which provided the impetus for "specialized" Catholic Action (Catholic Action groups focused on a particular profession or status in society). This modality grouped members of determinate social status: workers (YCW), high school and college students (YCS—Young Christian Students), agricultural workers (YCP—Young Christian Peasants), and workers with independent means or in banking or business offices (Young Christian Independent Workers). The work of these youth-based movements was then continued by adult organizations. The movement began in the First World War among young female workers in a parish in Brussels, where Joseph Cardijn (1882–1967) was the parish priest. Later it spread to boys and developed into other movements. During the interwar period, Cardijn came to the US and Canada, and in both countries the Fathers of the Holy Cross gave him a great boost. During the Second World War, these movements were destroyed in Europe and did not return until the end of the conflict. However, the methodological experience of the YCW subsisted in North America during the war, mainly in Quebec, and from there it spread to South America.[27]

It is interesting to note that Cardijn, the great driving force of the YCW and of specialization in Catholic Action, put the process of evangelization in the hands of the workers. His classic motto, "By them, between themselves, and for themselves" was adopted by all the specialized Catholic Action communities, as was the working methodology of the grassroots groups within specialized Catholic Action, which were no longer organized in the parish but rather in the environment of the militants. This methodology for the weekly meetings of the grassroots communities was called "Revision of Life," and it focuses on the militants' social milieu, in which the youth who shared a life of work and study faced social reality. They observed the common challenges facing the group and the daily realities of every kind that presented themselves. They then analyzed them in light of the church's social doctrine and, even more so, the scriptures, in order to discern how God was speaking in that moment and historical context. Finally, they determined how they should act in order to be faithful to the path proposed by Jesus. Those three moments of the methodology of the Revision of Life—"See-Judge-Act"—had a great impact on the communities and on the church. It is the methodological foundation of the church's approach, both during and after the Second Vatican Council, to discerning the will of God and understanding of how Christians should live the experience of his love in a concrete historical moment.

In the 1950s and '60s the weekly meetings of the students', workers', and peasants' grassroots communities, using the Revision of Life methodology, were complemented by other efforts, including survey campaigns (to learn directly about the social reality in which they had to act and the challenges it presented) and courses in biblical and theological formation and on the history of the church. This education served to prepare the laity to discern the voice of God in the events

27 Ana María Bidegain, "From Catholic Action to Liberation Theology: The Historical Process of the Laity in the Twentieth Century," Kellogg Institute Working Paper 048, University of Notre Dame, Notre Dame, Ind., 1985, https://kellogg.nd.edu/documents/1242.

they were living and to properly choose how to act. There was no lack of courses in the sociopolitical analysis of reality. Spiritual retreats and weekly celebrations of the Eucharist, which brought together the whole movement at the local level, were part of this great outpouring of lay spirituality. Diocesan, national, and international meetings and congresses of the laity organized by these movements were spaces of education, reflection, and decision-making. What was essential in this pedagogical effort of specialized Catholic Action was the education of people who, while living Christian values, would become subjects of their own history and help to transform it so that the love of God could be lived fully. This great mobilization of the laity was a precursor to the ecclesial changes proposed by the Second Vatican Council.

Also foreshadowing the Second Vatican Council, it is important to mention a few transformations in the life of the French church. The changes were exemplified by the creation in 1941 of the Mission of France, a response to the conclusions of the sociologist Le Bras that there had been an "apostasy of the masses." The publication by two priests linked to the YCW of the book *France pays de mission?* shocked the Catholic community in France and raised the need to change pastoral methods. It is in this context that the movement of the "worker priests" was born. These priests were supported by Cardinal Suhard and, theologically, by the work of M.D. Chenu.[28] In 1942 the Dominicans, headed by Louis Lebret, created the Economy and Humanism movement in France, which later spread to many Latin American countries. In 1958, Lebret founded the International Center for Development and Civilizations, a research and training institute dedicated to the problems of development in what were then called the countries of the third world. The work of this organization helped Catholics to understand why two-thirds of the world faced poverty and the other third was the site of such concentrated wealth, both of which had to do with the phenomenon of colonialism after the Second World War. The Center's studies on this topic contributed critical material to Paul VI's encyclical *Populorum Progressio*.

Pius XII called on the rich churches to support the churches with fewer material and intellectual resources. Important financial aid agencies were created to support diverse projects in the dioceses of the

28 De Bertier de Sauvigny and Hajjar, *De La Ilustración a La Restauración*, 515.

poorer countries,[29] and Catholic universities in the wealthy countries provided scholarships for the education of clergy, priests, nuns, and laity, not only in theology and philosophy, but also in the social sciences and other disciplines, for the purpose of promoting development in the poorer countries. An example of the latter is the scholarship fund for the youth of developing countries wishing to study at the University of Louvain established by Hélène and Lucien Morren, who were active members of specialized Catholic Action from the Belgian bourgeoisie.

In 1954, the Roman bureaucracy intervened to suspend the involvements of the worker priests. This had a great impact in France and in the countries where the experience had been successful. The Roman Curia was concerned with the encounters that necessarily occurred between the priests and Marxists in the organizations and social movements that had been established in the neighborhoods to defend the rights of the working and impoverished populations. However, similar experiences emerged in other contexts, including in the initiatives led by Paul Gauthier (1914–2002). Gauthier, a theology professor at the Paris seminary, felt that "at least socially, he did not live with or for Jesus in his manner and way of living. The rupture between the world of the poor and the church, and the world of labor and the church, appeared to him to be a 'schism,' a break with the body of Christ because Jesus identified himself not only with the church, but also with the poor."[30] So that Gauthier could commune with the poor of the church, he obtained authorization from his bishop to assume the role of a worker. The Melkite archbishop of Galilee, Georges Hakim, invited him to come to his diocese. Gauthier accepted the invitation and created a fraternity of male and female companions of Jesus in Nazareth.[31] The experience of this theologian impacted many laypersons, priests, and nuns. His proposal to build a church on the side of the poor also had an impact

29 Consider Adveniat and Misereor in Germany, CCFD in France, and Entre-aide et Fraternité in Belgium, among others.

30 Paul Gauthier, *Los Pobres, Jesús y la Iglesia* [The poor, Jesus, and the Church] (Barcelona: Estela, 1964), 35.

31 Enrique Dussel was one of the Latin Americans who lived as a worker with Gauthier. Following from the inspiration of Gauthier, which was renewed at the council and at the Medellín conference, in 1973 Dussel founded the Comisión para el Estudio de Historia de las Iglesias en América Latina y el Caribe (CEHILA) in order to write the history of the Latin American church from the perspective of the poor—in other words, to recover the prophetic history of Christianity in America.

in Latin America, where, in the sixties, many Christians from more privileged sectors of society went to live in the poorer neighborhoods. Many European and North American priests trained in this new pastoral perspective traveled to Latin America as missionaries, seminary professors, and leaders of parishes in the urban peripheries or remote rural places.

In January of 1959, John XXIII called for the celebration of an ecumenical council, a surprising announcement given the difficulties that previous pontiffs had had in organizing one and the efforts of the Roman Curia to control the life of the church from its fundamentalist, conservative perspective.[32] In a discourse prior to the opening of the council, on September 11, 1962, John XXII said, "For underdeveloped countries, the Church presents itself as it is and how it wants to be: the church of all and particularly *the church of the poor.*"[33]

We have seen that certain sectors of the church were already prepared to embrace the model of the church John XXIII called "the church of the poor." Although the points proposed for consideration by the council fathers for the preparation and first sessions of the council initially went in another direction, the bishops and their advisers were able to influence the proposed topics in order to broaden the basis of discussion. This allowed novel ways of discussing themes like poverty. There are two related aspects to this discussion about the church of the poor: that of the poverty that should be practiced by the church and the attention and service that it should give to the poor. *Lumen Gentium* (para. 8) and *Ad Gentes* (para. 5) are often cited as the council's explicit references to the church of the poor, but Planellas has emphasized the rich presence of the subject in several of the council documents.[34]

To understand what happened at the council concerning this topic, we must take into account the texts that emerged from it and the processes that generated these texts, including the discussions of the council fathers and their theologian advisors. During the first session in October 1962, at the request of Father Gauthier, council representatives met at the Belgian Pontifical College in Rome with an informal

32 De Bertier de Sauvigny and Hajjar, *De La Ilustración a La Restauración*, 553–55.

33 John XXIII, "Mensaje radiodifundido" [Broadcast message], November 9, 1962, cited in J. I. Planellas, *La Iglesia de los pobres en el Concilio Vaticano II* [The Church of the poor in the Second Vatican Council] (Barcelona: Herder, 2014), e-book, chap. 1.

34 Planellas, *La Iglesia de los pobres*, chap 3.

group of bishops and theologian advisors, with the idea of continuing to debate John XXIII's proposed concept of a church of the poor. The group in attendance was comprised of persons from various regions of the world, but no one from the Roman Curia was present; in addition to attending council sessions, the members of the Curia were required to attend to their daily responsibilities, while outsiders were fully available. This group, which grew in number during the initial sessions of the council, managed to enact several proposals. Cardinal Lercaro, who was considered the most important council father on the subject of poverty, was represented by his advisor, the theologian Giuseppe Dossetti. There were various Latin Americans, including bishops Manuel Larraín from Chile and Dom Hélder Câmara from Brazil, then the president and vice president of CELAM, respectively. In November 1965, a group of forty bishops met, among them many Latin Americans, to celebrate the Eucharist in the Catacombs of Domitilla. At the end of the meeting, they signed the Pact of the Catacombs, in which they committed themselves to adopting a humble life stripped of possessions after they returned to their dioceses and a new pastoral attitude toward the poor and workers.[35]

The theological concept of the church of the poor was taken up in Latin America in the great conferences of Medellín (1968) and Puebla (1979), both of which have been extensively studied[36] and whose ideas have been extensively developed by Latin American theology.[37] The

---

35 The Pact of Catacombs was signed in Rome in 1965 by a group of bishops who attended the Second Vatican Council. See Xabier Pikaza and José Antunes da Silva, eds., *El pacto de las Catacumbas: la misión de los pobres en la Iglesia* [The pact of the catacombs: The mission of the poor in the church] (Estella, Navarre: Verbo Divino, 2015), esp. part 1, http://www.verbodivino.es/hojear/4209/el-pacto-de-las-catacumbas.pdf. See also the works of J. I. Planellas, including *La Iglesia de los pobres*, chap. 7, and Óscar Beozzo, *Pacto das Catacumbas. Por Uma Igreja Servidora e Pobre* [The covenant of the catacombs: A serving and poor church] (Sao Paulo: CESEP, 2015).

36 With respect to Medellín, see Silvia Scatena, *In Populo Pauperum: la Chiesa Latinoamericana dal Concilio a Medellín (1962–1968)* [In populo pauperum: The Latin American church from the council to Medellín (1962–1968)] (Bologna: Il Mulino, 2008). Regarding Puebla, see Alberto Methol Ferré, *Puebla: Proceso y Tensiones* (Buenos Aires: Documenta, 1979), http://www.metholferre.com/obras/libros/capitulos.php?id=8.

37 The pioneering work of Gustavo Gutiérrez, *Teología de la Liberación: Perspectivas* (Salmanca: Sígueme, 1971), is widely known. His many works undoubtedly deepened the understanding of the concept. From the same period, the works of Juan Luis

reception of the concept was not only theoretical, but also experiential. In part, the effectiveness of this reception was made possible by the impacts that ecclesial movements, specialized Catholic Action, and others described above had in Latin America, and by the pressing realities of the poor masses of the continent, a constant and visible challenge for Christian ethics. These realities were without doubt decisive for the enthusiastic acceptance of the council's perspective among the Latin American people of God. It is the case, however, that the local churches of Latin America that became most committed to renewal were also those that suffered from the highest level of repression. We believe that this fact has not been recovered by the historiography in all its depth and richness.

In the decade of the seventies, many young couples educated in the Juventud Universitaria Católica (Catholic University Youth) and other ecclesial movements, decided to live in impoverished neighborhoods with and like the poor. Many priests and religious also asked to be sent to these neighborhoods. These pastoral projects of insertion counted on the support of those bishops who, upon returning from the council, accepted the challenge of living in a modest way, selling their episcopal palaces in order to finance projects to benefit the poor and moving into humble homes in the periphery.[38] Areas of urban misery continued to grow with the overcrowding of peasants pushed to move to cities by modernization and agrarian transformation. They lived in precarious housing and founded new parishes, often accompanied by lay and religious communities. Placed in the daily lives of poor neighborhoods, militant Catholics and pastoral workers focused on the formation of social movements and the empowerment of citizens in their struggle for fundamental rights: work, housing, education, health, transportation, and all types of public services.[39] In many cases,

Segundo, especially the five-volume *Teología abierta para el laicado adulto* (Buenos Aires: Lohlé, 1968–72), and those of Lucio Gera and Juan Carlos Scannone, developed the *teología del pueblo* and deepened the scope of the "preferential option for the poor," and most recently, "the preferential option for the excluded."

38 Beozzo, *El Pacto de las catacumbas*, sec. 2.

39 I could cite to many such cases and experiences from my personal experience, but I believe it is important to note that when Gutiérrez refers to "men and women" in the first paragraph of the introduction to *Teología de la Liberación*, he is specifically referring to the specialized Catholic Action of Latin America.

this work of social development became associated with revolutionary political projects and groups.[40]

The decisions of female religious communities to go to live among the poor in both urban and rural areas is noteworthy, especially in light of their widespread presence and continuity. The discernment of many of these women, performed in light of the conciliar document *Perfecta Caritatis* and the Gospel, involved a profound questioning of the social meaning of their institutional missions, which in many cases were at the service of the privileged classes. For this reason, many sisters experienced a Copernican turn, choosing to leave their rich institutions so they could live among the poor in neighborhoods devoid of public services. They would sustain themselves with wages paid to them as workers, peasants, rural teachers, and nurses, often serving in small health clinics. Their choice was often not based on their love of poverty or asceticism as a means of personal sanctification, but rather on solidarity. They made common cause with their neighbors, protesting against social injustice. They also supported community organizing so that their neighbors could leave behind the experience of social, political, cultural, and religious marginalization. Accompanying the decision to insert themselves into the lives of the poor was their support for pastoral work and the mission of the church, as requested by the bishops at the council and at Medellín. Pastorally, the sisters' proximity to the poor facilitated their task of bringing them the Good News and changed their way of speaking about the love of God. The most important pastoral task of these religious women was to establish and accompany the basic ecclesial communities. They worked to prepare these communities to live their experience of faith and to celebrate the presence of God while continuing to struggle for the rights that were being denied them.[41]

Those who built the church of the poor went from making the poor the center of their works of compassion to changing them into subjects

40 See the testimony of Solange Silvany, Salvador de Bahía, Brazil, July 5, 1996, in Ana María Bidegain, *Participación y Protagonismo de las Mujeres en la Historia del Catolicismo Latinoamericano* [Participation and leadership of women in the history of Latin American Catholicism] (Buenos Aires: San Benito, 2009), 123–38.

41 Ana María Bidegain, "Una historia silenciada, no reconocida, ignorada, ocultada, invisibilizada: La vida religiosa femenina en la historia brasileña e hispanoamericana" [A silenced, unrecognized, ignored, hidden, and invisible history: The female religious life in Brazilian and Hispano-American history], *Revista de Estudos da Religião (REVER)* 14, no. 2 (July–Dec. 2014): 13–73.

of social transformation, out of love and fidelity to the message of the Gospel, empowering them to become agents of their own historical project. Although the path was indicated by the council and the episcopal conferences, it was not well-received by many sectors among the powerful. They perceived the new pastoral experiences, which issued in aspirations for popular liberation, as antagonistic to the systems in which their privileges had been established. They made the church of the poor into a target of accusations and persecutions that often ended in the exile, prison, torture, and martyrdom of many of them. Great episcopal figures who had participated in the council or had signed the Pact of the Catacombs also suffered repression and even martyrdom, like Mons. Angelelli of Argentina, or exile, like Mons. Mendiharat of Uruguay. Unfortunately, ecclesial authorities defending a conservative model of the church often consented to these abuses. In other cases, from their positions of power, they repressed the experiences of those building the church of the poor.[42]

The coordinated condemnations put forth by the more conservative currents of Christianity and the reactionary oligarchs affected not only the enormous, varied, and widespread popular movements of the followers of Jesus. The very concept of the church of the poor, often heralded in the sixties and seventies, was repressed. In the eighties, it was often removed from theological, historical, and social science literature. It was seen as an unjustified criticism of the churches of the rich countries simply because they were bourgeois and established and because it was identified with liberation theology. Forms of theology that were supported by certain European and Latin American authors were relegated to the dustbin of history by many commentators in the US.

However, the church of the poor, under the leadership of Mons. Proaño in Ecuador, Mons. Bogarín in Paraguay, and Mons. Méndez Arceo in México, has been resilient, maintaining its vitality in many corners of the American continents. Today it receives Pope Francis with rejoicing. The trust that poor communities have in his message and the joy they show in receiving him, seeing that finally a pope came to visit in order to place himself by their side, is owed to their collective memory of the prophetic history of the church of the poor.

42 Sonia M. Scheuren Acevedo, "The Opposition to Latin American Liberation Theology and the Transformation of Christianity, 1960–1990" (master's thesis, Florida International University, 2016), https://digitalcommons.fiu.edu/etd/2454.

CHAPTER 5

POPE FRANCIS AND POPULAR MOVEMENTS IN LATIN AMERICA

Paulo Fernando Carneiro de Andrade

THE PASTORAL AND SOCIAL THEOLOGY of Latin America that was constituted on the basis of the Second General Conference of the Latin American Episcopate at Medellín, Colombia in 1968 and its gospel-based preferential option for the poor have as one of their central features the recognition and promotion of the poor as both ecclesial and social subjects. In particular, the Argentine current of liberation theology known as the "theology of the people" has emphasized the irreplaceable transformative social role of the poor when they are organized into popular movements.[1] These movements can promote the genuine transformation of social and economic structures. They belong to civil society and not to the structures of the state. They are comprised of people from the base of society, to which the movements give a voice and a force of action capable of leaving a decisive mark on the political sphere. The popular movements neither replace nor cancel out political parties. The movements are not an alternative to the parties, but are indispensable to democratic states; in fact, without them one cannot even conceive of a genuine representative democracy. Moreover, their impairment or destruction as is proposed today by diverse forms of populism leads inevitably to authoritarianism, as we can verify today in many countries.[2] The popular movements are

1 See Juan Carlos Scannone, *Theology of the People: The Pastoral and Theological Roots of Pope Francis* (New York: Paulist Press, 2021) and Emilce Cuda, *Para leer a Francisco: Teología, etica, y política* (Buenos Aires: Manantial, 2016), 155–214.

2 See Paolo Graziano, *Neopopulismi: Perché sono destinati a durare* (Bologna: Il Mulino, 2018), 45–85.

necessary for contemporary democracy, ensuring that the political activity of parties does not become something absolute, the sole form of politics, prone to denouncing and alienating a great part of the population, above all the popular sectors. They allow for just decision-making and constructing a more just and egalitarian society. Without the popular movements, politics tends to sclerosis, bureaucratization, and a lack of power to transform society—it is reduced to an instrument of domination and of maintenance of the status quo. For these reasons, the church in Latin America has always promoted a sustained engagement of the laity in popular movements, in order to empower the poor and marginalized sectors and to bring about social justice and the construction of a more just and egalitarian society, as called for by the church's social teaching. Pope Francis's high esteem for the popular movements originated in this context.[3]

Pope Francis Encounters the Popular Movements in Latin America

While visiting Ecuador, Bolivia, and Paraguay from July 5 to July 13, 2015, Pope Francis attended the Second World Meeting of Popular Movements, which was held on July 9 in Santa Cruz de la Sierra, Bolivia. The pope also attended the first meeting, which was held on October 28, 2014 in Rome. While the first meeting had 150 participants, the second gathered approximately 1,500 from every corner of the globe, including 600 Bolivians. Both meetings were organized by a group of popular organizations that met at the invitation of the

3 On this point, Austen Ivereigh writes:

> Francis wants the workers to organize for change, to band together against the new harsh winds of the global economy: "only by joining forces can we say 'no' to the unfairness which generates violence," he tells them. The following month in Bolivia he would give his second rousing speech to the "popular movements," mobilizing them in favor of another kind of globalized modernity, one that didn't make shareholder profit the main criterion of economic organization, but the right of all to land, labor, and lodging. When Francis spoke like this he was called Marxist, but it was an old call, repeated by popes across the twentieth century, for the markets to work for the many, not the few, the kind of thing President Juan D. Perón tried to create in Francis's childhood Argentina, or Franklin D. Roosevelt in the United States. *Wounded Shepherd: Pope Francis and His Struggle to Convert the Catholic Church* (New York: Henry Holt, 2019), 11.

Pontifical Council for Justice and Peace.[4] The goal was to provide an alternative to a globalization that excludes, which is a key theme in Francis's social thought.[5] Bolivia was chosen to host this second meeting because of the high level of organization of the popular movements in that country.

The pope's message at the second meeting expressed a deep sense of social Christianity in line with the address he gave at the first meeting in Rome, but also elaborated issues he had previously touched upon in the apostolic exhortation *Evangelii Gaudium* and in the encyclical letter *Laudato Si'* that were particularly relevant for the Americas. According to Sergio Rubin, the Argentinian journalist and biographer of Pope Francis, this was the most pointed social message he had given up to that time.[6]

Francis's message at the Second World Meeting of Popular Movements thus marked an important step forward in the development of Catholic social teaching, a tradition that dates back to Leo XIII's encyclical letter *Rerum Novarum* (1891). Pope Francis focused on a new strand in this tradition using a new interpretive lens. He highlighted a new form of criticism of the current forms of globalized capitalism. *Laudato Si'* inaugurated a third generation in the social doctrine of the church, emphasizing the close relationship between social and environmental issues and the poor as subjects in a new world. His message in Bolivia not only confirmed this emphasis, but also highlighted that the popular movements have a major role to play in the political life of the human family.

Land, Lodging, and Labor

Pope Francis's message in the first meeting stressed the importance of popular movements and their struggles and emphasized three

4 "What is WMPM?" Encuentro Mundial de Movimientos Populares website, http://movimientospopulares.org/quienes-somos/ (accessed July 25, 2016).

5 "What is WMPM?"

6 Fabiano Maisonnave, "Para biógrafo, fala do papa é a mais dura em teor social" [According to his biographer, the speech of the pope hits the hardest in its social teaching], *Folha de São Paulo* online, July 9, 2015, https://www1.folha.uol.com.br/mundo/2015/07/1653978-para-biografo-fala-do-papa-e-a-mais-dura-em-teor-social.shtml.

pillars that were to become the focus of his reflections in the second meeting: land, lodging, and labor. At the first meeting, Francis said, "I accompany you wholeheartedly on this journey. From our hearts let us say together: No family without housing, no farmworker without land, no worker without rights, no one without the dignity that work provides."[7]

According to Pope Francis, these three issues are at the heart of all of the major social and environmental problems of our time. The right to a piece of land on which one can work is based on the biblical and patristic principle of the universal destination of goods:

> At the beginning of creation, God created man and woman, stewards of his work, mandating them *to till and to keep it* (cf. Gn 2:15). I notice dozens of farmworkers (*campesinos*) here, and I want to congratulate you for caring for the land, for cultivating it and for doing so in community. The elimination of so many brothers and sisters *campesinos* worries me, and it is not because of wars or natural disasters that they are uprooted. Land and water grabbing, deforestation, unsuitable pesticides are some of the evils which uproot people from their native land. This wretched separation is not only physical but existential and spiritual as well because there is a relationship with the land, such that rural communities and their special way of life are being put at flagrant risk of decline and even of extinction. The other dimension of this already global process is hunger. When financial speculation manipulates the price of food, treating it as just another commodity, millions of people suffer and die from hunger. At the same time, tons of food are thrown away. This constitutes a genuine scandal. Hunger is criminal, food is an inalienable right. I know that some of you are calling for agrarian reform in order to solve some of these problems, and let me tell you that in some countries—and here I cite the *Compendium*

7 *Address of Pope Francis to the Participants in the World Meeting of Popular Movements*, October 28, 2014. All documents published by the Vatican, including this one and many others cited below may be found at the vatican.va website.

> *of the Social Doctrine of the Church*—"agrarian reform is, besides a political necessity, a moral obligation."[8]

Thus, the right to land and the prohibition against the wanton destruction of the environment are closely interrelated.

With reference to lodging, the pope emphasized in his first message the right of every family to housing and access to decent, socially and environmentally fit infrastructure. Exclusion and gentrification are outrageous phenomena:

> We live nowadays in immense cities that show off proudly, even arrogantly, how modern they are. But while they offer well-being and innumerable pleasures for a happy minority, housing is denied to thousands of our neighbours, our brothers and sisters including children, who are called elegant names such as "street people" or "without fixed abode" or "urban camper." Isn't it curious how euphemisms abound in the world of injustices! A person, a segregated person, a person set apart, a person who suffers misery or hunger: such a one is "urban camper." It is an elegant expression, isn't it? You should be on the lookout—I might be wrong in some cases; but in general, what lurks behind each euphemism is a crime.[9]

In noting the irony of the term "urban camper," the Holy Father uses the humorous, everyday language of the people to level a stinging social criticism of the forces that degrade the conditions of workers in cities. The euphemisms on people's lips conceal structural injustices that the subway rider and *porteño* (meaning a resident of Buenos Aires) pope wishes to bring to the light of day. With respect to labor, the pope stated in the first meeting of the popular movements that

> there is no worse material poverty—I really must stress this—there is no worse material poverty than the poverty which does not allow people to earn their bread, which deprives

8 *Address of Pope Francis to the World Meeting of Popular Movements.*

9 *Address of Pope Francis to the World Meeting of Popular Movements.*

> them of the dignity of work. But youth unemployment, informality [*sic*] or underground work, and the lack of labor rights are not inevitable. These are the result of an underlying social choice in favour of an economic system that puts profit above man. If economic profit takes precedence over the individual and over humanity, we find a throw-away culture at work that considers humanity in itself, human beings, as a consumer good, which can be used and then thrown away.[10]

Therefore, according to the pope, the phenomenon of labor exploitation takes on a new dimension: that of exclusion. Not only does labor allow someone to earn a living, but it is above all the normal way people achieve self-fulfillment. As had already been said by Pope Saint John Paul II, it is through work that human beings find purpose, thus becoming subjects in the world.[11] In his address, Pope Francis stated that millions of people today have no access to work and for this reason are disfigured in their humanity. They are discarded by an idolatrous economic system that is not centered around the human being, but rather around the god of money. In the name of higher profits, lives are sacrificed at the altar of this false god, creating unbridled consumerism and destroying nature.

An Economy That Kills and Excludes People and Destroys Mother Earth

In his message in Bolivia, about one-and-a-half months after the release of *Laudato Si'*, the pope went further. The current globalized economic system is idolatrous because it imposes a social principle of profit at all costs, sacralizing capital and treating it as if it were a god. This situation is intolerable and demands a real, structural change, and this is an urgent task:

> In your letters and in our meetings, you have mentioned the many forms of exclusion and injustice which you experience in the workplace, in neighbourhoods and throughout the

10 *Address of Pope Francis to the World Meeting of Popular Movements.*

11 John Paul II, Encyclical Letter *Laborem Exercens* (September 14, 1981), 5–6.

> land. They are many and diverse, just as many and diverse are the ways in which you confront them. Yet there is an invisible thread joining every one of the forms of exclusion. These are not isolated issues. Can we recognize that invisible thread which links them? I wonder whether we can see that those destructive realities are part of a system which has become global. Do we realize that that system has imposed the mentality of profit at any price, with no concern for social exclusion or the destruction of nature?
>
> If such is the case, I would insist, let us not be afraid to say it: we want change, real change, structural change. This system is by now intolerable: farmworkers find it intolerable, laborers find it intolerable, communities find it intolerable, peoples find it intolerable . . . The earth itself—our sister, Mother Earth, as Saint Francis would say—also finds it intolerable.[12]

The pope clearly states that this idolatrous economy kills, excludes people, and destroys the Earth: "Human beings and nature must not be at the service of money. Let us say NO to an economy of exclusion and inequality, where money rules, rather than service. That economy kills. That economy excludes. That economy destroys Mother Earth."[13]

Despite the fact that this economic system has reached a planetary dimension, we can find an alternative to it. The purpose of an economy should not be to promote accumulation and concentration of wealth, nor should it be reduced to the mere securing of a decent livelihood. The economy should guarantee that every human being will be given land, lodging and labor, but also more:

> The economy should not be a mechanism for accumulating goods, but rather the proper administration of our common home. This entails a commitment to care for that home and to the fitting distribution of its goods among all. It is not only about ensuring a supply of food or "decent sustenance." Nor,

---

12 Francis, *Address of the Holy Father at the Second World Meeting of Popular Movements in Santa Cruz, Bolivia*, July 9, 2015, no. 1.

13 *Address at the Second World Meeting of Popular Movements*, 3.1.

> although this is already a great step forward, is it to guarantee the three "L's" of land, lodging and labor for which you are working. A truly communitarian economy, one might say an economy of Christian inspiration, must ensure peoples' dignity and their "general, temporal welfare and prosperity." (Pope John XXIII spoke this last phrase fifty years ago, and Jesus says in the Gospel that whoever freely offers a glass of water to one who is thirsty will be remembered in the Kingdom of Heaven.) All of this includes the three "L's," but also access to education, health care, new technologies, artistic and cultural manifestations, communications, sports and recreation. A just economy must create the conditions for everyone to be able to enjoy a childhood without want, to develop their talents when young, to work with full rights during their active years and to enjoy a dignified retirement as they grow older. It is an economy where human beings, in harmony with nature, structure the entire system of production and distribution in such a way that the abilities and needs of each individual find suitable expression in social life.[14]

In this context, the pope refers to an expression that is frequently used nowadays to define the plan of a future society in Latin America—"to live well": "You, and other peoples as well, sum up this desire in a simple and beautiful expression: 'to live well,' which is not the same as 'to have a good time.'"[15] This concept is characteristic of the indigenous peoples from Bolivia. Despite its ancient roots, "living well" expresses a new paradigm that has been absorbed by popular movements in Latin America, in opposition to the "better living" or "having a good time" that is promoted by modern Western culture. It is all about living together in community, without asymmetries of gender, social level, or ethnicity, following alternative practices with respect to the economy and the exercise of power, always seeking to be in harmony with nature and valuing what people are, rather than what they have. This new paradigm distinguishes development from economic

14 *Address at the Second World Meeting of Popular Movements*, 3.1.

15 *Address at the Second World Meeting of Popular Movements*, 3.1.

growth in an attempt to break down the logic of neoliberal capitalism that focuses on production, consumption, and finally, disposal. In some Latin American countries, including Bolivia and Ecuador, popular movements were successful in including the concept of "living well" in their national constitutions. By using this concept in his address, Francis put himself on the same wavelength as contemporary Latin American popular movements, thus strengthening them and validating their trajectories.

Another fundamental concept in the pope's message at the second meeting is that of "the greater country" (*La Patria Grande*). Although it also has ancient roots, this concept has become particularly important in the recent struggles of Latin American peoples. It means fighting for Latin American integration, rejecting colonialism, and establishing a libertarian Latin American identity. It was the title of an important book, *La Patria Grande*, which was published in 1922 by Manuel Ugarte and which has been celebrated by a number of left-wing political leaders in Latin America, including the former presidents Evo Morales (Bolivia), Hugo Chavez (Venezuela), Rafael Correa (Ecuador), and José Mujica (Uruguay). The concept is used to express unity in the struggle for the sovereignty of Latin American countries and those countries' joint construction of economic, social, and environmental structures that can replace neoliberal capitalism. The pope clearly expresses this paradigm:

> The peoples of Latin America fought to gain their political independence and for almost two centuries their history has been dramatic and filled with contradictions, as they have striven to achieve full independence.
>
> In recent years, after any number of misunderstandings, many Latin American countries have seen the growth of fraternity between their peoples. The governments of the region have pooled forces in order to ensure respect for the sovereignty of their own countries and the entire region, which our forebears so beautifully called the "greater country." I ask you, my brothers and sisters of the popular movements, to foster and increase this unity. It is necessary to maintain unity in the face of every effort to divide, if the region is to grow in peace and justice.

> Despite the progress made, there are factors which still threaten this equitable human development and restrict the sovereignty of the countries of the "greater country" and other areas of our planet. The new colonialism takes on different faces. At times it appears as the anonymous influence of mammon: corporations, loan agencies, certain "free trade" treaties, and the imposition of measures of "austerity" which always tighten the belt of workers and the poor. We, the bishops of Latin America, denounce this with utter clarity in the Aparecida Document, stating that "financial institutions and transnational companies are becoming stronger to the point that local economies are subordinated, especially weakening the local states, which seem ever more powerless to carry out development projects in the service of their populations." At other times, under the noble guise of battling corruption, the narcotics trade and terrorism—grave evils of our time which call for coordinated international action—we see states being saddled with measures which have little to do with the resolution of these problems and which not infrequently worsen matters.[16]

Neocolonialism is a tangible reality. The old colonial structures were not actually overcome: they took on new shapes during the twentieth and now in the twenty-first century, allowing powerful capitalist countries to continue to exploit and subdue Latin America. These new forms of domination are ideologically supported by, among other things, the monopolistic concentration of mass media, a strong feature in several Latin American countries: "Similarly, the monopolizing of the communications media, which would impose alienating examples of consumerism and a certain cultural uniformity, is another one of the forms taken by the new colonialism. It is ideological colonialism."[17]

Like nineteenth-century colonialism, neocolonialism denies poor countries the right to full development, generating more poverty, environmental destruction, and violence:

16 *Address at the Second World Meeting of Popular Movements*, 3.2.

17 *Address at the Second World Meeting of Popular Movements*, 3.2.

> Colonialism, both old and new, which reduces poor countries to mere providers of raw material and cheap labor, engenders violence, poverty, forced migrations and all the evils which go hand in hand with these, precisely because, by placing the periphery at the service of the center, it denies those countries the right to an integral development. That is inequality, brothers and sisters, and inequality generates a violence which no police, military, or intelligence resources can control.
>
> Let us say NO, then, to forms of colonialism old and new. Let us say YES to the encounter between peoples and cultures. Blessed are the peacemakers.[18]

The issue of uncontrollable violence caused by the prevailing economic system and its structures of domination and exclusion had already been addressed by Pope Francis in *Evangelii Gaudium*:

> Today in many places we hear a call for greater security. But until exclusion and inequality in society and between peoples are reversed, it will be impossible to eliminate violence. The poor and the poorer peoples are accused of violence, yet without equal opportunities the different forms of aggression and conflict will find a fertile terrain for growth and eventually explode. When a society—whether local, national or global—is willing to leave a part of itself on the fringes, no political programmes or resources spent on law enforcement or surveillance systems can indefinitely guarantee tranquillity. This is not the case simply because inequality provokes a violent reaction from those excluded from the system, but because the socioeconomic system is unjust at its root. Just as goodness tends to spread, the toleration of evil, which is injustice, tends to expand its baneful influence and quietly to undermine any political and social system, no matter how solid it may appear. If every action has its consequences, an evil embedded in the structures of a society has a constant potential for disintegration and death. It is evil crystallized

18 *Address at the Second World Meeting of Popular Movements*, 3.2.

> in unjust social structures, which cannot be the basis of hope for a better future. . . .
>
> Today's economic mechanisms promote inordinate consumption, yet it is evident that unbridled consumerism combined with inequality proves doubly damaging to the social fabric. Inequality eventually engenders a violence which recourse to arms cannot and never will be able to resolve. It serves only to offer false hopes to those clamouring for heightened security, even though nowadays we know that weapons and violence, rather than providing solutions, create new and more serious conflicts.[19]

It is clear to Pope Francis that present-day violence cannot be resolved without social and environmental justice and that repressing this violence will only engender more violence. The pope has repeatedly condemned the fact that we are living today a "piecemeal world war," a war that differs from the two great wars of the twentieth century:

> A word that . . . is often repeated is "insecurity." But the real word is "war." For some time we have been saying: "the world is fighting a war piecemeal." This is war. There was the war of '14, with its methods; then that of '39–'45, another great war in the world; and now there is this one. It is not perhaps so organic; organized, yes, but organic... I say... But it is war. This holy priest, who died in the very moment when he was offering prayer for the whole church, is one (person): but how many Christians, how many innocents, how many children... We think of Nigeria, for example. 'But that is Africa...' It is war. Let us not be afraid to say this truth: the world is at war, because it has lost peace.[20]

Interrupting this state of violence requires urgent and realistic changes that should be conceived of as a process and not as a rapid

19 Francis, Apostolic Exhortation *Evangelii Gaudium* (November 24, 2013), 59–60.

20 Francis, *Greeting of the Holy Father to Journalists on the Flight to Krakow*, July 27, 2016. The second and third ellipses are in the original.

transformation. The so-called "end of the great utopias"[21] cannot result in the passive acceptance of the existing unfair and destructive social, environmental, and economic systems as the only possible paradigm. This would be a refusal to believe that change is possible. The pope embraces a new paradigm involving a process that is essential to the success of contemporary popular movements:

> Here in Bolivia I have heard a phrase which I like: "process of change." Change seen not as something which will one day result from any one political decision or change in social structure. We know from painful experience that changes of structure which are not accompanied by a sincere conversion of mind and heart sooner or later end up in bureaucratization, corruption and failure. There must be a change of heart. That is why I like the image of a "process," processes, where the drive to sow, to water seeds which others will see sprout, replaces the ambition to occupy every available position of power and to see immediate results. The option is to bring about processes and not to occupy positions. Each of us is just one part of a complex and differentiated whole, interacting in time: peoples who struggle to find meaning, a destiny, and to live with dignity, to "live well," and in that sense, worthily.[22]

Popular Movements and the Poor as Social Subjects

One month before the opening of the Second Vatican Council, on September 11, 1962, John XXIII astonished the world and the church in a historical radio message with the following words: "Where the underdeveloped countries are concerned, the Church presents herself as she is. She wishes to be the Church of all, and especially the Church of the poor."[23] This speech definitively placed "the church of the poor" on the agenda of the twentieth-century church. In response, in

---

21 Immanuel Wallerstein, *Utopistics: Or, Historical Choices of the Twenty-First Century* (New York: New Press, 1998), 1–64.

22 *Address at the Second World Meeting of Popular Movements*, 2.

23 John XXIII, "Radio Address Concerning the Second Vatican Council," September 11, 1962, EWTN website, https://www.ewtn.com/catholicism/library/radio-address-concerning-the-second-vatican-council-7925

October 1962, a number of bishops from all over the world started a study group that soon came to be known as "the church of the poor" at the Belgian Pontifical College in Rome. The purpose of this group was to advocate for issues related to the poor being given a higher priority in the agendas of the church and the council. At the end of the council, this group of bishops wrote and signed a document called the Pact of the Catacombs, establishing a firm commitment to the cause of the poor.[24] This document was to a large extent incorporated into Document XIV of the Final Conclusions of the Medellín conference, which declares, among other things:

> We ought to sharpen the awareness of our duty of solidarity with the poor, to which charity leads us. This solidarity means that we make ours their problems and their struggles, that we know how to speak with them. This has to be concretized in criticism of injustice and oppression, in the struggle against the intolerable situation which a poor person often has to tolerate, in the willingness to dialogue with the groups responsible for that situation in order to make them understand their obligations. We express our desire to be very close always to those who work in the self-denying apostolate with the poor in order that they will always feel our encouragement and know that we will not listen to parties interested in distorting their work. Human advancement has to be the goal of our action on behalf of the poor man and it must be carried out in such a manner that we respect his personal dignity and teach him to help himself. With that end in mind we recognize the necessity of the rational structuring of all our pastoral action and the integration of all our efforts with those of other entities. . . . We wish our houses and style of life to be modest, our clothing simple, our works and institutions functional, without show or ostentation. We asked priests and faithful to treat us in conformity with our mission

24 See Xabier Pikaza and José Antunes da Silva, eds., *El Pacto de las Catacumbas: La Misión de los Pobres en la Iglesia* (Estella, Navarre: Verbo Divino, 2015).

> as fathers and pastors, for we desire to renounce honourable titles belonging to another era.[25]

Championed by Latin American theology and reaffirmed after Medellín by the subsequent conferences at Puebla, Santo Domingo, and Aparecida, the option for the poor has two central meanings. First, it involves switching sides; that is, siding with the poor and adopting their perspectives, joys, and sufferings. In fact, true solidarity can only exist if people interact with the poor and the excluded. Second, it requires acknowledging the poor as privileged social and ecclesial individuals, subjects not only of necessary changes to the unfair structures oppressing, excluding, and destroying them, but also of changes in the methodology of evangelization. Pastoral guidance should follow that enables them to act as actual subjects, instead of mere objects of charitable practices that very often perpetuate mechanisms of domination.

From the beginning, Pope Francis has shown himself to be deeply aligned with the Latin American option for the poor and its two central meanings. This option does not arise from a simple theoretical or bureaucratic identification, but rather, through actual knowledge of the poor and the hardships they face:

> As members of popular movements, you carry out your work inspired by fraternal love, which you show in opposing social injustice. When we look into the eyes of the suffering, when we see the faces of the endangered campesino, the poor laborer, the downtrodden native, the homeless family, the persecuted migrant, the unemployed young person, the exploited child, the mother who lost her child in a shootout because the barrio was occupied by drug dealers, the father who lost his daughter to enslavement. . . when we think of all those names and faces, our hearts break because of so much sorrow and pain. And we are deeply moved, all of us. . . . We are moved because "we have seen and heard" not a cold

25 "Medellín, Columbia: II Conferencia General del Episcopado Latinoamericano 1968: Document XIV, The Poverty of the Church," in *Las Cinco Conferencias Generales del Episcopado Latinoamericano* (Paulinas: Bogotá, 2014), 195–205.

> statistic but the pain of a suffering humanity, our own pain, our own flesh. This is something quite different than abstract theorizing or eloquent indignation. It moves us; it makes us attentive to others in an effort to move forward together. That emotion which turns into community action is not something which can be understood by reason alone: it has a surplus of meaning which only peoples understand, and it gives a special feel to genuine popular movements.
>
> Each day you are caught up in the storms of people's lives. You have told me about their causes, you have shared your own struggles with me, ever since I was in Buenos Aires, and I thank you for that. You, dear brothers and sisters, often work on little things, in local situations, amid forms of injustice which you do not simply accept but actively resist, standing up to an idolatrous system which excludes, debases and kills. I have seen you work tirelessly for the soil and crops of campesinos, for their lands and communities, for a more dignified local economy, for the urbanization of their homes and settlements; you have helped them build their own homes and develop neighbourhood infrastructures. You have also promoted any number of community activities aimed at reaffirming so elementary and undeniably necessary a right as that of the three "L's": land, lodging and labor.[26]

The topic of the poor as subjects was highlighted in the pope's message delivered at the second meeting. When their lives are organized with the support and leavened by the wisdom of popular movements, the poor are enabled to be agents of necessary change:

> What can I do, as collector of paper, old clothes or used metal, a recycler, about all these problems if I barely make enough money to put food on the table? What can I do as a craftsman, a street vendor, a trucker, a downtrodden worker, if I don't even enjoy workers' rights? What can I do, a farmwife, a native woman, a fisher who can hardly fight the domination of the big corporations? What can I do from my little

26 *Address at the Second World Meeting of Popular Movements*, 2.

> home, my shanty, my hamlet, my settlement, when I daily meet with discrimination and marginalization? What can be done by those students, those young people, those activists, those missionaries who come to a neighbourhood with their hearts full of hopes and dreams, but without any real solution for their problems? They can do a lot. They really can. You, the lowly, the exploited, the poor and underprivileged, can do, and are doing, a lot. I would even say that the future of humanity is in great measure in your own hands, through your ability to organize and carry out creative alternatives, through your daily efforts to ensure the three "L's"—do you agree?—(labor, lodging, land) and through your proactive participation in the great processes of change on the national, regional and global levels. Don't lose heart![27]

At the end of the address, the pope emphatically repeated that the future of humanity lies in the hands of the poor: "The future of humanity does not lie solely in the hands of great leaders, the great powers and the elites. It is fundamentally in the hands of peoples and in their ability to organize. It is in their hands, which can guide with humility and conviction this process of change."[28]

Pope Francis had already cautioned in *Evangelii Gaudium* about attempts to tame the poor through initiatives aimed at preventing them from becoming subjects in history: "Some simply content themselves with blaming the poor and the poorer countries themselves for their troubles; indulging in unwarranted generalizations, they claim that the solution is an 'education' that would tranquilize them, making them tame and harmless."[29]

According to the pope, the poor who have been organized into popular movements have three urgent tasks: they must "put the economy at the service of peoples," "unite our peoples on the path of peace and justice," and "defend Mother Earth."[30] Popular movements should follow these common goals in the course of engaging in struggles around

27 *Address at the Second World Meeting of Popular Movements*, 1.

28 *Address at the Second World Meeting of Popular Movements*, 4.

29 Francis, *Evangelii Gaudium*, 60.

30 *Address at the Second World Meeting of Popular Movements*, 3.1–3.3.

specific topics, both local and national in scope. We have seen that the pope is concerned with both local and global issues, and while major concerns demand that the popular movements engage in international coordination, the globalization of an economic system that kills and excludes people and destroys the Earth requires both local and global solutions.

Finally, we should stress that Pope Francis believes that it is the duty of the church, given its mission, to cooperate with popular movements:

> The Church cannot and must not remain aloof from this process in her proclamation of the Gospel. Many priests and pastoral workers carry out an enormous work of accompanying and promoting the excluded throughout the world, alongside cooperatives, favouring businesses, providing housing, working generously in the fields of health, sports and education. I am convinced that respectful cooperation with the popular movements can revitalize these efforts and strengthen processes of change.[31]

The task of following popular movements is in profound harmony with the paradigm developed by Paul VI[32] in the apostolic letter *Octogesima Adveniens*[33] and with the traditions of the Latin American church. The fight for justice is part of evangelization. In light of the church's mission to evangelize, it is up to the church to support and follow popular movements instead of replacing them with something else or imposing itself on them. Walking side by side is mutually beneficial.

Conclusion: The Latest Statements on Economic Systems in Francis's Magisterium

Pope Francis's criticism of the reigning economic system in his address to the popular movements in Bolivia has been deepened in subsequent documents, speeches, and official pronouncements,

---

31 *Address at the Second World Meeting of Popular Movements*, 2.

32 See Paolo Fernando Andrade, "Um novo Paradigma na Doutrina Social da Igreja," *Revista Eclesiástica Brasileira* 79, no. 314 (Sept.–Dec. 2019): 615–36.

33 Paul VI, Encyclical Letter *Octogesima Adveniens* (May 14, 1971), 4.

especially in the document *Oeconomicae et Pecuniarie Quaestiones: Considerations for an Ethical Discernment Regarding Some Aspects of the Present Economic-Financial System*,[34] which was developed jointly by two important organs of the Holy See—the Congregation for the Doctrine of the Faith and the new Dicastery for the Promotion of Integral Human Development. It was published on January 6, 2018 after having received the approval of Pope Francis. A document of this sort about the current economic and financial system is of fundamental importance, for it expresses and deepens the new paradigm of the social doctrine of the church initiated under Francis's pontificate.[35] The words of Pope Francis directed to the popular movements acquire a doctrinal deepening in *OPQ*. The document is divided into three parts: an introduction, "Fundamental Considerations," and "Some Clarifications in Today's Context." Here we will focus on the introduction and the "Fundamental Considerations."

From a doctrinal point of view, the document highlights something that has always been very important in liberation theology and in Latin America more generally: the Good News of salvation revealed in Christ and for Christ does not speak merely to human persons but to the entirety of creation. In other words, God does not offer redemption to persons alone, but to all creatures and to the world and its social structures. The document affirms that "in the *fullness* of the good, which has its origin and consummation in God and is fully revealed in Jesus Christ, the head over all things (cf. Eph 1:10), lies the ultimate goal of every ecclesial activity. Such well-being flourishes as an anticipation

34 Congregation for the Doctrine of the Faith and Dicastery for the Promotion of Integral Human Development, *Oeconomicae et Pecuniarie Quaestiones: Considerations for an Ethical Discernment Regarding Some Aspects of the Present Economic-Financial System*, January 6, 2018, full text at Holy See Press Office Summary of Bulletin, May 17, 2018, https://press.vatican.va/content/salastampa/en/bollettino/pubblico/2018/05/17/180517a.html. Hereafter cited in text and notes as *OPQ*.

35 On this point, see also the speech of Pope Francis to those who participated in the international seminar titled, "The Changing Relationships between the Market, the State, and Civil Society." This seminar took place from October 19 to 21, 2017, under the auspices of the Pontifical Academy of Social Sciences and resulted in a two-volume publication, *Sociedad Civil y bien común: Hacia una nueva articulación del mercado, el estado y la sociedad civil*, ed. Juan Carlos Scannone (Córdoba, Argentina: Editorial de la Universidad Católica de Córdoba, 2018). The contributions to these volumes converge in large part with the content of *OPQ*. The pope's speech can be found in volume 1 at 13–15.

of the Kingdom of God, which the Church is called to proclaim and establish in every sphere of human enterprise."[36] Consequently, the document continues, "Love for society and commitment to the common good are eminent forms of a charity that affects not only relationships between individuals but also macro-relationships, social, economic and political ones."[37]

In this context, it lends precision to the matter to keep in mind a fundamental distinction that has always been present in Latin American theology and pastoral planning and has been adopted by Pope Francis: between social relationality (the relationship between individuals) and social relations (structural relations that are codified in laws, legal codes, and habits and sanctioned by the culture). The mission of the church cannot be reduced to religious affections and the conversion of souls. This mission includes by necessity promoting action that transforms social structures and social, economic, and financial relationships so that the world may be more just and conformed to the designs of the creator.

Today we live in a globalized economy. The concrete economy at its center is characterized by a hegemonic market that claims to be sovereign and rejects all forms of regulation, reducing individuals to consumers. The globalized economy is subordinated to financial capital and thus "it is impossible to ignore the fact that the financial industry, because of its pervasiveness and its inevitable capacity to condition and, in a certain sense, to dominate the real economy today, is a place where selfishness and the abuse of power have an enormous potential to harm the community."[38] Challenging the liberal and neoliberal vision, the document affirms clearly that markets are "not capable of governing themselves. In fact, the markets know neither how to make the assumptions that allow their smooth running (social coexistence, honesty, trust, safety and security, laws, and so on) nor how to correct those effects and forces that are harmful to human society (inequality, asymmetries, environmental damage, social insecurity, and fraud)."[39]

According to *OPQ*, we encounter in the actual market that governs our societies an inversion of the order of means and ends, whereby "work

---

36 *OPQ*, 2.

37 *OPQ*, 2.

38 *OPQ*, 14.

39 *OPQ*, 13.

as a good becomes an 'instrument,' and money an 'end.'"[40] This leads to a growing concentration of income and capital and the exclusion of broad sectors of the population, who are unemployed and deprived of decent labor, turning them into "the 'leftovers.'"[41] In continuity with the address that Pope Francis delivered in Bolivia to the popular movements, the document affirms that it is in this inversion of labor and capital that "the reckless and amoral 'culture of waste' finds a fertile ground."[42] The document affirms that this inversion is not in itself the product of a culture; rather, the economic reality produced by these heedless financial interests, in which a minority imposes this inversion on society, completes its task by normalizing the inversion and giving rise to a "culture of waste," a culture that considers it natural and necessary for the sake of social progress that a certain number of persons, who in reality occupy immense regions of the planet, are reduced to the status of "leftovers," deprived of all rights and of access to the most elementary necessities for their survival and dignity. This culture, which has its origin in a set of concrete economic practices and acts, reinforces and sustains this situation, sometimes unconsciously. Such a culture, like all cultures that reinforce or normalize exploitation, must be denounced and deconstructed. The concrete structures of our globalized economy produce a culture that promotes egoism and are for that reason (social) structures of sin. The mere goal of transforming the culture is not sufficient. Nor is it sufficient to transform interpersonal relations. Rather, it is necessary to go beyond these postures and to change the economic practices, social relations, and structures that lie at the root of these cultures, practices, and relations that are simultaneously their cause and result. According to *OPQ*, this new outlook derives from the mission of the church as a people of God and sacrament of salvation for humanity and the world, and thus, one can discern the ecclesial relevance of the teaching as well as its importance in helping the poor and marginalized organize themselves into popular movements.

On November 15, 2019, in an address at the XX World Congress of the International Association of Penal Law, Pope Francis returned to his criticisms of the contemporary social and economic systems

40 *OPQ*, 15.
41 *OPQ*, 15.
42 *OPQ*, 15.

that he advanced at the meeting with popular movements in Bolivia. In this address, the pope reaffirmed that in the contemporary context "the fragile, vulnerable person finds himself 'defenceless before the interests of a deified market, [interests] which become the only rule.' Today, some economic sectors exercise more power than the States themselves."[43] The pope also stated that "global financial capital is the source of serious crimes not only against property but also against people and the environment. It is organized crime that is responsible, among other things, for the overindebtedness of states and the plundering of the natural resources of our planet.[44]

In his recent contributions to the social magisterium, Francis is proposing a profound and radical form of critical thinking directed not at an abstract economic system, nor at an economic theory, but at a concrete economic system, the economy that truly rules today. This economy finds ideological justifications in certain philosophical and anthropological arguments that are in complete contradiction to the Catholic faith. The pope's criticisms of the concrete economic practices we see today focuses on the globalized economy's perverse structures. This economy, as he states, "kills, excludes, and destroys our Mother Earth."[45] The contemporary financial system that dominates the globalized economy participates in the "organized crime" that lies at the root of this economy's grave assaults against concrete persons, in particular against the poorest in society, against property, and against the environment. For Pope Francis, Christians have an obligation as part of their faith and the mission they received in baptism to fight to change economic structures in a profound way. For the pope, the popular movements are the best organizations in civil society to promote these changes.

---

43 *Address of Pope Francis to the Participants at the World Congress of the International Association of Penal Law*, November 15, 2019, no. 1 (citing *Evangelii Gaudium*, 56 and *Laudato Si'*, 56).

44 *Address to the World Congress of the International Association of Penal Law*, 2.

45 *Address at the Second World Meeting of Popular Movements*, 3.1.

CHAPTER 6

WHISPER TO THOSE IN DESPAIR

"The Best Wine Is Yet to Come"— Memory, Hope, and Resistance

Luis Herrera Rodríguez, SJ

FRANCIS BEGAN HIS 2015 visit to Ecuador with a celebration of the Eucharist for families. The Gospel chosen was that of the wedding at Cana, and the homily was centered on Mary's concern and appeal to Jesus because "there was no wine." There can be no celebration without joy, and wine is a sign of joy, and also of love, abundance, and messianic plenitude. In the context of this Gospel, Francis introduces one of the greatest concerns of his pontificate: the absence of "a wine" of shared love with the people who count for nothing in society, the insignificant and disposable ones like "abandoned single women," "adolescents and youth," and the "neglected elderly."[1] In the Gospel, the unexpected happens: the "sign" of Jesus. From the waters of the purification jars, new wine is born; according to the headwaiter, the best of wines. And that is the good news that the Gospel and Francis want to convey, even if everything says otherwise: "The best of wines is yet to be had, the most lovely, the most profound, and the most beautiful is yet to come"[2]—and the best wine is hope. That good news must be whispered to those in despair.

The story of the wedding at Cana appears once again in Francis's encounter with families in Cuba. There, a new element arises: memory. "In weddings, the past we inherit and the future that awaits us are

1 Francis, *Holy Mass: Homily of the Holy Father*, Guayaquil, Ecuador, July 6, 2015. All documents published by the Vatican, including this one and many others cited below, may be found at the vatican.va website.

2 *Holy Mass: Homily of the Holy Father*, Guayaquil, Ecuador.

always united. There is memory and hope."[3] There is *memory* for the parents because it is a privilege to see the product of their labor, of the years dedicated to the accompaniment of children as these children construct new lives; and there is *hope* in the young spouses because a new future is beginning in which "everything has the feel of a new house" (*todo tiene sabor a casa nueva*).[4] Francis concludes his words by alluding to the Eucharist as a memorial of the life of Jesus, a space where his presence is both the word and bread of life sustaining the family in the manner of Jesus's family—in faith, love, and hope.

Our intention in this chapter is to write about Francis's legacy in America with respect to memory and hope—expressions of the culture of encounter for those "that have remained without wine, those who only have dismay to drink"[5]—memory and hope that strengthen the ongoing active resistance against suffering and its structural causes.[6]

Grateful Memory and Resistance to Suffering

Angélica Mendoza de Ascarza, a woman of eighty-six years, called by all "Mama Angélica," is the public face of the relatives who disappeared during one of the most violent and degrading episodes in the republican history of Peru. Twenty years of internal conflict from 1980 to 2000 was triggered by the decision of the Communist Party of Peru (Sendero Luminoso) to begin an armed struggle against the Peruvian state, which launched "the history of a tragedy largely ignored in its most terrible aspects," but which was "at the same time, an exemplary proof of the resistance of human dignity in Peru."[7] About seventy thousand people were victims, and 75 percent of them spoke Quechua or other native languages as their mother tongue. By "victims," we

3 Francis, *Address of the Holy Father at the Meeting with Families at the Cathedral of Our Lady of the Assumption in Saantiago, Cuba*. September 22, 2015.

4 *Address at the Meeting with Families*, Santiago, Cuba.

5 *Holy Mass: Homily of the Holy Father*, Guayaquil, Ecuador.

6 I write this reflection having in mind the situation of the rural southern Andean Quechua population of Peru, with whom I have shared life and mission for twenty years, specifically in Quispicanchi, Cusco.

7 Hatun Willakuy, *Versión abreviada del Informe Final de la Comisión de la Verdad y Reconciliació* [Abbreviated version of the Final Report of the Truth and Reconciliation Commission] (Lima: Corporación Gráfica, 2004), back cover. See digital version at idehpucp.pucp.edu.pe/we-content/uploade/2012/11/hatun willakuy-cvr-espanol.pdf.

mean any person who suffered death, torture, rape, kidnapping, arbitrary detention, or enforced disappearance. At present, it is estimated that thirteen to fifteen thousand people remain missing. Arquímedes Ascarza Mendoza was nineteen years old when he was kidnapped on July 3, 1983, and, since then Mama Angélica has not stopped searching for her son. She said, "I have been to every place he could possibly be … We have all spent so many years searching and yet none of us have found our missing loved ones. We cannot forget them even as we grow old and die. How can we forget our sons, our husbands, our fathers? It's impossible."[8]

Two months after Arquímedes disappeared, Mama Angélica, along with five other women, founded the Asociación Nacional de Familiares de Secuestrados, Detenidos y Desaparecidos (ANFASEP) (the National Association of Relatives of those Kidnapped, Detained, and Disappeared). They managed to recruit eight hundred members. Presently, the Museum of Memory (*para que no se repita*, "so that it is not repeated") operates on the premises of ANFASEP in Ayacucho. A wooden cross has been placed in the central courtyard.

> The space is dedicated to the memory of the disappeared and killed in times of political violence. On the second floor there is a stylized representation of three extended hands that shows the relationship of missing family members to the ANFASEP partners. In the front of the space, there is a sanctuary with a small altar and a replica of the ANFASEP wooden cross, symbolizing its peaceful fight. Nearby there are small spaces embedded in the wall that can be used to commemorate the absent ones by lighting a candle.[9]

Mama Angélica, a woman of memory, hope, and resistance, is still looking for her son. "Many of our association's members are dying without ever having found out what happened, why their husbands

8 "Perú: Mamá Angélica, símbolo de lucha y fortaleza" [Peru: Mother Angélica, symbol of struggle and strength], Comité Internacional de la Cruz Roja website, March 4, 2016, https://www.icrc.org/es/document/peru-dia-mujer-mama-angelica-simbolo-lucha-fortaleza.

9 "Museo de la Memoria ANFASEP," Ayacucho Memoria website, http://ayacucho.memoria.website/espacios/museo-de-la-memoria-anfasep/ (accessed April 5, 2016).

and sons disappeared, why they were taken away. I will keep advocating for them for as long as I can. I want to ask the government the reason for all this suffering even today."[10] The report from the Truth and Reconciliation Commission (Comisión de la Verdad y Reconciliación) is not wrong to say that if those years of violence were among the most degrading in the history of republican Peru, they were also years of resistance on behalf of human dignity. Mama Angélica represents the two faces of this story: pain and resistance, but also memory and hope. Perhaps someone has whispered to her that the *best wine is yet to come.*

Transitional justice is an approach to applied justice in societies facing a necessary institutional reconstruction after intense periods of internal violence and systematic violations of human rights.[11] The principle guiding this type of justice is that every victim has a right to truth and reparation. One of the most useful tools of transitional justice is the public recovery of memory, for which "memory sites" are very important. We have already mentioned that a museum and a sanctuary of memory operate on the premises of ANFASEP. Let us now consider another memory site, the Ground Zero Memorial in New York, where Pope Francis delivered one of his most moving and striking speeches.

> The flowing water is also a symbol of our tears. Tears at so much devastation and ruin, past and present. This is a place where we shed tears, we weep out of a sense of helplessness in the face of injustice, murder, and the failure to settle conflicts through dialogue. Here we mourn the wrongful and senseless loss of innocent lives because of the inability to find solutions which respect the common good. This flowing water reminds us of yesterday's tears, but also of all the tears still being shed today.[12]

---

10 "Perú: Mamá Angélica, símbolo de lucha y fortaleza," Comité Internacional de la Cruz Roja website.

11 Cf. Gonzalo Gamio, *Tiempos de Memoria: Reflexiones sobre Derechos Humanos y Justicia Transicional* [Times of memory: Reflections on human rights and transitional justice] (Lima: CEP/IBC/IDEHPUCP, 2009). Cf. "Our Work," International Center for Transitional Justice website, https://www.ictj.org/our-work (accessed April 21, 2016).

12 Francis, *Interreligious Meeting: Address of the Holy Father*, Ground Zero, New York, September 25, 2015. In Lima, Peru, we have another memory site called "The Eye that Cries," which honors and preserves the memory of the victims of violence. It is a granite rock with another rock inserted in it like an eye that cries without stopping.

The water reminds us that the tears of yesterday and today are subversive and are a call to prevent history from repeating itself. It is subversive because it is a provocation to see history from the perspective of the vanquished. Official stories tend to suppress memory. The totalitarian regimes—writes Todorov—understood that the conquest of lands and men goes hand in hand with the conquest and appropriation of memory, even in its most hidden corners.[13] The public recovery of memory is opposed to official policies of silencing, bringing to light what was veiled, bringing to light the truth. The relationship between truth and memory has been present since the dawn of Western civilization. Faced with hubris, the excessive pride of men, an ethical demand arose that men not forget that they are not gods. Facing the pride of the triumphant, memory is necessary in order to illuminate and establish responsibility. "The truth that is memory only reaches its fullness in justice."[14]

In the Bible, memory is not exclusively or even primarily linked to the past; rather, it is linked to the present, which gives it depth, fullness, and momentum toward the future. We can say that it "makes memory" for the sake of action. Gustavo Gutiérrez points out that this memory "subverts any cynicism and indifference that has accumulated throughout the years in the name of the last ones of history, and it transforms itself into a permanent, demanding and creative present of the path to God."[15] After all, the biblical God is the God of memory, the God who does not forget his covenant nor his love for his people. Mary's Magnificat is the grateful memory of God's faithfulness to his people. Pope Francis remembered this in Cuba at the Sanctuary of the Virgin of our Lady of Charity. He said that Mary's prayer is grateful because "the living memory that God is in our midst is a perennial memory that God has seen the humility of his people and has helped his servant as he had promised to our fathers and their descendants forever."[16]

---

13 Cf. Tzvetan Todorov, *Los abusos de la memoria* [The abuses of memory] (Barcelona: Paidós Ibérica, 2000), 11.

14 Salomón Lerner, *La rebelión de la memoria: Selección de discursos 2001–2003* [The rebellion of memory: Selection of speeches 2001–2003] (Lima: CEP, 2004), 153.

15 Gustavo Gutiérrez, *The Option for the Poor in Christian Theology*, ed. Daniel G. Groody (Notre Dame, Ind.: University of Notre Dame Press, 2007), 19.

16 *Homily of His Holiness at the Minor Basilica of the Shrine Virgen de la Caridad del Cobre in Santiago*, September 22, 2015.

Memory, however, should not be idolized. The unearthing of memories does not always serve good causes. Todorov writes that it would be extremely cruel to continually remind someone of the most painful events of his life. He distinguishes, then, between *literal memory* and *exemplary memory*.[17] Literal memory is intransitive, it does not go beyond itself, it is incontrovertible and transforms the painful event into something insurmountable—the present and the future are inextricably bound to the past and all of the moments of existence are prisoners of the consequences of the initial painful event. Exemplary memory, on the other hand, compares, contrasts, and becomes a principle of action so that the "never again" does not actually happen again. It is the memory that resists, that liberates potentialities for people to live a good life that is committed to a future for victims. Exemplary memory is also grateful.[18] Here it is suitable to recall the analysis of Gonzalo Portocarrero, a Peruvian sociologist, of the work of José María Arguedas (1911–69): "[Arguedas] tried to tell the Peruvians and all oppressed peoples to have confidence in themselves; even if they are unaware of it, they are supported by a history full of happy moments."[19]

Indeed, all the peoples of America need exemplary memory, especially the Andean Quechua indigenous population, who live amidst "a disparate choir of shouts, in Quechua and in Spanish, of joy and pain, of liberation and oppression, of life and death" in Peru and elsewhere.[20] As we stated above, Mama Angélica represents the two sides of this story, of pain and resistance, but also of memory and hope. Francis found both at the Ground Zero Memorial. In front of that water that reminds us of the tears of yesterday and today, Francis also discovered the strength of love and memory, a strength that overcomes emptiness. Francis touched the heroic goodness of which man is capable, "the hidden force to which we must always appeal"—the strength of solidarity, of outstretched hands, of surrendered lives. He also said, "This place of death became a place of life too, a place of saved lives, a hymn to the

17 Todorov, *Los abusos de la memoria*, 21.

18 Todorov, 22.

19 Gonzalo Portocarrero Maisch, *Arguedas y el Perú de hoy* [Arguedas and the Peru of today] (Lima: Casa de Estudios del Socialismo, 2005) 26.

20 Gustavo Gutiérrez, *Entre las calandrias: Un ensayo sobre José María Arguedas* [Among the *calandrias*: An essay on José María Arguedas] (Lima: Bibliotéca Nacional del Perú, 2014), 243.

triumph of life over the prophets of destruction and death, to goodness over evil, to reconciliation and unity over hatred and division."[21]

Mama Angélica and Francis share what the American theologian David Tracy called the "Catholic analogical imagination." Faced with effervescent postconciliar theological pluralism, Tracy wondered in 1977 whether a shared vision among theologies should not be considered.

> What, if any, common vision is shared by such diverse theologies, for example, as Latin American liberation theologies, European transcendental theologies, North American experiential Catholic theologies? How do you define the heart of a religion which includes such distinct movements as the social justice apostolate, the charismatics, the ethnic revivals, the strong and vibrant mainline middle-class urban and suburban Catholics, the several forms of traditional and modern spirituality, the nationalist movements in African Catholicism, the different forms of prophetic witness of a Mother Teresa, a Dom Hélder Câmara, a Dorothy Day?[22]

His answer was to identify this shared vision in a "Catholic analogical imagination," a reality that does not define the essence of Catholic Christianity but refers to the "family resemblance" (Wittgenstein) of a prior horizon, a basic vision for the beliefs and practices of the Catholic community. The ultimate meaning of this view is that reality, despite overwhelming evidence to the contrary, is *finally benign*. He adduces a series of examples supporting this conclusion, but it is enough to point to one: he asks, "Do you believe, with Albert Camus, that there is more to admire in human beings than to despise?" If the answer is affirmative, then "you have a Catholic analogical imagination."[23]

The word "imagination" carries with it an invitation to creativity, to going further than what is apparent in the ordinary reality of everyday life. To imagine reality theologically, nourished by revealed faith, is to explore

---

21 Francis, *Interreligious Meeting: Address of the Holy Father.*

22 David Tracy, "Presidential Address: The Catholic Analogical Imagination," *Catholic Theological Society of America Proceedings* 32 (1977): 234–44. Tracy, then the president of the Catholic Theological Society of America (CTSA), aims to promote research in the Roman Catholic tradition related to the problems of contemporary society.

23 Tracy, "The Catholic Analogical Imagination," 235.

it by looking for the creative possibilities that reality can reveal. With analogical imagination, we re-create reality as a new series of possibilities arranged around a central point, a "focal sense" that sustains the whole of those possibilities. For Christians, this focal sense is the event of the life, death, and resurrection of Jesus Christ, which allows us to "reimagine" multiple sets of ordered relationships: those relationships existing between God and humanity, as well the interrelatedness of human beings with one another and with nature, society, and the cosmos. These relationships point to a reality that is finally sacramental, benign, and loving.

Reality thus reimagined is trustworthy; it does not involve us in error or illusion or death or sin but instead in radical love, "indeed as the final key to the order and trustworthiness of all reality."[24] Undoubtedly, we can affirm that Pope Francis is engaging in this kind of imagination in his encyclical *Laudato Si′* when, already in the first paragraphs, the benignity of creation appears: "Rather than a problem to be solved, the world is a joyful mystery to be contemplated with gladness and praise."[25]

That is why "the best wine is yet to come to those who today feel hopelessly lost," as Francis said in his homily to families in Ecuador; the Christian cannot fail to recognize a "yes" at the heart of the universe (Teilhard de Chardin) because "everything is grace."[26] In his homily at Holguín, Cuba on the day of St. Matthew, Francis asked if we believed that a tax collector could become a disciple, if a traitor could become a friend,[27] a very uncomfortable question in the face of our limited ability to trust in the power of love. In the current process in Colombia of seeking peace and reconciliation, do we believe that the unforgivable can be forgiven, that the victim can forgive the perpetrator? Do we believe in Mama Angélica's ability to forgive those who made her son Arquímedes disappear?

Nelson Mandela, in his farewell address as president of South Africa in 1999, proposed that we forgive but not forget.[28] Forgiveness is pos-

---

24 Tracy, "The Catholic Analogical Imagination," 237.

25 Francis, Encyclical Letter *Laudato Si'* (May 24, 2015), 12.

26 David Tracy, *The Analogical Imagination: Christian Theology and the Culture of Pluralism* (New York: Crossroad, 1991), 386.

27 *Homily of the Holy Father at the Plaza de la Revolución in Holguín, Cuba*, September 21, 2015.

28 "Speeches of Nelson Mandela," Nelson Mandela Memorial website, "Address by Nelson Mandela at Final Sitting of First Democratically Elected Parliament, Cape Town," March 26, 1999, www.mandela.gov.za/mandela_speeches/1999/990326_parlfinal.htm.

sible and necessary because a "yes" beats at the heart of the universe, but forgiveness does not suppress emblematic memories. The ethical demand not to forget is the greatest and best resistance to apartheids, holocausts, and the disappearance of people, the best hope that they cannot be repeated. As Agamben reminds us, "One cannot want Auschwitz to eternally return, just as one cannot ignore that what is essential about Auschwitz has not stopped repeating itself."[29]

"The Best Wine is Hope"

One of the best definitions of theology is that it is a "hermeneutic of hope." Peter formulated this definition when he told us to be ready to "give a reason" for the hope we have (1 Pt 3:15). The theologian Gustavo Gutiérrez is one of those theologians who likes to use the expression "hermeneutic of hope." During the hardest years of the internal conflict in Peru in the 1990s, Gustavo wrote that "only by maintaining silence, listening and sharing with the suffering of the poor, *will one be able to speak from the hope of the God that liberates*... From there, among us is born a contemplative language that recognizes that everything comes from the free love of the Father, and a prophetic language that reminds us of its demand for justice."[30] Mysticism and prophecy are at the heart of theology knitted out of the hope of the suffering.

Some years later, Gustavo returned to the subject of hope in a paper reflecting the trajectory and perspectives of Latin American theology on the occasion of the fiftieth anniversary of the beginning of the Second Vatican Council and the fortieth anniversary of the first formulations of liberation theology. He wrote that

> hope is a gift, it is a grace; to receive that gift calls us to build reasons to hope. *To hope is not to wait, it presupposes an*

29 Entrevista especial con Giorgio Agamben [Special interview with Giorgio Agamben], "O que resta de Auschwitz e os paradoxos da biopolítica em nosso tempo" [What remains of Auschwitz and the paradoxes of biopolitics in our time], Giacoia Junior Oswaldo, IHU online, August 21, 2013, www. ihu.unisinos.br/entrevistas/522762-o-que-resta-de-auschwitz-e-os-paradoxos-da-biopolitica-em-nosso-tempo-entrevista-especial-com-oswaldo-giacoia-junior.

30 Gustavo Gutiérrez, "¿Cómo hablar de Dios desde Ayacucho?" [How should we speak of God from Ayacucho?] *Concilium* 227 (January 1990): 131–42. Emphasis mine.

> *action, a creation.* It is about giving reasons for the love of God. From his perspective, Walter Benjamin said that the utopia of a just and fraternal world comes more from a compassion with respect to the suffering of so many today than from security in the future. *That compassion is a powerful reason to create in history reasons for hope.*[31]

Pope Francis delivered that message of hope on his apostolic trip to Ecuador, Bolivia, Paraguay, Cuba, and the US in July and September of 2015. In the usual press conference on the plane after he had concluded his visits to Ecuador, Bolivia, and Paraguay, he emphasized that the richness of the Latin American church came from its being a young, fresh church with a certain informality and a rich theology—it was a *searching* church. He said that he "wanted to give encouragement to this young Church" because it can contribute much to the universal church.[32] The words of Francis to the young people of the young Latin American church at the Father Félix Varela Cultural Center in Havana are well worth discussing.[33]

Francis first invites them to dream, because a young man who has no capacity to dream is closed in on himself. He reminds them of the words of the Guatemalan writer Miguel Ángel Asturias, who said that people have two eyes, one of flesh and one of glass. "With the eye of flesh, we see what is in front of us. With the eye of glass, we see what we dream of." "[D]ream…and share your dreams," he insists, because "the greater your ability to dream, the farther you will have gone; even if life cuts you short half way, you will still have gone a great distance." Without that "glass eye," we cannot give reasons for our hope. Neither can we walk, because hope is the virtue of the one on his way: "Hope is a path made of memory and discernment."[34]

Hope arises out of memory because we do not walk in life without an identity, without knowing who we are and where we come from;

---

31 Gustavo Gutiérrez, "La Teología Latinoamericana y Caribeña: Trayectoria y Perspectivas," [Latin American and Caribbean theology: Trajectory and perspectives] *Páginas* 38, no. 230 (June 2013): 29. Emphasis mine.

32 *In-Flight Press Conference of His Holiness Pope Francis from Paraguay to Rome*, July 13, 2015.

33 *Address of His Holiness Pope Francis to Students at the Fr. Félix Varela Cultural Centers in Havana, Cuba*, September 20, 2015.

34 *Address of Pope Francis to Students in Havana, Cuba.*

with the glass eye we see not only what we dream, but we also see an elaborate past of realized or frustrated dreams. Francis repeats to us something that the commissions of truth and reconciliation and policies aimed at transitional justice tell us at every moment: "Individuals or peoples who have no memory and erase their past risk losing their identity and destroying their future."[35] We need our spiritual, moral, and cultural heritage to have a direction. The technocratic paradigm, questioned so clearly by Francis in *Laudato Sí*, imposes its dominion in all fields of human existence in such a way that the capacity for decision, the most genuine freedom, and the space for coming up with creative alternatives, are severely limited.[36] Purely instrumental reasoning closes the doors to ethical-political conceptions, to questions about ends. What is observed then is the colonization of our lives, a colonization that destroys traditions, memories, resistance, and hope.[37] Hope comes from *discernment* because the walk of hope is not an erratic walk, but a walk directed toward an end that provides meaning and illuminates the path to be traveled—a path that is the product of a decision taken responsibly and freely after a search for what is most authentic and, in the case of a believer, in the light of the will of God. The believer confronts the choice of life and happiness versus death and unhappiness so that he or she can walk in the ways of God by listening to his will (Dt 30:15–16).

This path of hope, made from memory and discernment, has its price. In his homily in Santa Cruz de la Sierra (Bolivia), Francis, moved by the sight of the ladies carrying their children on their backs for hours, a scene so typical of the Andean culture of Quechua and Aymara, observed that the shoulders of those mothers also carry the disappointments, sorrows, scars, and bitterness of unaddressed injustices that never seem to end.[38] We can now recall the unanswered plea of Mama Angélica: "I want to ask the government the reason for all this suffering even today." We will not resign ourselves to suffering! Francis responds to

35 *Address of Pope Francis to Students in Havana, Cuba.*

36 Francis, *Laudato Si'*, 12.

37 Cf. David Tracy, *On Naming the Present: Reflections on God, Hermeneutics, and Church* (Maryknoll, N.Y.: Orbis, 1994), 9.

38 Francis, *Homily of the Holy Father at the Holy Mass at Christ the Redeemer Square in Santa Cruz de la Sierra, Bolivia*, July 9, 2015.

this suffering in his apostolic visit to America by whispering to the desperate that the best wine is yet to come!

In *Laudato Si'* we find another beautiful image announcing hope. Francis refers to the great power of the technocratic paradigm, in which life seems to be abandoned to and determined by technique, which becomes the chief means of interpreting existence.[39] But it is possible to broaden our outlook with our eyes of flesh and glass and free ourselves from this paradigm because authentic humanity "seems to dwell in the midst of our technological culture, almost unnoticed, *like a mist seeping gently beneath a closed door*. Will the promise last, in spite of everything, with all that is *authentic rising up in stubborn resistance*?"[40]

The Stubborn Resistance of the Authentic

Technocratic positivism conceives of history as linear, continuous, and teleologically oriented toward itself, and everything that happens is seen only as a moment within that scheme. Postmodernism, however, has put into crisis that teleological scheme of continuity and optimism by means of two relevant realities: the massive presence of universal suffering and the presence of the "others"—those who were excluded from the grand narrative of Eurocentric modernity. The real face of our era, as Levinas understood, is the face of the man on the side of the road or in a fragile raft trying to cross the Mediterranean, a face that cries out, "Don't let me die!"[41]

This presence of alterity has coincided with the return of an eschatological God who interrupts the writing of a history that is nothing more than blind chance (*una mano blanca*), who brings hope beyond all hope; He is an unpredictable, liberating, and incomprehensible hidden God. As David Tracy writes, it is the God who reveals himself in the occult, in the hidden, "in the mystics, in the religion of the people, in the cross and in negativity, above all in the suffering of all those 'others' whom the grand narrative of modernity has too often set aside as

39 Francis, *Laudato Si'*, 110.

40 Francis, *Laudato Si'*, 112. Emphasis mine.

41 Emmanuel Levinas, *Difficult Freedom: Essays on Judaism* (Baltimore: Johns Hopkins University Press, 1990), 8–10.

non-peoples, non-events, non-memory, in a word, as non-history."[42] This is in large part the God implicit in political and liberation theologies.

But evil also interrupts our history; we Christians call it sin, and sin is inauthentic existence, the radical alienation of the self in relation to itself, to nature, to society, and to God. In the term used by Saint Augustine, sin is *curvatus in se*, something turning upon itself in a dialectic of self-deception that rejects dependence on ultimate reality. But we will only fully understand what sin is if we understand what grace is—"the extraordinary process that emerges in the life of every person as a revealing gift in which the Ultimate Reality can be understood as God that is pure and unlimited Love."[43]

In the title of this section, "The Stubborn Resistance of the Authentic," we refer to authentic people who have accepted God's pure and unlimited love that has freed them *from* limiting situations and self-delusions *for* a new lifestyle, a life entrusted and devoted to God in love and solidarity with others. A person who lives authentically is someone who has experienced the salvation of God, who has revealed to us in Jesus Christ that the ultimate reality is the mystery of love, which, like a "mist seeping gently beneath a closed door" can make us subject to memory and hope, mystical and prophetic, and capable of leading a stubbornly active resistance against the dehumanizing status quo.[44]

We have suggested the name of a person who is emblematic of the Peruvian history of suffering—Mama Angélica. Pope Francis's speech before the US Congress was about other emblematic persons—Abraham Lincoln, Martin Luther King, Dorothy Day, and Thomas Merton—who "shaped fundamental values which will endure forever in the spirit of the American people. . . . In honoring their memory, we are inspired, even amid conflicts, and in the here and now of each day, to draw upon our deepest cultural reserves."[45] When Christianity or other religious traditions, including civil traditions, cease to produce mystical and

42 David Tracy, "O Deus Oculto: O resgate da apocaliptica," in *A Teologia na Universidade Contemporânea* [Theology at the contemporary university], ed. Inácio Neutzling (São Leopoldo: Unisinos, 2005), 88.

43 David Tracy, *Plurality and Ambiguity: Hermeneutics, Religion, Hope* (Chicago: University of Chicago Press, 1994), 74–75.

44 Francis, *Laudato Si'*, 112.

45 Francis, *Visit to the Joint Session of the United States Congress: Address of the Holy Father*, Washington, D.C., September 24, 2015.

prophetic or ethical-political people, then there will be reason to say that these traditions were pleasant and briefly enduring illusions, but only that.

For David Tracy, religions are radically ambiguous because in their histories we find a "strange mix of great good and horrible evil, of surprising beauty and repugnant cruelty."[46] Religion has liberated forces for good by generating spaces of solidarity, hope, and resistance to massive global suffering, but it has also allowed the deployment of demonic stratagems, of real terror in history, as we are observing in our days in various fundamentalisms. In the words of Pascal, "Men never do evil so completely and cheerfully as when they do it from religious conviction."[47]

When we fully take into account the "massive good and surprising beauty" of religions, Tracy believes that they have a great capacity to enable resistance to the status quo and that they must participate in resistance so that they are not tamed by power.[48] Francis makes an analogous affirmation: in our time, which is subject to the domination of the technocratic paradigm, pointing to a one-dimensional uniformity that eliminates all differences and traditions, "the religions thus have the right and the duty *to make clear that it is possible* to build a society where 'a healthy pluralism which respects differences and values them as such' is a 'precious ally in the commitment to defending human dignity… and a path to peace in our world.'"[49]

This impetus toward resistance within religions comes from their fundamental belief in ultimate reality, a belief that makes their adherents into militants fighting idolatry. In Christian terms, faith in a God who manifests himself in Jesus Christ as unconditional love that saves us so that we can live an authentic life in grace has the ability to discover ethical-political and cultural models of resistance to the irruptions of evil in history, resistance that is provoked by the lives of the poorest

---

46 Tracy, *Plurality and Ambiguity*, 70.

47 Blaise Pascal, *Pensées*, trans. W. F. Trotter (New York: E. P. Dutton, 1958), sec. XIV, no. 894.

48 Tracy, *Plurality and Ambiguity*, 83–84.

49 Francis, *Meeting for Religious Liberty with the Hispanic Community and Other Immigrants: Address of the Holy Father*, Independence Hall, Philadelphia, September 26, 2015, quoting Francis, Apostolic Exhortation *Evangelii Gaudium* (November 24, 2013), 255, 257.

and most vulnerable. "Our faith is revolutionary, because our faith challenges the tyranny of mammon."[50]

One of these strategies of greatest importance for Tracy is to "learn to listen to the narratives of others, especially those 'others' who have had to suffer our otherness imposed upon their interpretations of their own history and classics."[51] This listening, the beginning of all dialogue, offers the possibility of being able to discover a truth that can be an event of salvation for one who listens to the narratives of those who have never been taken seriously. Although it is difficult to believe, the best interpreters of all forms of evil, suffering, and pain, and also of hopes and joys, are not international agencies or humanitarian organizations or churches. The best interpreters of evil are the victims: the mothers searching for their missing children, the women who were sterilized against their will (in Peru), the Amazonian indigenous people who are denied rights in their land, and the Andean Quechua Indians and African Americans who continue to suffer the vilest discrimination.

Under the assumption that every attempt to develop a *logos* based on *theos* must begin by facing suffering and listening to horrors, Tracy offers a series of examples of hope discovered in "the subversive memory of the dead that remains alive in … popular stories,"[52] and in the "canticles of the suffering … in their patience and protests, in their struggles for justice, in the form of their prayers and lamentations, in the liturgies, in their laughs, in their readings of the Bible... in the tragic resonances, mournful and at the same time joyful, of a great part of popular Latin American music,... [and] in the magic realism of their literature."[53]

Now it is time to return to Francis and his words to the young people at the Father Varela Cultural Center in Havana because there the pope proposed two forms of "stubborn resistance."

The first is his statement that "hope is a path of accompaniment." He quotes the African proverb, "If you want to go quickly, walk alone,

---

50 Cf. Francis, *Address of the Holy Father at the Second World Meeting of Popular Movements in Santa Cruz de la Sierra, Bolivia*, July 9, 2015, no. 3.2.

51 Tracy, *Plurality and Ambiguity*, 72.

52 Tracy, *Plurality and Ambiguity*, 87.

53 David Tracy, "Salvarnos del Mal: La Salvación y El Mal Hoy" [Saving us from evil: Salvation and evil today] *Concilium: Revista internacional de teologia* 274 (February 1998): 147–59.

but if you want to go far, walk with another."[54] The meaning is this: closing in on oneself, depending on the self-centered ego, is infertile and does not generate hope; the bearer of hope is in fact proximity to and encounter and the capacity to dialogue with the other. Naturally, the culture of exclusion and of discarding people does not lead to anything good or authentic. Alone we do not get anywhere. A path of hope that resists the onslaught of technocratic culture and rejection of the other involves proximity to and encounter with the other. Put differently, as Tracy did, technocratic rationality "creates a desert and calls it peace. That peace is clearly not the peace that comes from the prophetic call to justice. It is a peace of sleepwalkers and the justice of bureaucrats."[55] What is the condition for hope as "a path of accompaniment"? It is respect for difference, diversity, and even the strange, seeing them as a kind of richness, not as a threat. The other name for hope as "a path of accompaniment" is the "culture of encounter," one of the great themes Francis has placed on the global and ecclesial agenda, to which we will return.

The second form of "stubborn resistance" is solidarity. There can be no encounter without solidarity; without it, there is no future other than, as Tracy says, that of the "deserts" of technocratic rationality. Solidarity for Francis "is the real and concrete preoccupation for the human being" who can be my friend, "but also someone who may think differently than I do," someone *different*. The solidarity he speaks of involves welcoming, collaboration, and service: "offering a helping hand, so that no one is excluded from the path."[56] Under this metaphor, being supportive means reaching out to someone who is out of the way. Francis goes beyond enlightened tolerance—solidarity is not to be found solely in our disposition and capacity to respect differences. To tolerate is more than to 'put up with'; it is to put yourself in the place of another so that the autonomy of the other is the limit of my autonomy—both autonomies can and must build "another course for the world."[57]

We have discussed three strategies for stubbornly resisting the technocratic culture's looting of memory and destruction of hope:

54 *Address of Pope Francis to Students in Havana, Cuba.*

55 Tracy, *On Naming the Present*, 6.

56 *Address of Pope Francis to Students in Havana, Cuba.*

57 Fidel Tubino, *La Interculturalidad en Cuestión* [The interculturality at issue] (Lima: Fondo Editorial, Pontifícia Universidad Católica del Perú, 2015), 32.

listening to the narratives of the "others," walking together with them, and stretching out one's hand to those outside the margins of the usual path. These strategies are capable of generating reasons for hope in those who despair—they are the "wine to be served to the unloved." These strategies are characteristic of Francis's dream of a "culture of encounter," a dream that he turns into a reality in his words and works, words and works that we heard and saw in his apostolic journey to America.

In his encounter with the popular movements in Bolivia, Francis pressed for a "culture of encounter." Francis affirmed that the future of mankind is largely in the hands of the humble, the poor, the excluded, and the exploited because active resistance to the idolatrous system lies in their ability to organize and generate alternatives, in their role as "harvesters of change." In their hands is also the cultivation and protection of the culture of encounter, "this ability to see yourselves in faces of others" in the proximity of the everyday, and a putting into practice of "the commandment of love."[58] In his homily at Madison Square Garden in New York City, a city that is on the one hand a symbol of diversity and plurality, and on the other, of the silenced faces of those without rights, Francis proclaimed that Jesus always proposes to his disciples to go out, "pushes them to leave to encounter others, where they really are and not where we would like them to be." Jesus incites us to go out and meet the other, as Francis says, without fear or disgust. This school of encounter frees us from a life without faces and the narcissism of self-reference and introduces us to the path of peace. "That peace which is born of accepting others, that peace which fills our hearts whenever we look upon those in need as our brothers and sisters."[59]

There is no encounter without dialogue. Raimon Panikkar left us the legacy of the "mysticism of dialogue" (*mística del diálogo*), a phrase that originated in the fact that dialogue is an act of trust in the other and expresses the spontaneity that is proper to purity of the heart.[60]

58 *Address at the Second World Meeting of Popular Movements*, no. 2.

59 *Holy Mass: Homily of His Holiness Pope Francis*, Madison Square Garden, New York, September 25, 2015.

60 Raimon Panikkar, "Hacia una teología de la liberación intercultural e interreligiosa," in *Interculturalidad, Diálogo Interreligioso y Liberación* [Interculturality, interreligious dialogue, and liberation], ed. Juan José Tamayo-Acosta and Raúl Fornet-Betancourt (Estella, Navarre: Verbo Divino, 2004), 67.

Dialogue taking place in an encounter, following Panikkar, is an act of love. Francis also told us this in his meeting with the popular movements in Bolivia. Both are telling us that "the way of encountering the other is by listening to him, and the way to listen so as not to misunderstand is to love him, and the way to love him is to empty my egoistic self-love."[61] Gadamer said it brilliantly: "In order to be capable of speech one must know how to listen. The encounter with the other is produced on a foundation of knowing how to self-eliminate." And he continued:

> Ignoring and mishearing occur for the same obvious reason: one who ignores or mishears is one who is constantly listening to himself, whose ears are so filled with the encouragement he is constantly giving himself and with which he pursues his drives and interests, that is he is unable to hear the Other. That is, I would insist, to some degree or other, a character trait we all share. Nevertheless, to become always capable of conversation—that is, to listen to the Other—appears to me to be the true attainment of humanity.[62]
>
> As we have shown at various points in this article, true humanity is authentic humanity; that is, humanity with memory and hope and that actively resists evil because it is a *grateful* humanity—grateful for the love of God in Jesus Christ. It is a humanity that has the authority to whisper in the ears of the desperate that the "best wine is yet to come."

Conclusion

It has been the intention of this chapter to show that one of the legacies of Pope Francis's apostolic visit to America in 2015 has been to strengthen the memory, hope, and stubborn resistance of the poor and those in despair. Francis has provoked us to go out to meet the "others" who are at the edge of the road and reach out, to engage in love in action, to announce that the "best wine is yet to come," that

61 Tamayo-Acosta and Fornet-Betancourt, *Interculturalidad, Diálogo Interreligioso y Liberación*, 67.

62 Hans-Georg Gadamer, *Verdad y Método* [Truth and method], trans. Ana Agud and De Rafael Agapito (Salamanca: Sígueme, 2006), 208.

everything has not yet been said about the fate of these "others," and that the possibilities for creating a good and authentic life are in the hands that have wiped their own tears and the tears of others. Memory, hope, and resistance are the threads that can weave a culture of encounter between peoples and cultures as they, as Panikkar wrote, express the spontaneity that is proper to purity of heart.

CHAPTER 7

THE PRESENCE OF GOD IN THE EXPERIENCE OF THE AMERINDIAN PEOPLES

A Reading of Pope Francis's Speeches in America (2015–16)

Roberto Tomichá Charupá

THE ORIGINAL INHABITANTS of Latin America (*pueblos originarios*) have lived for millennia, not without difficulties and ambiguities, in an experience of encounter with the mystery, as expressed in festive, communitarian, and human-cosmic symbols derived from constitutive, inclusive, and harmonious principles and relationships. In general, these symbols of life wisdom have often been not well understood and have gone unrecognized by the leaders of the societies in which these inhabitants have lived, including the leaders of the Christian churches. In the case of the Catholic Church, very few figures, especially among the hierarchy, have spoken with a prophetic voice in seeking to redirect faith to its biblical-evangelical origins, to rescue, in some way, the ancestral riches of both indigenous peoples and peoples of African origin.

After the Second Vatican Council, there began on the Latin American subcontinent and in the lands of the Caribbean a slow socioecclesial process of recovering the roots of an ancestral historical memory among these peoples. It has emerged only slowly and the process of decolonialization has faced numerous obstacles and ups and downs, especially since the "colonial mentality" is still very strong.[1] In recent

1 See the bishops' fourth revision of the *Aparecida Document*, the final document of the V General Conference of CELAM (the Episcopal Conference of Latin America and the Caribbean), specifically at n. 96 (*cuarta redacción*). The changes from the original to the fourth revision can be found in Ronaldo Muñoz, "Los Cambios Al Documento

years, however, there have been certain ecclesial signs, not only of opening but also of deepening that spiritual and theological proposal, which have been rooted not only the cultural and ethical realms but in the experience of the original peoples of the American continent.[2] The speeches of Pope Francis in his three visits to America illuminate this opening and deepening of the process of developing an Amerindian theology.

What follows seeks to approach the pope's speeches from the point of view of the experience of the native peoples, especially the Andean peoples, but to some extent also the Amazonian peoples, in order to highlight the affirmations, intuitions, and dreams that are capable of promoting the notion of "living well" (*vivir bien*), not only for the indigenous, but for all human beings living in the same creation. This involves a reading or rereading of his speeches in light of the very life of the native peoples (of course with their strengths and limitations), recovering those points of agreement between the pope's Christian vision and the indigenous project of living well and coexisting well with others.

The Search for God in the Speeches of Pope Francis: A Few Keys to Understanding

The search for God in America means, first of all, looking at the reality in which Christians must live, a diverse and plural reality with many contrasts and offering many opportunities to actualize and recreate the Gospel of Jesus, a message that reveals the trinitarian God, the source of life. It is important that this reality be read and understood in the way that Christian believers experience and perceive it.

De Aparecida," Redes Cristianas website, http://www.redescristianas.net/los-cambios-al-documento-de-aparecida-ronaldo-munoz/. Most of the citations to the *Aparecida Document* in this chapter come from Jorge Mario Bergoglio, ed., *Concluding Document, Aparecida, May 13–31, 2007* (Washington D.C.: United States Conference of Catholic Bishops, 2008). Citations to this document are to paragraph numbers.

2 One sign of this Amerindian theological deepening is the reactivation of the Symposia of Indian Theology organized by CELAM. Cf. *Teología India: IV Simposio Latinoamericano de Teología india—La teología de la creación en la fe católica y en los mitos, ritos y símbolos de los pueblos originarios de América Latina: El sueño de Dios en la creación humana y en el cosmos*, Lima, Perú, March 28–April 2, 2011 (Bogotá: Centro de Publicaciones del CELAM, 2013).

A few hermeneutical presuppositions or keys for achieving this goal are indicated by the magisterial documents of Pope Francis, as well as those emanating from the general conferences of the Latin American and Caribbean episcopate.[3]

"A Change of Cultural Epoch," the "Era of Knowledge and Information," and the "Search for Integral Solutions"

The Aparecida Document notes that "we live in an era of a change of epoch, the deepest level of which is cultural. . . . Individualism weakens community bonds and proposes a radical transformation of time and space, granting a primordial role to the imagination. Social, economic, and technological phenomena are at the foundation of the deep experience of time which is conceived as riveted on the present, thereby implying notions of insubstantiality and instability."[4] These observations, which were based on the assessments of diverse scholars and theologians, are reiterated by Pope Francis: "This era of change has been generated by great qualitative, quantitative, accelerated and cumulative leaps. . . . We are in the era of knowledge and information, the source of new forms of a power that are often anonymous."[5] Indeed, "the anthropological and cultural changes in our times influence all aspects of life and call for an analytic and diversified approach," and because of these changes, "individuals, in personal and family life . . . receive less and less support from social structures than in the past."[6] This change is profound and structural, not simply superficial or temporary, because it affects all of the interior, social, and relational dimensions of the human being. Christian communities often do not, however, want to accept this reality or, even if they do, draw the proper pastoral and missionary consequences.

---

3 With respect to the magisterial documents, see in particular the apostolic exhortation *Evangelii Gaudium* regarding the announcement of the Gospel in the real world, the encyclical letter *Laudato Si'* regarding the care for our common home, the earth, and the apostolic exhortation *Amoris Laetitia* regarding love in the family (see notes in the discussion below for full citations). All documents published by the Vatican, including these and many others cited below, including papal addresses, may be found at the vatican.va website.

4 Bergoglio, *Aparecida Concluding Document*, 44.

5 Francis, Apostolic Exhortation *Evangelii Gaudium* (November 24, 2013), 52.

6 Francis, Apostolic Exhortation *Amoris Laetitia* (March 19, 2016), 32.

In the religious-spiritual field, our contemporary times demonstrate that "a search for spirituality, prayer, and mysticism . . . expresses hunger and thirst for God" in the face of the superficialities and deficiencies of today's society.[7] This search is manifested in spiritualities, as much religious as secular, that it is necessary to be acquainted with in order to coexist with others in the midst of contemporary realities. Indeed, "in religious circles, the laity has taken on a greater role; there is a growing autonomy with respect to ecclesial authority and a personal search for religious meaning that is surpassing the boundaries of official beliefs and the rituals of established churches."[8] In any case, "Catholicism is no longer a hegemonic and monopolistic religion . . . The Latin American religious field is now pluralistic and its symbolic-semantic boundaries are no longer closed: there are today cross-influences that are constantly modifying the beliefs, rituals, ethics, and aesthetics of religious, spiritual, and magical content."[9] This is the context in which Christianity is called to be a meaningful and credible presence.

In addition to this anthropological-cultural and religious-spiritual change, we must add another of Pope Francis's urgent concerns—the continuous acceleration of changes to humanity's relationship to the planet.[10] Indeed, climate change, which affects all of humanity without exception, is a problem of such magnitude that "it is no longer possible to find a specific, discrete answer for each part of the problem. It is essential to seek comprehensive solutions,"[11] a search in which both developed and developing countries are actively involved and have "differentiated responsibilities."[12] For this, a pluralistic approach is needed to address the complexity of the present; it must be confronted from the point of view of diverse disciplines and sociospiritual senses of belonging and with a profound biblical-sapiential attitude that draws on the ancestral memory of our living peoples.

7 Bergoglio, *Aparecida Concluding Document,* 99g.

8 Cristián Parker Gumucio, "¿América Latina ya no es católica? Pluralismo cultural y religioso creciente," *América Latina Hoy*: *Revista de Ciencias Sociales* (Salamanca) 41 (December 2005): 41.

9 Parker Gumucio, "¿América Latina ya no es católica?" 47; Cf. Pierre Bourdieu, "Génese et structure du champ religieux," *Revue Francaise de Sociologie* 12, no. 3 (1971): 295–334.

10 Francis, Encyclical Letter *Laudato Si'* (May 24, 2015), 18.

11 Francis, *Laudato Si',* 139.

12 Francis, 52.

Reading the Signs of the Times and Discerning "What the Spirit is Saying to the Churches"

As missionary disciples we feel impelled to discern the "signs of the times" by the light of Jesus Christ and the Holy Spirit, which puts us in the service of the kingdom announced by Jesus, who came so that all may have life and "have it abundantly."[13] One sign of the times is an "appreciation of ethics . . . that indicates the necessity of surpassing hedonism, corruption, and the emptiness of values."[14] Paul VI refers to the necessity of an "always vigilant capacity to study the signs of the times," which is to be recognized communally by "listening to the Spirit," and to "what the Spirit is saying to the churches."[15] It is listening to persons with names, including the young and the elderly, the latter of whom "are the hope of peoples. The elderly provide the memory and wisdom of experience that invites us not to foolishly repeat the same errors of the past. The young call us to awaken and grow our hope, because they carry with them the new tendencies of humanity and open our future."[16] Memory, wisdom, and hope are missionary dimensions in the present.

To scrutinize and discern the signs of the times means, consequently, to seek out and embrace concrete faces even amidst the challenges posed by the changing stages of history. The concluding document produced by the Third General Conference of CELAM in Puebla, Mexico identified the suffering faces of Christ in the children, youth, indigenous, peasants, workers, underemployed-unemployed, marginalized, and elderly, while Aparecida pointed to the people living on the street, sick migrants, dependent addicts, and prisoners.[17] For Pope Francis, discipleship is lived in proximity to and encounter with the closest

13 Jn 10:10. See Bergoglio, *Aparecida Concluding Document*, 33.

14 Bergoglio, *Aparecida Concluding Document*, 99g.

15 Paul VI, Encyclical Letter *Ecclesiam Suam* (June 8, 1964), 632. See also Rv 2:29; Francis, *Evangelii Gaudium*, 14.

16 Francis, *Evangelii Gaudium*, 108.

17 Cf. Consejo Episcopal Latinoamericano (CELAM), "Puebla: III Conferencia General del Episcopado Latinoamericano, 1979" in *Las Cinco Conferencias Generales del Episcopado Latinoamericano* (Bogotá: Ediciones Paulinas, 2014), 31–39 [citations to this document are to paragraph numbers]; Bergoglio, *Aparecida Concluding Document*, 407–30.

faces—those of the family or the couple: this is "the encounter with a face, with a 'you' that reflects divine love."[18]

The signs of the times are discovered when the human being is encouraged to leave his own world and setting, or his own particular vision, in order to receive those who have been rejected by society and sometimes by the ecclesial space. The pope reminds us of Jesus's mandate to announce to "*everyone* . . . life as it is and not as you think it should be. Go out to the highways and byways, go out to tell the good news fearlessly, without prejudice, without superiority, without condescension, to all those who have lost the joy of living. Go out to proclaim the merciful embrace of the Father."[19] The concrete signs of the presence of God are perceived in this joyful announcement. Thus, the search for the signs of the times acquires meaning and depth for itself and for others when the human being—believer or not—is opened to the reality of others, a reality that fulfills and gives meaning to life in all its aspects.

A Trinitarian Interpretation: "In the World Everything is Connected" and "Everything is Related"

The faces we have mentioned are not just human; better, they are human in relationship with everything that exists: the animal, the created, and the cosmic world. The integral connection is a key for Francis's reading and analysis of reality: a central theme that runs through *Laudato Si'* is "the conviction that everything in the world is connected."[20] Indeed, Francis states a number of times in the encyclical that "everything is connected" or "everything is related"; in fact, "intimately related."[21] This connection is for Francis a key for a spiritual interpretation that allows an understanding of "all the factors of the global crisis."[22] This "everything" refers in one way to a just *human equilibrium* involving care for one's life, the promotion of fraternity

18 Francis, *Amoris Laetitia*, 12.

19 *Holy Mass and Canonization of Blessed Fr. Junípero Serra: Homily of His Holiness Pope Francis*, National Shrine of the Immaculate Conception, Washington D.C., September 23, 2015. Emphasis added.

20 Francis, *Laudato Si'*, 16.

21 Francis, 16, 70, 91, 117, 120, 137–38, 142, 213, 240.

22 Francis, *Laudato Si'*, 137.

and justice, an attention to marginalized persons or those with disabilities, and love for nature and human beings.[23] In another way it refers to an *integral ecology* in both its human-social dimensions and its physical, chemical, and biological dimensions as these affect the planet.[24] As a result, the particular relationship "between nature and society . . . prevents us from understanding nature as something separate from ourselves or as a mere setting in which we live. We are part of nature, included in it and thus in constant interaction with it."[25]

This intimate relationship between the human being and the environment acquires a final theological foundation in the intimate and permanent relationship existing between the divine persons in the trinitarian mystery. In other words, the visible created reality is a reflection "ad extra" of the invisible and eternal reality, the latter of which is manifested in time by means of the Son in the Holy Spirit. "The mystery of the Most Holy Trinity is the central mystery of Christian faith and life. It is the mystery of God in himself. It is therefore the source of all the other mysteries of faith, the light that enlightens them."[26] The fathers of the church saw the Trinity as *perichoresis* (the mutual indwelling of a person in others), *circumincessio* (the interpenetration of one person into others), or *circuminsessio* (the static and ecstatic being of persons in others). Contemporary theology is understood as expressing a communion of three divinities: family; the absolute, unfathomable, and indescribable mystery; and the "permanent integration, . . . eternal corelationality, [and] self-surrender" between divine persons.[27] Raimundo Panikkar called the last of these "cosmotheandrism" or God-human being-world interdependence: "The ultimate structure of reality [is] constitutively relational between three distinct, but inseparable, poles."[28] At the anthropological level, it should be remembered that the human being "is not primarily understood as a *substance* to which a relationship with

23 Francis, 70, 91, 117.

24 Francis, 137–38.

25 Francis, 139.

26 *Catechism of the Catholic Church* (Vatican City: Libreria Editrice Vaticana, 1994), 234.

27 Leonardo Boff, *La Trinidad, la Sociedad y la Liberación* (Madrid: Ediciones Paulinas, 1987), 11.

28 Raimon Panikkar, *Ecosofía Para Una Espiritualidad de la Tierra* (Madrid: San Pablo, 1994) 28.

God can later be added, but rather it is precisely constituted for this relationship."[29] For this reason, relationality becomes a constitutive human-theological-missionary dimension.

Pope Francis, following Saint Bonaventure, indicates that "the Trinity has left its mark on all creation . . . *each creature bears in itself a specifically Trinitarian structure,* so real that it could be readily contemplated if only the human gaze were not so partial, dark and fragile." The challenge is to "read reality in a Trinitarian key";[30] or in other words, to revisit the Christian tradition in a perichoretic, interrelational, and integrational way. In that manner, we could recover, for example, the relational paradigm of "living well," in all of its connotations and spiritual depth, from the cosmic experience of native peoples, especially the Andean people. Doing so would be very useful for a biblical-theological-missionary rereading of the Christian mystery.[31]

The Continual and Permanent Covenant of God with His People: "The Gifts and the Calling of God Are Irrevocable" (Rom 11:29)

The expression "ad extra" of the Uni-Triune mystery has been made explicit in history, concretely in the experience of the covenant that God wanted to establish with the people of Israel and, through it, with all the peoples of the earth. In fact, the Lord, freely and by his own initiative, imposes the duties of this covenant on himself, and therefore commits himself to be God for his people, bestowing the promised land on the descendants of Israel: "I will establish my covenant between me and you [self-imposed], and your offspring after you throughout their generations, for an everlasting covenant [*berit*/ self-imposed]. I will be your God and that of your future descendants."[32] The covenant will always be renewed by God despite the fact that the people and their kings are constantly rupturing it; God

29 Gonzalo J. Zarazaga, *Dios Es Comunión: El Nuevo Paradigma Trinitario* (Salamanca: Secretariado Trinitario, 2004), 58.

30 Francis, *Laudato Si'*, 239.

31 For more detail, see *Diálogos A: Revista de Culturas, Espiritualidades Y Desarollo Andino-Amazónico* 6, no. 8 (2015).

32 "*Alianza/pacto* [covenant/pact] (hebr. *berit*; gr. *diathēke*; lat. *testamentum*)," *Diccionario de la Biblia*, ed. Franz Kogler et al. (Santander: Sal Terrae, 2012), 26. cf. Gn 15:18; 17:1–4, 7.

continually establishes by his own initiative a "new beginning," a new relationship called the "new covenant."[33]

This covenant would continue in New Testament times, both at the linguistic level (in Greek *diathēkē*) and in content (as an agreement, contract, and obligation). It is the consummation of the first covenant—a "new action by God as an eschatological action [that] expresses the event of going to seek and reunite all of humanity by means of the mission and sacrifice of the Son, establishing the order of salvation created and realized in Jesus Christ; it is a supreme, sovereign, unconditional, and gratuitous act of God."[34] Jesus refers to himself as the "blood of the covenant" or the "new covenant" sealed with his blood.[35] It is from this point that Paul understands and affirms the covenant as a singular and definitive event, the source of salvation, a covenant of the spirit and of freedom.[36]

Much later, Irenaeus of Lyons would say that there "were four principal covenants given to the human race: one, prior to the deluge, under Adam; the second, that after the deluge, under Noah; the third, the giving of the law, under Moses; the fourth, that which renovates man, and sums up all things in itself by means of the Gospel, raising and bearing men upon its wings into the heavenly kingdom."[37] Therefore continuity and overcoming, opening and rupture are present, which manifest the salvific presence of the same God that made the covenant with Noah, a covenant that was not a "simple cosmic manifestation," as it is sometimes understood, but rather "a universal and personal intervention by God in the history of nations prior to the covenant with the chosen people."[38] In this covenant, the cultural and religious traditions of indigenous peoples are "chosen witnesses" to salvation and revelation.

Pope Francis, writing about Judaism, remembers the irrevocable continuity of that covenant with God and humanity, a unique God "who acts in history": "Their covenant with God has never been revoked, for

33 Cf. Gn 15:18; 17:7, 17; Ex 19:24; 32:4, 34; Jer 11:1–7; 31:31–33; Ezek 16: 59–62.

34 "Alianza/pacto [covenant/pact]," *Diccionario de la Biblia*, 27.

35 Mt 26:28, Mk 14:24, Lk 22:20, 1 Cor 11:25.

36 2 Cor 3:3–17.

37 Irenaeus of Lyons, *Adversus Haereses*, trans. Alexander Roberts and William Raambaut, in *The Apostolic Fathers with Justin Martyr and Irenaeus* (Buffalo, N.Y.: Christian Literature Publishing, 1885), III.11.8, https://www.newadvent.org/fathers/0103311.htm.

38 Jacques Dupuis, *Jesucristo Al Encuentro De Las Religiones* (Madrid: Ediciones Paulinas, 1991), 162. Cf. Gn 9:1–17.

'the gifts and the call of God are irrevocable' (Rom 11:29)."[39] Incidentally, this covenant willed by God considers human beings to be closely linked to their environment; these links have been lost over time and today require an authentic "environmental education" that disposes, motivates, and urges human beings to "leap towards the transcendent."[40] This involves a return to a "covenant between humanity and the environment," a covenant that has been maintained by and is living among the native peoples, based on their own ancestral wisdom.[41]

The Search for God among the Amerindian Peoples: "God Has Always Been Present"

In 1979, the Puebla conference held that "the indigenous cultures have unquestionable values; they are the richness of the peoples."[42] The Fourth General Conference of CELAM in Santo Domingo (1992) stated further that indigenous peoples "cultivate human values of great significance."[43] In 1992, Pope John Paul II referred to certain "positive aspects" of the indigenous peoples, such as an "openness to God's actions, a sense of gratitude for the fruits of the earth, the sacredness of human life and the value of the family, the sense of solidarity and co-responsibility in common work, the importance of culture, the belief in an afterlife."[44] Further, the Aparecida Document states that the church "especially values the indigenous for their respect for nature and love for mother earth as a source of nourishment, common home, and altar for human sharing."[45]

Among the "innumerable cultural riches" of the indigenous stands out an "openness to the action of God"[46] because "God has always been

39 Francis, *Evangelii Gaudium*, 247.

40 Francis, *Laudato Si'*, 210.

41 Francis, *Laudato Si'*, 209.

42 CELAM, "Puebla: III Conferencia General del Episcopado Latinoamericano," 1164.

43 CELAM, "Santo Domingo: IV Conferencia General del Episcopado Latinoamericano," in *Las Cinco Conferencias Generales del Episcopado Latinoamericano*, 245. Citations to this document are to paragraph numbers.

44 John Paul II, *Message to Indigenous Peoples*, December 10, 1992. Text reproduced in CELAM, "Santo Domingo: IV Conferencia General del Episcopado Latinoamericano," 17.

45 Bergoglio, *Aparecida Concluding Document*, 472.

46 CELAM, "Santo Domingo: IV Conferencia General del Episcopado Latinoamericano," 38; Bergoglio, *Aparecida Concluding Document*, 92.

present" in the indigenous life, and as such has been experienced and shared.[47] This presence has been perceived through a sacred vision of life and gratitude for that life, a gratitude that is expressed every day. This recognition of the presence of God is possible only under the conditions discussed in the four following sections.

Cosmic and Biocentric Relationality: The Andean Experience of the Pacha

In the Andean world, the principle, feature, and fundamental style of the cosmos, understood through experience, is "*the relationality of everything*"; in other words, "every element, being, and person is related to all the other elements, beings, and persons . . . everything is in some way related (linked, connected) to everything else."[48] The fundamental entity of the Andean cosmo-experience is not substantial "being," but relation, whose primordial structure permits the constitution of particular beings, not the reverse: "'Reality' (as a holistic 'whole') 'is' (exists) as *a group of 'beings' and interrelated events*."[49] According to one author, this principle is made explicit in at least five axioms of life, which render daily life deeply symbolic: complementarity, reciprocity, correspondence, completeness, and cyclicity.

From a theoretical point of view, the concept of relationality has much in common with the transdisciplinary approach presently proposed in a number of the sciences (human, social, physical, and others), an integrative and harmonious posture that seeks to overcome a certain rational and identity-exclusive vision of others (arising from social, cultural, generational, gender, or other factors) and of natural realities (i.e., the environment and the cosmos) because it seeks to include the other (e.g., the marginalized, the biodiverse). For the indigenous world, however, these considerations are not so much about philosophy or

---

47 Conferencia Episcopal de Bolivia, *Aporte de la Conferencia Episcopal de Bolivia a la IV Asamblea General del Episcopado latinoamericano* (La Paz: C. E. B, 1992), no. 4.

48 Josef Estermann, *Compendio de la filosofía occidental en perspectiva intercultural*, vol. 1, *Introducción al pensamiento filosófico* (La Paz: Instituto Superior Ecuménico Andino De Teología, 2011), 289–90.

49 In other words, "the 'principle of relationality' says that every 'being,' event, state of consciousness, feeling, action, and possibility is immersed in multiple relationships with other 'beings,' events, states of consciousness, feelings, actions, and possibilities." Estermann, *Introducción al pensamiento filosófico*, 290.

speculation, but rather a posture or attitude toward life that is in tune with the dream and project of living well: a more integrated life and sapiential way of thinking. This proposal will be taken up again at the end of this work.

In the Andean world, the symbolic expression that allows human beings to enter easily into dialogue with the transdisciplinary from the point of view of a religious-spiritual openness is probably the experience of *pacha*, a common Quechua-Aymara word with many meanings (earth, globe, world, planet, life space, universe, stratification of the cosmos). It includes the human being and the cosmos, and in synthesis can be translated as "cosmic relationality."[50] According to the Aymara thinker Calixto Quispe, *pacha* is "the cosmic nest that is vital to live well," and

> *pacha* is the living nest of cultures, communities, families and all that exists . . . it is the eternal vital nest of humanity . . . it is the eternal vital nest of existing animals . . . it is the nest of the eternal life of plants . . . it is the vital nest of the cloud, sun, moon, stars, and everything that exists in the cosmos . . . the nest of everything that exists in the womb of Pachamama; gold, silver, and water that flows like a fountain.[51]

Indeed, this relationality at every level, or transrelationality, acquires its ultimate meaning in care and respect for life in all of its expressions; it is about human life, but not limited to it; rather, it is human life in relation to its environment, the life of all the cosmos, of all creation. Pope Francis's convictions that there exists a mutually interconnected reality—"everything is related"—acquire concreteness in the Amerindian principles of relationality, which are expressed through a communitarian style, a celebratory integrative symbolism, and the

---

50 Josef Estermann, *Si el Sur fuera el Norte: Interculturales entre Andes y Occidente* (La Paz: Instituto Superior Ecuménico Andino De Teología, 2008), 78. Regarding Andean theology, see Josef Estermann, ed., *Teología Andina: El tejido diverso desde la fe indígena*, 2 vols. (La Paz: Instituto Superior Ecuménico Andino De Teología, 2006).

51 Vicenta Mamani Bernabé et al., eds., *Suma Qamaña–Vivir Bien*, Espiritualidades Originarias 8 (Cochabamba, Bolivia: Verbo Divina, 2012), 32.

logic of harmony-equilibrium and biocentrism, and are the foundation of Amerindian activity and work.[52]

Such notions are in line with the proposal of the church on the continent that favors a human-relational life in all of its dimensions and expressions, from the moment of its conception to its last days on this earth, passing through the concrete worries of the earthly life of human beings. This theme was the central motive for Francis's visit to the United States: "I appreciate the firm commitment of the Church in America to the cause of life and to that of the family, which is the primary reason for my present visit."[53]

Experience of Native Catholicity: A Communitarian and Plural Christianity That Recovers the Invisible and That Which Has Been Discarded

As is well-known, the most traditional native peoples live in an essentially communitarian way, a fact that is expressed in their daily experience of a relational community, which includes the human-cosmic. Living in this way overcomes a certain anthropocentrism and cosmocentrism—it is a way that Christianity contributed to. In this way of living, both human beings and the cosmos are subordinated to a reality that is present in the human-cosmic but at the same time rises to overcome this reality, establishing itself as a decisive means of judgment of it. This reality, which has been known by diverse names, has, in the Christian conception, a relationship with the ultimate, indescribable, and absolute mystery. It involves an inclusive, integrative, and open mystery in which opposites coincide and complement each other. Thus, for example, the divine feminine principle known by some native peoples is closely related to the divine vision symbolized by the earth, water, and other natural elements, although in the social sphere the masculine has tended to predominate, having been stressed by a clerical Christian vision.

This indigenous communitarian vision seeks dialogue and also the recovery of an authentic plural communitarian meaning of Christian

---

52 Francis, *Laudato Si'*, 70, 120, 142.

53 Francis, *Speech of Pope Francis to the Bishops of the United States*, St. Matthew's Cathedral, Washington, D.C., September 23, 2015.

origins, with a peculiar emphasis on the expressions of it described above and on invisible or rejected figures in their societies. Such is the proposal of Pope Francis, especially on the occasion of his visit to Mexico in 2016. In fact, this search for dialogue and authenticity makes it possible to experience the proximity to and election of God for people who "count for nothing" and are not "protagonists" at the social, cultural, and ecclesial level. For Francis, these people are the leaders, representatives, and witnesses of what Leonardo Boff calls the "maternal face of God" that is always present in the figure of the virgin-mother Mary. This phenomenon has been present from the beginnings of Christianity in America, on that morning in December 1531 when a mother chose Juan Diego as her ambassador to the church and society of that time to build a sanctuary for life, as well as authentic and integrative relationships. In this regard, Francis says that

> on that morning, Juancito experienced in his own life what hope is, what the mercy of God is. He was chosen to oversee, care for, protect and promote the building of this Shrine. . . . In this way, she [Mary] managed to awaken something he did not know how to express, a veritable banner of love and justice: no one could be left out of the building of that other shrine, the shrine of life, the shrine of our communities, our societies and our cultures.[54]

Indeed, "no one could be left out" implies, on the one hand, accepting the indigenous principle of hospitality, a very biblical one, which integrates the diversities of language, people, culture, and nation. On the other hand, it also implies a rereading and also overcoming of this principle so as to integrate and take in mental, paradigmatic, value-laden, and spiritual diversities and to advance toward a fuller, authentic, and more credible Catholicism.

54 *Holy Mass at the Basilica of Our Lady of Guadalupe: Homily of His Holiness Pope Francis*, Mexico City, February 13, 2016.

Memory As "Ancient Wisdom": "Do Not Forget Your Origins"

In 2007, the Latin American and Caribbean bishops said in the fourth revision of the Aparecida Document that "there remains in the collective imagination a *colonial mentality and gaze* with respect to the native peoples and Afro-Americans. Thus, decolonizing mentalities, knowledge, recovering historical *memory*, and strengthening spaces and intercultural relationships, are conditions for the affirmation of full citizenship of these peoples."[55] Pope Francis insists on the recovery of memory in many of his speeches, especially those delivered to the clergy and religious persons throughout America. Thus in Ecuador he said, "Do not fall into a spiritual Alzheimer's, do not lose your memory, especially the memory of where you were taken from. . . . Do not forget the faith that your grandmother and mother had. . . . Do not forget from where you were taken from, do not forget your roots, do not consider yourself to have been promoted."[56] He made similar comments in Paraguay: "A people which forgets its own past, its history and its roots, has no future, it is a dull people. Memory, if it is firmly based on justice and rejects hatred and all desire for revenge, makes the past a source of inspiration for the building of a future of serene coexistence. It also makes us realize the tragedy and pointlessness of war."[57] And in the US: "It will do us good to think back on our lives with the grace of remembrance. Remembrance of when we were first called, remembrance of the road travelled, remembrance of graces received… and, above all, remembrance of our encounter with Jesus Christ so often along the way. Remembrance of the amazement which our encounter with Jesus Christ awakens in our hearts."[58]

Something troubling occurred during the Christianization of this continent, which was realized in not only a context of political-economic

---

55 Fourth revision of the *Aparecida Document* (*cuarta redacción*) approved on May 31, 2007, n. 96. Emphasis is mine. In the official version of the expression "colonial gaze with respect to" is changed to "a certain gaze of less respect about." Bergoglio, *Aparecida Concluding Document*, 96.

56 Francis, *Meeting with Clergy, Religious, and Seminarians: Address of the Holy Father*, Quito, Ecuador, July 8, 2015.

57 Francis, *Meeting with Government Authorities and the Diplomatic Corps: Address of the Holy Father*, Asunción, Paraguay, July 10, 2015.

58 *Vespers with Priests and Religious: Homily of His Holiness Pope Francis*, St. Patrick's Cathedral, New York, September 24, 2015.

colonization, but of penetration and symbolic-spiritual suppression of the ancestral roots of various peoples. In this way, a colonial Christianity arose and spread, causing peoples to lose their memories, riches, wisdom, values, and spiritualities. Something troubling occurred, but despite this, much of the interior depth of the indigenous, mestizo peoples and peoples of African descent remained. These peoples have been working to recover their memory as part of their struggles experienced in diverse, organized civil and social movements with the participation of other Christians and in search of alternatives to a certain social-religious-spiritual monoculture with hegemonic pretensions. In order to counter histories of imposition, which have squelched diversity and biodiversity, Pope Francis insists that we should be guided by the Holy Spirit, which "builds up the communion and harmony of the people of God," and continues, "We would not do justice to the logic of the incarnation if we thought of Christianity as monocultural and monotonous. While it is true that some cultures have been closely associated with the preaching of the Gospel and the development of Christian thought, the revealed message is not identified with any of them."[59]

In February 2016, Francis insisted in Mexico on revisiting Latin America's roots, that "ancestral wisdom" which forms part of the rich and valued identity of its people, as one of its greatest "biographical resources" that must be esteemed and strengthened: "The ancestral wisdom shown by your multiculturalism is, by far, one of your greatest biographical resources. It is an identity that learned gradually how to shape itself amid diversity and that now constitutes, without any doubt, a rich patrimony to be valued, encouraged and protected."[60] The following day, the pope stressed the importance of returning to one's origins, to one's own roots, and from there giving thanks to God for life, relating a directive from Moses to the Israelites: "At harvest time, a [*sic*] the time of abundance and first fruits, do not forget your beginnings, do not forget where you came from. Thanksgiving is something which is born and grows among a people capable of remembering. It is rooted in the past, and through good and bad times, it shapes the present."[61] Francis

59 Francis, *Evangelii Gaudium*, 117.

60 Francis, *Meeting with Authorities, Representatives of Civil Soci,ety and the Diplomatic Corps: Address of His Holiness Pope Francis*, National Palace, Mexico City, February 13, 2016.

61 Francis, *Angelus Address*, Ecatepec, Mexico, February 14, 2016; cf. Dt 26:5–11.

also referenced this theme of identity when he instructed the bishops of Mexico to "protect the memory of the long journey undertaken so far—be *deuteronomical*—and know how to inspire the hope of attaining new heights . . . remembering the high standards which Mexico can attain when it learns to belong to itself rather than to others."[62]

Therefore, the search for God among the native peoples presumes the recovery of their ancestral memory, the source of an always dynamic and creative wisdom, a spiritual wisdom that is capable of overcoming both totalitarian ideologies, which have done so much harm among Christian peoples, and the visions of partial historical configurations of Christianity, which were imposed on Latin America and the Caribbean and have impeded the gestation of autochthonous (indigenous) Christian expressions. In other words, recovering, valuing, strengthening, and learning from the "ancestral wisdom" alive in the memory of indigenous peoples represents one of the urgent challenges, not only for believers, but for all of humanity, as a contribution to the building of new, more integrative, and fuller relationships.

Revisiting the Symbol of God in Light of Diverse Spiritualities

Relationality, community, and memory in the Amerindian experience always involve openness to experiences of the ultimate mystery, a mystery that is known as a symbol of life, a symbol that is embodied and celebrated in the everyday. Thus, the presence of the mystery is manifested in one way by the human-cosmic, concrete, and transparent closeness of everything that exists, but in another way it is also manifested in distance and mystery, for it expresses "something more" that is radically distinct and diverse—because it concerns the sacred. In any case, the mystery has to do with gestation, care, concern, and the promotion of life in its fullness and in all of its dimensions.

Therefore, one can understand from the Amerindian peoples that the search for God is a permanent rediscovery of the presence of ultimate meaning, a presence that is possible in the concrete experience of people living in harmony with the environment considered in its particularity and biodiversity. It is not, therefore, theory or speculation.

62 Francis, *Meeting with the Bishops of Mexico: Address of the Holy*, Metropolitan Cathedral of the Assumption, Mexico City, February 13, 2016.

From this principle of openness and recognition of "God" in daily experiences it is possible to find and receive him in the experiences of those who are searching for paths other than a personal "God," as the term is typically used in Christianity.

Indeed, many traditional communities have given and continue to give deep meaning to their lives from their experiences of encounter with a "God" that is not a person, responding profoundly to such an encounter, not only with their own searches for fullness of life, but especially with an ethic that promotes life between peoples and with the whole environment. Similarly, today there are those who seek true spiritual paths that are not always connected to traditional religious forms or historical codifications of spiritual (religious) experience. This is so-called secular spirituality, according to which "the finality is in things and persons taken for themselves, without any transcendent reference to sustain them . . . It encourages the ethical dimension and the ecological compromise, an interest in improving the collective environment through the arts and sciences, transforming the means by which we live."[63] Although it involves approaching the diverse mystery of the indigenous experience, it is worth pointing out the similarity between concerns and themes of indigenous and of more traditional spiritualities, especially as they impact on the field of ethics.

It is necessary to point out the importance of revisiting the traditional languages that bring us closer to what we conceive of as "God" and to recover the divine symbol, always open to and convergent with diverse human experiences, whether the symbol relates to a personal, impersonal, transpersonal, or "secular" "God," or even possesses varying and multiple meanings—all for the purpose of safeguarding a project of common life for all peoples and the cosmos.

Some Expressions of the Search for God: Common Horizons

Keeping in mind all of the above, it is possible to read the pope's speeches in light of the Amerindian peoples' search for God, an existential search in which the divine symbol is perceived and lived in daily expressions. A convergence between the pope's intentions and

63 Javier Melloni, *Hacia Un Tiempo De Síntesis* (Barcelona: Fragmenta, 2011), 171–72.

the experience of the indigenous peoples is possible. We see this convergence in the points that follow.

Interior Contemplative Silence: Presupposition for an Integral Encounter

The wonders of God manifest themselves as presence in attentive listening to the environment and in interior, contemplative silence, a listening and silence that is not limited to the intellectual, cognitive, volitional, and affective dimensions of the human being on this earth, but that also includes all other beings, including grandparents and ancestors and the cosmic environment, in their own particular natures. Francis emphasizes a deep and interior silence as the basis for every integral human-cosmic contemplation that transforms itself into an integral mysticism. In relation to the Virgin of Guadalupe, he says, "I think that some silence may do us good today as we pause to look upon her son . . . And in the silence, and in this looking at her, we will hear what she says to us once more, 'What, my most precious little one, saddens your heart?' just as she once asked, 'Yet am I not here with you, who have the honour of being your mother?'"[64]

Silent and contemplative prayer in the context of the everyday represents the principal way Amerindians live and express their encounter with God. Silence acquires a relational connotation as between son or daughter and mother, a connotation that expresses the feminine and maternal face of God. Of course, this relational connotation acquires relevance and sublimity in the personified figure of mother Mary, who embraces all of our everyday existence: interpersonal, familial, labor-related, festive, and cosmic relationships. The imprint of the feminine connotation of contemplative silence in the Amerindian tradition goes back to the dawn of American evangelization, as the pope well remembers: "*La Morenita* gathers together those who contemplate her, and reflects the faces of those who find her. It is essential to learn that there is something unique in every person who looks to us in their search for God. We must guard against becoming impervious

64 *Holy Mass at the Basilica of Our Lady of Guadalupe: Homily of His Holiness Pope Francis*. The pope quotes from the *Nican Mopohua*, 107, 118, and 119.

to such gazes but rather gather them to our hearts and guard them."[65] Therefore, contemplative silence encourages us to walk in reality and in the everyday toward missionary risk, hospitality, welcome, and full trust in the Holy Spirit, the lord and giver of life.

Nomadic Discipleship: Trust and Abandonment in That Living Presence

Pope Francis, referencing the Aparecida Document, pointed to the purpose of mission: "Life grows by being given away, and it weakens in isolation and comfort. Indeed, those who enjoy life most are those who leave security on the shore and become excited by the mission of communicating life to others."[66] Mission is expressed by giving life, in irradiating it passionately so that our peoples can have life.[67] There is, therefore, a "profound law of reality," the law of the maturation of a life that "is offered up in order to give life to others. This is certainly what mission means."[68]

This vision is in line with the Puebla conference regarding mission: "For Latin America the hour has arrived to intensify the mutual services between particular Churches and to project itself beyond its own frontiers 'ad gentes' . . . But we should give from our own poverty."[69] In reality it is not only about poverty, it is above all about exchange, reciprocity, and mutual learning because "our Churches can offer something original and important—their meaning of salvation and liberation, the richness of their popular religiosity, the experience of Base Ecclesial Communities, the flowering of their ministries, their hope and joy in their faith."[70] According to Francis, "missionary outreach is *paradigmatic for all the Church's activity*"[71] and liberates us "from our narrowness and self-absorption."[72] This is a nomadic and Abrahamic mission like the Exodus and Exile; it is communitarian,

65 *Address of the Holy Father in the Meeting with the Bishops of Mexico.*
66 Francis, *Evangelii Gaudium*, 10. Cf. Bergoglio, *Aparecida Concluding Document*, 360.
67 Cf. Jn 10:10.
68 Francis, *Evangelii Gaudium*, 10. Cf. Bergoglio, *Aparecida Concluding Document*, 360.
69 CELAM, "Puebla: III Conferencia General del Episcopado Latinoamericano," 368.
70 CELAM, "Puebla: III Conferencia General del Episcopado Latinoamericano," 368.
71 Francis, *Evangelii Gaudium*, 15.
72 Francis, 8.

prophetic, itinerant, and full of meaning, since the risen one and the Spirit accompany the missionary disciples.[73]

Pope Francis adds: "I dream of a 'missionary option,' that is, a missionary impulse capable of transforming everything, so that the Church's customs, ways of doing things, times and schedules, language and structures can be suitably channeled for the evangelization of today's world rather than for her self-preservation."[74] He urges, therefore, a return to the origins of the evangelical life, to the itinerant believing communities. Along their path, they allow themselves to be found by Jesus, who surprisingly appears to walk with them and thus manifests his closeness and resurrected presence. This is how modest people walk and move through their daily work, as well as how they attend great events and celebrations (like meeting with the pope). God is found on the path of life, in the midst of many trials and vicissitudes that, no matter how difficult, do not detract from the joy of the believer.

Much like the people of Israel, many indigenous peoples were travelers, itinerants, and nomads, and they conceived of a traveling and nomadic God, a dynamic God, tender, close to human reality, not subject to rigid ritual formalities. As Eleazar López, the "midwife" of Amerindian theology, said, "Nomadism is the point of departure and obligatory reference for all indigenous peoples in America . . . in the religious and theological scheme of nomadism, God is everything and everything has to do with God.[75]

Care for Creation: Ecological Formation as Self-Critique

"Praise be to you, my Lord," sang St. Francis of Assisi. In his beautiful *Canticle of the Creatures*, he reminds us that our common home is like a sister with whom we share existence, and like a beautiful mother who welcomes us into her arms: "Praise be to you, my Lord, through our Sister, Mother Earth, who sustains and governs us, and who

73 Lk 24:13–35.

74 Francis, *Evangelii Gaudium*, 27.

75 Eleazar López Hernández, *Teología India: Antología* (Cochabamba, Bolivia: Verbo Divino, 2000), 32–33. Regarding nomadism in the life of the Guaraní people of South America, see Memoria del IV Encuentro-Taller Ecuménico Latinoamericano de Teología India, *En busca de la tierra sin mal: Mitos de origen y sueños de futuro de los pueblos indios*. Asunción, Paraguay, May 6–10, 2002 (Quito: Abya-Yala, 2004).

produces various fruit with colored flowers and herbs."[76] The pope pointed out that "the earth herself, burdened and laid waste, is among the most abandoned and maltreated of our poor; she 'groans in travail' (Rm 8:22). We have forgotten that we ourselves are dust of the earth (cf. Gn 2:7); our very bodies are made up of her elements, we breathe her air and we receive life and refreshment from her waters."[77] In continuity with former pontiffs, who have spoken of a "global ecological *conversion*," an "authentic *human ecology*," and the truth that the human being "is spirit and will, but also nature," Pope Francis proposes "an integral ecology, lived out joyfully and authentically," a "broader vision" that incorporates "the human and social dimensions," including the cultural dimensions, and that opens itself up "to categories which transcend the language of mathematics and biology, and take us to the heart of what it is to be human."[78] In this way, we would be able to "contemplate the Creator, who lives among us and surrounds us."[79]

This "integral ecology" responds to an "integral education," to a diversified, interdisciplinary self-critique, beginning with one's own familiar environment, a space and place where one can practice "daily gestures which break with the logic of violence, exploitation, and selfishness"[80] and "learn to ask without demanding, to say 'thank you' as an expression of genuine gratitude for what we have been given, to control our aggressivity and greed, and to ask forgiveness when we have caused harm."[81] He urges the creation of educational spaces where we can learn to ask permission and say thank you, where we can live a "responsible simplicity of life, in grateful contemplation of God's world, and in concern for the needs of the poor and the protection of the environment."[82]

Such an ecological education has the potential to critically counteract "the dominant technocratic paradigm" and "an undifferentiated and one-dimensional paradigm" that is "efficiency-driven" and omnipresent

---

76 Francis, *Laudato Si'*, 1, quoting Saint Francis of Assisi, *Canticle of the Creatures*.

77 Francis, *Laudato Si'*, 2.

78 Francis, 4–6, 10, 11, 137, 143, 159.

79 Francis, 225.

80 Francis, 230.

81 Francis, 213.

82 Francis, *Laudato Si'*, 214.

in the "cult of unlimited human power."[83] Indeed, "the technological paradigm has become so dominant that it would be difficult to do without its resources and even more difficult to utilize them without being dominated by their internal logic."[84] He urges an education into an ecological culture that offers "a distinctive way of looking at things, a way of thinking, policies, an educational program, a lifestyle and a spirituality which together generate resistance to the assault of the technocratic paradigm."[85] It is urgent to understand "that certain mindsets really do influence our behavior. . . . Otherwise, the paradigm of consumerism will continue to advance."[86] We need to be critically attentive to the implicit preconceptions that underlie our actions, expressions, and pastoral and missionary projects.

Indeed, on the journey of life, the invitation is open to make a real commitment to the discarded, marginalized, and excluded. He recalls the words of the Virgin of Guadalupe: "Am I not your mother? Am I not here? Do not let trials and pains overwhelm you, she tells us. Today, she sends us out anew; as she did Juancito, today, she comes to tell us again: be my ambassador, the one I send to build many new shrines, accompany many lives, wipe away many tears."[87] The disciple of Jesus Christ thus becomes an apostle-ambassador and is responsible to put in practice the Gospel mandate of Matthew 25:31–46; that is, give food to the hungry, drink to the thirsty, shelter to the needy, clothes to the naked, and visits to the sick and the prisoner. The disciple must forgive those who hurt him, console those who are sad, have patience with others, and especially pray and petition to God for others.

Such a commitment also involves responsible care for the earth, "our common home," which, according to Francis, "has been part of this group of the excluded which cries out to heaven and which today powerfully strikes our homes, our cities and our societies."[88]

---

83 Francis, 101, 106, 122, 189; Cf. Francis, 16.

84 Francis, 108.

85 Francis, 111.

86 Francis, 215.

87 *Holy Mass at the Basilica of Our Lady of Guadalupe: Homily of His Holiness Pope Francis.*

88 Francis, *Welcoming Ceremony, South Lawn of the White House: Address of the Holy Father*, Washington D.C., September 23, 2015. http://time.com/4045956/pope-francis-us-visit-white-house-transcript/.

Living Well: An Integral Evangelical Project

In sum, the Amerindian search for God converges on the project of "living well," which is nothing other than "knowing how to relate oneself and coexisting with all forms of existence ... with the *cycles of Mother Earth, the cosmos, life and history.*"[89] More specifically, even though the Aymara expression "*suma qamaña*" and the Quechua expression "*sumaj kawsay*" (both meaning "living well") have only recently been coined and do not form part of everyday language, they nonetheless focus on the millenarian and communitarian experiences, searches for meaning, ancestral spiritualities, strategic projects, knowledge and dreams, and symbolic imagination of the various Latin American peoples. If what characterizes the peoples is an integral relationship, "living well" (*vivir bien*) also means "coexisting well," a concept that invites everyone to reach an understanding of an indigenous paradigm that aims to be an alternative to the hegemonic lifestyle proposed by the dominant Western trend. This paradigm allows us to revisit not only society in general, but also Christianity and its theologies.

In the Andean world this relational principle is expressed in the harmonious coexistence of the human being within his own community (*ayllu*), understood as a structure and space that generates life and receives and is connected to the whole environment: "Every part of the community, the mountain, the tree, the river, the insects; [...] the deterioration of any part is the deterioration of all."[90] This stance allows for an encounter with life in its communitarian, inclusive, integrative, and cosmic character, a life that is not reduced to a mere horizontal plane, but instead open to a depth of symbolic-spiritual meaning in the *pacha*. Therefore, the relationality of "living well" is expressed at all levels of reality as a communitarian principle of openness, respect, and inclusion of all of its parts that avoids centering itself on the simple projects of individuals.

If Christian theology allows itself to be questioned by the Andean notion of "coexisting well," a fruitful and convergent dialogue is possible,

89 Fernando Huanacuni, *Vivir Bien / Buen Vivir: Filosofía, políticas, estrategias y experiencias regionales* (La Paz: Convenio Andrés Bello, 2010), 15.

90 Fernando Huanacuni, "Buen Vivir-Vivir Bien," March 19, 2016, YouTube video, 12:17, at 2:00–2:17, https://www.youtube.com/watch?v=9oZHJMTcfOE.

as indeed characterizes the Amerindian experience. In short, as a noted Aymara thinker affirms, this indigenous project coincides with the project of Jesus of Nazareth called the kingdom of God, since both promote a full, authentic, and integrated life: "There is a coincidence of background content between the two utopias, a historical convergence toward the same objective, and inevitable suspicion of complementarity."[91] In particular, they coincide in the dimension committed to life and to a relational ecocentrism, which places the human being in its right biblical dimension and which at the same time is capable of overcoming anthropocentrism, which often becomes an exclusionary androcentrism. In this way, the Gospel of Jesus of Nazareth can be reread and lived from the perspective of other coordinates and autochthonous sensibilities, including those of the Amerindian peoples.

To a large extent, this defines Pope Francis's project: every one of us is nothing more than a part of a diverse and complex whole interacting in time; we belong to peoples struggling for meaning and destiny and attempting to live with dignity, to "live well."[92]

91 José María Vigil, "Sumak Kawsay Y Reino De Dios," *Diálogos A: Revista de Culturas, Espiritualidades Y Desarollo Andino-Amazónico* 6, no. 8 (2015), 11.

92 Francis makes clear that to "live well" is "not the same as 'to have a good time.'" Francis, *Address at the Second World Meeting of Popular Movements in Santa Cruz, Bolivia*, July 9, 2015, no. 3.1.

CHAPTER 8

THE FIRST AMERICAN POPE

William L. Portier

ONCE UPON A TIME, a pope coming to the United States would have been extraordinary.[1] Beginning with Pope Paul VI's historic address to the United Nations in 1965, however, all that has changed. Three of Pope Francis's four papal predecessors visited the US. During his twenty-five-year papacy, Pope John Paul II visited the US seven times. A former actor, John Paul II was the first media-savvy pope and something of a rock star. Nobel laureate Bob Dylan played for him in Bologna. Bono once gave him a pair of his signature sunglasses.

On the eve of Pope Francis's visit to the US at the end of September 2015, @Pontifex, the Twitter handle begun by Pope Benedict XVI in 2012, had twenty-two million followers, and Francis was the most retweeted leader in the world.[2] By comparison, on the day after New York's primary election in April 2016, @realDonaldTrump had a "mere" 7.7 million followers. Though only 55 percent of Americans have a "favorable impression" of the Catholic Church, 70 percent have a "favorable impression" of Francis. That includes 86 percent of Catholics and 74 percent of "nones"; that is, those with no religious affiliation.[3]

Amid intense media coverage, Pope Francis arrived in Washington, D.C., on Tuesday afternoon, September 23. With two other stops in New York City and in Philadelphia for the World Meeting of Families,

---

1 This chapter began as the inaugural lecture in the "Francis Factor" series at Alvernia University. I am grateful to President Thomas F. Flynn, who invited me to Alvernia, to the students and faculty for stimulating discussions and warm hospitality, and especially to Dr. Kevin Godfrey who suggested the title "The First American Pope."

2 Michelle Boorstein, "God's Message in a Digital Bottle," *The Washington Post*, September 22, 2016.

3 Michael S. Rosenwald, Michelle Boorstein, and Scott Clement, "Pope Begins a Journey to Bolster Church," *The Washington Post*, September 20, 2016.

his US visit lasted until the following Sunday. Global communications technology made Francis's every word, as well as extensive commentary, almost instantly available. As will become clear, I interpret Francis's visit primarily as a bicontinental encounter between South and North. In large measure, I think, that is how he saw it. He consistently referred to North and South America as one continent rather than two.

Pope Francis can be provocative. Despite his unique popularity, much ecclesial and political hand-wringing preceded his visit. He flew into the US from Cuba, a country with which the US government has been in bitter conflict for more than fifty years. In Bolivia the previous summer, Francis denounced the "unfettered pursuit of money" as the "dung of the devil." These words of St. Basil of Caesarea from the fourth century caught the favorable attention of presidential candidate Bernie Sanders.[4] And then, of course, there was Francis's description in his 2015 encyclical *Laudato Si'* of the earth becoming an "immense dung heap." This so exercised *The Washington Post*'s George Will that he devoted a whole column to the pope's "fact-free flamboyance."[5] Who knew what the pope might say when he got to the US?

Such worries were soon forgotten. During his five-day visit, Pope Francis struck a tone that attracted many different kinds of people in unexpected ways. If, as he insists, time is greater than space, and beginning a process is greater than controlling a space, this was an auspicious beginning, a beginning in which Francis built on the reservoir of goodwill that greeted him on Tuesday afternoon. He did not satisfy everyone. Nevertheless, with his gift for small gestures, such as riding in a little Fiat 500L rather than a limousine, and his tremendous ability to be really present to the people he encounters, he was more a pastor than the prophet some had hoped for. Rather than denouncing their country as harboring a "culture of death," Pope Francis exhorted people in the US to live up to their own ideals.

Along the way, Francis was drawn in by each person he met, whether it was the speaker of the House of Representatives, John Boehner, a former altar boy from Reading, Ohio, or Maryland governor Larry

4 Bernie Sanders, "I Annotated a Speech by Pope Francis, Here are the Ways his Words Show the Values We Have in Common," *The Washington Post,* April 15, 2016.

5 George Will, "Pope Francis's Fact-Free Flamboyance," *The Washington Post*, September 20, 2015.

Hogan, carrying on in office while undergoing cancer treatment, or Ricky Perry, a D.C. homeless man Francis greeted warmly at a shelter at St. Patrick's Church. To use two words dear to the pope, we might say that he *encountered* and *accompanied* each one of them.

Ecclesia in America, a South-North Encounter

Many in the nineteenth-century US wondered, in the words of George Will's "Fact-Free Flamboyance" column, how Catholics could "simultaneously honor the pope and celebrate their nation's premises." John F. Kennedy's 1960 affirmation of the separation of church and state before an assembly of Baptist pastors in Houston is best read as part of a long history of Catholic immigrants and their descendants negotiating a place in their country's unique political circumstances. These efforts came to a head in a series of late nineteenth-century controversies over the extent to which the US, with its signature political ideals of religious liberty and separation of church and state, was a benign or hostile place for Catholic immigrants.

These controversies involved everyday questions like work and school and beer. Should Catholic laborers participate in unions and other fraternal and benevolent societies? Such societies were secret and sometimes anti-Catholic, but they also offered benefits like insurance and credit. Should Catholics support the temperance movement promoted by the dominant evangelical Protestant culture of the day? After all, what could be wrong with Irish pubs and German beer gardens? The Irish wanted to know why German immigrants tried to preserve their own culture and language with German newspapers and organizations. Why didn't they just learn English? Catholics asked themselves whether they should have their own schools or send their children to public schools. Bishops who promoted rapid assimilation of Catholics into the culture of the US were called "Americanists." Their opponents, more distrustful of US political institutions, counseled caution and a certain measure of separatism.

During the 1890s, Americanist bishops tried to export their program to Europe, where they thought the separation of church and state would revivify the church and end its dominance by European governments, some of whom had the authority to nominate bishops and even to veto papal elections. However, these efforts of the Americanist bishops to expand into Europe, combined with the US's recent humiliation of Spain in the war of 1898,[6] led the Vatican to censure an error called "Americanism," which it vaguely described as an attempt to introduce greater liberty into the church in imitation of secular states. If nothing else, this censure sent the Americanists a clear message to back off. And they did. An embattled Vatican did not appreciate their efforts to create "a church in America different from that which is in other parts of the world." This papal censure came in a document known to history as *Testem Benevolentiae*—in English *A Witness to Our Benevolence.* It was signed on January 22, 1899.[7]

One hundred years later to the day, in Mexico City, on January 22, 1999, Pope John Paul II put his signature to his postsynodal apostolic exhortation *Ecclesia in America.*[8] The document's date suggests that its title was taken from *Testem Benevolentiae* and its reference to "a church in America [*ecclesia in America*] different from that which is in the rest of the world." But this time the pope was indeed calling for an *ecclesia in America* that was different. Most interestingly, however, he used the term "America" in a sense that combined both North and South America.

Ecclesia in America followed on and summed up the work of the Special Assembly for America of the Synod of Bishops, held in Rome in 1997. The exhortation is addressed to the church in North and South America, one church, one continent, one America. Speaking of America in the singular was a deliberate choice by which John Paul II hoped to express a unity that in some sense already existed, as well as a closer unity that might come about both through and for the sake

6 In an example of highbrow nativism, the same George Will began a more recent column with a reference to Puerto Rico as "an awkward legacy of the United States' 1898 testosterone spill, the Spanish-American War." George Will, "Contain Puerto Rico's Crisis," *The Washington Post*, April 28, 2016.

7 This quotation is from the conclusion of *Testem Benevolentiae*, which can be found at the Vatican.va website. The literature on Americanism is extensive. For a brief review of it and of *Testem Benevolentiae* and *Ecclesia in America*, see William L. Portier, "Americanism and Inculturation: 1899–1999," *Communio: International Catholic Review* 27, no. 1 (Spring 2000): 139–60. See also Peter Casarella, "Solidarity as the Fruit of Communion: *Ecclesia in America*, 'Post-Liberation Theology,' and the Earth," *Communio: International Catholic Review* 27, no.1 (Spring 2000): 98–123.

8 John Paul II, Postsynodal Apostolic Exhortation *Ecclesia in America* (January 22, 1999). All documents published by the Vatican, including this one and others cited below, including papal addresses, may be found at the vatican.va website.

of the church's mission.[9] Conspicuous for its language about culture and the evangelization of culture and for its refusal to separate cultural questions from economic critique and social analysis, this document is in clear continuity with those of the Latin American bishops going back to Medellín in 1968 and Puebla in 1979. The latter applied the teachings of *Evangelii Nuntiandi*, Pope Paul VI's 1975 apostolic exhortation on evangelization to the Latin American church. Puebla's language of "encounter," along with the references to *Evangelii Nuntiandi*, called by Francis shortly after his election "the greatest pastoral document ever written," recalls the Argentine movement that animates the words and gestures of Pope Francis: the "theology of the people."[10]

Since 1999, nothing approaching John Paul II's dream of a role for the church in unifying the peoples of North and South America has come to pass. *Ecclesia in America* lies largely forgotten,[11] but clearly, Pope Francis has not forgotten it. My argument here is that he imagined his visit to the US as the kind of encounter of South with North envisioned in *Ecclesia in America.* Such an encounter would be closely linked to immigration—speaking from Lampedusa and Lesbos, both Mediterranean islands of passage and confinement for immigrants, Francis has made advocacy for immigrants central to his papacy. His biographer claims that the pope "is convinced that the mass displacement of people at this time is the most important moral choice facing Western countries. Will we embrace the stranger in need or build new iron curtains?"[12]

9 John Paul II, *Ecclesia in America*, 5.

10 I have been unable to discover who drafted *Ecclesia in America.* On the Argentine influence on *Evangelii Nuntiandi,* and Pope Francis's estimate of it, see Austen Ivereigh, *The Great Reformer: Francis and the Making of a Radical Pope* (New York: Henry Holt, 2014), 122–23, 184–85. See also Juan Carlos Scannone, SJ, "Pope Francis and the Theology of the People," *Theological Studies* 77, no. 1 (March 2016): 118–35. In *Laudato Si'*, Francis cited Scannone with respect to "the values frequently found, for example, in the *villas*, *chabollas* or *favelas* of Latin America." See Francis, Encyclical Letter *Laudato Si', on Care for Our Common Home*, n. 117. On Lucio Gera and Rafael Tello, the chief architects of the theology of the people, see Allan Figueroa Deck, SJ, *Francis, Bishop of Rome: The Gospel for the Third Millennium* (New York: Paulist Press, 2016), chaps. 3 and 4.

11 David Morrison, "A Great Blueprint Left Unread," *Our Sunday Visitor* (April 11, 1999): 5.

12 Austen Ivereigh, as quoted in Griff Witte and Anthony Faiola, "Pope to Issue Moral Call to Europe on Migrants," *The Washington Post*, April 16, 2016.

About five months after his visit to the US, on February 16, 2016, Francis traveled to Mexico from Cuba. He said Mass at a fairground in Juárez, Mexico, just across the Rio Grande from El Paso, Texas. As thirty thousand people watched on simulcast from the Sun Bowl, a stadium in El Paso and with many thousands more on the Mexican side, Pope Francis walked to the edge of the river, paused, and prayed silently at the huge, dark memorial cross erected to the memory of those who have died along the border. Two women from Juárez, Daisy Flores Gámez and Evelia Quintana Molina, addressed Francis in Spanish about the working conditions there.[13] He waved to the immigrants in detention on the US side of the border and spoke in his homily of "poverty, violence, drug trafficking and lawlessness" as the root causes of migration from Central America and Mexico to the US.[14]

It is not hard to imagine that Francis believes that Latin American immigrants to the US will be the instruments of the church's role in unifying South and North America. With serious threats of mass deportations, a Muslim registry, and a massive (and partially completed) border wall between Mexico and the US, however, immigration is a controversial topic in the US. Nevertheless, from the beginning to the end of his five-day visit in September 2015, Francis emphasized the central theme of immigration. He portrayed it as a potential encounter in which Latin American peoples, following dreams of a better life, bring their faith and its popular expressions, part of a Catholic "culture" in the senses used by both Paul VI and John Paul II, as potential contributions to public life and the church in the US.

A Pilgrim from the South

Memoirist Richard Rodriguez has been writing for at least a decade about the "browning" of the US, about the historic shift from the traditional westward movement of Manifest Destiny to a new South to

13 Political Theology Network (website), "Speeches of Two Women Frame Pope Francis' Visit to the US-Mexico Border," July 10, 2016, http://www.politicaltheology.com/blog/speeches-of-two-women-frame-pope-francis-visit-to-the-us-mexico-border-neomi-deanda-and-nestor-medina/.

14 Manny Fernandez, "Pope Francis Visits U.S.-Mexico Border," *The New York Times* online, February 17, 2016, live coverage, http://www.nytimes.com/live/pope-francis-at-us-mexico-border.

North movement.[15] The US Census Bureau agrees, projecting that by 2060, one-third of the population will be Hispanic.[16] Most significant to note about Pope Francis's journey to the US is that he came from the South, immediately after a visit to Cuba. And it took him three years to get here—during his first three years as pope, Francis visited Brazil in 2013 and Bolivia, Ecuador, and Paraguay in 2015, but not the US.

Finally on September 22, 2015, the pope's white and green Alitalia jetliner touched down at Andrews Air Force Base. His flight originated not in Rome but in Santiago, Cuba, where at the Basilica of Our Lady of Charity of El Cobre, he urged a "revolution of tenderness." Four days earlier, he landed in Havana where he praised ongoing discussions aimed at a détente between the US and Cuba. While the US trade embargo remains in effect, the two countries had negotiated to ease restrictions on travel, trade, and banking. Francis called this process, in which the Vatican played a significant role, "a sign of the victory of the culture of encounter and dialogue."[17] On Sunday in Havana's Plaza of the Revolution, he said Mass "not far from the huge mural depicting the iconic gaze of fellow Argentine Ernesto 'Che' Guevara."[18]

After saying good morning to President Obama on the White House lawn, in Pope Francis's first public words in the US, he introduced himself as an immigrant, a pilgrim from the South: "As a son of an immigrant family, I am happy to be a guest in this country, which was largely built by such families."[19] He went on in this address to outline the topics he would treat while in the US, but he had sounded a central

15 See especially Richard Rodriguez, *Days of Obligations: An Argument with My Mexican Father* (New York: Penguin Books, 1992) and *Brown: The Last Discovery of America* (New York: Penguin Books, 2002).

16 Daisy Machado, "History and Latino/a Identity, Mapping a Past that Leads to our Future," in *The Wiley-Blackwell Companion to Latino/a Theology*, ed. Orlando Espín (London: John Wiley and Sons, 2015), 39.

17 Nick Miroff, "Pope Arrives in Havana, Praising U.S.-Cuba Thaw," *The Washington Post*, September 20, 2015.

18 Miroff, "Pope Arrives in Havana."

19 *Remarks of President Obama and His Holiness Pope Francis at Arrival Ceremony*, The White House, Washington, D.C. September 23, 2015, Aleteia website, "Read the Full Texts of all of Pope Francis' Addresses During His Visit to the US," September 28, 2015, http://aleteia.org/2015/09/28/read-the-full-texts-of-all-of-pope-francis-addresses-during-his-visit-to-the-u-s/. Unless otherwise noted, all the quotations from Pope Francis's addresses while in the US are from this source.

theme—that the US, following the title of President John F. Kennedy's posthumously published book, is a nation of immigrants.

South-North Encounter, Immigration, and Dreams

During his US visit, over five days in various settings in Washington, D.C., New York City, and Philadelphia, Pope Francis spoke seventeen times. His addresses varied in degrees of formality from brief greetings, unscripted remarks, and prayers to homilies and major addresses. The transcript of the addresses runs to more than forty single-spaced pages. The pope spoke about half the time as chief pastor and teacher of the church and half the time as a world leader, the capacity in which Speaker Boehner invited him to address Congress and in which he was invited to the United Nations. The two longest addresses, both running to about six pages, were his addresses to the UN and to the US Congress.

In addition to his roles as pastor and world leader, Pope Francis also clearly envisioned himself as somehow representing the people of Latin America to the people of the US. He represented the South in an integral way that combines what people in the US might distinguish as religion, politics, and culture. As a kind of icon of the hemispheric movement from South to North, described so eloquently by Rodriguez, he embodied the South-North encounter envisioned in *Ecclesia in America* back in 1999.

To the bishops in St. Matthew's Cathedral in Washington, he introduced himself as "from a land which is also American." "I must tell you," he continued, "I do not feel a stranger in your midst. I am a native of a land which is also vast, with great open ranges, a land which, like your own received the faith from itinerant missionaries." In speaking of the combined genius of pioneers and settlers, he quoted from the poem "Alexander Throckmorton" in Edgar Lee Masters' 1916 *Spoon River Anthology.*[20] The next day Francis thanked the Congress for their invitation to him to address a joint session "in the land of the free and the home of the brave." "I would like to think," he continued, "that the reason for this [invitation] is that I too am a son of this great continent, from which we have all received

20 *Speech of Pope Francis to the Bishops of the United States*, St. Matthew's Cathedral, Washington, D.C., September 23, 2015.

so much and toward which we share a common responsibility."[21] Both greetings presume one continent, one America.

Closely tied to this theme of South-North encounter is the contested theme of immigration. He concluded his address to the bishops in Washington with a moving plea for immigrants. He called them "pilgrims," to whose central place in US Catholic history he paid tribute. "Now," he told the bishops, "you are facing this stream of Latin immigrants," and speaking "as a pastor from the South," he thanked and encouraged them. "Perhaps it will not be easy for you to look into their soul; perhaps you will be challenged by their diversity. But know that they also possess resources meant to be shared. So do not be afraid to welcome them. Offer them the warmth of the love of Christ and you will unlock the mystery of their heart. I am certain that, as often in the past, these people will enrich America and its Church."[22] Clearly a major resource present in the South is the theology of the people, with its potential to enrich both ecclesial and public life in the US.[23]

At every stop along his journey in the US, Francis never missed an opportunity to talk about immigration. He spoke in terms of the South-North encounter, immigration enriching the whole unified continent, and our responsibility for its great resources. He closely tied the theme of immigration to the theme of dreams. These three themes of South-North encounter, immigration, and dreams came together in five-year-old Sophie Cruz of Los Angeles. As the motorcade made its way from the White House to St. Matthew's Cathedral on the morning of September 23, she darted out toward the popemobile from behind the barricades. Francis beckoned to her and, with a nod from him, she rushed past a guard to give him a letter and a T-shirt.[24]

In all three cities, Latinos made up a significant portion of Francis's audience. "Among us today are members of America's large Hispanic

---

21 *Visit to the Joint Session of the United States Congress: Address of the Holy Father*, Washington, D.C., September 24, 2015.

22 *Speech of Pope Francis to the Bishops of the United States.*

23 "In America, the *mestiza* face of the Virgin of Guadalupe was from the start a symbol of the inculturation of the gospel, of which she has been the lodestar and guide. Through her powerful intercession, the gospel will penetrate the hearts of the men and women of America and permeate their cultures, transforming them from within." John Paul II, *Ecclesia in America*, 70.

24 On Sophie Cruz, see the photo in "Notebook," *The Washington Post*, September 24, 2015.

population," the pope noted as he arrived in Philadelphia on Saturday, September 26, "as well as representatives of recent immigrants to the United States." With the Liberty Bell in the background, Francis spoke in his native Spanish: "I greet all of you with a particular affection. Many of you have immigrated to this country at great personal cost, but in the hope of building a new life. Do not be discouraged by whatever challenges and hardships you face." Locating them squarely in the story of immigrant struggles throughout American history, he urged Latinos not to be ashamed of their traditions: "Do not forget the lessons you learned from your elders … something you can bring to enrich the life of this American land …. You are called to be responsible citizens and to contribute, like others … did before you … fruitfully to the life of the communities in which you live."[25] The fact that the pope spoke in Spanish was hugely important. "Do you know how important it was that he came and spoke to us in Spanish?" Gladys Stillwagon, a Mexican American from New Jersey asked a reporter—in English! "He has affirmed us and given us the tools to take the next step."[26]

Pastoral Revolution and Responsibility for the Common Good

In addition to the three that I've highlighted—South-North encounter, immigration, and dreams—Pope Francis touched on many other themes. His address at Independence Hall in Philadelphia emphasized religious liberty, and as in the address to Congress, set religious liberty in the context of a general appeal to the founding principles of the US. As he did in *Laudato Si'*, he also spoke forcefully about the environment, encouraging President Obama, for example, in his initiative to reduce air pollution.[27] Finally, Francis also met with survivors of sexual abuse by priests and addressed the topic briefly in his remarks to bishops in both Washington, D.C. and movingly, in

25 All of the quotations in this paragraph to this point are from the *Meeting for Religious Liberty with the Hispanic Community and Other Immigrants: Address of the Holy Father*, Independence Hall, Philadelphia, September 26, 2015.

26 Manuel Roig-Franzia, Arelis Hernandez, and Pamela Constable, "Francis's Remarks on Immigration Hearten U.S. Latinos," *The Washington Post*, September 27, 2015.

27 *Remarks of President Obama and His Holiness Pope Francis at Arrival Ceremony*, September 23, 2015. Half of Francis's brief remarks on this occasion were devoted to the environment.

Philadelphia, and again to reporters on the return flight to Rome. However, he did not treat this topic with the seriousness that many had hoped for.[28] And though one of his homilies in Philadelphia focused on St. Katherine Drexel, he didn't address the situation of women in the church.

We might make sense of what Francis did say about these other themes by looking at them in terms of the pope's dual office as pastor and as a world leader having a unique political role. As his remarks to the bishops made clear, he came primarily as a pastor. Francis's words about marriage, religious liberty, and even the sexual abuse of children, are best understood in the context of the pastoral revolution he wants for the church, well-expressed in the apostolic exhortation *Amoris Laetitia* (April 2016).

Exhorting the bishops to a "culture of encounter" and "method of dialogue," he urged them to be first pastors and men of prayer. Like a good pastor, he did not put them down or shame them in public. In regard to the sexual abuse of children by priests, he praised them for their "courage" and "generous commitment to bring healing to victims"—comments that drew much criticism—but he also cautioned them pointedly that "harsh and divisive language do not befit the tongue of a pastor, it has no place in his heart." He urged them to be close to the sheep, to make of the church "a humble home, a family hearth which attracts men and women through the attractive light and warmth of love." He reminded them to recognize the Lord's voice "in the quiet pleas of so many of our brothers and sisters." When this certainty of Christ's presence weakens, he warned, "we end up being caretakers of ash and not guardians and dispensers of the true light and warmth which causes our hearts to burn within us (Lk 24:32)." He reminded the bishops of their "service to unity" and their role in working for the common good.[29]

28 See Karen Heller, Frances Stead Sellers, and Michael A. Ruane, "Philadelphia Visit Generates Excitement and Disruption," *The Washington Post*, September 27, 2015; Sarah Pulliam Bailey, Abby Ohlheiser, and Terrence McCoy, "'God Weeps': Pope Reveals Meeting with Five Sex Abuse Survivors," *The Washington Post*, September 28, 2015; "Obstruction on Child Sex Abuse," editorial, *The Washington Post*, April 20, 2016.

29 All of the quotations in this paragraph are from *Speech of Pope Francis to the Bishops of the United States*.

First Hispanic Saint

The day after addressing the bishops, in a ceremony on the lawn outside the National Shrine of the Immaculate Conception on the campus of The Catholic University of America, Pope Francis canonized the eighteenth-century Franciscan Fra Junípero Serra, founder of the California missions. Like most of Francis's actions and gestures, the canonization of the first Hispanic saint in US Catholic history brims with potential meanings. In his homily that day, Francis emphasized that Serra, who embodied "'a Church which goes forth' … to bring everywhere the reconciling tenderness of God," represented the kind of pastor and the kind of church he wants to encourage. Serra's motto was *siempre Adelante!*—"keep moving forward." He trod "the dust laden paths of history." He stood for the opposite of a "self-enclosed" church, "a church frozen into elites, clinging to their own security."[30]

Though Pope Francis tried to highlight Serra's efforts to "defend the dignity of the native community," he took some heat in Latino quarters on account of Serra's complicity in the coercive nature of the mission system.[31] Many hoped that the Argentine pope would have chosen a native of the Americas rather than another European. Perhaps Francis was thinking that Serra is widely recognized in the US not only as a Catholic missionary, but also as a contributor to California history and culture. Perhaps he was aware that, in the section of the Statuary Hall of the US Capitol honoring California, Fra Junípero's statue stands next to Ronald Reagan's.

The Address to Congress: Four Dreams

Pope Francis's vision of a pastoral church that goes forth and, along the way, contributes to the common life of the nation is on full display in his address to Congress. In his 1989 book *Public Catholicism*,

30 All of the quotations in this paragraph are from *Homily of Pope Francis*, Basilica of the Shrine of the Immaculate Conception, Washington, D.C., September 23, 2015.

31 See Jacqueline Hidalgo, "Serra's Actions Aren't the Only Reasons to Lament his Canonization," Religion Dispatches website, September 24, 2015, http://religiondispatches.org/serras-actions-arent-the-only-reason-to-lament-his-canonization/, and Joseph P. Chinnici, OFM, "Junípero Serra: A Hermeneutic of Holiness for the 21st Century," unpublished public lecture at The Catholic University of America, October 14, 2016, cited with author's permission.

historian David O'Brien describes various ways in which the church, through its members, is present in and engaged with society. He calls this presence "public Catholicism." O'Brien brilliantly weaves together the chronology, content, and ongoing dynamics of U.S. Catholic history to create a threefold typology of simultaneous and mutually self-correcting styles of public Catholicism: republican, immigrant, and evangelical. In Francis's historic address to Congress, all three styles are on display.[32]

To begin with, the very act of addressing Congress, with the expectation that he would speak, for the most part, in "publicly" accessible terms open to a pluralist audience, performs the republican style. Francis introduced himself with a reference to the line from the national anthem "the land of the free and the home of the brave" and went on to encourage the legislators in their political calling, whose "chief aim" is the "tireless and demanding pursuit of the common good." Then he veered in a slightly more biblical direction, likening the legislators to Moses. He pushed the republican envelope just a bit with this exhortation: "You are asked to protect by means of the law, the image and likeness fashioned by God on every human life."[33]

In 1966, sociologist Robert N. Bellah (1927–2013) borrowed from Rousseau's *Social Contract* (1762) to reflect, in what has become a classic essay, on civil religion in America. In Bellah's conception, subordination of the nation to higher ethical principles saves civil religion from the idolatry of national self-worship. Written during the Vietnam War, at a time of national crisis, Bellah's essay has inspired decades of subsequent commentary.[34] Historian Sidney Mead famously called

32 David J. O'Brien, *Public Catholicism* (New York: Macmillan, 1989), 247–52.

33 Like many of the quotations in this section, this one is from *Visit to the Joint Session of the United States Congress: Address of the Holy Father*.

34 Robert N. Bellah, "Civil Religion in America," *Daedalus* 96, no. 1 (Winter 1967): 1–21; reprinted with discussion in *The Religious Situation: 1968*, ed. Donald R. Cutler (Boston: Beacon Press, 1968), 388–93. In 1975, Bellah published a series of lectures on civil religion given in 1973 at Hebrew Union College in Cincinnati under the title *The Broken Covenant: American Civil Religion in Time of Trial* (New York: Seabury Press, 1975). The University of Chicago Press published a second edition of *The Broken Covenant* in 1992. Bellah's afterword to this work, at pp. 164–88, originally published in 1978, contains his sophisticated reflections on civil religion. For more recent engagement with the extensive literature on civil religion, see Raymond Haberski, Jr., *God and War: American Civil Religion Since 1945* (New Brunswick, N.J.: Rutgers University Press, 2012) and Jason A. Edwards and Joseph M.

the US "a nation with the soul of a church," speaking of a "religion of the Republic" potentially in tension with the nation's various denominational faiths and their theologies.[35] Such Protestant-inspired civic piety is perhaps the closest thing the US has to what in Argentina is called the theology of the people. By deploying O'Brien's republican style in his address to Congress, Pope Francis proved himself adept at the discourse of US civil religion.[36]

Invoking the method of dialogue he had urged upon the bishops, Francis told Congress that through them he hoped to address "the many thousands of men and women who strive each day to do an honest day's work, to bring home their daily bread, to save money and—one step at a time—to build a better life for their families." He wanted to engage in dialogue with all Americans "through the historical memory of your people." He picked "three sons and a daughter of this land, four individuals and four dreams": Abraham Lincoln, Martin Luther King, Jr., Dorothy Day, and Thomas Merton.[37]

The names of Lincoln, assassinated 150 years before the pope's 2015 address, and King, who marched from Selma to Montgomery fifty years before, with, as Francis put it, their dreams of "liberty" and "liberty in plurality and non-exclusion," respectively, are associated with national holidays and memorialized in iconic sculptures that are national landmarks. As public figures, Day and Merton do not approach the stature of Lincoln and King. The founder of the New York Catholic Worker, with her dream of "social justice and the rights of persons," and the Kentucky Trappist monk and mystic, with his dream of the "capacity for dialogue and openness to God," are less well-known and were perhaps even unknown to many in the congressional chambers. Lincoln, and especially King, had few peers as what historian Martin

---

Valenzano III, eds., *The Rhetoric of American Civil Religion: Symbols, Sinners, and Saints* (Lanham, Md.: Lexington Books, 2016).

35 Sidney Mead, *The Nation with the Soul of a Church* (New York: Harper and Row, 1975).

36 This raises the question of the source of the pope's facility with this discourse. It is rumored that, in addition to Cardinal Pietro Parolin, the Vatican secretary of state, cardinals Sean O'Malley and Donald Wuerl also worked on drafting Francis's address to Congress.

37 Luis D. Leon argues that Cesar Chavez has now joined Washington, Lincoln, and King among the recognized "saints" of civil religion in America. See "Cesar Chavez in American Religious Politics: Mapping the New Spiritual Line," *American Quarterly* 59, no. 3 (September 2007): 857–81.

Marty has called "public theologians."[38] As orators, they deployed the founding republican language of liberty seamlessly, as in King's 1963 "I Have a Dream" speech at the foot of the Washington Monument, and the biblical language in their speeches has been incorporated over time into American civil religion. Lincoln and King are the canonical public theologians of American civil religion.

In Philadelphia's Independence Hall on Saturday, Francis would speak from the lectern Lincoln used for the Gettysburg Address, which was identified by Bellah as the new covenant of civil religious scripture. In the Lincoln section of this speech, Francis spoke in the widely accessible language of freedom, peace, justice, combating violence, and eliminating "new global forms of slavery, born of grave injustices which can be overcome only through new policies and new forms of consensus"; that is, through politics. Appealing to the opening lines of the Declaration of Independence, for Bellah the foundational scripture of US civil religion, Francis concluded: "If politics must truly be at the service of the human person, it follows that it cannot be the slave of economy and finance."

Martin Luther King brought Francis to his recurring theme of dreams. "I am happy," he said, "that America continues to be for many a land of 'dreams.'" The next day, at Queen of Angels School in Harlem, he returned to King's "I have a dream": "Today we want to keep dreaming," he told the children.[39] With reference to King's dream, he recalled to Congress that: "We the people of this continent are not fearful of foreigners, … because most of us were once foreigners. I say this to you as the son of immigrants, knowing that so many of you are descended from immigrants." Recalling the tragedies and injustices associated with the "first contacts," he urged against repeating the mistakes of the past: "When the stranger in our midst appeals to us, we must not repeat the sins and errors of the past."

Invoking the Golden Rule of Matthew's Gospel (Mt 7:12), he urged Congress to treat the thousands "who are led to travel north in search of a better life for their loved ones, in search of greater opportunities"

---

38 Martin Marty, "Two Kinds of Civil Religion," in *American Civil Religion*, ed. Russell E. Richey and Donald G. Jones (San Francisco: Harper and Row, 1974), 139–57. Amazingly, Marty did not identify King as an example of a public theologian.

39 *Speech of Pope Francis*, Our Lady Queen of Angels School, Harlem, New York, September 25, 2015.

as they would want to be treated. "We must not be taken aback by their numbers, but rather view them as persons, seeing their faces and listening to their stories, trying to respond as best we can to their situation." The Golden Rule, he claimed, also grounded his continuing advocacy for the "global abolition of the death penalty."

In the King section of his address, Francis combined O'Brien's republican and immigrant styles, using republican language and his position as a world leader to advocate on behalf of immigrants, refugees, and prisoners. The explicitly Christian and pastoral appeals of his homilies in Washington, New York, and Philadelphia, which relied on Gospel witness in word and deed, epitomize O'Brien's evangelical style, but the evangelical style was not absent from the address to Congress. The pope wanted the legislators to know that faith drove Day's work on behalf of the poor and Merton's on behalf of peace and interreligious dialogue. He wanted them to know that the presence of people of faith in the body politic can enrich and elevate it.

He called Dorothy Day a "Servant of God," calling attention to the fact that her cause for sainthood in the Catholic Church is presently underway in New York. He emphasized that "her social activism, her passion for justice, and for the cause of the oppressed, were inspired by the Gospel, her faith, and the example of the saints." Day's example inspired him to speak at length of the tremendous task facing the world in the third millennium of "rais[ing] people out of extreme poverty," of giving hope to people "trapped in a cycle of poverty." It did not take him long to connect poverty to the environment. Though he spoke most substantively about the environment in his address to the United Nations on September 25, the address to Congress refers at length to *Laudato Si'*, urging a "culture of care" and "an integrated approach to combating poverty, restoring dignity to the excluded, and at the same time protecting nature."

Finally, he came to the Cistercian monk Thomas Merton, quoting his 1948 autobiography *The Seven Storey Mountain*. For Francis, Merton represents commitment to dialogue. He described him as "above all a man of prayer, a thinker who challenged the certitudes of his time and opened new horizons for souls and for the Church .... a man of dialogue, a promoter of peace between peoples and religions." He urged countries formerly at odds to "resume the path of dialogue," which for Francis entails a commitment to end "the many armed conflicts throughout our world" and the deadly arms trade which makes them possible.

Day and Merton are often looked to by many who, over the past decades, have felt pushed aside in the church. Both, however, as does the pope, combined service to the poor and to peace with deep personal commitments to prayer and the interior life. Their appearance in this address, not to mention their central places in it, was striking because their lives challenge everyone.

With its simultaneous appropriation, both celebratory and challenging, of civil religion and US Catholic history, delivered in Francis's signature style and voice, this address to Congress was certainly the highlight of his US trip.[40] Melding together O'Brien's three styles, the address to Congress ended with a summary of Francis's appeal, through these four figures, to the "richness of your cultural heritage" and the "spirit of the American people." "It is my desire," he concluded, "that this spirit continue to develop and grow, so that as many young people as possible can inherit and dwell in a land which has inspired so many people to dream. God bless America!" Often a perfunctory tag line to political speeches, "God bless America" became, when Francis spoke it, a prophetic utterance, his bicontinental perspective making it tremble with a new breadth of meaning.

The Family: A Factory of Hope

Francis original purpose for coming to the US was to attend the World Meeting on Families in Philadelphia. In Philadelphia, however, Francis did not focus on perceived threats to the family but on what is attractive and good about it. "For the Church," he told the bishops, "the family is not first and foremost a cause for concern, but rather the joyous confirmation of God's blessing upon the masterpiece of creation."[41]

40 It was not clear that all would go so well. On September 24, the day Francis addressed Congress, an organization called the Freedom From Religion Foundation took out a full-page ad on the back page of *The Washington Post*'s A section. "Why is the POPE Preaching to Congress?" the ad demanded to know. "POPE" appeared in bold. Inset above this question was John F. Kennedy's well-known affirmation of the separation of church and state, made during the 1960 presidential campaign.

41 *Meeting with the Bishops Taking Part in the World Meeting of Families: Address of the Holy Father*, St. Charles Borromeo Seminar, Philadelphia, September 27, 2015.

In earlier unscripted remarks to crowds in Philadelphia, speaking of God's creation, he proclaimed, "But the most beautiful thing God made, the Bible says, was the family." "And his Son," he continued, "where did God send Him? To a palace? To a city, to start a business? God sent him to a family! God came into the world in a family." God, he said, in a clear reference to US debates about the "undocumented," has given the family "a divine passport." He spoke of children and grandparents and another recurring theme, memory and remembrance: "A people that doesn't know how to care for the children and a people that doesn't know how to care for the grandparents is a people without a future, because it doesn't have the strength … the memory that will carry it forward." Family is a "factory of hope."[42]

Such language served as a dress rehearsal for Pope Francis's lengthy apostolic exhortation *Amoris Laetitia*, released on April 8, 2016. Introducing it to the press, Cardinal Christoph Schönborn of Vienna noted that, for him, *Amoris Laetitia* "is, first and foremost, a linguistic event …. Something has changed in ecclesial discourse." A child of divorced parents himself, Cardinal Schönborn especially appreciated the change in tone that "coherently overcomes that artificial, superficial, clear division between 'regular' and 'irregular' [marriages], and subjects *everyone* to the common call of the Gospel …: 'For God has consigned all to disobedience, that He may have mercy on all' (Rom 11:32)."[43]

The First American Pope: An Urban Gaucho

The change in church language initiated by Francis and noted by Schönborn extends far beyond marriage to other aspects of the church's life. It was on full display in the US. "By our own humble Christian apprenticeship in the familial service of God's people," he told the bishops in Philadelphia, "we will become more and more like fathers and mothers (as did St. Paul: cf. 1 Thes 2:7, 11), and less like people who have simply learned to live without a family."[44] Francis's

42 Francis, *Address to the Prayer Vigil for the Festival of Families: Address of the Holy Father,* Philadelphia, September 26, 2015.

43 "Cardinal Schönborn's Intervention at Presentation of Amoris Laetitia," Zenit.org website, April 8, 2016, https://zenit.org/articles/cardinal-schonborns-intervention-at-presentation-of-amoris-laetitia/.

44 *Meeting with Bishops Taking Part in the World Meeting of Families.*

down-to-earth, lyrical use of ordinary language for pastoral purposes strikes the ear as being different from what we usually hear from popes. If John Paul II was a philosopher pope and Benedict XVI a theologian pope extraordinaire, Francis is a poet pope. Not only does he quote Saint Thomas Aquinas and papal predecessors, he also quotes Jorge Luis Borges, *The Spoon River Anthology*, and *El Gaucho Martin Fierro*, an 1872 Argentine epic poem by José Hernandez that affirms solidarity in the face of social and material upheaval. He invoked the latter in urging the United Nations to stay strong in unity and avoid internal conflicts.[45] His feel for the narrative sense of Jesus's words and deeds as related in the Gospels, especially in the parables, and his ability to transpose them into ordinary situations of everyday life reflects his poetic gifts.

Early in his papacy, Francis described himself to a reporter as a "street priest," a lover of cities. He responded warmly to Washington. "They were so friendly. It was beautiful." But New York blew him away. To describe it, he needed an Italian phrase, *stra limitata*, "a superlative meaning beyond limit."[46] Perhaps we should attribute the "linguistic event" that is Francis in part to a unique appreciation for the urban landscape of Buenos Aires, its streets and neighborhoods, the people who live there, and the way they speak. Francis's homily at Madison Square Garden was a long meditation on encountering Jesus in the city. A Jesuit's lifetime of Ignatian mediation, the practice of regularly inserting himself imaginatively into the mysteries of Jesus's life, must have helped develop his poetic gifts as well. And no doubt there is in this gift with words much of the grace of God working with the pope's own unique personality.

In addition, Pope Francis's approach to language owes much to a Latin American "theology of the people" as developed in Argentina over the past forty years, which joins together a preferential option for the poor and a strong trust in and respect for popular Catholicism in Latin America. Perhaps we can attribute some of Francis's public ease with Gospel language and symbols to the fact that he comes from such

45 *Greetings of Pope Francis to United Nations Personnel,* United Nations Headquarters, New York, September 25, 2015.

46 These remarks are taken from a newspaper account of Francis's interview on the return flight from Philadelphia to Rome. See Brian Murphy, "Pope Expands Warnings about Clergy Sex Abuse Scandals," *The Washington Post,* September 29, 2015.

a people, from a Catholic culture. He urges immigrants from Latin America to the US to bring elements of this culture in order to enrich their new home. Francis's exhortations to an inclusive America made me think of Bruce Springsteen's quasi-liturgical 1999 performance of "Land of Hope and Dreams."[47] In the long run, however, it is not clear how Francis and his pastoral and linguistic revolution will translate into American English.

People from the US refer to themselves as "Americans." Francis's pastoral and linguistic revolution and his consistent use of both continents making up America in the singular, challenges citizens of the US to reimagine "America," to make it as wide as God's mercy. Aspects of our civil religion, such as the plea mounted on the pedestal of the Statue of Liberty, "Give me your tired, your poor, your huddled masses yearning to breathe free" and our history as a nation of immigrants, to which Francis appealed more than once, offer a bit of hope that citizens might find the resources to expand their sense of "America" and recognize the "divine passport" God has given to families. When Pope John Paul II died in 2005, and when Pope Benedict XVI resigned unexpectedly in 2013, the media buzzed about when or if we might ever have the first "American" pope. A sign that his pastoral and linguistic revolution has begun to bear fruit will come when people in the US begin to realize that Francis *is* the first American pope.

47 *The Essential Bruce Springsteen*, Columbia, 2003.

CHAPTER 9

A CENTURY OF MERCY

The Catholic Church and Immigration Along the US-Mexico Border

Julia G. Young

At approximately ten o'clock in the morning on February 17, 2016, Pope Francis arrived in the Mexican border city of Ciudad Juárez. During his historic visit—the first by any pope to the US-Mexico border region—he visited the city's Cereso prison, met with workers and employers at the Colegio de Bachilleres, and offered a mass at the fairgrounds of Ciudad Juárez, a few hundred feet from the US-Mexico border. The mass was simultaneously broadcast for an audience of thousands just north of the border, at the University of El Paso's Sun Bowl stadium.

During his homily, Pope Francis focused on the theme of divine mercy. Citing the story of the condemnation and redemption of the Biblical city of Nineveh, he called upon Catholics to remember and honor God's mercy by rejecting violence, oppression, and injustice. He also touched upon a theme that has been central to his papacy—the "humanitarian crisis" of migration. "Here in Ciudad Juárez," he noted, "there are thousands of immigrants from Central America and other countries." Specifically mentioning the victims of human trafficking, he appealed to his audience to help alleviate their suffering:

> Let us together ask our God for the gift of conversion, the gift of tears, let us ask him to give us open hearts like the Ninevites, open to his call heard in the suffering faces of countless men and women. No more death! No more exploitation! There is

Pope Francis prays before the cross on the border between Ciudad Juárez and El Paso (CNS)

> always time to change, there is always a way out and always an opportunity, there is always the time to implore the mercy of God.[1]

Pope Francis's request—that his audience open their hearts to the suffering of migrants at the US-Mexico border and to respond to their pain with mercy—was entirely in keeping with his commitment to migrants, as well as his continuous calls for Catholics to focus on the needs of the poor, the defenseless, and the underserved.[2] Indeed, this emphasis has been a hallmark of his papacy. His very first pastoral visit outside of Rome, on July 8, 2013, was to the island of Lampedusa, which had become a central port for migrants and refugees in

1 *Holy Mass: Homily of His Holiness Pope Francis*, Ciudad Juárez Fair Grounds, February 17, 2016. All documents published by the Vatican, including papal addresses, may be found at the vatican.va website.

2 For more on the centrality of migrants to Pope Francis's vision, see Allan Figueroa Deck, SJ, "Migrants and Refugees in Pope Francis's Transformative Vision of Church and Society" (The Fr. Lydio F. Tomasi, CS Annual Lecture on International Migration, San Diego, Calif., November 28, 2016), http://cmsny.org/publications/tomasilecture2016/.

the Mediterranean, many of whom were victims of trafficking. In his homily there, several weeks after yet another shipwreck in which hundreds of migrants had drowned, he strongly denounced migrant traffickers and challenged the citizens of the Western world to have compassion for migrants. In words that reflected his repeated focus on the "gift of tears," he pleaded, "[L]et us ask the Lord for the grace to weep over our indifference, to weep over the cruelty of our world, of our own hearts, and of all those who in anonymity make social and economic decisions which open the door to tragic situations like this. 'Has any one wept?' Today has anyone wept in our world?"[3]

Like Lampedusa, Ciudad Juárez is a place where tremendous suffering has occurred while the world's rich and powerful have turned away. Pope Francis's decision to come to the Mexican side of the border region thus perfectly fit with his mission to call attention to the global migration crisis. It was deeply symbolic that he chose to direct his message from south of the border to north of it. Just before offering mass, Pope Francis walked up to the edge of the Río Grande, where he knelt "before a large cross overlooking the border fence, made the sign of the cross and prayed before laying a bouquet of flowers on a small table before the cross." As he did so, a small group of people, some of them representatives of the US Catholic diocese of El Paso, watched from the US side of the border, "some peering at the spectacle through binoculars usually used to catch migrants trying to sneak over the border."[4]

Francis's visit to Ciudad Juárez and his call for mercy directed toward the Global North should also be considered within the context of his 2015 visit to South America, since it similarly helped to create, as well as to reinforce, the South-North dynamic that he had established during that trip. Indeed, Pope Francis had originally planned to visit Ciudad Juárez in 2015 before proceeding to the US. As he explained in an interview with Televisa's Valentina Alazraki, he decided not to do so (and went to Cuba instead) when his advisors pointed out that he could not visit Ciudad Juárez without first visiting the rest of Mexico—particularly the shrine to the Virgin of Guadalupe, Mexico's holiest

3 *Visit to Lampedusa, Homily of Holy Father Francis*, July 8, 2013.

4 Jim Yardley and Azam Ahmed, "Francis, at Border, Weighs in on American Debate over Immigration," *New York Times*, February 18, 2016.

site—or "it would cause a bit of a fuss." As a result, the border trip was delayed until he could make a longer visit to Mexico, and so he arrived in Ciudad Juárez after first visiting several other significant locations in Mexico: Mexico City, Ecatepec, Tuxtla Gutiérrez, San Cristobal de las Casas, and Morelia.[5] In any case, by staying on the Mexican side of the border and broadcasting his homily from south to north, Pope Francis was definitively reiterating the more global approach discussed in the introduction to this volume and in the accompanying chapters about his tour of South America in 2015.

Pope Francis's choice of Ciudad Juárez as the site for his border visit was also deeply significant because the area, including both Ciudad Juárez and its sister city across the border, El Paso, has long been one of the most important crossing sites for emigrants coming from Mexico and other parts of Latin America. It has also long been the site of illicit trade: in guns and weapons during the Mexican Revolution, in alcohol during the Prohibition years, and in illegal narcotics since at least the mid-twentieth century.[6] In more recent decades, the area has witnessed increasing violence, human trafficking, narcotrafficking, and—since the 1990s—a wave of femicides directed at young women factory workers, many of whom had migrated from other parts of Mexico. Indeed, ever since the modern border was established in 1848, migrant laborers have consistently been victimized by the violence and illicit trafficking that has occurred in the border region, as well as been subjected to constant surveillance from police forces on both sides of the border. Throughout this century-long history of violence and human rights violations, governments and much of the rest of society on both sides of the border have broadly failed to address the suffering of migrants at the border, offering instead, in the words of Nancy Pineda-Madrid, a "tacit acquiescence to these atrocities."[7]

Within this dark history, however, bright spots have appeared in which advocates have taken the side of migrants and attempted to

5 For a transcript of the interview, which took place on March 6, 2015, see Francis, "Two Years of a Pontificate—an interview with Televisa," *L'Osservatore Romano*, March 28, 2015, http://www.news.va/en/news/two-years-of-a-pontificate-an-interview-with-telev.

6 George T. Díaz, *Border Contraband: A History of Smuggling across the Rio Grande* (Austin: University of Texas Press, 2015).

7 Nancy Pineda-Madrid, *Suffering and Salvation in Ciudad Juárez* (Minneapolis: Fortress Press, 2011), 38.

bring them justice and respond to their needs with compassion. Some of these advocates have been members of the Catholic Church in the US, which has been actively assisting migrants in the region for almost a century. This long history of advocacy for migrants was, until recently, not well known outside of professional historical circles. As Allan Figueroa Deck states,

> Forty years ago there was very little familiarity with the breadth and depth of reflection on migration in the Catholic tradition... In the intervening years...knowledge and support for care and justice for immigrants and refugees have made tangible progress in Catholic social teaching. Indeed, one might argue that justice for migrants holds a place of high priority today in Catholic thought and action along with ecological concerns.[8]

It is certainly true that Catholic awareness of the need to respond to migrants with mercy has grown in recent years. Yet if we examine the activities of the US Catholic Church along the border in the early twentieth century, we can develop a fuller understanding of the long history of Catholic responses to the migrant experience. Indeed, this history shows that advocacy for migrants has been an integral part of US Catholic tradition.

In order to provide that fuller perspective, I offer here a historical overview of the Catholic Church's involvement with migrants and migration in the El Paso and Ciudad Juárez region, focusing in particular on the activities of the Immigration Bureau of the National Catholic Welfare Conference (NCWC) during the 1920s and 1930s. In doing so, I demonstrate that Catholic workers, clergy, and activists were forceful advocates for migrant welfare and rights along the US-Mexico border from the beginning of the twentieth century. A look at their actions, strategies, and motivations provides a more detailed and nuanced picture of Catholic activism in the field of immigration, while simultaneously demonstrating that the issues of great concern along the US-Mexico border today echo and mirror those of the early twentieth century. Knowing that history can be a tool for contemporary Catholics who

8 Deck, "Migrants and Refugees."

feel called to respond to Pope Francis's calls for mercy, especially in a political climate in which migrants are made the scapegoats of all of society's problems and in which the border is often described as a place more suited for walls than bridges.

The NCWC Immigration Bureau at the National Level

Since 1900, bishops and laypeople within the US Catholic Church have played a crucial role as advocates for the unprecedented number of immigrants who entered the country. During this period, the church was motivated by three major concerns. The most important of these was social welfare: foundational papal encyclicals like Pope Leo XIII's *Rerum Novarum* (1891) and Pope Pius XI's *Quadragesimo Anno* (1931) called for the just and humane treatment of working people and urged Catholics to work to improve the capitalist system, particularly with respect to the exploitation of labor. A second, related concern was the racism, discrimination, and prejudice that many migrants faced and the third was Protestant evangelization within immigrant communities, which was already ongoing during the first half of the twentieth century.

In 1920, the NCWC founded the Immigration Bureau in order to respond to the needs of these Catholic immigrants, many of whom arrived impoverished and without adequate support networks. In connection with assisting them in overcoming the travails associated with immigration, the Bureau was able to effectively minister to them and encourage them to remain within the church. The NCWC explicitly acknowledged this motivation in the pages of its monthly magazine, the *NCWC Bulletin* (a title that was later changed to the *NCWC Review* and subsequently to *Catholic Action*), when it stated that the "ultimate purpose of the Bureau [is to] protect the faith of the Catholic immigrant."[9]

9 "23,515 Immigrants Assisted by N.C.W.C. Bureau Last Year: Cooperating Catholic Groups Aid Work Locally, Nationally and Internationally," *NCWC Bulletin*, December 1929, 13. The *Bulletin* was the official publication of the NCWC and was published from June 1919 until January 1930 when its title was changed to *The NCWC Review*. After January 1932 it was renamed *Catholic Action* and it was published under that title until December 1953. All of the issues of the *NCWC Bulletin*, the *NCWC Review*, and *Catholic Action* cited in this chapter are found in the American Catholic History

Maintaining the faith of the immigrants was, however, only one of the factors motivating the NCWC to respond to their needs. Catholic advocates and many others at the time saw migrants as particularly vulnerable people, who, according to Immigration Bureau head Bruce Mohler, "have suddenly become separated from old established anchorages in their native countries, leaving behind all that was most precious, their old associations, their relatives, their friends, the homes which they…had learned to love and cherish." In particular, Mohler continued, it was of utmost importance to protect the immigrant family since "the nation itself was built upon a foundation of immigrant families…[and] [t]he spiritual well-being of the immigrant family determines to a very large degree its quality."[10] This belief in the vulnerability of migrants and the urgency of keeping their families healthy and united prompted the NCWC to create the Immigration Bureau.

The migrant laborers arriving at the time—coming primarily from southern and eastern Europe, as well as Mexico and migrating to the large cities of the US Northeast and Midwest— were indeed often impoverished, disadvantaged, and in need of welfare and assistance.[11] Increasingly after the turn of the century, these migrants and their family members also faced legal restrictions upon entering the US. The NCWC worked to assist them with finding jobs and secure, stable homes, and with navigating the complexities of the legal system.

Research Center and University Archives, The Catholic University of America [hereafter ACUA], Records of the General Secretary, Subseries 10.1.

10 Bruce M. Mohler, "The Immigrant and the Family," *NCWC Review*, January 1930, 25.

11 Immigration scholarship has increasingly come to acknowledge that immigrants had much more agency and adaptability than some historians, most importantly Oscar Handlin in his seminal work *The Uprooted*, have claimed. Nevertheless, during the first few decades of the twentieth century immigrant families did face many challenges, including urban housing shortages, unsafe working conditions, and nativist animosity. See Oscar Handlin, *The Uprooted* (New York: Grosset and Dunlap, 1951) and John Higham, *Strangers in the Land: Patterns of American Nativism, 1890–1925* (New Brunswick, N.J.: Rutgers University Press, 1955; repr., 1988). For an excellent general history of US immigrants and the Catholic Church, see Richard M. Linkh, *American Catholicism and European Immigrants, 1900–1924* (Staten Island, N.Y.: Center for Migration Studies, 1975). For more focused work on the Catholic Church and Mexicans, see Jay P. Dolan and Gilberto M. Hinjosa, eds., *Mexican Americans and the Catholic Church, 1900–1965*, Notre Dame History of Hispanic Catholics in the US 1 (Notre Dame, Ind.: University of Notre Dame Press, 1994) and Roberto R. Treviño, *The Church in the Barrio: Mexican American Ethno-Catholicism in Houston* (Durham: University of North Carolina Press, 2006).

Additionally, Catholic leadership was concerned that these migrants might be lost to Protestant evangelization. An organization devoted to migrants and their needs, then, would both assist Catholic migrants and keep them Catholic. According to the Immigration Bureau's *Official Catholic Year Book* (1928), the Bureau's mission at the national level "was to perfect a National Catholic Immigrant Aid organization to rank with and be recognized as the equal of other national immigrant aid organizations, both sectarian and non-sectarian, and to be a clearing house for matters relating to Catholic immigrants of all nationalities as well as for questions of migration with which the Catholic Church in America is particularly concerned."[12]

The activities of the national office, based in Washington, D.C. and headed by Bruce Mohler, largely included acting as an intermediary between various governmental departments, foreign embassies and consulates, and other national welfare groups; sending legal representatives to appear before the Secretary of Labor's Board of Review "in the interest of worthy immigrants who have been denied admission or those already here who have inadvertently broken the law"; applying to the State Department on behalf of specific immigrants; and filing applications for reentry permits, nonquota visas, and preference visas with the Department of Labor.[13] The Bureau also launched a port assistance program that met incoming ships, helped immigrants through the immigration process, and provided them with loans. Its staff members would also fill out paperwork, appeal to immigration authorities on behalf of individual migrants, and help with visa applications.

The Bureau and its officials also frequently spoke out publicly against immigration legislation that it deemed unjust or ineffective. In the decades after World War I, there were ample opportunities to critique new immigration laws. Heightened feelings of nationalism and distrust of outsiders, in combination with "a fear of being swamped with hordes of unassimilable people," prompted the US, along with many other nations, to move away from liberal immigration policies and toward new restrictions.[14] Prior to the First World War, these restrictions

12 "Immigration," a Statement Regarding Immigration to the United States, 1928, ACUA, Bruce Mohler Papers, series 4, box 29, folder 4.

13 "Immigration," a Statement Regarding Immigration to the United States.

14 Marilyn Bowman, "Labor Migration on Mexico's Southern Border, 1880–1941: The Quest for Regulation and Its Aftermath." (PhD. diss., University of Minnesota, 1987): 123–28.

were based on criteria such as physical or mental disability, poverty, or immorality, rather than race or nationality. (An exception—and a precursor to later national origin quotas—were restrictions against the immigration of Chinese natives.)

After the war, a nativist Congress passed new and more comprehensive restrictions. The 1917 Immigration Act established a literacy requirement and head tax on all immigrants entering the US. The Emergency Quota Act, which took effect on June 3, 1921, drastically reduced all immigration from Europe and European colonies by establishing numerical limits on the number of immigrants coming from specific countries. Even more explicit in its prohibitions against immigrants based on their nationality was the Johnson-Reed Act of 1924, which set an annual limit of 150,000 European immigrants, prohibited Japanese immigration, and established other targeted quotas. Once the law took effect in 1929, it caused the overall numbers of immigrants from southern and eastern Europe to decline sharply.[15] In the 1930s, restrictive legislation targeted immigrants, especially Mexican migrants along the border, for deportation.

Officials within the Immigration Bureau were outspoken critics of legislation that they saw as overly restrictive and punitive. The episcopate denounced the literacy test and sent written protests to Congress opposing the passage of the 1921 and 1924 bills. In the pages of the *NCWC Bulletin, NCWC Review*, and *Catholic Action*, the NCWC frequently offered strong criticisms of immigration legislation as well as updates about the activities of the Bureau.[16] A statement from 1953 summarized the attitude of the Bureau toward immigration legislation up to that point in the twentieth century:

> We believe in an affirmative Immigration Policy for America—one which will welcome, without racial, national, religious or other discriminations, those who seek to immigrate and become part of our national life; one which will

15 Compared to the total of 65,361 British immigrants allowed into the US each year after 1929, only 5,803 Italians, 6,534 Poles, and 2,784 Russians were eligible for admission in the same years. Alan M. Kraut, *The Huddled Masses: The Immigrant in American Society, 1880–1921* (Wheeling, Ill.: Harlan Davidson, 1982), 177.

16 Sarah Weadick, "Congress Revises the Immigration Laws," *Catholic Action*, August 1932, 9.

> provide the ever new life-blood which America needs and by which, throughout its history, it had been enriched; one which will assure to new immigrants the basic rights guaranteed to its citizens and will welcome permanent residents into citizenship; one which will express America's active concern to cooperate with other nations in providing a fair share of resettlement opportunities, in the USA, as well as in other countries, for those oppressed for freedom's sake.[17]

The Immigration Bureau in El Paso

The Washington office of the NCWC Immigration Bureau issued commentary on national immigration policy and processed visas and paperwork with the State Department and the Department of Labor. Yet the actual hands-on work of assisting and ministering to immigrants happened in the Bureau's local offices, established in key immigrant-receiving locales: New York, Philadelphia, San Francisco, and El Paso. The activities of regional office representatives included visiting and offering assistance to detained immigrants, furnishing clothing to those in need, helping immigrants to prepare affidavits or other legal papers, and forwarding information to the Washington office so that its legal staff would be able to submit appeals, among many other things.[18] Each regional office dealt with the populations and challenges specific to the region. For immigrants arriving from Mexico, the El Paso office of the Bureau provided a crucial haven.

The opening of the El Paso office was a direct response to the dramatic surge in the number of Mexican immigrants coming to the US. By the 1920s, as southern Europeans and other migrant groups were being restricted from entering the country, Mexican migration increased sharply. This is the period sometimes known as the first "Great Migration" of Mexicans to the US, which involved hundreds of thousands of Mexicans facing political and economic turmoil in their homeland crossing into the US to take jobs in railroads, agriculture, and industry. This decade also saw Mexican immigrants settling in urban areas

---

17 Sarah Weadick, "World Immigration–A World Problem," *Catholic Action*, April 1953, 7.

18 "Immigration," a Statement Regarding Immigration to the United States.

beyond the more traditional locations in the US Southwest, including Chicago, Detroit, and other cities of the Midwest.

The challenging landscape of Mexican immigration had a direct and dramatic impact on El Paso and Ciudad Juárez. While both border cities had been relatively sleepy places prior to the 1920s, by the end of the decade they had been transformed by Mexican immigration. El Paso County saw its population double between 1910 and 1930 from 52,600 to 130,600.[19] In 1928, at least 60 percent of the population of El Paso was of Mexican origin.[20]

The Immigration Bureau's office in El Paso opened in November of 1922. (A smaller "sister" office operated out of Juárez.) Its employees responded to the needs of immigrants along the entire US-Mexico border region, from Brownsville, Texas to San Diego, California. Despite the overwhelming demands of their task, the El Paso office's record was impressive: in its first fourteen years of operation alone, the El Paso office handled a total of 95,695 cases involving 130,987 people. Following the policies of the Immigration Bureau, the El Paso office handled all of its cases pro bono.[21]

The Work of the El Paso Office and its Director

The accomplishments of the El Paso office can be explained in large part by examining the life of its director, Cleofás Calleros, who ran the office for over four decades, from 1926 until 1968. Calleros was an extraordinary figure. Born in 1896, he would become a historian, writer, and community leader. A Mexican native, his family came to El Paso from Río Florido, Chihuahua in 1902. As a young man, Calleros served in World War I, and then became a railway worker. In this position, he helped process immigration paperwork for railway

19 County Information Program, Texas Association of Counties, "Texas County Profiles: Historic El Paso County Population," accessed September 10, 2020, https://txcip.org/tac/census/hist.php?FIPS=48141.

20 Lina Bresette, "Mexicans in the United States: A Report of a Brief Survey," box 148, folder 36, in ACUA, National Catholic Welfare Conference Records; "Immigration" a Statement Regarding Immigration to the United States.

21 "Address of Cleofás Calleros to the National Convention of the National Council of Catholic Women," October 21, 1936, series II, box 6, folder 14, Cleofás Calleros Papers, MS 231, C. L. Sonnichsen Special Collections Department of the University of Texas at El Paso Library (hereafter cited as UTEP-Calleros).

laborers. This led naturally to his assuming the position of Mexican border representative of the regional Bureau of Immigration office in 1926, working in that position until his retirement in 1968 (he died in 1973). During the same time period, he also served as the secretary and assistant to the bishop of El Paso, Anthony J. Schuler.

As one of the relatively few advocates for Mexican immigrants at this time, Calleros had his hands full in his first few decades on the job. This was a particularly eventful period for Mexican migration; as discussed above, the 1920 to 1940 period saw a raft of new immigration laws and restrictions. These had significant effects on the Mexican immigrant community—whereas the US-Mexico border had been almost completely unguarded before the 1920s, the establishment of the US Border Patrol in 1924 meant that Mexicans were increasingly asked to show visas, pay for permits, and pass inspections before coming into the US. Increasing numbers of Mexicans were refused entry. In addition, yet another violent conflict in Mexico—the Catholic rebellion known as the Cristero War—created new flows of religious refugees.[22] After the onset of the Great Depression in 1929, Mexican immigrants became scapegoats for widespread joblessness and local budget shortfalls. In many instances, Mexicans were rounded up and deported by local authorities, often despite the fact that they (or their children) were US citizens. All of these challenges at the border called out for a response by the US Catholic Church. It was Calleros's job, and the job of his office, to respond to each of these crises.

The Immigration Bureau's El Paso office rose to these challenges, becoming the premier Catholic migrant advocacy organization along the US-Mexico border. One of its most important (and time-consuming) tasks was to help immigrants complete visa applications, and then send the completed applications to the NCWC's Washington representatives, who then handled direct contact with the US Department of State. In additional, Calleros and his office took responsibility for communicating the content of US immigration laws to the Mexican migrant community; one pamphlet, produced in 1925, laid out "important Rules for immigrants crossing into the United States from the Mexican border," explaining the laws in layman's terms, offering words of counsel and

22 See Julia G. Young, *Mexican Exodus: Emigrants, Exiles, and Refugees of the Cristero War* (New York: Oxford University Press, 2015).

warning (such as to be careful with money, to watch out for smugglers, etc.), and providing the address of the NCWC's Immigration Bureau office in Juárez.[23]

The Bureau's effort to protect migrants was particularly onerous given the ever-shifting requirements of US immigration law. So that they could help immigrants navigate the legal processes and paperwork, the El Paso office's staff was required to remain abreast of every legislative change. Indeed, Calleros's papers are replete with bulletins from the NCWC's central office about changes impacting US immigration laws.[24] In an oral interview in the late 1960s, Calleros recalled how new regulations added to his workload: "[When] the immigration law went into effect, well, then the trouble started. The immigration act went into being in the early 1920's. Then came the head tax. Every alien had to pay a head tax of $8 to be immigrated. And then came the consular visas in addition to the head tax."[25]

Beyond Paperwork: Tales of the El Paso Office's Activities

The staff of the El Paso office of the NCWC Immigration Bureau had far more to do than simply filling out and processing visa application forms. Indeed, they responded to the needs of Mexican migrants with creativity, humanity, and—importantly—mercy. During the late 1920s and early 1930s, the US-Mexico border was a particularly turbulent place; for that reason, staff members in the office had to come up with solutions to many unprecedented problems and crises. These included the Cristero War and the resulting wave of refugees that resulted, the deportation/repatriation drives of the early 1930s, the religious needs of Mexican migrants, and the social welfare of the migrant population. In the following pages, I will discuss each of these challenges, and how the El Paso office responded to them.

---

23 Pamphlet, *Algunas Reglas de importancia para los inmigrantes que pasan por la frontera mexicana a los Estados Unidos,* 1925, series 1, box 7, folder 9, UTEP-Calleros.

24 See NCWC correspondence, box 4, UTEP-Calleros.

25 Cleofás Calleros, interview by Oscar J. Martinez, September 14, 1972, interview 157, 15, Institute of Oral History, University of Texas at El Paso.

"NCWC Border Worker assisting immigrants" Source: Catholic Action, January 1931, p. 18

"Waiting to Cross the Border" Source: Catholic Action, March 1931, p. 17

The Cristero War and Religious Refugees

Mexico's Cristero War began in 1926 when Catholic partisans took up arms against the Mexican government, prompting a large wave of migrants to arrive in Ciudad Juárez and El Paso. During the war years, the primary activity that Calleros and the Bureau undertook was the legalization, placement, and procurement of funding to support the hundreds of priests and religious that crossed the border during the years of persecution.

Often penniless, the exiled religious had to obtain the proper visas, and then be housed and given some kind of occupation. The paperwork was often challenging, for many religious crossed illegally due to the urgency of their situation. For example, the Good Shepherd Sisters, from the Bajio and Jalisco, inadvertently crossed illegally. Calleros also had to arrange charity train tickets for them, since they could not pay to get themselves anywhere else in the US. Similarly, the Sacred Heart Sisters were already in Laredo on visitor's visas by the time they made contact with Calleros; he managed to secure extensions on their visas and process their paperwork on time.[26]

Once their legal situations were resolved, the religious exiles had to be housed and fed. For example, nineteen Sisters of Perpetual Adoration, who had arrived in El Paso from Guadalajara, briefly camped out on Calleros's living room rug while he searched for more suitable housing for them.[27] (Eventually, the nuns were able to become economically self-sufficient: they opened a bakery in El Paso where they made tamales and enchiladas.) Like the nuns, refugee priests also arrived and needed help. Calleros and the Immigration Bureau's El Paso office helped them support themselves in any way they could.[28]

During the Cristero War period, Calleros was also involved in helping Mexican Catholics who sought to cross the border temporarily in order to attend mass and receive other Catholic sacraments that they could not access in Mexico. The Catholic Church in El

26 The client cases for religious orders arriving in El Paso during the Cristero War period can be found in box 11, UTEP-Calleros.

27 Cleofás Calleros, interview 157, 19.

28 The case files of the many priests, nuns, and clergy who sought help from the Immigration Bureau office in El Paso can be found in series I, box 10, folders 4-7, and box 11, folders 1-5, UTEP-Calleros.

Paso welcomed thousands of Mexicans from Juárez and northern Chihuahua who came to the US side of the border.[29] Although Calleros was involved in orchestrating their crossing, he warned an Immigration Bureau official in the NCWC's Washington office not to publicize his office's role in helping Mexicans come to the US for services: "Persons paroled to us for confession, are persons who are inadmissible owing to illiteracy, senility, etc. If we were to boast of the fact that such 'inadmissible aliens' were permitted to come, I believe it would be considered as a criticism to the American authorities.[30] It is clear that at times the Bureau's El Paso office was willing to bend the rules in order to allow Mexicans to participate in their religious faith.

In 1929, when the Catholic Church in Mexico reached a truce with the Mexican government, the El Paso office reported in the *NCWC Bulletin* that it "experiences a feeling of satisfaction in looking back on the services it was privileged to render to those who took refuge in this country." In particular, the office pointed out that it had been very successful in interceding with the Department of Labor in order to access extensions of temporary stay for religious refugees. "Over this period of years many hundreds of such appeals were handled by the Bureau, and *invariably with success*," the report continued.[31] This was particularly important in the case of a group of religious sisters, originally from Spain, who had fled Mexico for the United States and were technically ineligible for visas because of the quota system that had been implemented in 1921 and 1924. As a result, "they could not hope to obtain permanent admission." The Bureau assured the Department of Labor that the sisters would return to Mexico whenever they could safely do so; the US government accepted this intercession "as a sufficient guarantee" and granted them the visas they needed.[32]

---

29 Ransom Patrick Cross, "Hands across the Border: The Role of the Catholic Church on the Border in Assisting Mexican Catholics during the Religious Crisis in Mexico, 1926–29" (master's thesis, University of Texas, 1994).

30 Cleofás Calleros to Bruce Mohler, memorandum (regarding activities of the Mexican border office), February 13, 1929, series I, box 5, folder 4, UTEP-Calleros.

31 "N.C.W.C. Activities in the Field of Immigration," *NCWC Bulletin*, August 1929, 19.

32 "N.C.W.C. Activities in the Field of Immigration," *NCWC Bulletin*, August 1929, 19.

Deportation and Repatriation

One of the biggest obstacles to the well-being of Mexican migrants during the late 1920s and early 1930s was crossing the border but being unable to remain in the US. As stated previously, immigration laws aimed at controlling the US-Mexico border and restricting Mexican immigration had proliferated during this period. In the early 1930s, Mexican families were frequently subject to deportation (more commonly labeled "repatriation") by local authorities across the US.[33]

Whenever it could, the El Paso office helped Mexican migrants avoid such deportations. In one instance, an eighteen-year-old girl got on a streetcar in El Paso that crossed into Mexico without her noticing. When it returned to the border, an immigration officer asked the girl to show proof of residency in the US, but she had none. "Fortunately, the story has a happy ending," the Bureau reported, "as the Department of Labor acceded to the Bureau's request that she be paroled for six months in order that she might apply for registration of entry and thus legalize her residence in this country."[34] In another case, the Bureau tried to help a Mexican man who had been deported petition for readmission. Although his petition was granted, he did not receive the letter until after the Deportation Act of 1929, a law that made it a felony for people arrested and deported to attempt to reenter the country, had gone into effect. Ultimately, the man was not able to enter the US.[35] Finally, in March 1931, the office helped Mexican children obtain alien identification cards so that they could continue to cross from Juárez and attend schools in El Paso.[36]

When families returned to Mexico—either voluntarily or as a result of deportation—the El Paso and Ciudad Juárez offices of the Immigration Bureau were there to help them with the difficult logistical and financial details involved in their return. This was a daunting task. In 1932, the office in Juárez reported that at least fifty families per day were appealing for help with repatriation "in the hope that they will fare better in their own land." The Juárez office described how providing

33 See Francisco Balderrama and Raymond Rodríguez, *Decade of Betrayal: Mexican Repatriation in the 1930s* (Albuquerque: University of New Mexico Press, 2006).

34 "N.C.W.C. Activities in the Field of Immigration," *NCWC Review*, January 1931, 18.

35 "N.C.W.C. Activities in the Field of Immigration," *NCWC Bulletin*, June 1929, 12.

36 "N.C.W.C. Activities in the Field of Immigration," *NCWC Bulletin*, March 1931, 17.

this assistance required "not only a knowledge of the technical requirements, but the far more difficult task of finding ways and means to provide for the hundreds of families who ever so often are stranded in Juárez."[37] To help impoverished Mexicans return to Mexico, the Bureau office sometimes provided free transportation for returning migrants traveling into the interior of Mexico, as well as "conveying the personal belongings of the emigrants to Mexico free of duty." In addition to this, the office helped migrants prepare the necessary paperwork, and provided "the innumerable additional services necessary in the many complicated situations that invariably arise."[38]

In addition to subsidizing transportation for returning migrants, the Immigration Bureau in El Paso sometimes made arrangements to house Mexicans in need of shelter during the deportation drives. In 1929, it was reported in the *NCWC Bulletin* that the office had arranged for a number of Mexican women and children awaiting deportation proceedings to stay with the Sisters of the Sacred Heart, who were in charge of St. Joseph's Day Nursery in El Paso.[39] (Prior to that, they had been housed in the jail, at times for several weeks—a situation that is startlingly analogous to the detention of immigrant women and children on the US-Mexico border in the early twenty-first century.)

By providing these migrants with housing, the Immigration Bureau was not only assisting with their well-being, but was meeting their spiritual needs as well—"Practically all are Catholics and the weeks spent in the convent have had in many cases a most beneficial effect." The report stated that the chapel's services were "well attended" by families; that children were able to attend "classes and nursery activities," and that "one old lady who had not been to the Sacraments for twenty years went to confession and received Holy Communion the day after her arrival."[40]

Beyond simply responding to the humanitarian crisis, the NCWC and the border office representatives publicly decried the deportations, which disproportionately affected Mexicans. Bruce Mohler commented on immigrants who had married and become fathers in the US, but

37 "IN THE FIELD OF IMMIGRATION: Contributed by the Bureau of Immigration, N.C.W.C.," *Catholic Action*, September 1932, 27.

38 "N.C.W.C. Activities in the Field of Immigration," *NCWC Review*, July 1931, 19.

39 "N.C.W.C. Activities in the Field of Immigration," *NCWC Bulletin*, November 1929, 27.

40 "N.C.W.C. Activities in the Field of Immigration," *NCWC Bulletin*, November 1929, 27.

were now being deported or denied reentry: "The situation is a serious one as far as the families here (most of them American citizens) are concerned. It surely seems *poor policy* and *poor judgment* as well as *poor humanity* to enforce what is, after all, merely administrative procedure, in cases of this kind."[41] Mohler strongly criticized the Deportation Act. It was, according to Mohler, "the most fanatical immigration legislation ever to pass the US Congress ... The law should be repealed or amended at the earliest possible time."[42] Calleros, too, criticized harsh immigration laws, stating that "further restrictive laws will accomplish nothing in curbing illegal entries across the border. They will merely serve to antagonize Mexico."[43]

Religious Ministry

By advocating for Mexican migrants and assisting them with their immigration travails, the Bureau was able to effectively minister to them, providing them with a direct connection to their Catholic faith, as well as discouraging them from converting to Protestantism. As one writer put it in the pages of the *NCWC Bulletin*: "The opportunity afforded for religious influence at the same time that technical assistance is being rendered to immigrants is a matter which is constantly being emphasized by the N.C.W.C. Bureau, and is the reason why Catholic immigrant aid for Catholic immigrants is so earnestly advocated."[44]

To this end, NCWC workers, many of them volunteers, did mission work with Mexican laborers. In Amarillo, Texas, the bishop recruited lay Catholic women to do "catechetical instruction, religious vacation schools, the teaching of English, etc." An article in the *NCWC Bulletin* describes the work of one missionary and asks readers to help contribute to "a special fund for enlarging the work."[45]

In this way, the El Paso office, in the process of assisting migrants with paperwork and bureaucratic hurdles, often found itself attending

41 "Hardships in Immigration Regulations Noted by N.C.W.C. Bureau," *Catholic Action*, March 1932, 15.

42 Bruce M. Moher, "The Immigrant and the Family," *NCWC Review*, January 1930), 26.

43 "N.C.W.C. Activities in the Field of Immigration," *NCWC Review*, September 1930), 21.

44 "In the Field of Immigration," *NCWC Bulletin*, February 1929, 11.

45 "The N.C.C.W. and the Mexican Problem: Crying Need for Educational and Social Workers in Southwest Partially Met," *NCWC Bulletin*, February 1929, 17–18.

to their religious needs as well. In one case, when a representative of the Bureau, "while preparing affidavits to prove legal United States residence for a Mexican couple and their three children, discovered that no church marriage ceremony had ever been performed...[and that] the man, during his entire lifetime, had never learned to pray." As a result, the Bureau offered the migrants catechetical instruction and arranged for the couple to be married by a priest and for their infant to be baptized.[46]

In a similar instance, a Mexican father of an American-born twenty-one-year-old woman who had gone back to Mexico to be married was worried about his daughter; he wanted to check on her and return her to the US. The problem was referred to NCWC, "and the bureau at once asked its corresponding agency in Mexico to get in touch with the girl and her child and learn what the circumstances were." As it turned out, the young woman and child were fine and did not want to come back to US, but the woman did want to be married in the church and receive first communion, as well as have her child baptized. In the end, everyone was satisfied, as "[the] father in New York expressed himself as well content when he read of the sympathetic assistance that had been rendered to his daughter and her son."[47] In these two cases, the El Paso office was fulfilling the Bureau's stated goal of providing not only material care for migrants, but spiritual care as well.

Social Justice and Social Welfare

With Calleros's guidance, the Immigration Bureau's El Paso office also attempted to seek social justice and social welfare for Mexican migrants. In a speech about Mexican labor, he called Mexicans "an unappreciated asset in the Southwest... [who are] cheated on all sides." He then went on to mention cases in which migrants were fired from their railroad jobs because they had refused to buy overpriced goods from company stores.[48] In some instances of worker exploitation, the border office appealed directly on behalf of the workers, as

46 "In the Field of Immigration," *NCWC Bulletin*, February 1929, 11.

47 "In the Field of Immigration," *Catholic Action*, April 1933, 23.

48 "Mexican Labor Leading Topic at Los Angeles Conference: Need of Organization Stressed by Bishop Cantwell at C.C.I.P. Meeting," *NCWC Review*, May 1930, 18.

when it wrote a letter to the Mexican consul "in favor of a workman who had been injured while in the service of the Santa Fe Railway." The man had spent seven months in the hospital and wanted to go home. The Bureau handled the case up to the point of "settlement ... with the Santa Fe Railroad Company."[49]

The Mexican border office also made an effort to help Mexican immigrants secure an education. In El Paso, the Knights of Columbus opened a citizenship school and placed Cleofás Calleros in charge. "The purpose of the school," stated an article in *Catholic Action*, "is primarily to teach the advantages and duties of American citizenship to Spanish-speaking residents of El Paso."[50] In other cases, the border office directly intervened with government officials to make sure that Mexican children were able to attend schools along the border. In 1933, the NCWC's Mexican border representative reported that a large number of American-born children of Mexican parents had been deported to Mexico. In one case, a ten-year-old girl who was born in New Mexico, along with her two other American-born siblings and her parents (who had lived in the US for fifteen years) were sent to Mexico. From Ciudad Juárez, the family tried to enroll the girl in an El Paso school, but administrators refused to allow her to attend. "The N.C.W.C. bureau's representative appealed to the assistant superintendent of schools and appeared before the school board with the relative and the child. As a result of his explanation the board ruled favorably and authorized the school to accept the little girl."[51]

Conclusion

By working proactively during several decades of challenging conditions for Mexican migrants, the El Paso border office of the NCWC Immigration Bureau proved itself an enthusiastic and effective advocate for a population that often faced discrimination, racism, poverty, and the constant threat of deportation. While a primary motivation for its actions was to keep Mexicans from abandoning their Catholic

49 "In the Field of Immigration," *NCWC Bulletin*, February 1929, 11–12.

50 "In the Field of Immigration," *NCWC Bulletin*, March 1929, 17.

51 "In the Field of Immigration: Contributed by the Bureau of Immigration, N.C.W.C.," *Catholic Action*, February 1933, 27.

faith, this by no means crowded out the NCWC's larger goal of assisting and advocating for the migrant family. Its work was particularly meaningful and important at a time when migrants and migration were viewed unfavorably by lawmakers and the US public.

The work of the El Paso Immigration Bureau office also received the support and approbation of the NCWC and the Catholic hierarchy. In 1927, NCWC director John Burke commended Calleros's efforts on behalf of Mexican migrants, and made sure that he had the budget he needed.[52] Throughout the late 1920s and early 1930s, officials at the NCWC continued to correspond frequently with Calleros so they could keep track of his work, and they frequently highlighted his work in the pages of the *NCWC Bulletin*, the *NCWC Review*, and *Catholic Action*.[53]

The activities of the NCWC Immigration Bureau's El Paso office during the late 1920s and early 1930s mark only a brief moment in a longer history of efforts by the US Catholic Church to respond to the needs of migrants. Indeed, many other examples could be discussed in which US Catholic bishops, agencies, and community-based groups have responded by advocating on behalf of migrants and engaging in outreach to assist with their welfare. These extend from the beginning of the century (for example, Bishop Francis C. Kelley's work with the Extension Society in the early 1900s) to midcentury (Archbishop Robert E. Lucey's work with the Bishops' Committee for the Spanish-Speaking during the 1945–65 period) to the present-day work of countless Catholic organizations—including the Catholic Legal Immigration Network, Catholic Charities, and the USCCB's office of Migration and Refugee Services, to name just a few.

The challenges that today's migrants face are many, but in some ways, they are not entirely different from those of the past. In both the late 1920s and today, the US saw a surge in nativism (often encouraged by politicians), casting immigrants as a threat to the native-born. This nativism was often accompanied by violence against migrants, unlawful deportations, and scapegoating of those within immigrant communities. In the face of that nativism, some Catholics—and some key

52 Letter from Bruce Mohler to Cleofás Calleros, September 17, 1927, in NCWC correspondence, box 4, UTEP-Calleros.

53 NCWC correspondence, boxes 4–5, UTEP-Calleros.

players within the US church—responded to the needs of immigrant communities with mercy and advocacy.[54]

In today's contentious political environment, when it seems that few can agree on how to meet the needs of immigrants who enter the country along the US-Mexico border, perhaps there are lessons to be learned from the efforts of the NCWC's Immigration Bureau. During the 1920s and 1930s, Catholics in Ciudad Juárez and El Paso channeled and expressed God's mercy in their responses to the plight of immigrants along the border. In 2015, Pope Francis called upon Catholics to do the same thing again. History, in this case, provides a template and a guide.

54 For a detailed discussion of nativism in the past vs. the present, see Julia G. Young, "Making America 1920 Again? Nativism and US Immigration, Past and Present," *Journal on Migration and Human Security* 5, no. 1 (March 2017), 217–35.

CHAPTER 10

POPE FRANCIS AND LATINO COMMUNITIES IN THE US

Spiritual Empowerment in the Americas through Language

Luis Ricardo Fraga and Kiku Huckle

THE SELECTION OF POPE FRANCIS as the 266th pontiff of the Roman Catholic Church was an unexpected decision in several respects. He was the first Jesuit pope. The Jesuit order, founded by the Spaniard Ignatius of Loyola in 1540, has always had a special place in the hearts of many Catholics, but not always in the Vatican, which suppressed it from 1773 to 1814. Francis was also the first pope ever selected from a Latin American country. Although a number of Latin American cardinals had been considered seriously over the years by the cardinal electors, his selection represented a clear acknowledgement of the importance of Latin America to the contemporary Catholic Church. Latin America is the only region of the world where an overwhelming majority of the population, 72 percent, identifies as Catholic; in Europe the number is down to 35 percent.[1] It was also the case that his leadership in the development and practice of *la teología del pueblo*, "the theology of the people," strongly differentiated him from most recent popes and especially his immediate predecessor Benedict XVI. The theology of the people and its grounding in popular piety guided him when he led the Archdiocese of Buenos Aires, Argentina, moving him to adopt a very simple lifestyle, embrace a preferential option for the poor, and develop a propensity to always

1 Pew Research Center, "The Global Catholic Population," February 13, 2013, http://www.pewforum.org/2013/02/13/the-global-catholic-population/.

acknowledge those at the margins of society, including prisoners and the homeless.[2]

Of equal significance, and perhaps most relevant to any consideration of the influence of Pope Francis in all of the Americas, is whether his selection had special meaning and special impact on Catholics in the United States having origins, across generations, in Spanish-speaking countries. Although it is well understood that the countries of Latin America have distinct origins, cultural traditions, and at times their own regional vocabularies, once they arrive in the US, many immigrants from these countries begin to find that they are identified by many in the receiving society as marginalized others,[3] perpetual foreigners,[4] and impossible subjects,[5] which pushes them to focus more on what they have in common than what makes them different. Among the clearest indications of this propensity is the substantial percentage of people of Latin American origin in the US who identify as Hispanic and Latino, easily reconciling their strong identification with their countries of origin to their linked fates and common destinies with their fellow Latin American immigrants. The Latino National Survey conducted in 2006 found that 35 percent of respondents preferred the term "Hispanic," 14 percent preferred "Latino," and 51 percent preferred either or did not care.[6] Among the most significant characteristics of what many Latinos have in common is the Spanish language. Although Latinos lose their ability to speak Spanish across generations in the US, it is

---

2 Austen Ivereigh, *The Great Reformer: Francis and the Making of a Radical Pope* (New York: Henry Holt, 2014), 112, 148; Rafael Luciani, *Pope Francis and the Theology of the People* (Maryknoll, N.Y.: Orbis, 2017), 10.

3 Otto Santana, *Brown Tide Rising: Metaphoric Representations of Latinos in Contemporary Public Discourse* (Austin: University of Texas Press, 2013), 1–11. See also Leo Chavez, *The Latino Threat: Constructing Immigrants, Citizens, and the Nation*, 2nd ed. (Stanford, Calif.: Stanford University Press, 2002), 3.

4 Ray Rocco, *Transforming Citizenship: Democracy, Membership, and Belonging in Latino Communities* (Lansing, Mich.: Michigan State University Press, 2014), 50.

5 Mae M. Ngai, *Impossible Subject: Illegal Aliens and the Making of Modern America* (Princeton, N.J.: Princeton University Press, 2004), xxv, xxvii, 12.

6 Luis Ricardo Fraga et al., *Latinos in the New Millennium: An Almanac of Opinion, Behavior, and Policy Preferences* (New York: Cambridge University Press, 2012), 81. We use the terms Hispanic and Latino interchangeably in this essay.

still the case that an estimated 73 percent of Latinos above the age of five speak Spanish.[7]

A story by CNN reporters Cindy Y. Rodriguez and Alicia W. Stewart in 2013 was entitled "Is the New Pope Latino?"[8] The authors note that he is Argentine and describe the fact that many Argentines have close ties to Italy because many Italians moved there in the twentieth century. It is perhaps the fact that Pope Francis is the son of Italian immigrants that makes his life experience similar to those of many Latinos in the US—although the overwhelming majority of Latinos in the US are citizens, estimated at 74 percent,[9] 51 percent of Latino adults in the US were born in another country. Twenty percent of Latino adults were born in the US and have at least one parent who was born in a Latin American country, and 29 percent were born in the US, with both of their parents born in the US, and yet have at least one grandparent who was born in another country.[10] Thus, the immigrant experience is part of the life of most Latino families in the US. As one leader of Hispanic ministry in the Catholic Church, Rev. Juan J. Molina, the associate director of the church in Latin America for the US Conference of Catholic Bishops, stated, "He [Pope Francis] is also the son of migrants. And for us Hispanics in the US, this is very important. I think that this topic of migration is going to be very important for him. And we the Hispanics, the Latinos who now live in the United States…we can also take some hope and pride that this pope intimately knows and has deeply lived the life of a migrant."[11]

There is no doubt that Pope Francis is Latin American, but might his being raised in Latin America and learning and practicing his faith

---

7 "Hispanic Americans By the Numbers," Infoplease (website), last modified, February 28, 2017, http://www.infoplease.com/spot/hhmcensus1.html. Data from the US Census Bureau.

8 Cindy Y. Rodriguez and Alicia W. Stewart, "Is the New Pope Latino?" *Latino in America* (blog), March 15, 2013, http://inamerica.blogs.cnn.com/2013/03/15/is-the-new-pope-latino/.

9 Arturo Vargas, (PowerPoint presentation to the Latino Civic Engagement meeting, National Association of Latino Elected and Appointed Officials [NALEO] conference, Aspen Institute, Washington, D.C., August 10, 2015).

10 Pew Research Center, Second Generation Americans, chap. 2, "Demographic Portrait of the Adult Children of Immigrants," February 7, 2013, http://www.pewsocialtrends.org/2013/02/07/chapter-2-demographic-portrait-of-adult-children-of-immigrants/.

11 As quoted in Rodriguez and Stewart, "Is the New Pope Latino?"

in Spanish allow him to be understood in a culturally compatible yet culturally distinct way by Spanish-speaking Latino Catholics in the US? Might Pope Francis in Spanish be understood differently than Pope Francis in English translation? Might Latino Catholics in the US gain a special enrichment of their own spirituality because they hear him differently than those who read him only in English translation? If this is the case, might Latino Catholics in the US be a bridge between US Catholics and Catholics in Latin America, seeing as they are the future of the Catholic Church in the US? Might Pope Francis be serving as the engineer of that bridge because of his Latin American and immigrant background?

In this essay we consider these questions through the analytical lens of language, its intimate relationship to religious worship, and the ways in which language is the thread that weaves religion into culture, meaning, and spirituality. We do so by focusing on the differences between how Pope Francis's speeches in the US were delivered in Spanish and how they were translated into English. To a certain extent, these differences cannot be avoided since it is impossible to perfectly translate sentiments and expressions from one language to another. Yet an examination of the pope's speeches in the US reveals a much greater disparity between the messages given in Spanish and their English translation than can be attributed to the usual difficulties involved in translation. There is a cultural component to language as much as there is a cultural component to religious expression. As a result, English translators seem to not only convert the language, but also to "translate out" the *culture* in Pope Francis's speeches. As a result, we argue that Spanish-speaking audiences can hear the message of and experience Pope Francis in a way that is very distinct from those relying on English translations alone. We conclude by arguing that Francis's messages provide a unique type of spiritual empowerment for Spanish-speaking Latino Catholics that is different from what they provide to their anglophone brothers and sisters. This empowerment is directly related to their experiences in the US in that it reverses the general tendency to marginalize, segregate, and "other" those, especially immigrants and their children, who speak languages other than English. What is often considered a disadvantage can become a resource that builds and enriches faith in the US and across Latin America. In this way, Pope Francis's leadership truly reaches across all of the Americas.

Latinos, Latino Catholics, and Language Use in the US

The Latino population in the US is now estimated at 56.6 million, which represents about 17.6 percent of the country's population.[12] In 2014, the US Census determined that about 73 percent of all Hispanics living in the US above the age of five spoke some Spanish at home.[13] Based on the results of the 2012 National Survey of Latinos, the Pew Hispanic Center determined that 82 percent of all Latino adults speak Spanish very/pretty well and 72 percent read Spanish very/pretty well.[14] Not surprisingly this varies by generation, with 91 percent of first generation Latinos—those born outside of the United States—indicating that they speak and read Spanish very/pretty well; 82 percent of the second generation—the first in their families to be born in the US—reporting that they speak Spanish very/pretty well and 71 percent that they read Spanish very/pretty well; and 47 percent of the third or more generations indicating that they speak Spanish very/pretty well and 41 percent that they read Spanish very/pretty well.[15] Spanish is thus still a very important part of the lives of a very substantial percentage of Latinos who currently live in the US.

Relatedly, the same Pew study also asked questions about respondents' primary language (the language in which a respondent indicates that she is more proficient than other languages) and about whether they are bilingual (highly competent in both languages). Of all Hispanic adults, 38 percent are Spanish-dominant, 38 percent are bilingual, and 24 percent are English-dominant. Again, this varies by generation, with the first generation indicating that 61 percent are Spanish-dominant, 33 percent are bilingual, and only 6 percent are English-dominant. In the second generation the percentage that indicates they are Spanish-dominant drops to a mere 8 percent, with 53 indicating that they are bilingual and a substantial 40 percent indicating that they are English-dominant. Not surprisingly, the third generation is clearly English-dominant:

---

12 "Hispanic Americans By the Numbers," Infoplease.

13 "Hispanic Americans By the Numbers," Infoplease.

14 Pew Research Center/Pew Hispanic Center, "Language Use Among Latinos," April 4, 2012, http://www.pewhispanic.org/2012/04/04/iv-language-use-among-latinos/.

15 Pew Research Center/Pew Hispanic Center, "Language Use Among Latinos."

only 1 percent indicates that they are Spanish-dominant, 29 percent report being bilingual, and 69 percent of Latino adults report being English-dominant.[16]

A final characteristic that helps us to better understand the significance of Spanish to the lived experiences of many Latinos in the United States is captured by the responses to the question, "When you think, is it mostly in Spanish or English?" asked in the Pew 2012 survey. Of all Hispanic adults living in the US, 45 percent indicated that they think mostly in Spanish, 16 percent in both equally, and 37 percent in English. Again, generation makes a very substantial difference. In the first generation, 65 percent think mostly in Spanish, 18 percent in both languages, and only 15 percent mostly in English. This is very different from the second generation, in which 18 percent think mostly in Spanish, 18 percent in both equally, and a substantial 63 percent mostly in English. Not surprisingly, these numbers are even greater among the third or more generations, in which only 13 percent think mostly in Spanish, 7 percent in both equally, and an overwhelming 80 percent mostly in English.[17] This reinforces the conclusion that Spanish is still a very important part of the lives of Latinos in the US, although this importance declines substantially with each generation.

These patterns of Latinos' use of the Spanish language become even more salient when one looks at the self-identified Catholic population in the US. Although estimates vary, a reasonable estimate of the percentage of the US adult[18] population that self-identifies as Catholic is 20 percent.[19] It is also the case that Catholics are more likely to be either immigrants or the children of immigrants. An estimated 27 percent of all Catholic adults in the US were born outside of the country, and an additional 15 percent have at least one parent who was born outside of the US.[20]

---

16 Pew Research Center/Pew Hispanic Center, "Language Use Among Latinos."

17 Pew Research Center/Pew Hispanic Center, "Language Use Among Latinos."

18 It is important to note that this estimate is only for adults because they are the ones who respond to surveys concerning religious affiliation.

19 Pew Research Center, "A Closer Look at Catholic America," September 14, 2015, https://assets.documentcloud.org/documents/2426898/a-closer-look-at-catholic-america-pew-research.pdf.

20 Pew Research Center, "A Closer Look at Catholic America."

Latinos are estimated to comprise 40.1 percent, or 30.4 million, of all self-identified Catholics in the United States.[21] Pew estimates that this percentage is even greater among Catholic millennials, in which Hispanics are already the largest group at 46 percent with white Catholics comprising only 43 percent.[22] It is also estimated that 57 percent of all adult Hispanics in the US identify as Catholic.[23] As with language use there is a significant generational variation in the identification of Latino adults as Catholic. A Pew survey of Hispanic adults conducted in 2013 found that 61 percent of first generation Latinos identify as Catholic, but that the figure goes down to 50 percent among the second generation and drops slightly more to 46 percent of the third generation.[24] There is also a very interesting regional variation among white and Latino Catholics. In the Northeast, the traditional center of Catholicism in the US, 75 percent of Catholics are white and in the Midwest it is 82 percent, but in the South it is only 50 percent with Latinos comprising 42 percent. In the West, Latinos are the clear majority at 57 percent, with whites being only 31 percent and Asians 8 percent.[25] Among Hispanic Catholics, 85 percent indicate that their faith is an important part of their daily lives, and 83 percent report that they are proud to be Catholic.[26]

A very high percentage of Hispanic Catholics use the Spanish language. Based upon the Pew 2013 National Survey of Latinos, 80 percent of Latino Catholics use mostly Spanish or are bilingual. This percentage is higher than among non-Catholic Hispanics.[27] Of special importance is the fact that this same survey found that 39 percent

21 Center for Applied Research in the Apostolate (CARA), "Frequently Requested Church Statistics," accessed August 17, 2020, http://cara.georgetown.edu/frequently-requested-church-statistics/; CARA, "Fact Sheet: Hispanic Catholics in the U.S," 2014, http://cara.georgetown.edu/staff/webpages/Hispanic%20Catholic%20Fact%20Sheet.pdfPew estimates that Latinos comprise 34 percent of all Catholic adults in the US.

22 Pew Research Center, "A Closer Look at Catholic America."

23 CARA, "Fact Sheet: Hispanic Catholics in the U.S."

24 Jens Manuel Krogstad, "Many US Catholics Will Understand Pope Francis's Spanish-Language Mass," Pew Research Center, September 22, 2015, http://www.pewresearch.org/fact-tank/2015/09/22/many-u-s-catholics-will-understand-pope-francis-spanish-language-mass/.

25 Krogstad, "Many US Catholics Will Understand Pope Francis's Spanish-Language Mass."

26 CARA, "Fact Sheet: Hispanic Catholics in the U.S."

27 Pew Research Center/Pew Hispanic Center, "Language Use Among Latinos."

of all Hispanic Catholics who attend church do so only in Spanish. Although this number is down from a reported 60 percent in 2007, it is still quite substantial.[28]

In sum, what these data indicate is that Spanish is still a very significant part of the lives of Latinos in the US. Not surprisingly, this is much more the case for those who are immigrants from Spanish-speaking countries, but it is still an important part of how Latinos in the second generation, and some in the third generation, communicate. What all of these data outline is a Latino reality in the US in which Pope Francis's native language of Spanish and his propensity to identify himself as an immigrant allows Latino Catholics to hear and experience him in intimate and personal ways. When the pope speaks Spanish, he is understood by most Latino Catholics. When he identifies himself as an immigrant, in Spanish, he places his own life experience in direct alignment with that of many Latino Catholics, whether they are immigrants themselves or are sons and daughters or grandsons and granddaughters of immigrants.

What Is Lost in Translation: Pope Francis in Spanish in the US

Pope Francis gave eighteen official speeches in his six-day visit to the US. Of those, only three were in English, one was in Italian, and the rest in Spanish. He chose politically significant events to speak in English: his arrival at the White House on his first day in the US, his visit to Congress, and his meeting with the staff of the United Nations in New York. Reports have indicated that there was no particular symbolism in his decision to speak in one of his mother tongues for the rest of the speeches; rather it was more a matter of practicality given his limited English ability.[29] The Vatican prepares translations of all of the pope's speeches into a number of languages so that his words can be nearly instantly accessible to all audiences regardless of the language in which he chooses to deliver them.

However, the pope's preference for speaking in Spanish, combined with his Argentine dialect and his propensity for spontaneity, make

28 Pew Research Center/Pew Hispanic Center, "Language Use Among Latinos."

29 Elizabetta Povoledo, "Msgr. Mark Miles, Pope's English Translator, Braces for the US Spotlight," *New York Times*, September 15, 2015, http://nyti.ms/1Nvow52.

translations difficult to obtain at times. Further, Vatican correspondent Robert Mickens noted that translations "very often miss the point. They miss the nuances."[30] This is striking because "the Holy Father likes to have direct control over the message he gives," so he is very careful and intentional in crafting all of his speeches himself.[31] To that end, Pope Francis devoted most of the month of July to preparing for his trip to the US and Cuba, not only doing research but also talking with both religious and nonreligious authorities in the countries he was to visit.[32]

Given the pope's significant effort to craft his communications, it is reasonable to expect that the Vatican's translations are as accurate as possible. Even when the pope speaks spontaneously, he is still intentional because he is aware of the impact and significance of his words. For this reason, all translations of both prepared and spontaneous speeches should preserve the pope's tone and tenor.

Of the fourteen speeches Pope Francis delivered in Spanish, the translations of eleven of them that were done close to the time of the speeches contained minor discrepancies, which is to be expected due to the large number of stylistic preferences and judgment calls necessary to produce any translation.[33] However, there is a pattern to these discrepancies that changes the overall tone of the pope's carefully crafted

30 Henry Chu, "Pope's Interpreter Learns Job Brings Surprises and Fans," *The Seattle Times*, September 26, 2015, http://www.seattletimes.com/nation-world/translator-for-pope-francis-a-job-with-surprises/

31 Bart Jones, "Reporter's Notebook: The Pope's Speechwriter, the Pope's Translator, a Press Corps Roadblock," *Newsday*, September 27, 2015.

32 Jones, "Reporter's Notebook."

33 We extensively researched the speeches, verified the validity of our translations into English, and then once discrepancies were found, cross-checked the translations against various sites, including those of the National Federation of Priests' Councils (NFPC) and the United States Conference of Catholic Bishops (USCCB), where people in the US may commonly look for the pope's speeches. We also verified the accuracy of the Spanish language texts by watching video of his speeches in order to ensure that the discrepancies were not due to an error with the Spanish transcripts provided by the Vatican. We performed these tasks in 2017. It is our understanding that the Vatican website has, apparently, been updated and reorganized since we collected the translations analyzed here, and we are pleased that the Vatican updated the language to more accurately reflect the words spoken by the pope during his visit, but our findings reflect the translations that were performed and widely publicized *at the time* of the pope's visit, when they would have had the most weight and significance. A table with all of the identified Spanish and English texts that are the focus of our analysis is available from the authors.

messages. The notable differences involve changes to verb tenses and the omission of words, phrases, and repetitions added for emphasis. Many of his jokes and personal comments were also omitted.

The English versions rely on the passive or subjunctive tense, but in the Spanish version the pope usually uses the active or imperative tense. The result of this simple switch, while seemingly minor, has the effect of diminishing the intensely personal and direct mode of communication that characterizes Pope Francis's speeches. For example, the English translation of his homily during Vespers at St. Patrick's Cathedral in New York reads that "[another] danger comes when we become jealous of our free time." The Spanish, however, uses the present tense: "when we *are jealous* of our free time." In his remarks at the interreligious ceremony at the Ground Zero memorial, the English translation has "here, amid pain and grief, we also have a palpable sense of the heroic goodness which people are capable of, those hidden reserves of strength from which we can draw" while the Spanish has a distinctly normative intention. A better translation of the Spanish would read: "Here, amidst excruciating pain, we can feel the heroic goodness that is part of being human, a hidden strength that we should always draw on." There are a total of twelve instances of the English version deliberately changing the verb tense of the pope's texts, and in each of these cases the change was not necessary to the sentence structure or to maintain consistency with the rest of the speech.

More significant are the many omissions in the English text. Often phrases that are left out were included by the pope to provide emphasis, to highlight a topic, or to connect themes between his speeches. The English text of his homily at the canonization of Junípero Serra reads, "Jesus said: Go out and tell the good news to everyone." A better translation of the Spanish would be "to *everyone*, said Jesus, to everyone, go out and tell the good news."

The English-speaking prisoners at the Curran-Fromhold Correctional Facility heard the pope say (from a previously prepared translation): "I encourage you to have this attitude (to care for and help those in need) with one another and with all those who any way are part of this institution. May you make possible new opportunities, new journeys, new paths." If the prisoners spoke Spanish, they heard, "I want to encourage you to have this attitude amongst yourselves and with everyone that has some role in this institution. Be forgers of opportunity, be forgers of pathways, be forgers of new trails." The repetition in the Spanish is stronger and produces a more powerful effect than in the English translation.

The English translations also removed some short phrases included by Francis for emphasis, even if they were not exactly repetitious like those set forth above. The English translation of Pope Francis's talk with survivors of sexual abuse in the church reads, "In some cases the trust was betrayed by members of your own family, in other cases by priests who carry a sacred responsibility for the care of the soul," but in Spanish the pope highlighted that the priests were "members of the church." When Pope Francis spoke of homelessness at St. Patrick's Church in Washington D.C., in the translation he is quoted as saying: "We can find no social or moral justification, no justification whatsoever, for lack of housing." Yet in Spanish, he is much more emphatic: "I want to be very clear. There is no type of social, moral, or any other kind of justification for accepting homelessness." The problem is not just a lack of housing, but also our *acceptance of* the lack of housing.

While the English translations sans emphatic repetition are much more concise, they miss the inspirational cadence of Pope Francis's prose, soften his mandate for action, and diminish his emphasis on how the church *should* be.

Interestingly, another common omission from the English translations is the pope's jokes. While not technically necessary to communicate a pastoral message, such levities reveal the pope's personality and accessible nature. While visiting the students in Harlem, he thanked the school for allowing him to "steal" instructional time, but the English transcripts omit his quip that "the teachers are really happy about this, I can tell!" At the Curran-Fromhold Correctional Facility he opened with a remark that he would speak in Spanish because "this guy speaks English very well," referring to his interpreter, Msgr. Mark Miles. He told the bishops at the World Meeting of Families about the Argentinian woman who asks him what to do about her thirty-, thirty-two-, or thirty-four-year-old son who still lives at home, "Stop ironing his shirts!"

Taken together, these changes in tense, omission of emphatic phrases and repetitions, and removal of his jokes alter the intensely personal nature of Pope Francis's speeches. It is possible to make the case that this conglomeration of minor discrepancies simply come with the territory of translation, a difficult task that must take into account a variety of cultural norms and expectations, colloquialisms, and interpretations of the pope's intent. Yet this is the crux of our argument: that Pope Francis has a distinctly Latin American Catholicism that is carefully and deliberately expressed in his Spanish language. In translating the pope's speeches into English, a part of that unique cultural perspective is effectively translated out, so that those who only hear or read him in English see a different picture from those who share the Spanish tongue.

Further emphasizing this cultural translation and loss are the three remaining speeches Pope Francis gave in Spanish in which there are major discrepancies and omissions in the English texts. These include his talk with students in East Harlem, his speech on religious liberty at Independence Mall, and his remarks to the bishops at the World Meeting of Families. At first we anticipated that there would be a pattern to which types of speeches would have the most discrepancies, and that his impromptu or informal speeches would have more inaccuracies in translation than his formal talks or homilies. We did not find this to be the case. There was only a single, minor discrepancy in the translation of the pope's impromptu speech at the Festival of Families, but his speech at Independence Mall (which was prepared and translated ahead of his visit) had twelve. The tone also was also not a factor—his talks with the students and inmates were both very informal in nature as compared to his talk with the bishops, in which he was necessarily speaking as the leader of the Catholic Church.

An alternate hypothesis lies with the demographics of the audiences. A speech given to a predominantly Latino or Catholic crowd might be intentionally translated to remove the cultural and religious nuance that a wider audience would miss. This theory is also readily disproven. Though it is natural to assume that mostly Catholics would be interested in attending the pope's appearances, he also spoke in secular spaces (e.g., Independence Mall and Madison Square Garden) and to expressly nonreligious audiences (including at the UN), as well as to interreligious audiences (at the Ground Zero memorial). The only verifiably Catholic audiences were at the Festival of the Families, but only one of the pope's speeches at the Festival contained multiple discrepancies. Further, the only Latino-dominant audience appeared to be at the school in East Harlem,[34] enabling us to dismiss the possibility that his audience affected the accuracy of subsequent translations.

In examining the three remaining speeches referenced above, what is most striking is what is simply omitted from the English translation. The omissions are not stylistic preferences and go beyond the jokes and personal notes that we see removed from his other speeches. Instead, what is left out are Francis's comments that intentionally and directly recognize marginalized groups, his comments about the role and responsibility of leaders, and his comments that demonstrate a radical departure from the US Catholic Church's presentation of religious ideals. We address the discrepancies in each of the three speeches individually because each addresses a distinct topic.

First of all, in his talk with immigrant children and their families in East Harlem the pope, logically, addressed the topic of immigration. In Spanish, he made it clear that he personally understands the pain and difficulty that results from leaving one's home country. Pope Francis also took pains to emphasize the role and importance to immigrants of a welcoming community—the people who provide kindness and compassion and who make them feel at home in someplace new. "All of this is the work of people who help us feel at home. Even though sometimes our mind strays home, we find good people who help us feel at home [here]." This text, omitted from the English translation, could only have been written by someone who either experienced or is extremely empathetic to the immigrant experience and is a strong signal to immigrant communities that the pope is one of them.

Pope Francis also emphasized the importance of dreaming, evoking the memory of Martin Luther King Jr. From the English text: "His dream is that many children like you could get an education. It is beautiful to have dreams and to be able to fight for our dreams." But in Spanish the pope continues by describing the centrality of *community* to these dreams. "And many people I have met and who have come to me also dream with all of you, they have the same dream. And for this reason

34 As a side note, it is interesting that all of the English-language descriptions of the pope's speeches refer to it as his "talk with East Harlem Students." However, the Spanish-language description refers to it as a "Visit to the School of Our Queen of the Angels and Meeting with Immigrant Children and Families." This also appears to be the only speech he gave without an in-time English translation, since many attendees spoke and understood Spanish.

they are involved in this work. They are involved in your lives to help you along this path. We all dream. Always." He clearly emphasizes to these immigrant children and to their families that *they are not alone.* This is a powerful message to give to an otherwise marginalized population that is often left without support, even from the church.

Perhaps more interesting, though less explicable, is the omission of the pope's discussion of the devil. He links dreaming with Jesus: "Wherever there are dreams, there is joy, Jesus is always present." This is where the English text ends and moves on to the next, concluding paragraph. Yet in the Spanish text, the pope continues: "In turn, who is the one who sows sadness, the one who sows insecurity, the one who sows jealousy, the one who sows bad intentions? What is his name? The devil. The devil always sows sadness because he does not want us to be happy, does not want us to dream." Even more interesting is that even the Spanish text is a slightly abbreviated version of what the pope actually said. The video of this talk shows Pope Francis asking, "What is his name?" not as a rhetorical question, but as question that the children should answer. He quickly receives an answer and then says, "The devil, eh? *The devil.* The devil always sows sadness." Though this lesson about the devil might appear dark, in general his speech was not. His interaction with the children was quite lighthearted, following the tone of the entirety of his visit to the school. This striking pastoral lesson on the devil and darkness, encouraging the children and all others present (another sentence that was omitted from the English text) to dream as Jesus wishes for them, is simply erased.

As a result of both minor translation discrepancies and major text omissions, the pope's message is unquestionably altered to remove his emphasis on his connection with and esteem for the immigrant, his direct acknowledgement of the presence of immigrants, his affirmation that there is a community present to welcome and love them, and his pastoral encouragement for all present to keep dreaming.

The pope's speech at Independence Mall in Philadelphia strikes a more political tone. There are three notable alterations from the Spanish to the English texts: his redefinition of religious liberty, his discussion of the benefits and drawbacks of globalization, and his reminder to the US of its historical dedication to the ideal of liberty.

It is simple to address the discrepancies in the texts regarding religious liberty and globalization because much of the pope's presentation was simply omitted from the English text. What are the differences? First, Pope Francis works to reconceptualize the idea of religious liberty as the right of *any* tradition to worship as it sees fit. Then, in the Spanish (but not English) text, he emphasizes that liberty is the result of free, interreligious dialogue: "The ideal of interreligious dialogue, where all men and women of different religious traditions can talk without fighting. This is what creates religious liberty." This indirectly challenges American Catholics to expand their definition of religious liberty beyond a debate about family values and sexuality.

Regarding globalization, the English text includes only a perfunctory mention of its connection to the "healthy pluralism" Pope Francis discussed in *Evangelii Gaudium*.[35] However, in Spanish the pope provides an extended metaphor about the benefits of globalization[36] when it allows individuals to maintain their uniqueness, but states that globalization is bad and harmful when it works to make everyone the same.

Moreover, the pope also took advantage of his presence on the Independence Mall to remind the American public of this country's founding principles of liberty and challenged them to apply those principles today to their treatment of immigrants. This message is significantly weakened and watered down in the English translation. In Spanish the pope said, "When a country guards the memories of its roots, it continues to grow, to renew, and to take in to its breast new communities and new people that come to it." In the conclusion of his speech he urged his audience, "Do not lose the memory of what happened here more than 200 years ago. Do not lose the memory of this Declaration of Independence that proclaimed that all men and women

35 Francis, Apostolic Exhortation *Evangelii Gaudium* (November 24, 2013), 255.

36 The full, translated text of the omitted quote is as follows:

> A moment ago, I spoke of the tendency towards globalization. Globalization is not bad. On the contrary, the tendency to globalize is a good one, it brings us together. What can be bad is the manner of doing it. If globalization pretends to equalize everyone, as if it were one sphere, this globalization destroys the richness and uniqueness of every person and every country. If a globalization tries to unite everyone, but respects everyone and their person, their richness, their uniqueness, and respects every country, every richness, every uniqueness, this globalization is good, will help all of us develop, and bring peace. I would like to use a little geometry here. If globalization is a sphere, where every point is equal, equidistant from the center, it cancels each out, it is not good. If globalization unites as a polyhedron, where there are many united but each one retains its own identity, it is good and the nation grows, and grants dignity and rights to all men.

were created equal, that they are given by God certain inalienable rights and that governments exist to protect and defend those rights." These omitted texts, combined with the (also omitted) exhortations to recognize the positive contributions of immigrants to American society, constitute an undeniable and, in some ways, uncomfortable message to the American public.[37] According to the pope, the US, by insisting on the assimilation or removal of immigrants, is not living up to the ideal of liberty that it professes to hold dear.

In Pope Francis's speech to the bishops at the World Meeting of the Families, we found a total of nineteen discrepancies between the English and Spanish translations. Some were minor but still affected the tone and strength of the pope's message. Others were major, including the deletion of entire sentences or paragraphs. While there are a few themes that could be addressed under this category, here we focus only on the inconsistencies regarding the role and condition of the survivors of sexual abuse.

Pope Francis met with the survivors of sexual abuse on the same day he spoke with the bishops. This fact and his comments about the survivors were not completely omitted from the English translation, but his message was significantly weakened and altered. For instance the English translation states that the pope said: "I have in my heart these stories of suffering of those youth that were sexually abused." The Spanish is, however, much more dramatic. "*Llevo grabado en mi corazón las historias, el sufrimiento y el dolor de los menores que fueron abusados sexualmente por sacerdotes.*" (I carry engraved in my heart the stories, the suffering, and the pain of the children who were sexually abused by priests.) Further, in the Spanish, Pope Francis ends this paragraph with, "*Lo lamento profundamente*" (I regret this deeply), a personal sentiment that is simply removed from the English version.

This emotional connection is consistently diminished in the English translation. Take for example this paragraph: "God weeps for the sexual abuse of children. These cannot be maintained in secret, and I commit

37 "*Please* do not ever be ashamed of your traditions. Do not forget the lessons you learned from your elders, *and that you can enrich the life of this American land.* I repeat: do not be ashamed of *that which is an essential part* of you." (The omitted text is in italics.)

to a careful oversight to ensure that youth are protected and that all responsible will be held accountable." A closer translation from the Spanish reads, "God weeps. The crimes and sins of sexual abuse of children can no longer be kept secret, I commit to the jealous vigilance of the church [or, I commit the church to a jealous vigilance] to protect the youth and I promise that all who are responsible will be held accountable." While this difference *could* represent a stylistic preference, the diminished emotional capacity of the words is undeniable and in line with the overarching pattern of the English translation to make the pope's message more abstract than it is in Spanish.

In the next paragraph, the English translation reads, "Those who have survived this abuse have become true heralds of mercy. Humbly, we owe each of them our gratitude for their great value as they have had to suffer this terrible abuse, sexual abuse of minors." Note the difference not only in meaning, but also the implications for the larger church in the Spanish text: "The survivors of abuse have become true heralds of hope and ministers of mercy. We humbly owe each of them and their families our gratitude for their immense bravery in making Christ's light shine on the terrible sexual abuse of children." The English version only names the survivors as "heralds of mercy," which frames the victims as having an obligation to forgive the church because that is where their value lies. In contrast, in the Spanish version the pope acknowledges the survivors as beacons of *hope* as well as mercy and also recognizes the role of their families in their ordeal.

Finally, on the topic of the survivors of abuse, the pope's address in Spanish (but not in the English translation) makes clear that they are actual people, not an abstract concept: "And I say this because I have just met with a group of people who were abused as children." Comments like this one, which simply and directly acknowledge people's existence, were also omitted from other speeches. In talking with the students in Harlem, he said that he heard that many of the students were immigrants, using the words "some of *you*," an emphasis omitted from the English text. At Independence Mall, he said: "Among us today are members of America's large Hispanic population, as well as representatives of recent immigrants to the United States. *Thank you for opening the doors.*" The text in italics was omitted from the English translation. This simple, direct form of address is one of the most effective ways the pope has of empowering his audiences, specifically members of groups that have traditionally been marginalized and ignored, and it is removed from the English translations being analyzed here.

What our analysis reveals is that those who heard and understood the pope in Spanish had the opportunity to experience an active, personal, engaged, empathetic, immigrant leader of the Catholic Church. This type of experience is directly aligned with how many Catholic Latinos, especially Spanish-speaking immigrants and those raised in immigrant households, with family, work, and church connections to immigrant communities, live their Catholicism. Through his language and its reflection of culture, Pope Francis showed that he lives his faith in ways that are familiar to most Latino Catholics. The leader of the worldwide Catholic Church proved that he is, in a very real sense, one of them.

Spiritual Empowerment through Language across the Americas

In describing the difference between mainstream ways of practicing Catholicism in the US and Mexican American practice of the faith, Fr. Virgilio Elizondo wrote:

> The Euro-American ways of the established church were not the ways of our people. The clergy, religious, and theologians were still foreigners and strangers to our way of life and to our expressions of the faith. Their language of God did not reflect our experiences of God and their priorities of Church life did not reflect our experiences of church. We had to articulate, proclaim, and sing the praises of the Lord of life in ways that were truly native and natural to our people.[38]

This quote captures our central thesis. We suggest that a Latin American and Latino way of practicing Catholicism, such as that embodied in Pope Francis's use of the Spanish language and in the messages he conveyed and lessons he taught while in the US, as well as the cultural context that gives rise to how he uses the language, resonate in a special way with many Spanish-speaking Latino Catholics in the country. What is important about this is that it may in fact allow many

38 Virgilio Elizondo, *The Future Is Mestizo: Life Where Cultures Meet*, rev. ed. (Boulder, Colo.: University Press of Colorado, 2000), 70. First published 1988.

Spanish-speaking Latinos to compensate in part for their marginalized status in the US. Pope Francis's visit to the US may have served to empower their spirituality in ways that are in direct contradiction to what they often experience in everyday life.

Linguistic anthropologists have already put forth well-developed theories of how language is used to marginalize and disempower groups in the US. In effect, this occurs through the establishment of language hierarchies that value English over all other languages. Spanish is certainly often placed at the bottom of these hierarchies. Sociolinguist Michael Silverstein offers the term "indexicality" to allow us to understand how social context provides the cultural frames that give language its relational meaning.[39] He states that "[w]henever languages and other perilinguistic semiotic systems are used in their ubiquitous human habits, cultures as well as people can be said to be communicating…we are at the same time experiencing culture by communicating through this exemplar, medium, and site: language-in-use."[40] Hillary Parsons Dick links indexicality to the ways in which language hierarchies develop into language ideologies that can serve to disempower transnational migrants when they speak a language other than the one that is in the mainstream of the receiving society.[41] She states that "US indexical orders position migrants as outsiders primarily by racializing them," and "[r]acialization is a form of social marking that distinguishes normative actors by dehumanizing them, representing them as undifferentiated, immoral, dangerous, and inherently Other."[42] This process of social marking can have two very distinct consequences. First, it can lead to groups being marginalized and not worthy of participating in society where "lack of skill in English [is treated] as an index of 'backwardness' and 'irrationality.'"[43] But, Parsons Dick continues, it can also lead to Latino immigrants building bonds

39 Michael Silverstein, "Indexical Order and the Dialectics of Sociolinguistic Life," *Language and Communication* 23, no. 3/4 (2003): 193–229. We thank Alex Chávez, Assistant Professor, Department of Anthropology, University of Notre Dame, for pointing us to this literature on linguistic anthropology.

40 Michael Silverstein, "Cultural Concepts and the Language-Culture Nexus," *Current Anthropology* 45, no. 5 (December 2004): 621.

41 Hillary Parsons Dick, "Language and Migration to the United States," *Annual Review of Anthropology* 40 (2011): 227–40.

42 Parsons Dick, 229.

43 Parsons Dick, 231.

across national boundaries at the same time that the language marker allows them to also identify strongly with their countries of origin. She states, "Speaking Spanish is not a sign only of being a US Latino/a, but also of being Mexican, Puerto Rican, etc."[44]

We learn from this literature that language and culture are inextricably linked and can serve purposes of both empowerment and disempowerment. This helps us understand that the language and cultural frames used by Pope Francis, in Spanish and as a Latin American, can serve to link the Vatican to Spanish-speaking Latino communities in the US in ways that compensate for the alienation and lack of responsiveness they often experience in the US Catholic Church.[45]

There is no doubt that Latino immigrants have very high aspirations and dreams of a better quality of life when they come to the US. Many make incredible sacrifices, taking the risk of crossing national borders, often dealing with prejudice and discrimination driven by language and race after arriving in the US, and not knowing whether the risks that they are taking and the burdens they are bearing will ever pay off. Interestingly, the need to migrate is largely driven by the globalization of capital generated by multinational corporations, international banking, and information technology. This need often leads to economic displacement and resulting devastating impacts on traditional areas of work and economic subsistence.[46] It is a fact, however, that the marginalizing and othering that can occur to Spanish-speaking migrants from other countries can lead them toward a deeper spiritual life, one that allows them to cope with the challenges and especially the unknowns of transnational migration.

By speaking Spanish and bringing his Latin American cultural framework to the US, Pope Francis gave respect, meaning, validation,

---

44 Parsons Dick, 234.

45 Kiku Huckle, "Es Su Casa Mi Casa? [Is your house my house?]: Latinos, Socialization, and the Catholic Church" (PhD diss., Department of Political Science, University of Washington, 2016). See also Timothy Matovina, *Latino Catholicism: Transformation in America's Largest Church* (Princeton, N.J.: Princeton University Press, 2012), esp. 248–50, and Carmen Nanko-Fernández, *Theologizing en Espanglish: Context, Community, and Ministry* (Maryknoll, N.Y.: Orbis, 2010), esp. chap. 1, "We Are Not Diversity, We Are the Church!" 1–20.

46 Douglas S. Massey, Jorge Durand, and Nolan J. Malone, *Beyond Smoke and Mirrors: Mexican Migration in an Era of Economic Integration* (New York: Russell Sage Foundation, 2003), 144–49.

and an unquestionable spiritual empowerment to Spanish-speaking, Latino communities of immigrant origin and, through them, perhaps to all Latino Catholics regardless of their language preferences and how strongly they identify with their immigrant origins. He spoke eloquently and often about being a person of immigrant origins himself and of the need for all immigrants to have an unquestioning sense of dignity and self-worth. Most importantly, perhaps, he called to Latino and all communities of immigrant origin to dream about and to persevere in their work to realize those dreams, with the Vatican, through his leadership, validating both their dreams and their sacrifices.

Is not this spiritual empowerment to both individuals and communities the central message of the Gospel? The words of Fr. Virgilio Elizondo are again relevant.

> As Jesus is the Savior of all peoples, he is the personal savior of the Mexican-American people as he speaks directly to the deepest level of our human suffering and to our most fervent aspirations. His way liberates us from false aspirations and opens up unimagined possibilities. He liberates us by giving a totally new signification to our identity and a challenging mission to our movements. In him, curse is transformed into blessing and rejection becomes election for a sacred mission.[47]

Is not the primary message of Jesus that it is those who are the most marginalized that he came to empower and that he wanted them to see themselves as full beings equal to everyone in the eyes of God? At least now, with Pope Francis, this central message can be heard, and *lived*, in Spanish. For Latino communities in the US, and especially for those Latinos who live significant parts of their lives in Spanish, the leader of the Catholic Church validates and empowers them as no previous pope has been able to do. In this way, Pope Francis is yet again an example of a pope for all of the Americas.

47 Elizondo, *The Future Is Mestizo*, 86.

CHAPTER 11

CLERICALISM

A Neuralgic Point for Church Reform

Allan Figueroa Deck

THIS ARTICLE WILL EXPLORE Pope Francis's repeated expressions of concern about clericalism and the sources of this concern in the Second Vatican Council's ecclesiology of the People of God. It is no secret that Pope Francis hardly misses an opportunity to criticize clericalism. He condemns it in the most direct and uncompromising manner as "the fruit of a mistaken way of living out the ecclesiology proposed by Vatican II ...and one of the greatest distortions that Latin America has to confront."[1] While rooted in the ecclesial context of Latin America, the pope's concern with clericalism is surely not limited to that region of the world. Clericalism's wider grip on the church is hardly disputed, and the pope's urgent denunciations cannot be dismissed as mere aberration or idiosyncrasy. What is at the heart of his insistence on naming and condemning clericalism with such urgency?

I want to suggest that Francis's unrelenting critique of clericalism constitutes a "neuralgic point" for advancing what the conference of Aparecida calls *conversión pastoral*, a Gospel-centered structural reform of the Catholic Church starting with and from the Americas.[2] This

1 *Letter of His Holiness Pope Francis to Cardinal Marc Ouellet, President of the Pontifical Commission for Latin America*, March 19, 2016. All documents published by the Vatican, including this one and many others cited below, including papal addresses, may be found at the vatican.va website.

2 "All ecclesial structures and all pastoral plans of dioceses, parishes, religious communities, movements, and any Church institution must be imbued with this firm missionary decision. No community should excuse itself from entering decidedly with all its might into the ongoing processes of missionary renewal and from giving up outdated structures that are no longer useful for handing on the faith." See Jorge Mario

article is a wide-ranging discussion of clericalism, how it works, and why it is a central issue for the church today. As Richard R. Gaillardetz claims in speaking of the first Latin American and Jesuit pope, "His pontificate represents the most ambitious and comprehensive effort of the postconciliar papacy to bring to life the reforming vision of the Council."[3] Understanding clericalism's hold on the ministerial structures of the church and that it is a fundamental obstacle to reform provides a pathway to discovering the nature of this pope's vision of and for the worldwide church in the third millennium.

Clericalism and Evangelization

Any analysis of clericalism must begin with an acknowledgement that the concern about it arises as a logical consequence of the church's portentous decision at the Second Vatican Council to conceive of its mission and identity in terms of evangelization. Its landmark pastoral constitution *Gaudium et Spes* and Pope Paul VI's 1975 apostolic exhortation *Evangelii Nuntiandi* reformulated the church's self-understanding in terms of evangelization and mission.[4] Consequently, a process was set in motion that has led to a serious rethinking and reimagining of every aspect of the church, including the nature and configuration of ministries, from the point of view of its missionary purpose. That process surely has a long way to go. While the council set the church down this path, the simple fact is that for decades after the council various forms of resistance and foot-dragging impeded the process of transformation it contemplated. In his description of the "new evangelization," Pope Saint John Paul II insisted that the church is, *in its entirety*, missionary.[5] Fr. David

---

Bergoglio, ed., *Concluding Document, Aparecida, May 13–31, 2007* (Washington D.C.: United States Conference of Catholic Bishops, 2008), 365. Citations to this document herein are to paragraph numbers.

3 Richard R. Gaillardetz, "Conclusion," in *Go Into the Streets: The Welcoming Church of Pope Francis*, ed. Thomas P. Rausch and Richard R. Gaillardetz (New York: Paulist Press, 2016), 177.

4 This emphasis was unequivocally affirmed by Pope John Paul II in his encyclical *Redemptoris Missio* (December 7, 1990), esp. 26–27.

5 John Paul II, Postsynodal Apostolic Exhortation *Ecclesia in America* (January 22, 1999), chap. VI, "The Mission of the Church in America Today: The New Evangelization," 66–76.

Power captured the radical implications of reading ecclesiology and ministry in the key of mission in his magisterial study of ministry as it has developed in various parts of the world in the decades after Vatican II. The main title of his study is quite evocative: *Mission, Ministry, Order*.[6] The order of these three concepts in the title says it all: first comes mission, the call to "go out," a foundational value that is the originating point of the church's life. Then comes ministry, the action that flows from the church's missionary identity, and then order (hierarchy), which is the manner in which this call and response is structured or organized in history.

The US missiologist Stephen Bevans helps us grasp the profound implications of the church's deeper realization of its missionary nature with a quotation from John Paul II in which he powerfully expresses how mission defines the ministerial priesthood itself in relation to the more fundamental notion of the common priesthood of the faithful: "Christ gives to priests, in the Spirit, a particular gift so that they can help the People of God to exercise faithfully and fully the common priesthood which it has received."[7] The point is that the sacrament of orders is not the starting point—the most foundational and significant of all of the sacraments is baptism because the one vocation of all the faithful, and their fundamental equality, flow from it. All share in a common priesthood conferred in baptism, which is the source of the entire Christian identity. Taking inspiration from *Lumen Gentium*, Pope Francis alludes to this in these emphatic words: "Our first and fundamental consecration is rooted in our Baptism. No one has been baptized a priest or a bishop. They baptize us as lay people and it is the indelible sign that no one can ever erase…the Church is not an elite of priests, of consecrated men, of bishops, but … everyone forms the faithful Holy People of God."[8]

In the same document Francis laments clericalism's antipathy toward an evangelizing church that is *siempre en salida*, "always going out," noting that "clericalism is more concerned with dominating spaces

6 David N. Power, *Mission, Ministry, Order: Reading the Tradition in the Present Context* (New York: Continuum, 2008).

7 John Paul II, Postsynodal Apostolic Exhortation *Pastores Dabo Vobis* (March 15, 1992), 17.

8 *Letter of His Holiness Pope Francis to Cardinal Marc Ouellet.*

than with generating initiatives."[9] By "dominating spaces" he means occupying positions of control and power.

For a number of reasons, over two thousand years of church history the evangelizing and missionary purpose of the church has tended to be undermined and "outsourced," as it were, in various ways, relegated to one sector or elite group; for instance, to clerics, monks, or consecrated persons. The universal call to missionary discipleship has been repeatedly devalued, but at various times in its history, the church has pursued correctives to this tendency by renewing and reforming structures and pastoral praxis. One might think of the rise of the mendicant orders as one example of this. Indeed, the church is living such a moment now under the Petrine leadership of Francis.

Ultimately, the context of ecclesial mission—a constant "going out" and ongoing encounter with others—is dynamic and subject to change. That divine mission must inevitably shape the contour of ministries and the configuration and structure of the church. Stephen Bevans has reminded us that the mission has a Church and not the Church a mission.[10] According to the Second Vatican Council's Decree on the Mission Activity of the Church (*Ad Gentes*), that mission is rooted in nothing less than the trinitarian life of the Godhead itself.[11] A truly evangelizing, missionary church, therefore, always looks outward, is always "going out"; the way in which it practices ministry cannot become self-referential and narcissistic, but must rather remain nimble, open to "the signs of the times" and to the demands imposed by change and new circumstances. Pope Francis sees all of this with unusual clarity and for that reason points to clericalism as an enormous stumbling block to successful mission, or, in popular English, the elephant in Holy Mother Church's living room!

To repeat the formulation of David Power, mission comes first, ministry second, and order or hierarchy third. Implicit in this ordering of priorities is the need to be open to the reconfiguration of ministries so that the church can reach out most effectively in fidelity to the one

9 *Letter of His Holiness Pope Francis to Cardinal Marc Ouellet.*

10 Stephen Bevans, "The Mission Has a Church: Invitation to the Dance" (paper presented at the Institute of the Sisters of Mercy Lecture Series: The Mission Has a Church, 2009), https://pdfs.semanticscholar.org/2f40/b924345bd1e2faa24a30d98c-89bcde8bec9f.pdf.

11 Vatican II, Decree *Ad Gentes* (December 7, 1965), 2.

baptismal call. In this regard, John Paul II made two points whose full weight is only now being grasped in the pontificate of Pope Francis. First, speaking to a conference of the Latin American bishops, he spoke of a "new evangelization," which he defined as proclaiming the Gospel with "new ardor, with new expressions, and with new methods."[12] It is not difficult to understand what he meant by "ardor," but what did he mean by "new expressions and methods"? What did the Holy Father have in mind and how might it relate to clericalism? He did not clarify, but it can be argued that in the age of Francis, those new expressions and methods (as well as the "new ardor") are emerging as perhaps never before in the post–Vatican II church. They are expressions and methods linked, for example, to a kerygmatic emphasis being given to mercy, to changes in pastoral practice related to the difficult cases of divorce and remarriage, and to the pastoral care of gay and transsexual persons. One might also add a growing recognition of the negative effect of clericalism on the church's outreach to others as a result of the usurpation of proper roles by clergy or a handful of clericalized laity—clerical elites who attempt to substitute themselves for the wider ecclesial community.

The second point pertinent to our discussion raised by John Paul II relates to the role of the laity in embracing the church's identity as a community of evangelizers: "The renewal of the Church in America will not be possible without the active presence of the laity. *Therefore, they are largely responsible for the future of the Church*."[13] Clericalism works against the active participation of the laity, so Francis's denunciations of clericalism and his persistent call to the laity to assume its rightful role is thoroughly in agreement with his predecessor's urgent concern. Francis, however, adds a significant new point regarding the laity's essential role in carrying out the church's mission, suggesting that they and not the clergy are indispensable transmitters and guarantors of the continuity of faith across generations:

> Once the Gospel has been inculturated in a people, in their process of transmitting their culture they also transmit the

12 John Paul II, *Opening Address of the Nineteenth General Assembly of CELAM*, March 9, 1983, Port-au-Prince, Haiti, *L'Osservatore Romano* English edition 16/780 (April 18, 1983), 9.

13 John Paul II, *Ecclesia in America,* 44. Author's emphasis.

> faith *in ever new forms*; hence the importance of *understanding evangelization as inculturation*. Each portion of the People of God, by translating the gift of God into its own life and in accordance with its own genius, bears witness to the faith it has received and enriches it with new and eloquent expressions. One can say that "a people continuously evangelizes itself."[14]

At Aparecida, the Latin American bishops applied this logic to their understanding of ministry in the church. They suggested that the distinction between clerics and laity is not very useful and boldly proposed a new category for better expressing the vocation of all the faithful: *missionary disciples*. At an October, 2013 ministry conference held at the University of Dallas, Cardinal Oscar Rodríguez vigorously asserted the need to give pride of place to the radical equality of all the baptized:

> The whole church, the people of God, continues the priesthood of Jesus without losing their lay character in the realm of the profane and the unclean, the "cast out," a priesthood not centered exclusively in the cult of the temple but *in the entire world*, with a Samaritan praxis of justice and love. This priesthood belongs to the substantive plane; the other—the presbyterium—*is a ministry and cannot be conceived apart from the common priesthood.*[15]

He went on to suggest that "the clergy are neither the 'men of God' nor are the laity the 'men of the world.' That is a false dichotomy. To speak correctly we should not speak of clergy and laity but instead of community and ministry."[16]

What this means is that a church which is missionary in its entirety, completely missionary in nature, can no longer think of itself as divided between clerics and laity. This division creates a false dichotomy that undermines the sense of real responsibility that the baptized exercise in carrying out the mission, and the sacramentality of their actions

---

14 Francis, Apostolic Exhortation *Evangelii Gaudium* (November 24, 2013), 122.

15 Cardinal Rodríguez's address to the conference was later published. See Oscar Rodríguez Maradiaga, "The Importance of the New Evangelization," *Origins* 43, no. 24 (Nov. 14, 2013): 374–75. Author's emphasis.

16 Rodríguez, 374–75.

in doing so. At the heart of this misleading, dualistic, and essentialist way of thinking at the heart of clericalism is a failure to adequately appreciate the centrality of the common priesthood of the faithful as stressed by *Lumen Gentium*.[17]

In a finely researched article, David Coffey points out the limitations in thinking that led to the formulation of the relationship between the ordained and the common priesthood in *Lumen Gentium*, a limitation that contributes to the persistent tendency to downplay the greatness and meaning of the common priesthood.

> Because the Council was unable to reconcile its judgments about the ordained and the common priesthood in the person of Christ, it settled for the idea of the ordained priesthood as referred immediately to Christ, indeed to his headship, which did nothing to correct the popular perception of the priest *as above the Church rather than as part of it, and unlike Mediator Dei, it left the common priesthood rather vague.*[18]

In *Ratio Fundamentalis Institutionis Sacerdotalis*, a definitive document on the formation of priests, the Congregation for the Clergy expresses Pope Francis's teaching on this matter; namely, that the ministerial priesthood must first of all be understood in relation to the church itself and not first of all in relation to Christ: "As the Second Vatican Council reminds us, the nature and mission of priests must be understood *within the Church*, the People of God, the Body

---

17 See Vatican Council II, Dogmatic Constitution *Lumen Gentium* (November 21, 1964), 10–11. Those who desire to put the ordained priesthood somehow above or beyond the common priesthood cite the following statement at *Lumen Gentium* 10: "Though they differ essentially and not only in degree, the common priesthood of the faithful and the ministerial or hierarchical priesthood are nonetheless interrelated; each in its own way shares in the one priesthood of Christ." What is important to note is that the teaching of Vatican II regarding the common priesthood, as stated by Cardinal Rodríguez Maradiaga above, pertains to the substantive or more essential plane, while the ordained priesthood or *presbyterium*, as he refers to it, is a function, real and distinct, but still a function relative to the common priesthood and not vice-versa.

18 David Coffey, "The Common and the Ordained Priesthood," *Theological Studies*, 58, no. 3 (June 1997): 235. Author's emphasis.

of Christ, the Temple of the Holy Spirit, for the service of which they consecrate their lives."[19]

A renewed conception of the ministerial priesthood, one that grounds it in the common priesthood of all the baptized and intimately links the priest *first* to the wider church and *then* to the *persona Christi* will go far to correct a debilitating dichotomy and elitism that have afflicted the church for centuries. While acknowledging the importance of the identification of the ministerial priest with Christ as the head of the church, Thomas P. Rausch insists that both the ministerial and the common priesthood have a Christological reference and cautions that "it is important to avoid any suggestion that the priest is over the Church or prior to the Church rather than part of it."[20]

More Problems with Clericalism

Perhaps the most important sources for grasping Pope Francis's concerns regarding clericalism are described in his July 28, 2013 address to the leadership of the Episcopal Conferences of Latin America (CELAM) in Rio de Janeiro. He clearly sees the 2007 gathering of the Latin American bishops at Aparecida and the substantive document they produced as a significant resource for grasping the universal church's current challenges. He frames his comments about the church's reform and renewal in terms of what Aparecida calls the "continental mission" embraced by the Latin American bishops in response to their analysis of the contextual realities of the region. The missionary activities of the church, according to Francis, will follow two lines of development, one *programmatic* and another *paradigmatic*. The programmatic aspect refers to the missionary activities themselves. The paradigmatic refers to "setting in a missionary key all the day-to-day activities of the Particular Churches," which "entails a whole process of reforming ecclesial structures,"[21] as part of which

19 Congregation for the Clergy, "The Gift of the Priestly Vocation," *Ratio Fundamentalis Institutionis Sacerdotalis* (Vatican City: L'Osservatore Romano, December 8, 2016), 30. Author's emphasis.

20 For more on this, see Thomas P. Rausch, "Priestly Identity: Priority of Representation and the Iconic Argument," *Worship* 73, no. 2 (March 1999): 175.

21 Francis, *Address to the Leadership of the Episcopal Conferences of Latin America* (CELAM), July 28, 2013, 3.

a straightforward confrontation with the temptation of clericalism is essential. In his talk with the bishops of CELAM, Francis stressed the need to clearly articulate the real challenges facing missionary discipleship, and identifies two sets of challenges: the church's inner renewal (*ad intra*) and the church's dialogue with the wider world (*ad extra*). Both include challenges touching on the subject of clericalism, and Francis sheds light on why it is so harmful to the church's mission.

The first challenge has to do with the tendency of priests to act like and become administrators rather than pastors. The priest becomes focused on the institution and its functionality rather than on the concrete persons making up the faithful. Pope Francis has used the terms "customs house official" or "NGO executive" to refer to the priests, bishops, and other pastoral agents who exhibit this behavior.[22] An example of this clericalizing tendency toward administration instead of pastoral care is the resistance of some priests and other ministers to refocusing their pastoral approaches or making timely adaptations that truly benefit people merely because implementing these modifications is inconvenient or bothersome. Yet the responsibility of responding to the needs of the faithful is in a very real sense a common responsibility of all the baptized, and the faithful must also be challenged to do their part.

In Latin America as well as in Hispanic ministry in the US, the concept of *pastoral de conjunto*—coordinated and participative pastoral planning and action—has been developed and can serve as an alternative to the clerical or lay leader who behaves like an officious bureaucrat. Do priests and other ministers actually recognize that the faithful become *sharers and agents* in missionary activities and not just *objects* of them? Is the need for pastoral discernment continuously acknowledged in practice by means of ongoing consultations and planning with respect to pastoral, financial, and organizational matters? Are parish and diocesan pastoral and financial councils truly working? Francis asserts quite clearly that "on this score, we are far behind."[23] More pointedly, he asks whether clerics and other ministers see themselves as *accompanying* the faithful, rather than manipulating or, worse, infantilizing them. Do

22 "Pope Francis Warns Church Could Become 'Compassionate NGO,'" *BBC News*, March 14, 2013, bbc.com/news/world-europe-21793224; "Francisco: La Iglesia no es una aduana, quiere las puertas abiertas," *CNN Español*, September 9, 2017, cnnespanol.cnn.com/2017/09/09/Francisco-la-iglesia-no-es-una-aduana-quiere-las-puertas-abiertas/.

23 Francis, *Address to the Leadership of the Episcopal Conferences of Latin America*, 3.

priests see themselves as open to challenges coming from an engaged missionary outreach? Or is there still something of the old formula that sees the role of the faithful as simply to "pray, pay and obey?" Is there a sense that the baptized faithful are not merely collaborators with the priest and other ministers in the apostolate but *agents in their own right*?

Francis goes on to assert in the address to CELAM that the pastoral conversion he is proposing in accord with the indications of the council is a matter of attitudes. He highlights the need for affective maturity and a desire to reform one's life through an ongoing process of discernment. The implication is that clericalism will not be overcome without a change of attitude on the part of both the clergy and the baptized faithful, a change that pays attention to pastoral practices and spiritual growth as well as ecclesial and ministerial structures. For example, for bishops Francis proposes a threefold relationship with their flock that encourages and preserves a proactive agency on behalf of the baptized faithful. "The Bishop has to be among his people in three ways: in front of them pointing the way; among them, keeping them together and preventing them from being scattered; and behind them, ensuring that no one is left behind, but also, and *primarily, so that the flock can sniff out new paths.*[24]

In the same address, Francis goes on to describe in some detail for the bishops his understanding of clericalism. He refers to it as "a temptation" that flourishes as a result of a terrible complicity; indeed, he calls it "a sinful complicity: the priest clericalizes the lay person and the lay person kindly asks to be clericalized, because deep down it is easier."[25] He goes on to say that clericalism explains in great part the lack of maturity and freedom in some Latin American laity. Clericalism, he says, holds people back from taking responsibility for their lives and truly growing as human beings. The lack of regard for one's own baptismal vocation and an unhealthy dependence on clerics, together with a corresponding lack of freedom, can contribute to a thoughtless adherence to ideologies that blind people to concrete human realities in favor of a doctrinal or disciplinary "safety" that does not allow them to cast their gaze ahead to see what is directly in front of them. Francis

24 Francis, *Address to the Leadership of the Episcopal Conferences of Latin America*, 5. Author's emphasis.

25 Francis, 4.

thus links clericalism to a kind of blindness and suggests that it is not evangelical, given that "curing the blind" was central to the activities of Christ himself.[26]

In the address, Francis goes on to list narrow ideologies to which clericalism can contribute: sociological reductionisms of either left or right, psychologizing, modern-day forms of the ancient heresies of neo-Pelagianism and gnosticism, and a functionalism that "more than being interested in the road itself, it is concerned with fixing holes in the road."[27]

In a thought-provoking reflection on clericalism's reach in Latin American Catholicism, Francis makes the point in the address that there is an area of freedom and relative maturity for the baptized faithful found precisely in their "communal experiences." He notes that in popular Catholicism there is great autonomy, which he insists is "on the whole … a healthy thing."[28] This Catholicism is primarily expressed in popular piety, which is described at length in the Aparecida Document.[29] Various developments in the life of Catholic communities in Latin America over the past fifty years exemplify a healthy dynamic away from clericalism. Francis mentions in this connection bible study groups, base ecclesial communities, and pastoral councils. It is interesting that the Holy Father does not mention in this connection movements like the Neocatechumenal Way or Communion and Liberation, perhaps because there is some suspicion, as Massimo Faggioli suggests, that these movements have to some extent been manipulated by sectors in the church for the purpose of promoting a questionable interpretation of Vatican II and an ecclesial vision inspired by clericalism.[30]

At the root of the significance Pope Francis assigns to his critique of clericalism is a tectonic shift from the church's focus on hierarchy and organization, a focus permeated by ideology, doctrine, and order during the past five hundred years of post-Tridentine and Enlightenment Catholicism, to something fresh and new. His message and ways of communicating all point to a synodality and expressivity that give

26 *Letter of His Holiness Pope Francis to Cardinal Marc Ouellet.*

27 Francis, *Address to the Leadership of the Episcopal Conferences of Latin America*, 4.

28 Francis, 4.

29 Bergoglio, *Concluding Document*, 258–65.

30 Massimo Faggioli, *The Rising Laity: Ecclesial Movements since Vatican II* (New York: Paulist Press, 2016), 120.

pride of place to experience, accompaniment, witnessing, performance, and charism. By indicating this preference, Francis is pursuing changes that were inspired by the council but became sidetracked over the last fifty years by internal resistance and mixed signals from Rome and other sectors of the church.[31] Sam Rocha explains the change of focus espoused by Francis as grounded in *radical realism.*[32] Rocha, interestingly enough, connects this turn to realism with the distinctive trend in American philosophy toward concreteness and pragmatism exemplified by the philosophers William James and C. S. Peirce. Rocha argues that this connection makes sense because Francis is an "American," the first American pope, if one uses that term to refer broadly to the Americas, North and South.[33] Rocha, however, goes further to make a point not yet adequately grasped by the many interpreters of Francis:

> Yet, in a more direct way, the geopolitical situation of Latin America over the past hundred years has produced a sense of the concrete that is more than purely philosophical in nature. The comparative political history of modernity in Europe and the Americas makes this very clear. Whereas the European story is driven by an intellectual progression of *ideas* (e.g., rationalism, empiricism, idealism, and so on), the Latin American version is a postcolonial response to political *situations*...Francis reflects this situation-based approach in a very direct and pointed way... He describes the distinction between realities and ideas by giving ontological priority to the former. Realities simply are, whereas ideas are worked out...The ontological simplicity of reality gives way to a

31 "History may well look back on the pontificate of Francis as that decisive moment in the history of the church in which the full force of the Second Vatican Council's reformist vision was finally realized." Gaillardetz, "Conclusion," 178.

32 Pope Francis uses the term "healthy realism." Francis, *The Holiness of Negotiation, Morning Meditation in the Chapel of the* Domus Sanctae Marthae, June 9, 2016, http://www.vatican.va/content/francesco/en/cotidie/2016/documents/papa-francesco-cotidie_20160609_the-holiness-of-negotiation.html.

33 Sam Rocha, "Francis's Radical Realism: Performance v. Ideology," *Ethika Politika*, March 11, 2014, https://ethikapolitika.org/2014/03/11/franciss-radical-realism-performance-v-ideology/.

> "principle of reality," an incarnational order between word and flesh that favors the *practice* of evangelization.[34]

Francis's notion of where the emphasis must be placed in the church's historical journey is, according to Rocha, on *performance*. His ecclesiology is inspired by a drive toward reality, concreteness, and witness, not propositions, doctrines, formulations, standardizations, rules, and speculations. Hence the church as field hospital and bishops out on the streets (*callejeros*) smelling of sheep! Where, we may ask, did Francis get this orientation, this nitty-gritty vision of and for the church?

As a child of the drama of Latin American history during the tumultuous second half of the twentieth century, including his own Argentine history, Jorge Mario Bergoglio was deeply marked and schooled by events, realities, situations, and experiences that flow from social, economic, political, and cultural developments. This includes suffering on a scale perhaps unknown by people in the centers of power but common among the Latin American masses on the margins of wealth and influence. The second half of the twentieth century in Latin America, the period of Francis's most formative life experiences, was filled with struggles, dangers, and violence that resulted from economic disasters, political conflicts, and war.[35] As a Jesuit priest he belonged to the body of church leaders in Latin America who made a decisive and distinctive commitment to pursue the vision of Vatican II in ways that differed from his contemporaries in other parts of the world. It was the vision of Dom Hélder Câmara, Eduardo Pironio, Manuel Larraín, and several other outstanding Latin American prelates that laid the foundation for CELAM, the largest and most collegial organization of bishops in the world.

This foundation had already been laid in 1955 at the time of CELAM's first conference in Rio de Janeiro. The second conference, however, in Medellín in 1968, set the church in Latin America on a course that for fifty years, if properly appreciated and understood, explains at least partially the evocative and creative impact that Pope Francis has had upon the global church. The Latin American church at the highest

---

34 Rocha, "Francis's Radical Realism."

35 Austen Ivereigh, *The Great Reformer: Francis and the Making of a Radical Pope* (New York: Henry Holt, 2014), 140–65.

levels opted to focus its attention on the drama of social, economic, and political realities, as well as move away from a Christendom that operated on the basis of an outmoded and exhausted colonial pastoral praxis. The obsessive defensiveness characteristic of the Eurocentric Tridentine church was not shared by the Latin American faithful, for whom the threat of Protestantism and the assault of the Enlightenment had been mitigated by the isolation of three centuries of Spanish and Portuguese rule and by the monopoly on official religion enjoyed by Catholicism well into the twentieth century. During these dramatic decades of struggle, moreover, Latin American Catholicism became the crucible for the creation of contextual theologies, better known as "liberation" theologies. One of the more distinctive forms of this theology is what has been called the "Theology of the People" (*Teología del pueblo*), developed by two Argentine theologians dear to the heart of Pope Francis: Lucio Gera and Rafael Tello.[36]

The relative freedom from the fortress-church mentality of the West as expressed in the pre–Vatican II tendency toward dogmatism, circling the wagons, and defensively drawing lines in the sand in an orientation focused on apologetics and orthodoxy resulted, in Latin America, in a new focus on praxis. The rising influence of vigorous contextual theologies also contributed to an existential and forward-looking attitude among church leaders that carried them beyond the status quo and the pastoral/theological maintenance modes that the clerical system tends to reproduce. The long history of hybridity and *mestizaje* resulting from the encounter of cultures at the very birth of Latin American civilization explains in large part the particular character and originality of the evangelization of the Americas. Such an inculturated Catholicism, a product of the encounter of numerous cultures going back centuries, is instinctively suspicious of any kind of "culture war" mentality. Rather, the turn to realism, contextuality, and hybridity characteristic of Latin American Catholicism required engagement with the other and with the demands of epochal change, not allowing a retreat into the shell of traditionalism. This stance demanded a renewed emphasis on the here and now. Concretely, this meant engaging the poor, the youth, and

36 On Gera and Tello, see Allan Figueroa Deck, SJ, *Francis, Bishop of Rome: The Gospel for the Third Millennium* (New York: Paulist Press, 2016), 36–59.

the marginal and vulnerable, as well as a serious revision of pastoral methods in a search for effective ways to reach out and serve under these particular circumstances.

At the heart of this turn toward praxis was a movement away from a deductive reasoning that placed received tradition, doctrinal formulations, rules and regulations, and a rigid clerical order at the center of the church's attention. Instead, the focus was on the fact that the thrust of the church's mission in history and in the world is deeply incarnational and horizontal, a focus that addressed the realities of the times by promoting contact, mutual give-and-take, and, above all, dialogue with and among the people and their contemporary cultures. As Rafael Tello put it, evangelization occurs not only with and among the poor but from (*desde*) the poor.[37]

It must not be forgotten that Latin American Catholicism is unique within worldwide Catholicism because it is deeply hybrid, the result of a prolonged and largely successful blending of indigenous and African elements with medieval and baroque Iberian Catholicism. As Tello insisted, Catholicism in Latin American was the result of a striking process of inculturation grounded on *popular* rather than ecclesiastical culture. As a result, the real faith of Latin Americans is a popular Catholicism standing in considerable contrast (not opposition) to the standard Catholicism of textbooks and official teachers without, of course, falling into heterodoxy.[38]

In a collection of essays shedding light on various aspects of the Aparecida Document, Cardinal Bergoglio contributed a lively piece on popular religion as inculturation of the faith. In it, he highlights the distinctive role of popular culture as the locus of the church's mission to evangelize in an inculturated manner. One can detect in it some interesting implications that go to the question of why Francis is so concerned about clericalism. Clericalism creates a rarefied ecclesiastical environment, ethos, and culture that is removed from most people's ordinary lives. In such a context, the Gospel message may not find effective ways to really sink into the everyday practices

37 Omar Albado, "Volverse al Hombre Concreto: Una Aproximación a la Cultura Popular en la Teología del Padre Rafael Tello," *Vida Pastoral* 283 (2010): 4–11.

38 Enrique Ciro Bianchi, *Pobres en este mundo, ricos en la fe* (Buenos Aires: Agape, 2012), 93.

of life, to take root in what US Latina theologians call *lo cotidiano*, daily life.[39] He quotes John Paul II in his inaugural speech to the Pontifical Council for Culture: "The synthesis between faith and culture is not just a demand of culture but also of faith. A faith that does not become culture is a faith not fully embraced, nor totally grasped, nor faithfully lived."[40]

Consequently, culture, especially popular culture, becomes the way, indeed, the privileged way, in which evangelization truly takes shape and faith becomes life. In *Gaudium et Spes* (nos. 57–62) and *Evangelii Nuntiandi* evangelization clearly implies inculturation. Francis likes to use the emphatic term "inculturated evangelization," a coinage that strongly suggests engagement with culture, but especially popular culture, and accords with the school of Tello's and Gera's *Teología del pueblo*.[41]

The inductive, contextualizing methodology espoused by *Gaudium et Spes* was widely welcomed and applied in Papa Bergoglio's Latin America in terms of a renewed emphasis on the "pastoral circle" methodology—"See-Judge-Act-Celebrate-Evaluate"—which had already taken root before the council in hugely popular ecclesial movements like the Young Christian Workers.[42] This methodology, which was embraced by CELAM, gained considerable traction at Medellín (1968), flourished at the Puebla conference (1979), and was vigorously reaffirmed at Aparecida (2007) by none other than Pope Benedict XVI himself after some elements in the church had tried but failed to redirect the Aparecida gathering away from the inductive, pastoral approaches of Vatican II, Medellín, and Puebla and turn back to the hidebound, deductive mentality of the Tridentine past.[43]

---

39 Jorge Mario Bergoglio, "Religiosidad Popular Como Evangelización de la Fe," in *Testigos de Aparecida*, vol. 2 (Bogotá: CELAM, 2008), 281–325. On *lo cotidiano* as *locus theologicus* see Ada María Isasi-Díaz, *En la Lucha/In the Struggle, Elaborating a Mujerista Theology*, 2nd ed. (Minneapolis: Fortress Press, 2003).

40 Bergoglio, "Religiosidad Popular," citing John Paul II, *Speech at the Foundation of the Pontifical Council for Culture*, May 20, 1982.

41 Deck, *Francis, Bishop of Rome*, 36–59.

42 Joe Holland, "Roots of the Pastoral Circle in Personal Experiences and Catholic Social Tradition," Introduction to *The Pastoral Circle Revisited*, ed. Fans Wijsen, Peter Henriot, and Rodrigo Mejía (Maryknoll, N.Y.: Orbis, 2005), 1–14.

43 Benedict XVI, *Address Of His Holiness Benedict XVI to the Inaugural Session of the Fifth General Conference of the Bishops of Latin America and the Caribbean*, May 13, 2007, 2.

Argentine theologian Carlos María Galli reminds us of the realism of Pope Francis's methodology, echoing in some way Sam Rocha's observations noted above. Galli, however, connects the focus on realism in Francis's thinking not to American pragmatism but to the renewal of Thomism in Argentina in the last half of the twentieth century. Thomas Aquinas endorsed the Aristotelian emphasis on experience and science, even as other powerful philosophical and theological trends in Christianity preferred Plato's idealism. Galli shows how mercy as understood by Aquinas is the hermeneutical key for understanding Francis's pontificate.[44] Mercy brings with it a powerful, existential orientation toward reality, toward what one is undergoing in the real world of sensory experience and affective response. In *Evangelii Gaudium*, Francis observes that

> Saint Thomas Aquinas taught that the Church's moral teaching has its own "hierarchy" in the virtues and in the acts which proceed from them. What counts above all else is faith working through love.....Thomas thus explains that, as far as external works are concerned, mercy is the greatest of all the virtues...it is proper to God to have mercy, through which his omnipotence is manifested to the greatest degree.[45]

Galli describes mercy as "the historic form of love." Mercy arises out of the concrete experience of humanity in history, in time, and requires the ability to attend to the existential rather than to the theoretical and speculative challenges faced by humans. It plunges us into the very heart of reality as Francis explains it:

> Sometimes we are tempted to be that kind of Christian who keeps the Lord's wounds at arm's length. Yet Jesus wants us to touch human misery, to touch the suffering flesh of others. He hopes that we will stop looking for those personal or communal niches which shelter us from the maelstrom of human

44 Carlos María Galli, "Diez claves de la Exhortación *Evangelii Gaudium* en el contexto del pontificado reformador y misionero de Francisco" (unpublished manuscript, Faculty of Theology, Universidad Católica Argentina, 2014), nos. 8.5, 15.

45 Francis, *Evangelii Gaudium,* 37.

> misfortune and instead enter into the reality of other people's lives and know the power of tenderness.[46]

This renewed emphasis on realism may also spring in some way from the shift that has occurred from a vertical and organizational way of thinking about the church, from one that gives pride of place to stasis and hierarchy and the *cursus honoris* to one that is synodal and thus concerned with motion (the root of the word "synod" relates to "journey") and with the plurality and diversity of situations and perspectives that characterize the existential rather than the theoretical church. This framework and attitude stresses nearness rather than distance between the pastor and the sheep. Synodality is encouraged by a collaborative "walking with" each other in which both the faithful, and most importantly their leaders, participate, a walking together that reaches down to all levels of the church, not merely remaining at the level of the pope or the bishops or even regional gatherings of bishops or presbyters.

In this connection the impact of the emphasis on solidarity within Catholic social teaching should also be mentioned. Solidarity requires attentiveness to the nitty-gritty, to whatever diminishes the life of one's neighbor. Both solidarity and synodality are immensely meaningful ways of being church that must permeate the workings of dioceses, parishes, schools, and other Catholic institutions. All of this suggests a turn toward a more horizontal and less vertical and clerical way of proceeding. What is at play is a turn toward Gospel realism as found in experience and concrete situations as well as in pastoral methodologies generated by the most penetrating expressions of ecclesial vision in Latin America over the past fifty years, especially those contained in the documents of Medellín, Puebla, and Aparecida.

Ministerial Structures and Clericalism

One of the major obstacles to the turn toward Gospel realism is an entrenched mind-set among both clergy and faithful regarding the ministerial structures of the church. In *Evangelii Gaudium*, Pope

46 Francis, 270.

Francis speaks of how clericalism, a lack of a sense of true responsibility for one's baptismal calling, comes about.

> A clear awareness of this responsibility of the laity, grounded in their baptism and confirmation, does not appear in the same way in all places. In some places it is because lay persons have not been given the formation needed to take on important responsibilities. In others, it is because in their particular Churches room has not been made for them to speak and to act, *due to an excessive clericalism which keeps them away from decision-making.*[47]

Even though clericalism is a significant aspect of our present-day experience of the church, it was not always so. It is clear that ministry for the first two or three centuries of Christianity was centered in the home, and Latin American popular Catholicism has been described in depth by Orlando Espín, Virgilio Elizondo, and others as a highly contextual reality; that is, deeply rooted in practices that are taught and repeated over and over again in the family at home, practices that are presided over more by mother and grandmother than by father or parish priest.[48]

In early Christianity, ministerial roles were fluid and not subject to a clearly defined priesthood, diaconate, or episcopacy, all of which arose over time. The particular configuration of ministries we have today is the result of many historical factors that can and do change over time. Jesus Christ did not provide the fledgling community with a clear organizational structure beyond the designation of apostles and the "the seventy-two" (Lk 10:1–24) and other disciples, none of whose functions were clearly delineated. The early record of ministerial outreach in the Acts of the Apostles and the Pauline letters demonstrates the active participation of lay women and men like Aquila and Priscilla, Andronicus and Junia, Tabitha, Lydia, Phoebe, Philemon, and many others.

---

47 Francis, *Evangelii Gaudium*, 102. Author's emphasis.

48 Orlando O. Espín, "Popular Catholicism among Latinos," in *Hispanic Catholic Culture in the U.S.: Issues and Concerns*, ed. Jay P. Dolan and Allan Figueroa Deck, SJ (Notre Dame, Ind.: University of Notre Dame Press, 1994), 308–59.

Carlos G. Alvarez outlines the evolving and fluid context of ministry in the earliest period of Christianity as recorded in the letters of St. Paul and the Acts of the Apostles. He provides a biblical and theological interpretation of the participation of the baptized in ecclesial service and leadership:

> It is clear that for the third Gospel (Luke's) the Lord's disciples in the successive periods of the ecclesial community have the same mission and same authority that Jesus gave to the Twelve to communicate the Gospel in all places and make the Reign of God present...This discipleship is a right and a duty that later the Church assumes in the context of the sacrament of Baptism: thanks to that, each and every believer participates in and continues the same mission of Jesus in the world. As the people of God, all believers constitute the Church *in fundamental equality*, and are chosen, holy, disciples and brothers and sisters; they all are a royal priesthood.[49]

Spanish pastoral theologian Juan Pablo García Maestro focuses on the underlying causes of the movement away from that sense of fundamental equality, participation, and agency enjoyed by all the baptized in the early Christian communities and later clericalism and clericalization. Following the lead of Edward Schillebeeckx, he notes that for the first one thousand years of Christianity, the ecclesial dimension is indeed the determining element for ordination or the ministerial institution. In the second millennium, however, "the connection to community gets lost and attention is centered on the Christological connection acting directly on the candidate without the mediation of community."[50]

García Maestro suggests that Pope Benedict XVI, in closing the year 2009 dedicated to priestly ministry, made the point that two of the important outcomes of the year of prayer and reflection on the ordained

---

49 Carlos G. Alvarez, "Ministerios confiados a los laicos en América Latina y el Caribe: Aporte bíblico y teológico," in *Boletín CELAM* 326 (December 2009): 41–79.

50 J. P. García Maestro, *Eclesiología de la Praxis Pastoral* (Madrid: PPC, 2012), 161. See Edward Schillebeeckx, *Ministry: Leadership in the Community of Jesus* (New York: Crossroad, 1981), 48–58, and *The Church with a Human Face* (New York: Crossroad, 1985), 141–51. See also David N. Power, "The Evolution of the Priesthood," *Church* (Fall 1988), 16–21.

priesthood are a renewed sense of ministry as service to the ecclesial community and the enabling of lay ministries to function more widely and better.[51] What was at stake was the retrieval of the conviction that all the baptized are, simply, Christians. García Maestro refers us to *Lumen Gentium* (nos. 10 and 11) and to the distinction between the *substantive* realities that underlie all differences and *relative* ones that define particular differences. The common priesthood, as Cardinal Rodríguez reminded us in his Dallas talk, pertains to the *substantive* reality and the ordained priesthood to the *relative* one. Perhaps St. Augustine was getting at this, at the foundational greatness of simply being a baptized Christian, when he wrote, "Where I'm terrified by what I am for you, I am given comfort by what I am with you. For you I am a bishop, with you, after all, I am a Christian. The first is the name of an office undertaken, the second a name of grace; that one means danger, this one salvation."[52]

In his analysis of the development of ministry in early Christianity, Carl A. Volz notes that there were forces already at work undermining the sense that all Christians are radically equal and the significance of the common priesthood. One was the increasingly important analogy made between the Old Testament ritual and hierarchical Levitical priesthood and the Christian priesthood, and the other was the growing concept in the West that the priest's charism is a personal possession independent of the community.[53] Both of these developments undoubtedly fed into the distancing of clerics from the rest of the people of God and offered possibilities and incentives for abuse of power and exploitation of underlings.

Clericalism and Women

The identification of the clerical role with men alone is, of course, a major factor contributing to a harmful clerical mind-set that excludes half the human race from consideration for ordained ministry and leadership in the church. Francis has raised the issue of how women

51 J. P. García Maestro, *Eclesiología de la Praxis Pastoral*, 165.

52 St. Augustine of Hippo, *Sermons 20–50*, trans Edmund Hill, ed. John E. Rotelle, The Works of Saint Augustine: A Translation for the 21st Century, Part 3, vol. 2 (Brooklyn: New City Press, 1990), 292–94.

53 Carl A. Volz, *Pastoral Life and Practice in the Early Church* (Minneapolis: Augsburg Press, 1990): 45–47.

are treated in the church repeatedly and he has set in motion important changes; for example, he has appointed women to several pontifical commissions and to leadership roles in pontifical institutes, pastoral and financial councils, Catholic organizations, schools, and the theological academy. He has insisted on the more prominent presence of women in the leadership of the church.[54] In February 2016 he announced the creation of a commission to study the diaconate of women, and in July 2016 the make-up of that commission was announced: six men and six women.[55] Thus he has opened the possibility of reestablishing women deacons and resolving the outstanding issue about the appropriateness of admitting women to orders (at least to the Order of Deacon), a development that would open the doors to women in a number of areas of church governance. At a February 2015 gathering in Rome, Francis said that "I am convinced of the urgency of offering spaces for women in the Church and to welcome them…A more capillary and incisive presence in the community is desirable, so that we can see many women involved in pastoral responsibilities, in the accompaniment of persons, families and groups, as well as in theological reflection."[56] He then added these intriguing but controversial words: "Women know to incarnate the tender face of God, his mercy, which translates into *availability to give time more than to occupy spaces, to welcome instead of excluding.*[57]

Moral theologian Lisa Fullam has developed a serious criticism of what she sees as Francis's inconsistent reasoning. She points out that Francis fails to prioritize women and their concerns, voices, and needs. While championing the equal dignity of women, he has often pursued

54 "More must be done to include women in roles of advising and governance, but without reducing them to having just a functional role." See Carol Glatz, "More Must Be Done to Include Women in Church Bodies, Pope Says," *Crux*, November 19, 2019, quoting Pope Francis's November 16, 2019 speech to the first plenary assembly of the Dicastery for Laity, the Family and Life.

55 Vatican Radio website, "Pope Institutes Commission to Study the Diaconate of Women," August 2, 2016, http://www.archivioradiovaticana.va/storico/2016/08/02/pope_institutes_commission_to_study_the_diaconate_of_women/en-1248731.

56 Joshua J. McElwee, "Pope Calls Again for 'Incisive' Women's Presence in Church, Offers No Specifics," *National Catholic Reporter* online, February 7, 2015, https://www.ncronline.org/news/vatican/pope-calls-again-incisive-womens-presence-church-offers-no-specifics.

57 McElwee, "Pope Calls Again for 'Incisive' Women's Presence." Author's emphasis.

the status quo and unwittingly used stereotypical language that reinforces the exclusion of women from leadership. The pope also fails to adequately make the connection between poverty and the uneven distribution of the world's wealth, his number one priority, and the status of women, who happen to constitute the majority of the world's poor.[58] While some processes have been set in motion and decisions made that will result in the broader participation of women in the life of the church and even in its decision-making, there are features of the Holy Father's approach that some find questionable, if not contradictory. In the statement quoted above, for example, Francis suggests that because women are given to being more welcoming, they will also be inclined to give of their time while not being concerned about "occupying a space."[59] Is it possible that this will be interpreted as just another way to rationalize the exclusion of women from leadership?

While the question of women's roles in the church touches on how clericalism works in tandem with the historical diminishment of women's participation in church life, it goes well beyond that to broader issues of patriarchy and evolving understandings of how gender really works. The problem is imbedded in deep-seated cultural attitudes that vary from country to country and region to region. These are serious matters of epochal change that go beyond the limits of this article. The question of women's equality and their rights and roles in the church is, nevertheless, a key factor in addressing the harm done to the church's identity and mission by clericalism. This question presents a real challenge to Pope Francis's call for reform and his concern about clericalism. This challenge will for various reasons surely take many more years to resolve. One might argue, however, that at least the process has begun.

Clericalism: The Other Side of the Coin

It would be a mistake not to mention the other side of the coin. Surely concern about maintaining certain distinctions, not clericalism *per*

58 Lisa Fullam, "Francis, Women, and the Church for the Poor," in *Pope Francis and the Future of Catholicism in the United States*, ed. Erin Brigham, David E. DeCosse, and Michael Duffy (San Francisco: University of San Francisco Press, 2016), 73–84.

59 Jamie Manson, "It's Time to Be Honest about Pope Francis and Women," *National Catholic Reporter*, May 19, 2016, ncronline.org/blogs/grace-margins'its-time-to-be-honest-about-pope-francis-and-women.

se as an ideology, can be associated with the legitimate and necessary function of organizational leadership connected to the practice of establishing norms and criteria for positions of service and leadership in the church. After all, as the *Ratio Fundamentalis* reminds us, "the priest is placed not only in the Church but also in the forefront of the Church."[60] It must be understood that the evolution of the concept of priesthood and its clericalization were often motivated by good intentions and important factors that justified some of these developments. Foremost was the need to eliminate unworthy and/or false leadership in the Christian communities and to guard against heterodoxy.

While it is true that in the Middle Ages the addition of mandated celibacy for the ordained priesthood in the West contributed mightily to the setting apart of priests and to the false idea that they are somehow superior to other Christians, it is also true that it was called for as a discipline safeguarding church leadership from the corruption of lay investiture and that it was conducive to upgrading the quality of the ministerial priesthood. Important elements of clericalization came about as a direct result of the Gregorian Reform, for instance, which sought to confront and resolve the organizational challenges to the church posed by a corrupt clergy *and* laity.[61] The Council of Trent also introduced many practices that contributed to clericalization, but arguably these were necessary to respond to legitimate criticisms coming from the Protestant reformers. The requirement of seminary training for all men seeking ordination, for example, was intended to raise the intellectual and spiritual quality of the ordained.[62] But unfortunately it created a wider chasm between the clergy and the ordinary faithful.

Conclusion

Today the church, however, faces a new and totally different moment of reform involving developments in the evolution of priesthood and ministry in the church. Pope Francis's call for an end to clericalism is an invitation to reconfigure the various ways in which leadership

---

60 Congregation for the Clergy, "The Gift of the Priestly Vocation," 32.

61 J. Gaudemet, "Gregorian Reform," in *New Catholic Encyclopedia*, vol. 6 (New York: Thomson Gale: 2003), 468–73.

62 John W. O'Malley, *Trent: What Happened at the Council?* (New York: Belknap Press at Harvard University Press, 2013), 204–40.

is practiced in the church. The underlying values of synodality, collegiality, subsidiarity, and Samaritanism certainly provide inspiration and direction useful for pursuing the radical reforms proposed by the Second Vatican Council and urgently promoted by Francis. These values point to a renewed stress on the horizontal rather than the vertical; the charismatic, ministerial, and missionary rather than the hierarchical; and the inclusive rather than the exclusive. In some sense, hierarchical structures are being challenged to subordinate themselves to the wider church as community and faithful people of God in history. The church in Latin America with its insistence on the radical equality of all the baptized as *discípulos misioneros,* and in its robust ecclesiology of pastoral praxis, is beckoning the universal church toward the path ahead.

Rich neologisms promoted by Francis give shape and an inviting, upbeat tone to the reform movement emerging under his charismatic leadership: *pastoralidad* (pastorality), *misioneidad* (orientation toward mission), and *samaritanidad* (Samaritanism). At the heart of this reform is the elimination of clericalism, with its tendencies to usurp the proper roles of service that all baptized persons are called to exercise both within the church and most especially outside it in the world of family, work, the professions, politics, economics, and culture. Certainly the parish and diocese as key institutions will look much different in ministerial environments characterized by collaboration, mutuality, a persistent recognition of the radical equality of all the baptized, and a strong orientation to mission.

In such a reformed context, a new focus on pastoral care or praxis rather than abstract doctrinal formulations is the order of the day. Pope Francis's hermeneutic of Vatican II gives first place to the culture of encounter: to missionary outreach rather than proselytism and apologetics, to engaging the world as it is, to relationality and dialogue, and in the truest spirit of *Ad Gentes* and, by the way, of the Ignatian exercises, to finding truth in the propositions of others. By *samaritanidad* (Samaritanism), Francis refers to the primacy of witness and action in pursuit of social justice above abstract teachings as the way par excellence to demonstrate fidelity to the Gospel. Priority is given to the vulnerable, the weak, and the excluded. Those previously considered unqualified; for example, the despised Samaritan outsider, are lifted up as also being capable of exemplifying the way of Christ.[63]

In an ecclesial world structured around these evangelical values, the phenomenon of clericalism will be simply out of place and even bizarre because it tends to produce distance from rather than nearness to God's people. It isolates and removes the minister from collaborating with others to further God's reign and is a direct impediment to the church's mission to evangelize. Clericalism clashes with Gospel values and limits the outreach of the church to ever-smaller circles; it imprisons the Holy Spirit, who blows where he will. Clericalism acts in synergy with a sick narcissism and a deadening territoriality and self-referentiality, all of which is contrary to the deepest and most authentic truths of the Christian faith.

63 Vatican Radio website, "Pope Francis: Love Thy Neighbour like the Good Samaritan," April 27, 2016, http://www.archivioradiovaticana.va/storico/2016/04/27/pope_francis_love_thy_neighbour_like_the_good_samaritan/en-1225767

CHAPTER 12

FRANCIS AND THE WITNESSES OF AMERICA

Maria Clara Lucchetti Bingemer

SINCE THE BEGINNING OF his pontificate, Pope Francis has adopted a very peculiar style for governing the church. He prefers gestures to words, actions to speeches, testimonies rather than a lot of talking. When he speaks, he usually refers to saints, whether they are canonized or not. He uses figures of great virtue and courage as examples, witnesses to both yesterday and today, and he maintains that reflecting on our lives helps us understand that living virtuously and courageously is the true way for a Christian to follow Jesus. These witnesses inspire the people of God, helping them always to be a more "holy people" or a "people who are holy," expressions that are dear to the pope.[1]

In this essay, we will reflect on the central importance of testimony to the Christian faith. We will examine it in the spirituality of the Jesuit Jorge Mario Bergoglio—a spirituality that has its roots in the *Spiritual Exercises* of Saint Ignatius of Loyola (born Iñigo López de Loyola, only later known as "Ignatius"), in which the testimony of the saints is of vital importance.[2] We will see how emulating the life of Christ and of the saints shaped the whole life of Ignatius as a pilgrim and apostle

1 For Pope Francis, the poor constitute the holy people of God. Cf. Francis, *The Poor Man Cried, and the Lord Heard Him: Message of His Holiness Pope Francis, Second World Day of The Poor* (November 18, 2018). Available from Zenit, https://zenit.org/articles/popes-message-for-2nd-world-day-of-the-poor.

2 As the *Exercises* put it, "During the Second Week and thereafter, it will be very profitable to read some passages from the *Following of Christ,* or from the Gospels, and from the *Lives of the Saints.*" Ignatius of Loyola, *The Spiritual Exercises,* trans. Louis J. Puhl, SJ (Westminster, Md.: The Newman Press, 1951), 100 n2.

of the will of God. To do so, we will examine sections of the *Spiritual Exercises* as well as other writings by Ignatius.

We will then turn to the pope's visit to America (Cuba and the US). In our review of the pontiff's stay in Cuba, we will pay special attention to his assessment of the country and most importantly its people as an example, a testimony, for the world, despite all the shortcomings present on the island. Then we will examine Francis's speech to the US Congress. There we will see how Francis applies the Ignatian directive to "read the lives of the saints" in order to inspire conduct and life as part of his dialogue with the politicians of the greatest nation of the Americas.[3] In the case of the US congressmen, this involved motivating and moving their consciences to change important policies in the country.

We conclude by seeing how the pope's desire that there should be an ever more unified America, a unity that would promote the globalization of solidarity, can become a reality—a desire expressed by another pope, John Paul II, in his encyclical *Ecclesia in America*.[4]

The Imitation of Christ and of the Saints in *The Spiritual Exercises*

The first person that Ignatius wants to imitate is undoubtedly Jesus. In the *Exercises* there are countless mentions of the imitation of Christ in everything.[5] But in addition to Jesus Christ, the model of excellence, the eternal King and universal Lord, Ignatius also sees in the *Exercises* the fruit that he can bring to the spiritual and apostolic life of the practitioner by imitating others who in turn imitated Jesus.[6] The first of these "others" to be imitated is of course Mary, Our Lady, the mother of Jesus, who is present in all the important invocations and conversations in the *Exercises*. In Exercise 248, in explaining the manner of prayer in the application of the senses, Ignatius says that the practitioner entrusts himself to the Virgin in order to imitate her.[7]

---

3 Ignatius of Loyola, 100 n2.

4 The desire for American unity originated in 1997 at the Special Assembly for America of the Synod of Bishops, which at that time started working on the postsynodal exhortation *Ecclesia in America*, promulgated in 1999.

5 Ignatius of Loyola, *The Spiritual Exercises*, 98, 109, 139, 147, 167, 168, 214, and 248.

6 Cf. Ignatius of Loyola, 91–98.

7 "If anyone wishes to imitate Christ our Lord in the use of the senses, he should recommend himself to His Divine Majesty in the preparatory prayer, and after the consideration of each sense say a Hail Mary or an Our Father. / If he wishes to imitate our Lady

The saints are invoked many times in the *Exercises* as intercessors and personal "mediators," sometimes called the "heavenly court."[8] This is how they help in the "imitation of Christ" and in continuing to open the Christian to the action of the Spirit, which has no other purpose except to sanctify and Christianize him.[9]

Ignatius would experience in his life the desire for holiness that is proper to saints. That desire moves saints in search of establishing a relationship of spiritual closeness and intimacy with Christian figures that the church proposes as models for following Christ. Ignatius is not an exception to this phenomenon, and in him these relationships acquired a singular importance inasmuch as they constituted the first impulse of his conversion and a continuous reference point throughout his life.[10]

During a period in which Loyola was convalescing, his devoted sister-in-law gave him, instead of the novels featuring knights that he wished to read, readings about the life of Christ and the saints.[11] That is how from the beginning of his conversion, Ignatius accepted and followed an ideal ruled by him whom the Gospels call, including in the mouth of demons, "the Saint of God"[12]—Jesus Christ—but also by those men and women who have followed him most lovingly and closely. Faithful to what Paul said in his Second Letter to the Corinthians (3:3), the lives of the saints "are for Ignatius a second gospel, or said in another way, the historical plausibility of living a radical gospel, without a gloss of accommodation."[13] The source of this strenuous path,

---

in the use of his senses, he should recommend himself to her in the preparatory prayer that she obtain for him this grace from her Son and Lord, and after the consideration of each sense say a Hail Mary." Ignatius of Loyola, 248.

8 Ignatius of Loyola, 98, 232

9 Today in theology one speaks more of "following" instead of "imitation," since imitation is more literal, while following is more creative and less informed by education. Cf. Maria Clara Bingemer, *Em tudo amar e servir: Mística trinitária e práxis cristã* (São Paulo: Edições Loyola, 1990), among many other works. With respect to following, see José Maria Castillo, *El seguimiento de Jesucristo* (Salamanca: Sígueme, 1998).

10 Cf. Guillermo Arana, "Santidad," in *Diccionario de espiritualidades ignaciana* [Dictionary of Ignatian spirituality], ed. José Garcia de Castro (Santander: Sal Terrae, 2006).

11 Ignatius of Loyola, *The Autobiography of St. Ignatius,* ed. J. F. X. O'Connor, SJ (New York: Benziger Brothers, 1900), para. 5.

12 Mt 8:29, Lk 4:34, and parallels.

13 "You are a letter of Christ written by us, not written with ink, but with the living Spirit of God; not in rock tablets, but the tablets of human hearts." Arana, "Santidad."

lived in the madness of love and faith, is the Gospel centered on the person of Christ and manifested in his historical existence. With this Gospel, Ignatius passed from being an emulator of the honor of the noble knight to an imitator of the faithful of the Lord Jesus Christ.[14]

It is worth recalling that Ignatius's imitation of Christ was at the beginning largely ignored and contained vestiges of willfulness, in which spiritual desire was clearly mixed with a certain vanity that made him say, for example, "Saint Dominic did this; therefore I have to do it also."[15] Nevertheless, this goal of modeling holiness widened him internally and deepened his capacity for desire, awakening him to a horizon of total giving and love as he carried out his destiny of serving God.

Having passed through and overcome the temptation to vanity, he was given the grace to always have a great devotion and love of the saints. He never forgot the good that this devotion had done for him, and consistently presented himself to men and women as an example of someone whose only ideal of life was to do everything in and for the will of God. He strongly advised reading about the lives of witnesses and saints, especially Thomas à Kempis's *Imitation of Christ* and the Gospels. With respect to the contemplations of the second, third, and fourth weeks of the *Exercises*, he recommended "the historical plausibility of those persons" and "appropriat[ing] them in the contemplative path from the second week."[16]

The *Exercises* were not the only way Ignatius brought the saints into his spiritual life. The Constitutions of the Company of Jesus also have recourse to the example of the saints in a number of their disciplinary objectives for Jesuits in formation.[17] Similarly, the authority of the first theologians that the church considered saints and the authority of the church fathers—often referred to as the "holy fathers"—are frequently referred to in the Constitutions and in the vast Ignatian epistolary.[18]

14 Cf. Arana, "Santidad."

15 Ignatius of Loyola, *The Autobiography of St. Ignatius*, paras. 7–10.

16 Ignatius of Loyola, *The Spiritual Exercises*, 100, 215; Arana, "Santidad."

17 Ignatius of Loyola, *Constitutions of the Society of Jesus and Their Complementary Norms*, ed. John W. Padberg, SJ (St. Louis: The Institute of Jesuit Sources, 1996), para. 134.

18 Ignatius of Loyola, *Constitutions of the Society of Jesus*, para. 368; Letters of Ignatius of Loyola, I, 275; II, 57, 59–60, 482; IV, 679; VIII, 13, 472, 475; X, 717; XII, 63, 490.

According to Guillermo Arana in the *Diccionario de espiritualidades ignaciana*, following saints "is an instrument of great utility because it nourishes the cauldron of fervor, in other words, the affective and effective dynamic of adherence to Christ, in such a way that it can be recognizable in the proper conduct of what is taught in the beatitudes, as occurs in the life of the saints."[19]

Like Saint Paul, Ignatius does not hesitate to designate Christians of the past as "saints," especially those persons who made serious and radical choices for living the Gospel,[20] but he greatly resists identifying living persons as saints. How can one, for example, regard the rules for thinking and feeling with the church (in the original Spanish, *sentir con la iglesia*) without looking at the dynamics and challenges of a life of holiness? Ignatius still recognizes the distinction in English between sanctity and holiness, suggesting that "we should be cautious of making comparisons of those of us who are living to the past beatitudes . . .: this one knows more than Saint Augustine, he is another or more than Saint Francis, he is another Saint Paul in goodness, holiness, etc."[21]

However, despite this instance of Ignatius's rarely praised prudence, he believes a great deal in the power of good example to help one grow in the Christian life and therefore in holiness. As he says, for example, in the important "Letter of Perfection" to the scholars of Coimbra, "Every day, passing forward in total perfection, [one needs] to grow, *without searching for it*, the holy [scent] and edification of the one whom follows."[22] As an example of this wise counsel, Ignatius guides his Jesuits toward treating everyone with a frugality that is stripped of titles, a mode of conduct that puts into practice the equal treatment of all by the Lord.[23] Ignatius sought to avoid immature enthusiasms with regard to persons as well as the risk of pulling attention away from the substantive aspects of holiness and directing it toward the social

19 Arana, "Santidad."

20 On Paul, see for example Rom 1:7; 8:27, 12:13; 15:25–26, 31; 16:2, 15; Eph 1:14, 15, 18; 2:19; 3:5, 8, 18; 4:12; 5:3; and 6:18, among many others, including references to saints in the First Letter to the Corinthians and the Letter to the Philippians. The Spanish word *santidad* means both "sanctity" and "holiness," and both meanings can be seen in the Epistolary. Letters of Ignatius of Loyola, VIII, 684 and XII, 559. Cf. Arana, "Santidad." *Santidad* does not imply canonization.

21 Ignatius of Loyola, *The Spiritual Exercises*, 364.

22 Letters of Ignatius of Loyola, I, 509.

23 Cf. Mt 23:8–10.

"fame" that it can give. That is to say, social esteem is valued for what it edifies whenever it is based on true holiness. It is not to be sought directly, because it would feed a disordered demand of the ego that is incompatible with the aim of holiness.[24]

Ignatius desired for himself and his followers a real and concrete holiness based on the perfection of the virtues that appear in many of the passages of the Constitutions.[25] With his finely tuned and strong spirit of discernment, the saint of Loyola knew that even though the examples of heroes, saints, and the wise can inspire human beings to give the best of themselves in following Jesus Christ and in building the kingdom of God, the ambiguity of everything human, even of the most holy and virtuous examples, requires prudence in judgment and a steadfast faith in God alone.

This was the spirituality that nourished Jorge Bergoglio, now Pope Francis. He applies it constantly in his ordinary magisterium as the bishop of Rome, as well as in his extraordinary magisterium as the universal shepherd of the Roman, Catholic, and Apostolic church. We can see the fruits of this spiritual methodology in his formation and apostolic mission: it was clearly applied in his visit to Cuba and the US.

Cuba, the Testimony of Justice, and the Challenge of Reconciliation

Francis was awaited in Cuba as the person who had built bridges that would open dialogue between the US and Cuba. President Obama, when announcing alongside President Raúl Castro the opening of dialogue between the two countries, clearly stated that if it were not for His Holiness Pope Francis, what they were experiencing that day would not have been possible.[26]

When the old adversaries Cuba and the US announced the beginning of an easing of tensions, bells rang in Catholic churches over the whole island. The church was celebrating the success of eighteen months

24 Cf. Arana, "Santidad."

25 See for example the paragraphs mentioning "solid and perfect virtues," "solid and true virtues," and "true virtues." Ignatius of Loyola, *Constitutions of the Society of Jesus*, paras. 117, 260, 813.

26 White House Office of the Press Secretary, "Statement by the President on the Re-Establishment of Diplomatic Relations with Cuba," July 1, 2015.

of secret negotiations, during which the Vatican had been one of the most important mediators that strengthened the will of both sides to pursue reconciliation.

The Castros' Cuba needed this to bring oxygen to their model of government—it was bureaucratized and in danger now that Venezuela, its last and only sponsor, was collapsing in slow motion and threatening to disappear from this role. The US needed it in order to rid itself of an uncomfortable isolationist policy dating from the middle of the last century that put Washington on its heels in a region of global importance. This policy, with its cruel economic embargo that it imposed on Cuba so long ago, had stamped the powerful country as antidemocratic in the eyes of the world. The world paid close attention to Francis's trip to the Caribbean island.

It is symbolic that the pontiff's visit to America had begun in Cuba: his visit to the powerful empire of the US came after the visit to the small island, which has been hit by so many hardships in recent times. In visiting Cuba first, Francis reaffirmed what had been an important precept of his pontificate: those who go through greater difficulties, the poor, and those who suffer, will be first.

The content of what he said and, overall, what he did on this trip to Cuba was abundant and rich: the cordial greeting to Raúl Castro, the fraternal and intimate visit to the old leader Fidel and their exchange of books, and the visit "as son and pilgrim" to the sanctuary of the Virgin of Charity of El Cobre, "Chachita," as she is lovingly called by the Cuban people.

In sum, it was a visit full of meaningful gestures. The pope sealed the rapprochement between Cuba and the US with his presence. The path left to walk was still great and there would be continuing resistance from both sides. Because of these challenges, on arriving Francis spoke the word that would guide his entire visit: "reconciliation." At the José Martí International Airport, in his first speech on Cuban soil, the pope affirmed the theme of exemplary models, stating that "the process of normalizing relations between two peoples following years of estrangement" is a concrete example for the world.[27] And he reiter-

27 *Address of Pope Francis at José Martí International Airport*, Havana, September 19, 2015. All documents published by the Vatican, including this one and many others cited below, may be found at the vatican.va website.

ated the importance of this example, stating that the new relationship between the US and Cuba was "an example of reconciliation for the entire world. The world needs reconciliation in this climate of a piecemeal third world war in which we are living."[28] Furthermore, he stated that the new approach being taken by the two countries, which had had broken relations for decades, was a victory of dialogue.[29]

On the second day of his visit, the keynote of the pope's words was on the topic of service. He emphasized how important it is that this service not be ideological, since one does not help ideas, but people. He then highlighted the form that this service should take: taking care of people's weaknesses; that is, addressing those who are most vulnerable, who are unprotected and exposed to the harshness of life. According to the pontiff—always faithful to the primacy of the poor—the greatness of a country is measured by the way it treats those who are most easily broken.[30]

Although he did not mention it explicitly, one can detect the pope's approval of a number of positive achievements of the Cuban regime, in particular regarding care for children and the elderly; in other words, the most vulnerable. With the opening of the country to relations with its northern neighbor, among the pope's concerns was the latent danger of a crazed consumerism that dominates the affluent societies, invading and seducing the population. This has happened in Eastern Europe by means of a well-known process.[31] For decades Cuba has built a model that, with all its defects, looks for justice through its people living an austere and sober life, a life of great dignity but not without sacrifices.[32] The Cubans are an example of austerity and sobriety for the world, and Francis did not miss the opportunity to value this fact, a fact that is generally not understood and is often overlooked in discussions about Cuba.

A reconciliation that would mean the end of the US's embargo imposed on the island and the return of Guantanamo, which remains a

28 *Address of Pope Francis at José Martí International Airport.*

29 *Address of Pope Francis at José Martí International Airport.*

30 *Address of His Holiness Pope Francis to Students at the Fr. Félix Varela Cultural Center in Havana, Cuba*, September 20, 2015.

31 See Carl Bernstein and Marco Politti, *His Holiness* (New York: Penguin, 1997), especially the chapter titled "The Angry Pope."

32 This theologian witnessed this in the ten years in which she did pastoral work in Cuba, traveling to Cuba twice a year to present Ignatius's *Spiritual Exercises* to the laity.

military base, could restore to the Cubans a peace for which they have hoped for a long time. Despite the strength with which Cubans raise their heads, refusing to lower them to their adversaries, and the joy with which they insist on living, it is well known that life has not been easy for the people of the island. For this reason, Francis paternally said that "despite the wounds it has like any other people [the Cuban people] knows how to open its arms, walk with hope, because it is called to greatness."[33] In the words of the pope, we can see the value of the vocation of the brave Cuban people to being witnesses to a life that is not measured by having, but by being.

A reconciliation that would open the doors to communication and free trade between Cuba and the US surely implies concessions from both sides. If the North Americans were asked for concrete measures that would have an impact on the opening of commercial relations and on the US's effective recognition of the island's sovereignty, the Cuban government would be asked to grant greater liberty to its people and to democratize the regime by means of elections and other democratic institutions.

The pope knows that democratization will not be easy or quick to arrive in Cuba. It involves a slow and delicate process that can only come to fruition with much care. That is surely one of the reasons why on the last day of his visit, he went to lay his intentions at the feet of the Virgin Mambisa, mother of all Cubans. In Santiago, Cuba, home of the sanctuary of el Cobre, Francis had praised Mary as the personification of a "revolution of tenderness" and urged Cubans to follow her example, so as "to build bridges, to break down walls, to sow seeds of reconciliation," clearly alluding to the important and delicate process of reconciliation that the church helped to initiate.[34]

Addressing himself filially to Our Lady, he has called her the "Mother of Reconciliation."[35] He asked her to unite all the dispersed peoples of the world and to make the Cuban nation a home for all of its brothers

33 *Homily of His Holiness Pope Francis*, Plaza de la Revolución, Havana, Cuba, September 20, 2015.

34 *Holy Mass: Homily of His Holiness Pope Francis at the Minor Basilica of the Shrine Virgen de la Caridad del Cobre in Santiago, Cuba*, September 22, 2015.

35 CNA Newsletter, "Mary is the 'Mother of Forgiveness,'" *Catholic News Agency*, January 1, 2016, https://www.catholicnewsagency.com/news/pope-francis-mary-is-the-mother-of-forgiveness-25646.

and sisters. He issued a challenge: in a country capable of a revolution that brought many successes for justice for an oppressed and crushed people, he said that they must have the courage to create a "revolution of reconciliation," both internally and externally. This work is demanding and difficult, but surely liberating.

The Argentine pope was able to move the Cuban ecclesiastical hierarchy toward an unprecedented rapprochement with the Castro regime, easing relations that had for a long time been strained, making a desired and needed dialogue difficult. It is no wonder that the most important invitation he made to the Cuban people during his visit was to engage in dialogue, an encounter with the human being. In keeping with the spirit of this invitation, he avoided controversies—although risking the disappointment of some—and taught a Cuba facing difficulties the option of opening itself to the world. With these tasks in mind, he gracefully went in search of what Fidel Castro spoke of regarding the inevitability of changes in the country. He did this while valuing the testimony and example that Cuba already is for the world, with its undeniable success in pursuing justice and equality.

An opinion poll found that in Cuba only 27 percent of people consider themselves Catholic, but also that eight out of ten people have a positive image of Pope Francis. It also found that the Cuban people in general have trust in the Church as an institution, perhaps in large part because of their view of the pope.[36]

It is interesting to note how the dynamic of exemplary models and testimony function creatively in Francis's teaching. Even though it is not easy to recognize, this dynamic is strongly present. Francis did not point to many concrete examples of individual Cubans who inspire and serve as role models; rather, the examples and testimony that he employs is collective: the Cuban people who, despite all that they have suffered and continue to suffer, lift up their faces with dignity to seek justice in a profoundly unjust and exploitative world. It is also the pope himself and the institution he represents that are serving as an inspiration and example for Cubans. With the many years of lived

36 Nick Miroff, "As Ideology Fades in Cuba, Spirituality and Popes Intervene," *Washington Post* online, June 1, 2015, https://www.washingtonpost.com/world/the_americas/as-ideology-fades-in-cuba-spirituality-and-popes-intervene/2015/06/01/c337174a-04b8-11e5-93f4-f24d4af7f97d_story.html.

difficulties the inhabitants of the island have experienced, to be able to trust in the person of the pope and the church is surely comforting, invigorating movements of reconciliation and openness with a view toward a new era for Cubans and for the whole world.

The US: Four Children of the Earth

Francis's speech delivered to the US Congress displayed another interesting communicative strategy. Francis touched with his words all the open wounds in the economic, social, and political fabric of the most powerful country in the world. At the core of what he said was the well-known Golden Rule, which is present throughout the Bible, beginning with the Law of Holiness described in Leviticus: "Speak to all the congregation of the sons of Israel and say to them: You shall be holy, because I, Yahweh your God, am Holy" (Lv. 19:2). That holiness consists in loving God with your whole heart and strength, and your neighbor as you would love yourself. The Golden Rule is also present in the New Testament at Mt 7:12: "Do to others whatever you would have them do to you." What seemed like a saying at the level of personal conversion carried with it clear and important political repercussions.

Just as in Cuba, the keynote of Francis's visit to the great power of the north was reconciliation. Although all of his speeches in the US were of great importance, we must emphasize the speech to the US Congress, during which he received much applause and several standing ovations. The first pontiff to speak to the US Congress, Francis gave, in the view of all of the commentators, an historic speech. He touched on all of the critical points of the internal and external politics of the country without touching on anything that could be considered polemical or risky. He spoke as an immigrant whose family came from Italy to the south of the American continent, and he reminded the members of Congress that all or almost all of them were also immigrants. That is why he asked for the end of a "mindset of hostility" against migrants and for a step forward toward "reciprocal subsidiarity." With respect to the migrants, he advised: "We must not be taken aback by their numbers, but rather view them as persons, seeing their faces and listening to their stories."[37]

In addition, he stressed the theme of climate change and environmental stewardship, a theme he clearly and cogently addressed in the encyclical *Laudato Si'*. Regarding this issue, which divides Republicans and Democrats in the US, Francis affirmed that Congress has an important role to play in the struggle against harm to the environment. Francis asked for "brave actions" on the issue, stating that he is convinced that such actions can make a difference.[38]

As the speech progressed, the pope went further and more deeply into burning polemical issues. The moment had arrived to touch the wound of the death penalty, still widely applied in the US. The pope spoke clearly against the death penalty, asking for its global abolition, saying that he was convinced that this would be the right decision because every life is sacred. On this point, he placed himself more radically in favor of life than the text of the new *Catechism of the Catholic Church*, which allows the use of the death penalty if it is the only way to effectively defend human life against an unjust aggressor.[39]

---

37 Francis, *Visit to the Joint Session of the United States Congress: Address of the Holy Father*, September 24, 2015.

38 Francis, *Visit to the Joint Session of the United States Congress.*

39 The position of the Catholic Church is found in nos. 2266 and 2267 of the second edition of the *Catechism of the Catholic Church* (1997). No. 2266 states that

> the efforts of the state to curb the spread of behavior harmful to people's rights and to the basic rules of civil society correspond to the requirement of safeguarding the common good. Legitimate public authority has the right and duty to inflict punishment proportionate to the gravity of the offense. Punishment has the primary aim of redressing the disorder introduced by the offense. When it is willingly accepted by the guilty party, it assumes the value of expiation. Punishment then, in addition to defending public order and protecting people's safety, has a medicinal purpose: as far as possible, it must contribute to the correction of the guilty party.

And 2267 continues:

> Assuming that the guilty party's identity and responsibility have been fully determined, the traditional teaching of the Church does not exclude recourse to the death penalty, if this is the only possible way of effectively defending human lives against the unjust aggressor. If, however, non-lethal means are sufficient to defend and protect people's safety from the aggressor, authority will limit itself to such means, as these are more in keeping with the concrete conditions of the common good and more in conformity to the dignity of the human person. Today, in fact, as a consequence of the possibilities which the state has for effectively preventing crime, by rendering one who has committed an offense incapable of doing harm—without definitely taking away from him the possibility of redeeming

The pope's position directly and flatly rejecting everything that produces violence and assaults human life was further reinforced with his brave, vehement denunciation of the arms trade. In front of the elected representatives of the US, which occupies first place in the global ranking of arms commerce, the pope asked, "Why are deadly weapons being sold to those who plan to inflict untold suffering on individuals and society?"[40] He then suggested an answer: "Sadly, the answer, as we all know, is simply for money: money that is drenched in blood, often innocent blood."[41]

The whole world followed Francis's calm and courageous speech. The profound strength of his words came not just from him—he invoked four people to accompany him, four heroes in their humanity, four great citizens of the US who represent values that oppose the countervalues that today threaten the life and harmonious coexistence of the great nation of the north. He identified them as "three sons and a daughter of this land."[42]

The first figure was President Abraham Lincoln, who defended liberty and worked tirelessly so that the nation could know a new dawn of freedom. During his presidency, he abolished slavery and brought an end to the Civil War, the great conflict that divided the nation.[43] Lincoln was not religious and was never a member of a church. He knew the Bible well and believed in God, and referred to his faith in a number of his speeches, but he never made a clear demonstration of Christian faith, remaining silent about it out of a respect for religious diversity. Lincoln was assassinated in 1865.

The second figure was Martin Luther King, the Protestant pastor and political activist.[44] He became one of the most important leaders of the movement to secure the civil rights of people of African descent in the US and in the world, and his campaign was based on nonviolence. He

---

himself—the cases in which the execution of the offender is an absolute necessity "are very rare, if not practically nonexistent."

40 Francis, *Visit to the Joint Session of the United States Congress.*

41 Francis, *Visit to the Joint Session of the United States Congress.*

42 Francis, *Visit to the Joint Session of the United States Congress.*

43 Among the many biographies of Abraham Lincoln, see David Herbert Donald, *Lincoln* (London: Random House, 1996).

44 Clayborne Carson, *Eu tenho um sonho: A autobiografia de Martin Luther King* (Rio de Janeiro: Zahar, 2014); Martin Luther King, *Why We Can't Wait* (New York: Harper and Row, 1963).

led the March on Washington in 1963, where he delivered his famous "I Have a Dream" speech.[45] In 1964, he received the Nobel Peace Prize for his work. He was assassinated in 1968 in Memphis, Tennessee.

Referencing the "I Have a Dream" speech, in which the great activist spoke of his lifelong dream and ideal of attaining full civil and political rights for African Americans, Francis called the US a land of dreams and reminded the members of Congress about the dreams of immigrants, the men and women who came en masse to the country in search of the "American Dream" and to transform their lives.[46]

The third figure Francis mentioned is a Catholic woman for whom a cause for canonization has been opened in the Vatican and who is already a Servant of God: Dorothy Day. Day was a North American activist who spent her life serving the poor. Francis described her as an example of a Gospel-inspired passion for justice and for the cause of the oppressed. She protested against all forms of violence, including the wars in which her country was involved, and was imprisoned several times as a result of these protests. She died of old age, living with the poor, eating and dressing like the poor.[47]

Finally, the fourth witness was a contemplative: the Trappist monk Thomas Merton, whose centenary of birth was celebrated in 2015, the same year of Francis's visit. Merton converted to Catholicism as an adult and entered the Trappist order. He was a man of deep prayer, as well as a brilliant thinker and great writer. He challenged the certainties of his time from his cell in the monastery, communicating with the whole world through his writings and opening new horizons for the church. Merton's writings touched on problems that only now constitute priorities for the church, like ecology and interreligious dialogue.

45 See this speech online at https://www.americanrhetoric.com/speeches/mlkihaveadream.htm.

46 The expression "American Dream," coined by James Truslow Adams in 1931, is a national ethos in the US. It includes a variety of ideals, not only liberty, but also the opportunity for success, prosperity, and social mobility for families and children, to be achieved by hard work in a society without barriers. It implies that life should be better and richer for all, with everyone having opportunities to succeed based upon their abilities and achievements, independent of their social class or circumstances of birth.

47 See her autobiography, Dorothy Day, *The Long Loneliness* (New York: HarperOne 2009).

He had a profound relationship with Eastern monasticism.[48] Merton died in an accident in Bangkok in 1968; he was fifty-three years old. The pope recalled him as a man of dialogue and a promoter of peace between peoples and religions.[49] His writings continue to inspire men and women struggling today to reconcile their faith with their lives in a modern, secular society.

Francis, supported by those figures, by those heroes and saints of yesterday and today, finished his speech under a shower of applause. He made it clear to his audience that everything he said took on greater meaning because of the cloud of witnesses that surrounded him. He called attention to the fact that a nation is great not because it is the richest or greatest power in the world, the possessor of the most weapons of war, nor because it makes the weakest and most vulnerable tremble at its power, nor because it truculently defends its borders. On the contrary, the greatness of a nation becomes clear when it defends freedom as Lincoln did; when it creates a culture that allows one to dream of the fullness of rights for all as Martin Luther King did; when it identifies itself fully with justice and the cause of the oppressed like Dorothy Day; and when it lives with a faith that engenders dialogue and sows peace as Thomas Merton did.

He summarized the witnesses in this way: "Three sons and a daughter of this land, four individuals and four dreams: Lincoln, liberty; Martin Luther King, liberty in plurality and non-exclusion; Dorothy Day, social justice and the rights of persons; and Thomas Merton, the capacity for dialogue and openness to God. Four representatives of the American people." Francis left behind him the perfumed scent that emanates from the Letter to the Hebrews (12:1): "Therefore, since we are surrounded by so great a cloud of witnesses, let us also lay aside every weight and the sin that clings so closely and let us run with perseverance the race that is set before us."

Pope Francis concluded his speech by returning to the witnesses as people that inspire others to dream: "It is my desire that this spirit continue to develop and grow, so that as many young people as

48 Daniel Horan, "Merton (Still) Matters: How the Trappist Monk and Author Speaks to Millennials," *America: The Jesuit Review* online, January 19–26, 2015, https://www.americamagazine.org/faith/2015/01/07/merton-still-matters-how-trappist-monk-and-author-speaks-millennials.

49 Francis, *Visit to the Joint Session of the United States Congress.*

possible can inherit and dwell in a land which has inspired so many people to dream."[50]

Conclusion: The Witnesses that Helped Build America

Through their lives and examples, exceptional persons, whether or not they have been declared saints, propose an ideal of being human that is made up simultaneously of a profound interior life, an unshakable freedom, and a concern for acting on behalf of others, thereby becoming the visible and concrete fruit of the work of God. Their freedom is expressed in a real context but at the same time transcends that context. It is a liberating freedom, not only on the spiritual plane, but also in the social world, and may be seen in their work and decisions, as well as in the societal changes they follow or anticipate.

Holiness is a vocation and destiny that are not only personal but also communitarian and collective. It results less from the execution of an ascetical-moral program than from an absolute and radical loving response to the call and the will of God. It is quite independent of any kind of social projection or desire for unity and is open to those of different levels of education, different cultures and socioeconomic conditions, and even different psychological states.

The desire and effort to respond to God, choosing a path that brings a person closer to others, to their needs and sufferings, means a commitment to search for spiritual and moral radicality. The call of God is unforeseeable and irreducible to the circumstances of life, which can be seen in the personal and concrete examples of the saints as well as in the common projects of collectivities that pursue an ideal and bear witness to it.

The visit of Pope Francis to Cuba and the US pointed toward the direction we must walk so that the continent in which we live can be one America: we must be witnesses to the world. For that, it is necessary to be inspired by the testimony and example of heroes, saints, and the witnesses that abound in America, both north and south. Throughout his formation, Francis contemplatively read the lives of the saints and was inspired by their testimony and example. This marked him for the

50 Francis, *Visit to the Joint Session of the United States Congress.*

rest of his life, and it is what he wants to convey when he addresses men and women everywhere.

His message for America is that for a Christian, the best path is following in the footsteps of the testimony of the holy people of God and of Jesus, the faithful witnesses par excellence. Following this path will result in the individual Christian and the Christian community becoming witnesses. That may imply having to, at a determined moment, give one's life, because following Jesus is not a choice, but a destiny. As the pope said so well, "One cannot understand a Christian without his witness and this testimony. We are not a 'religion' only of ideas, of pure theology, of aesthetics, of commandments. We are a people who follow Jesus Christ and bear witness, who want to bear witness to Jesus Christ."[51]

51 Francis, *Bearing Witness to Christ, Morning Meditation in the Chapel of the* Domus Sanctae Marthae, May 6, 2014.

Works Cited of Pope Francis / Jorge Mario Bergoglio

Bergoglio, Jorge Mario. *Meditaciones Para Religiosos*. Buenos Aires: Diego de Torres, 1982. Rev. ed., Bilbao: Mensajero, 2014.

———. "Prólogo." In Guzmán Carriquiry, *Una Apuesta por América Latina*. Buenos Aires: Sudamericana, 2005.

———. "Prólogo." In Guzmán Carriquiry, *En Camino hacia la V Conferencia de la Iglesia Latinoamericana*. Buenos Aires: Claretiana, 2006.

———. "Religiosidad Popular Como Evangelización de la Fe." In *Testigos de Aparecida,* vol. 2, edited by Consejo Episcopal Latinoamericano, Bogotá: CELAM, 2008.

———, ed. *Concluding Document, Aparecida, May 13–31, 2007*. Washington, D.C.: United States Conference of Catholic Bishops, 2008.

Francis, Pope. *Address to the Latin American Conference of Religious* (CLAR). June 10, 2013.

———. *Lumen Fidei*. Encyclical Letter. June 29, 2013.

———. *Visit to Lampedusa, Homily of Holy Father Francis*. July 8, 2013.

———. *Holy Mass in the Basilica of the Shrine of Our Lady of Conception of Aparecida, Homily of His Holiness Pope Francis*. July 24, 2013.

———. *Meeting with Brazil's Leaders of Society: Address of Pope Francis*. Rio de Janeiro, July 27, 2013.

———. *Meeting with the Bishops of Brazil: Address of Pope Francis*. Rio de Janeiro, July 28, 2013.

———. *Address to Leadership of the Episcopal Conferences of Latin America*. Rio de Janeiro, July 28, 2013.

———. *Address to the Leadership of the Episcopal Conferences of Latin America* (CELAM). July 28, 2013.

———. *Evangelii Gaudium*. Apostolic Exhortation. November 24, 2013.

———. *Bearing Witness to Christ, Morning Meditation in the Chapel of the* Domus Sanctae Marthae. May 6, 2014.

———. *Address of Pope Francis to the Participants in the World Meeting of Popular Movements*. October 28, 2014.

———. *In-Flight Press Conference of His Holiness Pope Francis from the Philippines to Rome*. January 19, 2015.

———. *Laudato Si'*. Encyclical Letter. May 24, 2015.

———. *Holy Mass: Homily of the Holy Father*. Guayaquil, Ecuador, July 6, 2015.

———. *Homily of the Holy Father at Samanes Park, Guayaquil*. July 6, 2015.

———. *Holy Mass for the Evangelization of Peoples: Homily of the Holy Father*. Quito, Ecuador, July 7, 2015.

———. *Welcome Ceremony: Address of the Holy Father*. La Paz, Bolivia, July 8, 2015.

———. *Meeting with Clergy, Religious, and Seminarians: Address of the Holy Father*. Quito, Ecuador, July 8, 2015.

———. *Meeting with Clergy, Religious, and Seminarians: Address of the Holy Father*. Santa Cruz de la Sierra, Bolivia, July 9, 2015.

———. *Address of the Holy Father at the Second World Meeting of Popular Movements in Santa Cruz de la Sierra, Bolivia*. July 9, 2015.

———. *Homily of the Holy Father at the Holy Mass at Christ the Redeemer Square in Santa Cruz de la Sierra, Bolivia*. July 9, 2015.

———. *Meeting with Government Authorities and the Diplomatic Corps: Address of the Holy Father*, Asunción, Paraguay. July 10, 2015.

———. *Holy Mass: Homily of the Holy Father*, Marian Shrine of Caacupé, Paraguay. July 11, 2015.

———. *Meeting with Representatives of Civil Society: Address of the Holy Father*, Asunción, Paraguay. July 11, 2015.

———. *In-Flight Press Conference of His Holiness Pope Francis from Paraguay to Rome*. July 13, 2015.

———. *Address of Pope Francis at José Martí International Airport*, Havana. September 19, 2015.

———. *Address of His Holiness Pope Francis to Students at the Fr. Félix Varela Cultural Center in Havana, Cuba*. September 20, 2015.

———. *Homily of His Holiness Pope Francis*, Plaza de la Revolución, Havana, Cuba. September 20, 2015.

———. *Celebration of Vespers with Priests, Men and Women Religious and Seminarians: Homily of His Holiness Pope Francis*, Cathedral, Havana. September 20, 2015

———. *Homily of the Holy Father at the Plaza de la Revolución in Holguín, Cuba*. September 21, 2015.

———. *Address of the Holy Father at the Meeting of Families at the Cathedral of Our Lady of the Assumption in Santiago, Cuba*. September 22, 2015.

———. *Homily of His Holiness at the Minor Basilica of the Shrine Virgen de la Caridad del Cobre in Santiago, Cuba*. September 22, 2015.

———. *Speech of Pope Francis to the Bishops of the United States*, St. Matthew's Cathedral, Washington, D.C. September 23, 2015.

———. *Remarks of President Obama and His Holiness Pope Francis at Arrival Ceremony*, September 23, 2015. https://obamawhitehouse.archives.gov/the-press-office/2015/09/23/remarks-president-obama-and-his-holiness-pope-francis-arrival-ceremony.

———. *Address of the Holy Father at the Welcoming Ceremony*, South Lawn of the White House, Washington, D.C. September 23, 2015.

———. *Homily of Pope Francis*, Basilica of the Shrine of the Immaculate Conception, Washington, D.C. September 23, 2015.

———. *Holy Mass and Canonization of Blessed Fr. Junípero Serra: Homily of His Holiness Pope Francis*, National Shrine of the Immaculate Conception, Washington D.C. September 23, 2015.

———. *Visit to the Joint Session of the United States Congress: Address of the Holy Father*, Washington, D.C. September 24, 2015.

———. *Vespers with Priests and Religious: Homily of His Holiness Pope Francis*, St. Patrick's Cathedral, New York. September 24, 2015.

———. *Speech of Pope Francis*, Our Lady Queen of Angels School, Harlem, New York. September 25, 2015.

———. *Interreligious Meeting: Address of the Holy Father*, Ground Zero, New York. September 25, 2015.

———. *Meeting with the Personnel of the United Nations: Greeting of the Holy Father*, United Nations Headquarters, New York. September 25, 2015.

———. *Holy Mass: Homily of His Holiness Pope Francis*, Madison Square Garden, New York. September 25, 2015.

———. *Meeting for Religious Liberty with the Hispanic Community and Other Immigrants: Address of the Holy Father*, Independence Mall, Philadelphia. September 26, 2015.

———. *Address to Prayer Vigil for the Festival of Families: Address of the Holy Father*, Philadelphia. September 26, 2015.

———. *Meeting with Bishops Taking Part in the World Meeting of Families: Address of the Holy Father,* St. Charles Borromeo Seminary, Philadelphia. September 27, 2015.

———. *Holy Mass at the Basilica of Our Lady of Guadalupe: Homily of His Holiness Pope Francis*, Mexico City. February 13, 2016.

———. *Meeting with Authorities, Representatives of Civil Society, and the Diplomatic Corps: Address of His Holiness Pope Francis*, National Palace, Mexico City. February 13, 2016.

———. *Meeting with the Bishops of Mexico: Address of the Holy Father*, Metropolitan Cathedral of the Assumption, Mexico City. February 13, 2016.

———. *Angelus Address,* Ecatepec, Mexico. February 14, 2016.

———. *In-Flight Press Conference of His Holiness Pope Francis from Mexico to Rome*. February 17, 2016.

———. *Holy Mass: Homily of His Holiness Pope Francis*, Ciudad Juárez Fair Grounds, Mexico. February 17, 2016.

———. *Amoris Laetitia.* Postsynodal Apostolic Exhortation. March 19, 2016.

———. *Letter of His Holiness Pope Francis to Cardinal Marc Ouellet, President of the Pontifical Commission for Latin America.* March 19, 2016.

———. *General Audience*. April 27, 2016.

———. *Conferral of the Charlemagne Prize: Address of His Holiness Pope Francis*. May 6, 2016.

———. *The Holiness of Negotiation, Morning Meditation in the Chapel of the* Domus Sanctae Marthae. June 9, 2016.

———. *Letter of His Holiness Pope Francis for the Bicentennial of Independence of the Argentine Republic*. July 8, 2016.

———. *Greeting of the Holy Father to Journalists on the Flight to Krakow*. July 27, 2016.

———. *Message of His Holiness Pope Francis for the V Encuentro*. United States Conference of Catholic Bishops website. November 15, 2016. http://www.usccb.org/about/leadership/usccb-general-assembly/2016-november-meeting/message-of-his-holiness-pope-francis-for-the-v-encuentro.cfm.

———. "Presentación." In Guzmán Carriquiry, *Memoria, coraje y esperanza: A la luz del Bicentenario de la Independencia de América Latina*. Granada: Editorial Nuevo Inicio, 2017.

———. *Latinoamérica: Conversaciones con Hernán Reyes Alcaide.* Buenos Aires: Planeta, 2017.

———. *Prayer to the Black Christ of Bojayá*, Las Malocas Park (Villavicencio), Colombia. September 8, 2017.

———. *The Poor Man Cried, and the Lord Heard Him: Message of His Holiness Pope Francis, Second World Day of The Poor*. November 18, 2018.

———. "The Changing Relationships between the Market, the State, and Civil Society." In *Sociedad Civil y bien común: Hacia una nueva articulación del mercado, el estado y la sociedad civil*, 2 vols., edited Juan Carlos Scannone, 1: 13–15. Córdoba, Argentina: Editorial de la Universidad Católica de Córdoba, 2018.

———. *En tus ojos está mi palabra: Homilías y discursos de Buenos Aires, 1999–2013*. Madrid: Ed Claretiana, 2018.

———. *Address of His Holiness Francis to a Group from the Pontifical Commission for Latin America*. March 4, 2019.

———. *Address of Pope Francis to the Participants at the World Congress of the International Association of Penal Law*. November 15, 2019.

———. "Prologue." In *La irrupción de los movimientos populares: "Rerum Novarum" de nuestro tiempo*, edited by Guzmán Carriquiry and Gianni La Bella, 1–8. Rome: Libreria Editrice Vaticana, 2019.

———. *Fratelli Tutti: On Fraternity and Social Friendship*. Encyclical Letter. October 4, 2020.

———. "A un ejército invisible: Carta a los movimientos populares, 22 de abril de 2020." In Francis, *La vida después de la pandemia*, 39–44. Rome: Libreria Editrice Vaticana, 2020.

Works Cited

Albado, Omar. "Volverse al Hombre Concreto: Una Aproximación a la Cultura Popular en la Teología del Padre Rafael Tello." *Vida Pastoral* 283 (2010): 4–11.

Alberigo, Giuseppe. *Historia del Concilio Vaticano II*. Salamanca: Ediciones Sígueme, 1999.

Alvarez, Carlos G. "Ministerios confiados a los laicos en América Latina y el Caribe: Aporte bíblico y teológico." *Boletín CELAM* 326 (December 2009): 41–79.

Arana, Guillermo. "Santidad." In *Diccionario de espiritualidad ignaciana*, edited by José Garcia de Castro. Santander: Sal Terrae, 2006.

Asturias, Miguel Ángel. *El Señor Presidente*. New York: Atheneum, 1964.

Augustine of Hippo. *Sermons 20–50*. Translated by Edmund Hill, edited John E. Rotelle. The Works of Saint Augustine: A Translation for the 21st Century, Part 3, vol. 2. Brooklyn: New City Press, 1990.

Balderrama, Francisco and Raymond Rodríguez. *Decade of Betrayal: Mexican Repatriation in the 1930s*. Albuquerque: University of New Mexico Press, 2006.

Battalion, Marcel. *Erasmo en España*. Madrid: FCE, 1950.

Bellah, Robert N. "Civil Religion in America." *Daedalus* 96, no. 1 (Winter 1967): 1–21; reprinted with discussion in *The Religious Situation: 1968*, edited by Donald R. Cutler, 388–93. Boston: Beacon Press, 1968.

———. *The Broken Covenant: American Civil Religion in Time of Trial*. New York: Seabury Press, 1975. Reprinted with an afterword by Robert Bellah, Chicago: University of Chicago Press, 1992.

Benedict XVI, Pope. *Deus Caritas Est*. Encyclical Letter. December 25, 2005.

———. *Address of His Holiness Benedict XVI to the Inaugural Session of the Fifth General Conference of the Bishops of Latin America and the Caribbean*. May 13, 2007.

———. *Verbum Domini*. Postsynodal Apostolic Exhortation. September 20, 2010.

Beozzo, J. Óscar. *Pacto das Catacumbas. Por Uma Igreja Servidora e Pobre*. Sao Paulo: CESEP, 2015.

Bergoglio, Jorge Mario. *See* Francis, Pope.

Bernstein, Carl, and Marco Politti. *His Holiness*. New York: Penguin, 1997.

Berthem-Bontoux. *Sainte Françoise Romaine Et Son Temps (1384–1440)*. Paris: Bloud and Gay, 1931.

Bertier de Sauvigny, Guillaume de and Joseph N. Hajjar. *De La Ilustración a La Restauración*. 2nd ed. Vol. 4 of *Nueva Historia de la Iglesia*, edited by L. J. Rogier, Roger Aubert, and David Knowles. Madrid: Cristiandad, 1984.

Bianchi, Enrique Ciro. *Pobres en este mundo, ricos en la fe*. Buenos Aires: Agape, 2012.

Bidegain, Ana María. "From Catholic Action to Liberation Theology: The Historical Process of the Laity in the Twentieth Century." Kellogg Institute Working Paper 048, University of Notre Dame, Notre Dame, Ind., November 1985, https://kellogg.nd.edu/documents/1242.

———. *Participación y Protagonismo de las mujeres en la historia del catolicismo latinoamericano*. Buenos Aires: San Benito, 2009.

———. "Una historia silenciada, no reconocida, ignorada, ocultada, invisibilizada: La vida religiosa femenina en la historia brasileña e hispanoamericana." *Revista de Estudos da Religião (REVER)* 14, no. 2 (July–Dec. 2014): 13–73.

Bingemer, Maria Clara. *Em tudo amar e servir: Mística trinitária e práxis cristã*. São Paulo: Edições Loyola, 1990.

Boff, Leonardo. *La Trinidad, la sociedad y la liberación*. Madrid: Ediciones Paulinas, 1987.

Bourdieu, Pierre. "Génese et structure du champ religieux." *Revue Francaise de Sociologie* 12, no. 3 (1971): 295–334.

Bowman, Marilyn. "Labor Migration on Mexico's Southern Border, 1880–1941: The Quest for Regulation and Its Aftermath." PhD. diss., University of Minnesota, 1987.

Buckley, Michael. *At the Origins of Modern Atheism*. New Haven, Conn.: Yale University Press, 1987.

Camus, Albert. *The Myth of Sisyphus and Other Essays*. Translated by Justin O'Brien. New York: Vintage 1948.

Carriquiry, Guzmán. *En Camino hacia la V Conferencia de la Iglesia latinoamericana: Memoria de los 50 años del CELAM*. Buenos Aires: Claretiana, 2006.

———. *El bicentenario de la independencia de los países latinoamericanos*. Madrid: Encuentro 2011.

———. "Desde Aparecida a la *Evangelii Gaudium*." In de Mier, *Instauremos el reino del padre*, 49–64.

———. *Una apuesta por América Latina*. Buenos Aires: Sudamericana, 2015.

———. *Memoria, coraje, y esperanza. A la luz del Bicentenario de la Independencia de América Latina*. Granada: Editorial Nuevo Inicio, 2017.

Carriquiry, Guzmán and Gianni La Bella, eds. *La irrupción de los movimientos populares: El "Rerum Novarum" de nuestro tiempo*. Rome: Libreria Editrice Vaticana, 2019.

Carson, Clayborne. *Eu tenho um sonho: A autobiografia de Martin Luther King*. Rio de Janeiro: Zahar, 2014.

Casarella, Peter J. "Solidarity as the Fruit of Communion: *Ecclesia in America*, 'Post-Liberation Theology,' and the Earth." *Communio: International Catholic Review* 27, no.1 (Spring 2000): 98–123.

Castillo, José Maria. *El seguimiento de Jesucristo*. Salamanca: Sígueme, 1998.

Catechism of the Catholic Church. Vatican City: Libreria Editrice Vaticana, 1994.

Chavez, Leo. *The Latino Threat: Constructing Immigrants, Citizens, and the Nation*. 2nd ed. Stanford, Calif.: Stanford University Press, 2002.

Christophe, Paul, *Les pauvres et la pauvretê*. Paris: Desclee, 1987.

Coffey, David. "The Common and the Ordained Priesthood." *Theological Studies* 58, no. 3 (June 1997): 209–36.

Conferencia Episcopal de Bolivia. *Aporte de la Conferencia Episcopal de Bolivia a la IV Asamblea General del Episcopado latinoamericano*. La Paz: C. E. B., 1992.

Congregation for the Clergy. "The Gift of the Priestly Vocation." *Ratio Fundamentalis Institutionis Sacerdotalis*. Vatican City: L'Osservatore Romano, December 8, 2016.

Congregation for the Doctrine of the Faith and Dicastery for the Promotion of Integral Human Development. *Oeconomicae et Pecuniarie Quaestiones: Considerations for an Ethical Discernment Regarding Some Aspects of the Present Economic-Financial System*, January 6, 2018, full text at Holy See Press Office Summary of Bulletin, May 17, 2018. https://press.vatican.va/content/salastampa/en/bollettino/pubblico/2018/05/17/180517a.html.

Consejo Episcopal Latinoamericano (CELAM). *Teología India: IV Simposio Latinoamericano de Teología india—La teología de la creación en la fe católica y en los mitos, ritos y símbolos de los pueblos originarios de América Latina: El sueño de Dios en la creación humana y en el cosmos*. Lima, Perú, March 28–April 2, 2011. Bogotá: Centro de Publicaciones del CELAM, 2013.

———. *Las Cinco Conferencias Generales del Episcopado Latinoamericano*. Bogotá: Ediciones Paulinas, 2014.

———. "Medellín, Colombia: II Conferencia General del Episcopado Latinoamericano 1968: Document XIV, The Poverty of the Church." In *Las Cinco Conferencias Generales*, 195–205.

———. "Puebla: III Conferencia General del Episcopado Latinoamericano, 1979." In *Las Cinco Conferencias Generales*, 31–39.

———. "Santo Domingo: IV Conferencia General del Episcopado Latinoamericano, 1992." In *Las Cinco Conferencias Generales*, 497–662.

———. "Aparecida: V General Conference of the Bishops of Latin America and the Caribbean, 2007." In *Las Cinco Conferencias Generales*, 663–880.

———. *Promoviendo la colegialidad episcopal y la integración latinoamericana*. Bogotá: CELAM, 2016.

Council of Trent. *De Regularibus et Monialibus*, *Actas Apostolicas Sedes*, ann. 43, ser. 2, vol. 18 (January 1951), 38–40.

Cross, Ransom Patrick. "Hands across the Border: The Role of the Catholic Church on the Border in Assisting Mexican Catholics during the Religious Crisis in Mexico, 1926–29." Master's thesis, University of Texas, 1994.

Cuda, Emilce. *Para leer a Francisco: Teología, ética y política*. Buenos Aires: Manantial, 2016.

Day, Dorothy. *The Long Loneliness*. New York: HarperOne, 2009.

Deck, Allan Figueroa, SJ. *Francis, Bishop of Rome: The Gospel for the Third Millennium*. New York: Paulist Press, 2016.

———. "Migrants and Refugees in Pope Francis's Transformative Vision of Church and Society." The Fr. Lydio F. Tomasi, CS Annual Lecture on International Migration (San Diego, Calif., November 28, 2016), http://cmsny.org/publications/tomasilecture2016

Denzinger, Heinrich, and Peter Hünnermann. *El Magisterio de la Iglesia = Enchiridion symbolorum definitionum et declarationum de rebus fidei et morum.* Translated by Bernabe Dalmau, OSB, Constantino Ruiz-Garrido, and Eva Martin Mora. 38th ed. Barcelona: Herder, 2000.

Diálogos A: Revista de Culturas, Espiritualidades Y Desarollo Andino-Amazónico 6, no. 8 (2015).

Díaz, Bárbara. "Alberto Methol Ferré: una influencia fundamental en el pensamiento del Papa Francisco." *Cuadernos del CLAEH*, 2a series, año 34, no. 101 (2015–1): 63–85.

Díaz, George T. *Border Contraband: A History of Smuggling across the Rio Grande.* Austin: University of Texas Press, 2015.

Dick, Hillary Parsons. "Language and Migration to the United States." *Annual Review of Anthropology* 40 (2011): 227–40.

Dolan, Jay P. and Gilberto M. Hinojosa, eds. *Mexican Americans and the Catholic Church, 1900–1965.* Notre Dame History of Hispanic Catholics in the US 1. Notre Dame, Ind.: University of Notre Dame Press, 1994.

Donald, David Herbert. *Lincoln.* London: Random House, 1996.

Ducourneau, Jean Yves. *Jesus, l'Eglise et les pauvres.* Nouan-le Fuzelier: Beatitudes, 2010.

Dupuis, Jacques. *Jesucristo Al Encuentro De Las Religiones.* Madrid: Ediciones Paulinas, 1991.

Dussel, Enrique D. *El Episcopado Latinoamericano y la Liberación de los Pobres, 1504–1620.* México, D.F.: Centro de Reflexión Teológica, 1979. http://biblioteca.clacso.edu.ar/clacso/otros/20120131104309/espiscopado.pdf

Edwards, Jason A. and Joseph M. Valenzano III, eds. *The Rhetoric of American Civil Religion: Symbols, Sinners, and Saints.* Lanham, Md.: Lexington Books, 2016.

Elizondo, Virgilio. *The Future Is Mestizo: Life Where Cultures Meet*, rev. ed. Boulder, Colo.: University Press of Colorado, 2000. First published 1988.

Espín, Orlando O. "Popular Catholicism among Latinos." In *Hispanic Catholic Culture in the U.S.: Issues and Concerns,* edited Jay P. Dolan and Allan Figueroa Deck, SJ, 308–59. Notre Dame, Ind.: University of Notre Dame Press, 1994.

Estermann, Josef, ed. *Teología Andina: El tejido diverso de la fe indígena*. 2 vols. La Paz: Instituto Superior Ecuménico Andino De Teología, 2006.

———. *Si el Sur fuera el Norte: Interculturales entre Andes y Occidente*. La Paz: Instituto Superior Ecuménico Andino De Teología, 2008.

———. *Introducción al pensamiento filosófico*. Vol. 1 of *Compendio de la filosofía occidental en perspectiva intercultural*. La Paz: Instituto Superior Ecuménico Andino De Teología, 2011.

Faggioli, Massimo. *The Rising Laity: Ecclesial Movements since Vatican II*. New York: Paulist Press, 2016.

Farmer, William R. and Roch Kereszty, O.Cist. *Peter and Paul in the Church of Rome: The Ecumenical Potential of a Forgotten Perspective*. New York: Paulist Press, 1990.

Fernández, Victor and Carlos Galli. *Discípulos Misioneros*. Buenos Aires: Agape, 2006.

Fraga, Luis Ricardo, John A. Garcia, Rodney E. Hero, Michael Jones Correa, Verlerie Martinez-Ebers, and Gary M. Segura. *Latinos in the New Millennium: An Almanac of Opinion, Behavior, and Policy Preferences*. New York: Cambridge University Press, 2012.

Fullam, Lisa. "Francis, Women, and the Church for the Poor." In *Pope Francis and the Future of Catholicism in the United States*, edited by Erin Brigham, David E. DeCosse, and Michael Duffy, 73–84. San Francisco: University of San Francisco Press, 2016.

Gadamer, Hans-Georg. *Verdad y Método.* Translated by Ana Agud and De Rafael Agapito. Salamanca: Sígueme, 2006.

Gaillardetz, Richard R. "Conclusion." In *Go into the Streets: The Welcoming Church of Pope Francis,* edited by Thomas P. Rausch and Richard R. Gaillardetz, 175–78. New York: Paulist Press, 2016.

Galli, Carlos María. "El aporte de la fe cristiana a la formación de la comunidad iberoamericana de naciones." In *El mundo iberoamericano antes y después de las independencias,* edited by

M. A. Peña González, 449–79. Salamanca: Publicaciones de la Universidad Pontificia, 2011.

———. "El Viento Del Sur de Aparecida a Río: El proyecto misionero latinoamericano en la teología y el estilo pastoral de Francisco." *Seminarios sobre los ministerios de la Iglesia* (España) 60, no. 211 (2014): 9–48.

———. "Lectura teológica, espiritual y pastoral de la exhortación *Evangelii Gaudium* de Francisco." In de Mier, *Instauremos el Reino del Padre*, 13–48.

———. "Diez claves de la Exhortación *Evangelii Gaudium* en el contexto del pontificado reformador y misionero de Francisco." Unpublished manuscript, Faculty of Theology, Universidad Católica Argentina, 2014.

Gamio, Gonzalo. *Tiempos de memoria: Reflexiones sobre derechos humanos y justicia transicional.* Lima: CEP/IBC/IDEHPUCP, 2009.

García, Maestro, J. P. *Eclesiología de la Praxis Pastoral.* Madrid: PPC, 2012.

Gaudemet, J. "Gregorian Reform." In *New Catholic Encyclopedia*, vol. 6, 468–73. New York: Thomson Gale, 2003.

Gauthier, Paul. *Los Pobres, Jesús y la Iglesia.* Barcelona: Estela, 1964.

Gera, Lucio. *Escritos teologico-pastorales de Lucio Gera.* Vol. 1 of *Del preconcilio a la conferencia de Puebla (1956–1981)*, edited by Virginia Raquel Azcuy, C. M. Galli, and Manuel Gonzalez, 113–19. Buenos Aires: Agape, 2006. Containing a written text by Gera from 1957.

Gomes Moreira, José Aparecido. *Conquista y Conciencia Cristiana: El Pensamiento Indigenista y Jurídico Teológico de Don Vasco de Quiroga.* Quito: Abya-Yala, 1990.

Gonzalo, Portocarrero, *Arguedas y el Perú de hoy*. Lima: Casa de Estudios del Socialismo, 2005.

Grande, SJ, Rutilo. *Homilies and Writings.* Edited and translated by Thomas Kelly. Collegeville, Minn.: Liturgical Press, 2015.

Graziano, Paolo. *Neopopulismi: Perché sono destinati a durare.* Bologna: Il Mulino, 2018.

Gutiérrez, Gustavo. *Teología abierta para el laicado adulto.* 5 vols. Buenos Aires: Lohlé, 1968–72.

———. *Teología de la liberación. Perspectivas.* Lima: CEP, 1971.

———. *La fuerza histórica de los pobres.* Lima: CEP, 1979.

———. *Hablar de Dios desde el sufrimiento del inocente*. Salamanca: Ediciones Sígueme, 1986.

———. "¿Cómo hablar de Dios desde Ayacucho?" *Concilium* 227 (January 1990): 131–42.

———. *In Search of the Poor of Jesus Christ*. Maryknoll, N.Y.: Orbis, 1993.

———. "The Meaning and Scope of Medellin." Chapter 3 in *The Density of the Present: Selected Writings*. Translated by Margaret Wilde, James B. Nickoloff, and Francis McDonagh. Maryknoll, N.Y.: Orbis, 1999.

———. *The Option for the Poor in Christian Theology*. Edited by Daniel G. Groody. Notre Dame, Ind.: University of Notre Dame Press, 2007.

———. "La Teología Latinoamericana y Caribeña. Trayectoria y Perspectivas." *Páginas* 38, no. 230 (June 2013): 14–29.

———. *Entre las calandrias en ensayo sobre José María Arguedas ; incluye dos nuevos ensayos en conmemoración del centenario del nacimiento de Arguedas*. Lima: Biblioteca Nacional del Perú, 2014.

Haberski, Jr., Raymond. *God and War: American Civil Religion Since 1945*. New Brunswick, N.J.: Rutgers University Press, 2012.

Haidt, Jonathan. "When and Why Nationalism Beats Globalism." *The American Interest* 12, no.1 (July 10, 2016).

Handlin, Oscar. *The Uprooted*. New York: Grosset and Dunlap, 1951.

Hatun Willakuy Versión abreviada del Informe Final de la Comisión de la Verdad y Reconciliació. Lima: Corporación Gráfica, 2004.

Higham, John. *Strangers in the Land: Patterns of American Nativism, 1890–1925*. New Brunswick, N.J.: Rutgers University Press, 1955. Reprint 1988.

Holland, Joe. "Roots of the Pastoral Circle in Personal Experience and Catholic Social Tradition." Introduction to *The Pastoral Circle Revisited*, edited by Fans Wijsen, Peter Henriot, and Rodrigo Mejía, 1–14. Maryknoll, N.Y.: Orbis, 2005.

Horan, Daniel. "Merton (Still) Matters: How the Trappist Monk and Author Speaks to Millennials." *America: The Jesuit Review* online (January 19–26, 2015). https://www.americamagazine.org/faith/2015/01/07/merton-still-matters-how-trappist-monk-and-author-speaks-millennials.

Huanacuni, Fernando. *Vivir Bien / Buen Vivir: Filosofía, políticas, estrategias y experiencias regionales*. La Paz: Convenio Andrés Bello, 2010.

Huckle, Kiku. "Es Su Casa Mi Casa?: Latinos, Socialization, and the Catholic Church." PhD diss., Department of Political Science, University of Washington, 2016.

Ignatius of Loyola. *The Spiritual Exercises*. Translated by Louis J. Puhl, SJ. Westminster, Md.: Newman Press, 1951.

———. *The Autobiography of St. Ignatius*. Edited by J. F. X. O'Connor, SJ. New York: Benziger Brothers, 1900.

———. *Constitutions of the Society of Jesus and Their Complementary Norms*. Edited by John W. Padberg, SJ. St. Louis: The Institute of Jesuit Sources, 1996.

———. *Letters of St. Ignatius of Loyola*. Translated by William J. Young, SJ. Chicago, Ill.: Loyola University Press, 1959.

Irenaeus of Lyons. *Adversus Haereses*. Translated by Alexander Roberts and William Rambaut. In *The Apostolic Fathers with Justin Martyr and Irenaeus*, 309–567. Ante-Nicene Fathers 1. Buffalo, N.Y.: Christian Literature Publishing, 1885. https://www.newadvent.org/fathers/0103311.htm.

Irvin, Dale T. and Scott W. Sunquist. *History of the World Christian Movement*. Maryknoll, N.Y.: Orbis, 2001.

Isasi-Díaz, Ada María. *En la Lucha/In the Struggle, Elaborating a Mujerista Theology*. 2nd ed. Minneapolis: Fortress Press, 2003.

Ivereigh, Austen. *The Great Reformer: Francis and the Making of a Radical Pope*. New York: Henry Holt, 2014. Reprinted and expanded. New York: Picador, 2015.

———. *Wounded Shepherd: Pope Francis and His Struggle to Convert the Catholic Church*. New York: Henry Holt, 2019.

———. "We Belong to a People." In *Pope Francis: A Voice for Mercy, Justice, Love and Care for the Earth,* edited by Barbara E. Wall and Massimo Faggioli, 128–54. Maryknoll, N.Y.: Orbis, 2019.

John Paul II, Pope. *Laborem Exercens*. Encyclical Letter. September 14, 1981.

———. *Speech at the Foundation of the Pontifical Council for Culture*. May 20, 1982.

———. *Redemptoris Missio*. Encylical Letter. December 7, 1990.

———. *Pastores Dabo Vobis*. Postsynodal Apostolic Exhortation. March 15, 1992.

———. *Ecclesia in America*. Postsynodal Apostolic Exhortation. January 22, 1999.

———. *Opening Address of the Nineteenth General Assembly of CELAM*, Port-au-Prince, Haiti. March 9, 1983.

———. "Message to Indigenous Peoples." December 10, 1992.

John XXIII, Pope. *Adiomensaje de su Santidad Juan XXIII. Un mes antes de la apertura del Concilio Vaticano II*." September 11, 1962. English: *Pope's Address to World Month before Council Opened*. In *Council Daybook: Vatican II, Session I and Session 2*, edited by Floyd Anderson, 18 –21. Washington, D.C.: National Catholic Welfare Conference, 1965.

Kasper, Walter. *Theology and the Church*. New York: Crossroad, 1972.

King, Martin Luther. *Why We Can't Wait*. New York: Harper and Row, 1963.

Knowles, M. D., D. Obolensky, C. A. Bouman. *La Iglesia en la edad media*. 2nd. ed. Vol. 2 of *Nueva Historia de la Iglesia*, edited by L. J. Rogier, Roger Aubert, and David Knowles. Madrid: Cristiandad, 1983.

Kraut, Alan M. *The Huddled Masses: The Immigrant in American Society, 1880–1921*. Wheeling, Ill.: Harlan Davidson, 1982.

Lacordaire, Henri Baptiste. *Lettres a un jeune homme sur la vie chretienne*, rev. ed. Paris: Cerf, 1988. First published 1858.

Leo XIII, Pope. *Testem Benevolentiae Nostrae*. Letter. January 22, 1899.

Leon, Luis D. "Cesar Chavez in American Religious Politics: Mapping the New Spiritual Line." *American Quarterly* 59, no. 3 (September 2007): 857–81.

Lerner, Salomón. *La Rebelión de la Memoria. Selección de discursos 2001–2003*. Lima: CEP, 2004.

Levinas, Emmanuel. *Difficult Freedom: Essays on Judaism*. Baltimore: Johns Hopkins University Press, 1990.

———. *Otherwise than Being: Or Beyond Essence*. Dordrecht: Springer, 1991.

Linkh, Richard M. *American Catholicism and European Immigrants, 1900–1924*. Staten Island, N.Y.: Center for Migration Studies, 1975.

Lohfink, Gerhard. *No Irrelevant Jesus: On Jesus and the Church Today*. Translated by Linda M. Moloney. Collegeville, Minn.: Liturgical Press, 2014.

López Hernández, Eleazar. *Teología India: Antología*. Cochabamba, Bolivia: Verbo Divino, 2000.

Luciani, Rafael. *El Papa Francisco y la teología del pueblo*. Madrid: PPC, 2016. Translated by Phillip Berryman as *Pope Francis and the Theology of the People*. Maryknoll, N.Y.: Orbis, 2017.

Luther, Martin. *Temporal Authority: To What Extent It Should Be Obeyed*. In *Luther's Works* 45: *The Christian in Society II*, edited by Walter I. Brandt and Walter T. Lehmann, 77–133. Philadelphia: Fortress Press, 1962.

———. *Against the Murderous, Thieving Hordes of Peasants*. In *Martin Luther*, Documents of Modern History, edited by E. G. Rupp and Benjamin Drewery, 121–26. London: Edward Arnold, 1970.

Machado, Daisy. "History and Latino/a Identity, Mapping a Past that Leads to our Future." In *The Wiley-Blackwell Companion to Latino/a Theology*, edited by Orlando Espín, 35–52. London: John Wiley and Sons, 2015.

Mamani Bernabé, Vicenta et al., eds. *Suma Qamaña–Vivir Bien*. Espiritualidades Originarias 8. Cochabamba, Bolivia: Verbo Divina, 2012.

Marcel, Gabriel. *The Mystery of Being*. Translated by G. S. Fraser. South Bend, Ind.: St. Augustine's Press, 2001.

Marty, Martin. "Two Kinds of Civil Religion." In *American Civil Religion*, edited by Russell E. Richey and Donald G. Jones, 139–57. San Francisco: Harper and Row, 1974.

Massey, Douglas S., Jorge Durand, and Nolan J. Malone, *Beyond Smoke and Mirrors: Mexican Migration in an Era of Economic Integration*. New York: Russell Sage Foundation, 2003.

Matovina, Timothy. *Latino Catholicism: Transformation in America's Largest Church*. Princeton, N.J.: Princeton University Press, 2012.

Maximus the Confessor. *Maximus the Confessor: Selected Writings*. Translated and edited by George C. Berthold. New York: Paulist Press, 1985.

McDonagh, Francis M. *Dom Helder Camara: Essential Writings*. Maryknoll, N.Y.: Orbis, 2009.

Mead, Sidney. *The Nation with the Soul of a Church*. New York: Harper and Row, 1975.

Melloni, Javier. *Hacia un tiempo de síntesis*. Barcelona: Fragmenta, 2011.

Memoria del IV Encuentro-Taller Ecuménico Latinoamericano de Teología India. *En busca de la tierra sin mal: Mitos de origen y sueños de futuro de los pueblos indios*. Quito, Ecuador: Abya-Yala, 2004.

Methol Ferré, Alberto with Alver Metalli. *El Papa y El Filósofo*. Buenos Aires: Biblios, 2013.

Methol Ferré, Alberto. *La Crisis de Uruguay y el Imperio Británico*. Buenos Aires: A. Peña Lillo, 1959.

———. "La revolución verde oliva, Debray y la OLAS." *Víspera* 1, no. 3 (October 1967): 17–45. http://www.metholferre.com/obras/articulos/capitulos.php?id=1_

———. "Marco histórico de la religiosidad popular." In *Iglesia y Religiosidad Popular en América Latina*, 45–75. Bogotá: CELAM, 1977.

———. *Puebla: Proceso y Tensiones*. Buenos Aires: Documenta, 1979. http://www.metholferre.com/obras/libros/capitulos.php?id=8.

———. *De río a puebla: Etapas históricas de la Iglesia en América Latina (1945–1980)*. Bogotá: CELAM, 1980.

———. "El resurgimiento católico latinoamericano." In *Religión y cultura: Perspectivas de la evangelización de la cultura desde Puebla*. Bogotá: CELAM, 1980.

———. "Terceros incluidos y excluidos." *Nexo* 1, no. 2 (March 1984): 6–45. http://www.metholferre.com/obras/articulos.php#obr_3_

———. *Perón y la alianza Argentino-Brasileña*. Córdoba, Argentina: Ediciones Del Corredor Austral, 2000.

———. *Los estados continentales y el Mercosur*. Montevideo: HUM, 2013.

Metz, Johann Baptist. *A Passion for God: The Mystical-Political Dimension of Christianity*. Translated by Matthew Ashley. New York: Paulist Press, 1998.

———. *Memoria Passionis. Ein provoziriendes Gedächtnis in pluralistischer Gessellschaft*. Freiburg: Herder, 2006.

Mier, Eugenio Gomez de. *Instauremos el Reino del Padre y su Justicia: Comentarios a la* Evangelii Gaudium. Buenos Aires: Docencia, 2014.

Mitre, Bartolomé. *Historia de San Martín y de la emancipación sudamericana*. Buenos Aires: Felix Loujane, 1890.

Morandé, Pedro. "En simposio de Humanitas sobre el bien común global. Presentación libro *El Papa y El Filósofo*." *Humanitas* 20, no. 79 (2015): 594–600.

Nanko-Fernández, Carmen. *Theologizing en Espanglish: Context, Community, and Ministry*. Maryknoll, N.Y.: Orbis, 2010.

Ngai, Mae M. *Impossible Subject: Illegal Aliens and the Making of Modern America*. Princeton, N.J.: Princeton University Press, 2014.

O'Brien, David J. *Public Catholicism*. New York: Macmillan, 1989.

O'Malley, John W. *Trent: What Happened at the Council?* New York: Belknap Press of Harvard University Press, 2013.

Panikkar, Raimon. *Ecosofía para una espiritualidad de la tierra*. Madrid: San Pablo, 1994.

———. "Hacia una teología de la liberación intercultural e interreligiosa," In *Interculturalidad, Diálogo Interreligioso y Liberación*, edited by Juan José Tamayo-Acosta and Raúl Fornet-Betancourt, 61–68. Estella, Navarra: Verbo Divino, 2004.

Pannenberg, Wolfhart. *Jesus, God and Man*. Translated Lewis Wilkins and Duane Priebe. Philadelphia: Westminster, 1968.

Parker Gumucio, Cristián. "¿América Latina ya no es católica? Pluralismo cultural y religioso creciente." *América Latina Hoy: Revista de Ciencias Sociales* (Salamanca) 41 (December 2005): 35–56.

Pascal, Blaise. *Pensées*. Translated by W. F. Trotter. New York: E. P. Dutton, 1958.

Paul VI, Pope. *Ecclesiam Suam*. Encyclical Letter. June 8, 1964.

———. *Address During the Last General Meeting of the Second Vatican Council*, December 7, 1965.

———. *Octogesima Adveniens*. Encyclical Letter. May 14, 1971.

———. *Evangelii Nuntiandi*. Apostolic Exhortation. December 8, 1975.

Pelton, CSC, Robert. "Learning from the Cuban House Churches." In *Small Christian Communities Today: Capturing the New Moment*, edited by Joseph G. Healey and Jeanne Hinton, 22–27. Maryknoll, N.Y.: Orbis, 2005.

Pikaza, Xabier and José Antunes da Silva, eds. *El pacto de las Catacumbas: La misión de los pobres en la Iglesia*. Estella, Navarre:

Verbo Divino, 2015. http://www.verbodivino.es/hojear/4209/el-pacto-de-las-catacumbas.pdf.

Pineda-Madrid, Nancy. *Suffering and Salvation in Ciudad Juárez*. Minneapolis: Fortress Press, 2011.

Planellas, Joan I. *La Iglesia de los pobres en el Concilio Vaticano II*. Barcelona: Herder, 2014.

Podetti, José Ramiro. "Confluencias entre Francisco y Alberto Methol Ferré: Iglesia, evangelización y mundo contemporáneo." Paper given at the Semana Teológica del Uruguay, Fac. Teología, Inst. Mariano Soler, Montevideo, September 22, 2014.

Politi, Sebastián. *Teología del pueblo: Una propuesta Argentina a la teologia Latinoamérica*,. Buenos Aires: Docencia, 2015. Originally published in 1992.

Portier, William L. "Americanism and Inculturation: 1899–1999." *Communio: International Catholic Review* 27, no. 1 (Spring 2000): 139–60.

Portocarrero Maisch, Gonzalo. *Arguedas y el Perú de hoy*. Lima: Casa de Estudios del Socialismo, 2005.

Power, David N. "The Evolution of the Priesthood." *Church* (Fall 1988): 16–21.

———. *Mission, Ministry, Order: Reading the Tradition in the Present Context*. New York: Continuum, 2008.

Rahner, Karl. *Grundkurs des Glaubens. Einführung in den Begriff des Christentums*. Freiburg: Herder, 1976.

———. *Further Theology of the Spiritual Life*. Vol. 7 of *Theological Investigations*. Translated by David Bourke. New York: Seabury, 1977.

Ratzinger, Joseph. *Introducción al Cristianismo*. Translated by José L. Domínguez Vilar. Salamanca: Sígueme, 2005.

Rausch, Thomas P. "Priestly Identity: Priority of Representation and the Iconic Argument." *Worship* 73, no. 2 (March 1999): 169–79.

Restán Martínez, Javier. *Alberto Methol Ferré: Su pensamiento en* Nexo. Buenos Aires: Dunken, 2010.

Rocco, Ray *Transforming Citizenship: Democracy, Membership, and Belonging in Latino Communities*. Lansing, Mich.: Michigan State University Press, 2014.

Rocha, Sam. "Francis's Radical Realism: Performance v. Ideology." *Ethika Politika*. March 11, 2014.

Rodriguez, Richard. *Days of Obligations: An Argument with My Mexican Father*. New York: Penguin Books, 1992

———. *Brown: The Last Discovery of America*. New York: Penguin Books, 2002.

Rodríguez Maradiaga, Oscar. "The Importance of the New Evangelization." *Origins* 43, no. 24 (Nov. 14, 2013): 374–75.

Rourke, Thomas R. *The Roots of Pope Francis's Social and Political Thought: From Argentina to the Vatican*. London: Rowman and Littlefield, 2016.

Santana, Otto. *Brown Tide Rising: Metaphoric Representations of Latinos in Contemporary Public Discourse*. Austin: University of Texas Press, 2013.

Scannone, Juan Carlos. "El Papa Francisco y la Teología del Pueblo." In de Mier, *Instauremos el Reino del Padre*, 77–96.

———. *Il Papa del Popolo. Bergoglio raccontato dal confratello teologo gesuita e argentino. Colloqui con Bernadette Sauvaget*. Rome: Librería Editrice Vaticana, 2015.

———. "Pope Francis and the Theology of the People." *Theological Studies* 77, no. 1 (March 2016): 118–35.

———, ed. *Sociedad Civil y bien común: Hacia una nueva articulación del mercado, el estado y la sociedad civil.* 2 vols. Córdoba, Argentina: Editorial de la Universidad Católica de Córdoba, 2018.

———. *La Teología del pueblo: Raíces teológicas del Papa Francisco*. Maliaño, Cantabria: Sal Terrae, 2017. Translated as *Theology of the People: The Pastoral and Theological Roots of Pope Francis*. New York: Paulist Press, 2021.

Scatena, Silvia. *In Populo Pauperum: la Chiesa Latinoamericana dal Concilio a Medellín (1962–1968)*. Bologna: Il Mulino, 2008.

Scheuren Acevedo, Sonia M. "The Opposition to Latin American Liberation Theology and the Transformation of Christianity, 1960–1990." Master's thesis, Florida International University, 2016. https://digitalcommons.fiu.edu/etd/2454.

Schillebeeckx, Edward. *Ministry: Leadership in the Community of Jesus*. New York: Crossroad, 1981.

———. *The Church with a Human Face*. New York: Crossroad, 1985.

Segundo, Juan Luis. *Teología abierta para el laicado adulto*. 5 vols. Buenos Aires: Lohlé, 1968–1972.

Silverstein, Michael. "Indexical Order and the Dialectics of Sociolinguistic Life." *Language and Communication* 23, no. 3/4 (2003): 193–229.

———. "Cultural Concepts and the Language-Culture Nexus." *Current Anthropology* 45, no. 5 (December 2004): 621–52.

Sobrino, Jon. "Extra Pauperes Nulla Salus." In *No Salvation Outside the Poor: Prophetic-Utopian Essays*, translated by Margaret Wilde, Joseph Owens et al., 35–76. Maryknoll, N.Y.: Orbis, 2008.

Tamayo-Acosta, Juan José, and Raúl Fornet-Betancourt. *Interculturalidad, diálogo interreligioso y liberación*. Estella, Navarre: Verbo Divino, 2004.

Thomas Aquinas. *Commentary on the Epistle to the Hebrews*. Translated by Chrysostom Baer, O. Praem. South Bend, Ind.: St. Augustine's Press, 2006.

———. *Summa Theologiae*. Translated by the Fathers of the English Dominican Province. New York: Benziger Brothers, 1947.

Todorov, Tzvetan. *Los abusos de la memoria*. Barcelona: Paidós Ibérica, 2000.

Tracy, David. "Presidential Address: The Catholic Analogical Imagination." *Catholic Theological Society of America Proceedings* 32 (1977): 234–44.

———. *The Analogical Imagination: Christian Theology and the Culture of Pluralism*. New York: Crossroad, 1991.

———. *On Naming the Present: Reflections on God, Hermeneutics, and Church*. Maryknoll, N.Y.: Orbis, 1994.

———. *Plurality and Ambiguity: Hermeneutics, Religion, Hope*. Chicago: University of Chicago Press, 1994.

———. "Salvarnos del Mal: La Salvación y El Mal Hoy" *Concilium: Revista internacional de teología* 274 (February 1998): 147–59.

———. "O Deus Oculto: O resgate da apocalíptica." In *A Teologia na Universidade Contemporânea*, edited by Inácio Neutzling, 85–97. São Leopoldo: Unisinos, 2005.

Treviño, Roberto R. *The Church in the Barrio: Mexican American Ethno-Catholicism in Houston*. Durham: University of North Carolina Press, 2006.

Tubino, Fidel. *La interculturalidad en cuestión*. Lima: Fondo Editorial, Pontifícia Universidad Católica del Perú, 2015.

Tüchle, Hermann, and Cornelis Adrianus Bouman. *Reforma y contrarreforma*. Vol. 3 of *Nueva Historia de la Iglesia*, edited by L.J. Rogier, Roger Aubert, and David Knowles. Madrid: Cristiandad, 1966.

Várnagy, Tomás. "El pensamiento político de Martín Luther." Chapter 7 in *La filosofía política clásica: De la antigüedad al renacimiento*, edited by Consejo Latinoamericano de Ciencias Sociales. Buenos Aires: CLACSO, 1999. http://biblioteca.clacso.edu.ar/clacso/se/20100609123955/8varnagy.pdf

Vatican Council II. *Lumen Gentium*. Dogmatic Constitution. November 21, 1964.

———. *Ad Gentes*. Decree. December 7, 1965.

Vigil, José María. "Sumak Kawsay Y Reino de Dios." *Diálogos A: Revista de Culturas, Espiritualidades Y Desarollo Andino-Amazónico* 6, no. 8 (2015): 8–13.

Vincent, Marcel. *Ozanam: Une Jeunesse Romantique, 1813–1833*. Paris: Médiaspaul, 1997.

Volz, Carl A. *Pastoral Life and Practice in the Early Church*. Minneapolis: Augsburg Press, 1990.

Wallerstein, Immanuel. *Utopistics: Or, Historical Choices of the Twenty-First Century*. New York: New Press, 1998.

Young, Julia G. *Mexican Exodus: Emigrants, Exiles, and Refugees of the Cristero War*. New York: Oxford University Press, 2015.

———. "Making America 1920 Again? Nativism and US Immigration, Past and Present." *Journal on Migration and Human Security* 5, no. 1 (March 2017): 217–35.

Zarazaga, Gonzalo J. *Dios Es Comunión: El Nuevo Paradigma Trinitario*. Salamanca: Secretariado Trinitario, 2004.

Archbishop Christophe Pierre was born on January 30, 1946 in Rennes, France. He completed his primary education in Antisirabé, Madagascar, and his secondary schooling in Saint-Malo, France and Marrakech, Morocco. He attended the major seminary of the Archdiocese of Rennes (1963–69) and the Catholic Institute of Paris (1969–71). He performed military service from July 1965 to October 1966. He was ordained a priest on April 5, 1970, in Saint-Malo, France and incardinated in the Archdiocese of Rennes. He was the parochial vicar of the St. Peter and St. Paul Parish in Colombes, Diocese of Nanterre, France (1970–73). He has a master's degree in sacred theology (Paris, 1971) and a doctorate in canon law from the Pontifical Lateran University in Rome (1973–77). He completed his studies at the Pontifical Ecclesiastical Academy in Rome (1973–77), and began his service in the diplomatic corps of the Holy See on March 5, 1977. He was appointed first to the pontifical representation in New Zealand and the Islands of the Pacific Ocean (1977–81). Subsequently he served in Mozambique (1981), in Zimbabwe (1982–86), in Cuba (1986–89), in Brazil (1989–91), and at the permanent mission of the Holy See to the United Nations in Geneva, Switzerland (1991–95). He was elected Titular Archbishop of Gunela on July 12, 1995, and received the episcopal consecration on September 24, 1995, in Saint-Malo, France. Archbishop Christophe Pierre was appointed apostolic nuncio to Haiti on July 12, 1995, where he served until 1999. He served as the apostolic nuncio to Uganda (1999–2007) and then to Mexico (2007–16). He was appointed as apostolic nuncio of the United States of America by His Holiness Pope Francis on April 12, 2016.

Peter J. Casarella is a professor at the Duke University Divinity School with an expertise in Latinx theology and pneumatology. Before coming to Duke in 2020, he served as the director of the Latin American/North American Church Concerns Project at the University of Notre Dame and as a professor of Catholic studies at DePaul University, where he was also the founding director of the Center for World Catholicism and Intercultural Theology. He has published almost one hundred essays in scholarly journals or books on a variety of topics, including medieval Christian Neoplatonism, contemporary theological aesthetics, intercultural thought, and the Hispanic/Latino presence in the US Catholic

Church. He has published a monograph, *Word as Bread: Language and Theology in Nicholas of Cusa* (2017) and edited or coedited *Cuerpo de Cristo: The Hispanic Presence in the U.S. Catholic Church* (1998), *Christian Spirituality and the Culture of Modernity: The Thought of Louis Dupré* (1998), *Cusanus: The Legacy of Learned Ignorance* (2006), *A World for All? Global Civil Society in Political Theory and Trinitarian Theology* (2011), *Jesus Christ: The New Face of Social Progress* (2015), *Finding Beauty in the Other: Theological Reflections Across Religious Traditions* (2019), and, most recently, *The Whole is Greater Than its Parts: Encountering the Interreligious and Ecumenical Other in the Age of Pope Francis* (2020). He is currently working on a second monograph entitled *The God of the People: A Latinx Theology.*

Austen Ivereigh is a British writer, journalist, and Fellow in Contemporary Church History at Campion Hall, University of Oxford. He also holds a doctorate in Argentinian history from Oxford. He is the author of two biographies of Pope Francis—*The Great Reformer: Francis and the Making of a Radical Pope* (2014) and *Wounded Shepherd: Pope Francis and His Struggle to Convert the Catholic Church* (2019). Recently, he has collaborated with Pope Francis on his vision for a post-COVID world, to be published as *Let Us Dream: The Path to a Better Future (In Conversation with Austen Ivereigh)* by Simon & Schuster in December 2020.

Sixto García received his Ph.D. in 1986 from the University of Notre Dame in systematic and philosophical theology. He then served as a professor of systematic theology and New Testament studies at St. Vincent de Paul Regional Seminary in Boynton Beach, Florida for thirty-one years. Dr. García has served as president of ACHTUS, taught candidates for the permanent diaconate in the Permanent Diaconate Program of the Archdiocese of Miami, and presented seminars on Hispanic American theology at the annual convention of the Catholic Theological Society of America. His publications include "Hispanic Theologians as Actors, Poets, and Prophets of their Communities," *The Journal of Hispanic/Latino Theology* (1999) and contributions to *We are a People! Initiatives in Hispanic American Theology* (2013) and *The Wiley Blackwell Companion to Latino/a Theology* (2015). He has recently retired and is completing a monograph titled *Faith and Grace in Francisco de Vitoria's Theology*.

Ana María Bidegain is a professor in the department of religious studies at Florida International University, where she specializes in studies of Christianity in Latin America, women in Latin American religions, and the history of religion in Latin America. She developed her academic career in Colombia, where she taught for over twenty years, founded the history department at the University of Los Andes, and opened a department of religious studies at the National University of Colombia. Dr. Bidegain has published extensively on various themes related to religion, society, politics, and Latin American history and has participated in numerous research teams in South America, Europe, and the US. She is currently working as the editor of volume six of the *Edinburgh Companions to Global Christianity* on Latin America and the Caribbean, and she is the program director for research at the Latin American and Caribbean Center at Florida International.

Paulo Fernando Carneiro de Andrade is a professor at the Pontifícia Universidade Católica in Rio de Janeiro (PUC-Rio), where his research and teaching focus on liberation theology, faith and politics, ecclesial social doctrine, and Christian social ethics. Dr. Carneiro de Andrade has served as president of the Society of Theology and Sciences of Religion, vice president of the International Network of Societies for Catholic Theology, and a member of the board of directors of the Globethics Network. He has contributed to multiple published volumes on the themes of religion and modernity and liberation theology, among others, and is the author of *Capitalism and Socialism: Dialogue Between Liberation Theology and the Social Doctrine of the Church* (1993) and *Faith and Effectiveness: The Use of Sociology in Liberation Theology* (1991).

Luis Herrera Rodríguez, SJ, currently holds a research position at the Loyola Center in Ayacucho, Peru. He earned a PhD in theology from the Faculdade Jesuita de Filosofia e Teologia in 2014 and has taught theology, humanities, and philosophy at the Jesuit School of Theology in Berkeley (US), the Pontifícia Universidad Católica de Peru, and the Universidad Católica de Santiago de Chile. As a Jesuit priest, Dr. Herrera has worked as a rural pastor in Quechua indigenous communities and coordinated the Social Centers Network and the social apostolate of the Peruvian province of the Jesuits. He participates in the Theological Commission of the Society of Jesus in Latin America and the Latin American Reflection Team of the Society of Jesus on indigenous cultures and religions. His current interests include Christology, intercultural and interreligious dialogue with indigenous traditions, theological hermeneutics, and Latin American theology.

Roberto Tomichá Charupá is the director of the Latin America Institute of Missiology at the Catholic University of Bolivia (Cochabamba) and the representative of Latin America to the International Association of Catholic Missiologists. He has served as a visiting professor at the Pontifical University of St. Bonaventure (Rome), a partner of the Bolivian Academy of Ecclesial History, and an advisor to CELAM on topics of indigenous missiology and theology. Father Tomichá, a Bolivian of the Chiquitana indigenous family, is a priest in the order of Conventual Franciscans. He has published several books and articles on history, missions, and indigenous culture and religious life in Latin America and Europe. He is the editor of the South American collection *Scripta Autochtona–An Indigenous History of the Lowlands.*

William L. Portier is the Mary Ann Spearin Chair of Catholic Theology and director of the PhD program in religious studies at the University of Dayton, Ohio. His interests include generational differences among Catholics and Pope Francis's impact on the American church. He is the 2015 recipient of the American Catholic Historical Association's Distinguished Scholar Award, a 2016 Distinguished Visiting Scholar at Mount Saint Mary's University in Emmitsburg, Maryland, and a member of the national board of the Lilly Fellows Program Network. Dr. Portier has served on multiple editorial boards and published numerous works, including *Tradition and Incarnation* (1994) and *Divided Friends: Portraits of the Roman Catholic Modernist Crisis in the United States* (2013).

Julia G. Young holds a PhD in Latin American history from the University of Chicago and serves as an associate professor of history at the Catholic University of America. As a historian of migration, Mexico and Latin America, and Catholicism in the Americas, Dr. Young is well-published in many scholarly journals, author of the award-winning *Mexican Exodus: Emigrants, Exiles, and Refugees of the Cristero War* (2015), and coeditor of *Local Church, Global Church: Catholic Activism in Latin America from* Rerum Novarum *to Vatican II* (2016). She has served as a fellow at the Kluge Center at the Library of Congress and at the Institute for Policy Research at Catholic University. Her work in progress focuses on twentieth-century right-wing Catholicism in Mexico.

Kiku Huckle is an assistant professor of political science at Pace University, New York, where she specializes in the fields of race and ethnic politics, Latino politics, and religion and politics. With a PhD in political science from the University of Washington and multiple MAs in political science and biblical studies, her current research is focused on the intersections of culture, values, and identity and their effect on political beliefs and engagement. Dr. Huckle is working on multiple book projects in these research areas that address the place of the American Catholic Church in Latino and Latino-immigrant populations, as well as the effect of community-level factors on immigrant political incorporation and engagement.

Luis Ricardo Fraga is an American Catholic political scientist living in South Bend, Indiana. He is the Joseph and Elizabeth Robbie Professor of political science and Reverend Donald P. McNeill, C.S.C., Professor of Transformative Latino Leadership at the University of Notre Dame. Prior to joining the faculty at Notre Dame, he was vice president of the American Political Science Association and taught at the University of Washington, Stanford University, and the University of Oklahoma. In 2011, President Obama appointed Dr. Fraga to the President's Advisory Commission on Educational Excellence for Hispanics. He currently serves as director of the Institute for Latino Studies and fellow at the Institute for Educational Initiatives at Notre Dame. He has published numerous works, including most recently coediting *Latinos and the 2016 Election: Latino Resistance and the Election of Donald Trump* (2020).

Allan Figueroa Deck is a recipient of multiple awards for excellent scholarship and teaching in the field of Catholic Hispanic theology. He is currently the Distinguished Scholar of Theology and Latino Studies and professor of theological studies at Loyola Marymount University, where he has served in many leadership and administrative roles. Father Deck belongs to the board of directors of the Jesuit School of Theology at Santa Clara University as well as the Center for Applied Research in the Apostolate at Georgetown University. He was cofounder and first president of the Academy of Catholic Hispanic Theologians of the United States and the

National Catholic Council for Hispanic Ministry. In 2007, he was called to serve as the executive director of the Secretariat of Cultural Diversity in the Church within the United States Conference of Catholic Bishops (USCCB) in Washington, D.C. His current research engages the Latin American and Jesuit roots of Pope Francis and Latin American influences on Hispanic ministry in the US, and he has recently published a monograph titled *Francis, Bishop of Rome: The Gospel for the Third Millennium* (2016).

Maria Clara Bingemer is a well-known Brazilian theologian who is widely published in multiple languages. She has previously worked with Peter Casarella to edit another work, *Witnessing: Prophecy, Politics, and Wisdom* (2014), and most recently published *Simone Weil: Mystic of Passion and Compassion* (2015), *The Mystery and the World: Passion for God in Times of Unbelief* (2016), and *Latin American Theology: Roots and Branches* (2016). Dr. Bingemer is a professor and the director of Cátedra Carlo María Martini at the Pontifícia Universidade Católica in Rio de Janeiro (PUC-Rio), where she is focused on systematic theology, mysticism, and Latin American and liberation theology. She has previously served as a Kellogg Institute visiting fellow at the University of Notre Dame and as dean of the Center of Theology and Human Sciences at Pontifícia, and together with Dr. Casarella, Dr. Bingemer cofounded the network Ecclesia in America.

Index